D1694734

REPUBLICANISM, COMMUNISM, ISLAM

REPUBLICANISM, COMMUNISM, ISLAM

Cosmopolitan Origins of Revolution in Southeast Asia

John T. Sidel

CORNELL UNIVERSITY PRESS ITHACA AND LONDON

First published 2021 by Cornell University Press

Library of Congress Cataloging-in-Publication Data

Names: Sidel, John Thayer, 1966– author.
Title: Republicanism, communism, Islam : cosmopolitan origins of revolution in
    Southeast Asia / John T. Sidel.
Description: Ithaca, [New York] : Cornell University Press, 2021. |
    Includes bibliographical references and index.
Identifiers: LCCN 2020043164 (print) | LCCN 2020043165 (ebook) |
    ISBN 9781501755613 (hardcover) | ISBN 9781501755620 (epub) |
    ISBN 9781501755637 (pdf)
Subjects: LCSH: Revolutions—Vietnam. | Cosmopolitanism—Southeast Asia. |
    Philippines—History—Revolution, 1896–1898. | Indonesia—History—
    Revolution, 1945–1949.
Classification: LCC DS682 .A274 2021 (print) | LCC DS682 (ebook) |
    DDC 303.6/4095909041—dc23
LC record available at https://lccn.loc.gov/2020043164
LC ebook record available at https://lccn.loc.gov/2020043165

For Ben

Contents

Acknowledgments

This book has been extremely long in the making, and the accumulated debts of gratitude are commensurately large and deeply felt. First, there are institutions that deserve my thanks for their encouragement and assistance in the many years of research and writing that have gone into the production of this book. The School of Oriental and African Studies (SOAS), where I worked between 1994 and 2004, provided the nurturing intellectual environment in which I first began to conceive of this book project, and its musty but trusty library has continued to enable my research on Southeast Asia to this day. The British Academy funded a generous Research Readership from 2003 to 2005 that gave me two full years to embark on this project and granted me the freedom to focus on other projects, including other books, at the same time. The London School of Economics and Political Science (LSE), where I have worked since 2004, has greatly facilitated the subsequent progress over the years that eventually brought this book to completion, through sabbatical leave, research funding, and library resources, with unrestricted interlibrary loans enabling access to diverse and otherwise unavailable (and at times esoteric) sources.

More important, I also owe heartfelt thanks to a wide range of individuals whose influence, encouragement, and assistance have made the research and writing of this book not only possible but also highly enjoyable over the many years since the inception of the project. My significant other, Lotta, provided much inspiration for this book through her own earlier thinking and writing about transnational social movements and blocs of social forces; she has shaped the development of my own investigations and understandings on this front in many ways, even as her own work has moved far more adventurously beyond these concerns. At the outset of the research, she also very helpfully facilitated my access to the Bodleian Library at the University of Oxford, where I fully enjoyed the medieval scholastic ambiance and indulged myself in months of dilettantish dabbling on multiple fronts, however tangentially related to the book. In those early days, our daughter Matilda was spending many of her days immersed in finger painting and the like at the Little Scholars Nursery (seriously!) in Oxford. As of this writing, she is now a wise and worldly young woman with many interests and abilities, and a budding young scholar in her own right, now reading History at Cambridge. The accumulating breadth, depth, and pace of her personal and intellectual development has been a happily humbling source of admiration, vicarious enjoyment, and parental pride. Over the intervening years, Lotta and Matilda have proved to be fully reliable sources of companionship, support, and distraction as I have worked—and not worked—on this book and other academic pursuits. My gratitude to and for them exceeds not only the boundaries of this book project but also the expressive capacities of words.

Meanwhile, I am also deeply grateful for the encouragement and assistance I have received from elsewhere as I have struggled over the years to bring this book to completion. Jim Siegel deserves special mention here, both for the formative influence of his brilliant book *Fetish, Recognition, Revolution* on my thinking and for the affection and enthusiasm that he has imparted over the years through intermittent communications and occasional conclaves in London and Paris. Jim Conwell has provided a steady source of guidance and support over many years, and his encouragement has helped to sustain my progress on the book in more ways than I can fully understand. Roger Haydon has once again lived up to his worldwide reputation as a formidable editor, showing both ample patience as I dithered and deferred "closure" in the writing of this book and then considerable astuteness of judgment in navigating the manuscript through the processes of review, revision, editing, and production. Many thanks to Sue Sakai for her astute and attentive copyediting, to Mary Ribesky for production editing, and to Ken Bolton for his fine work on the index.

Broader and more long-standing debts of gratitude are owed to a wide range of historians of Southeast Asia. As a graduate student in the Cornell University Southeast Asia Program, I was very fortunate to have Takashi Shiraishi as a mentor and teacher, and both his introduction to the comparative historical sociology of the region and his classic study *An Age in Motion* have profoundly influenced and enabled the writing of this book. At SOAS, I was blessed to have many good colleagues, but among them Ian Brown stands out in particular for his generous encouragement of my "historical turn." I remain enormously grateful for the friendship, generous hospitality, and multifarious personal kindnesses of other leading historians of Southeast Asia—Vince Rafael, Geoff Robinson, Jim Rush, Eric Tagliacozzo, and Peter Zinoman—which date back many years, span three continents, and extend far beyond the call of duty, not to mention the history of Southeast Asia. These are serious debts, and I must admit that I am very glad to be living in an era of historically low interest rates, given the unlikelihood of repayment for the foreseeable future. In the case of Peter Zinoman, these debts, and the accumulated interest on them, have been compounded by his retrospectively self-revealed role as a reviewer of the book manuscript and his many astute suggestions for revisions, which have saved me from a number of needless errors, especially with regard to Vietnam. The other second, still anonymous reviewer also deserves heartfelt thanks for other insightful comments and helpful nudges on various fronts.

Here a more general if no less grateful note of appreciation is due to the broader archipelago of historians of Southeast Asia extending across the globe. After all, this book is largely a synthesis of the impressive and illuminating research and writing of these historians, and it has been written in large measure as an admiring tribute to their work, as the many endnotes should make abundantly clear. Here I owe special thanks to Michael Laffan for sharing microfilm of Jawi newspapers from the early 1900s and to Chris Goscha for sharing his Sorbonne PhD thesis, and to both for the eye-opening and otherwise inspiring insights provided by their pioneering scholarship on transoceanic and transcontinental linkages extending across and beyond Southeast Asia. I also remain very grateful to Henk Schulte Nordholt for his scholarship, for hosting a very helpful book workshop in Leiden, for engaging very constructively and creatively with the manuscript, and for otherwise reminding me of the real pleasures of "going Dutch." Guest lectures at the University of Washington, UCLA, and elsewhere have also provided opportunities for engagement with a wide range of other Southeast Asia specialists, whose comments, questions, and suggestions have helped me in various ways in the development of this book.

Beyond such easy and uncomplicated acknowledgments remains an enduring sense of gratitude mixed with lingering sadness at the passing of four very special people over the years since I first embarked on this book project. Nancy Sidel, my ardently Francophile (if not quite Francophone) late mother, encouraged the aspirations to "cosmopolitanism" through travel and language study that enabled and impelled the research and writing of this book. That bright-eyed ancient mariner Lennart Hedman, my late father-in-law, helped to inspire the recurring digressions on maritime trade, shipping routes, and seamen's travels in the book through his deep love for sailing and the sea, an enthusiasm he has successfully imparted over two generations of the loving family he left behind. The late and much mourned Jeff Hadler, my college Bahasa Indonesia classmate and fellow Yale-Cornell mafia "made man," helped me to understand the history of Islam in the Indonesian archipelago, to appreciate the importance of the so-called Outer Islands beyond Java, and to acknowledge and enjoy the many ironies of Southeast Asian Studies and the many idiosyncrasies of Southeast Asianists.

Last but not least, the late great Ben Anderson has provided the overarching source of inspiration not only for this book but for so much of my many years of studying Southeast Asia. As teacher, supervisor, and mentor, he provided invaluable advice, encouragement, and assistance on multiple fronts, and thereafter he remained amply supportive, both on this book project and more broadly. But beyond all this, and beyond my awestruck admiration for him and the underlying affection and affinities we shared, there were also the ideas and ideals that Ben embodied and articulated in his scholarship: breadth of erudition, elegance of expression, sharpness of insight, depth of engagement, and recurring strokes of original genius. To mourn the loss of Ben is also to mourn the passing of an era, not only for me but also for Southeast Asian Studies. There is much to be grieved, but also much for which to remain grateful. It is in this spirit that I dedicate the book to his memory.

Finally, I would also like to acknowledge an accumulated wellspring of gratitude for my home here in London, a city for which I have developed an enormous affection over the years since I commenced the research and writing of this book. Bits and pieces of this book were researched in Oxford, in Penang, and on lake Mälaren in Sweden. But this book has largely been written—and lived—in a house once occupied by the Communist Party of Great Britain (CPGB) leader and National Unemployed Workers' Movement organizer Walter Hannington (1896–1966), just five minutes away from a well-established left-wing salon and home once frequented by Hồ Chí Minh during his brief stint here in the 1910s, and a ten-minute stroll to the street where Karl Marx lived in the 1860s. To the northeast, Highgate Cemetery, where Marx is buried, can be seen from Parliament Hill at the end of my daily morning run around Hampstead Heath. Southwest from us in nearby Primrose Hill, down the street from our family's favorite pub, stands the house where José Rizal lived in the late 1880s, literally around the corner from the home of Friedrich Engels throughout the same period. It was on Lincoln's Inn Fields, where I teach my LSE students about Southeast Asia and other parts of the world, that Sun Yat-sen was abducted in 1896 and briefly detained at the Chinese embassy on Great Portland Street, drawing unprecedented protests and press attention from around the world to his cause.

Such traces of London's history as a city of refuge and revolution have helped to add an extra layer of nostalgic enchantment to the revolutionary contexts I have immersed myself in through my readings and attempted to evoke in this book, even as the decidedly nonrevolutionary comforts and pleasures of our home, the streets of our neighborhood, and the paths, fields, and woods of Hampstead Heath have provided the setting for a life lived beyond books about faraway places in bygone days. A life enfolded within and indebted to an appealingly "cosmopolitan" city cared for by a National Health Service with its thousands of Filipino doctors and nurses and by a mayor born to immigrant parents from Pakistan. It is for this life and its loves that I shall remain most grateful as I bid a belatedly and begrudgingly fond farewell to this book and move on into the uncertain future that lies ahead.

REPUBLICANISM, COMMUNISM, ISLAM

BEYOND NATIONALISM AND REVOLUTION IN SOUTHEAST ASIA

Of all the regions of the world, Southeast Asia is arguably the most impressive, interesting, and important in terms of its nationalist revolutions. The Philippine Revolution at the turn of the twentieth century led to the establishment, however briefly, of Asia's first independent republic, a development that Chinese intellectuals followed with great interest and excitement on the eve of the revolution that would overthrow the Qing dynasty in 1911 and usher in a protracted period of conflict and contestation in China and East Asia as a whole.[1] It took an American invasion and the violent colonization of the archipelago to undo the Philippine Revolution, deferring independence and national sovereignty for the Philippines until 1946 while drawing the United States into expanded imperialist adventures in Asia and beyond. The Indonesian Revolusi (Revolution) of 1945–1949, moreover, was of similar significance, establishing the fourth most populous and largest majority-Muslim nation-state in the world. In its success in uniting ethnically, religiously, and linguistically diverse populations across the archipelago in a Republik Indonesia and in its persistent struggle against successive Dutch schemes for stage-managed and circumscribed decolonization, the Revolusi stood as a source of inspiration for other struggles for independence across the colonized world. It was thus the Indonesian nationalist leader and first president, Soekarno, who hosted the famous Bandung Conference of 1955, which drew

---

1. Rebecca E. Karl, *Staging the World: Chinese Nationalism at the Turn of the Twentieth Century* (Durham, NC: Duke University Press, 2002), 83–115.

together the leaders of new nation-states in Asia, Africa, and the Middle East to voice their opposition to colonialism and neocolonialism, and helped to set the stage for the Non-Aligned Movement and the broader era of Third Worldism.[2] Finally, the Vietnamese Revolution set in motion the dissolution of the French Empire, provided a model for armed guerrilla struggle against colonialism and imperialism across the developing world, and, in the 1960s and early-mid 1970s, helped to stir up mass protests and controversies in American society and to raise new doubts and questions about US power across the world. When the famous Argentinian Marxist revolutionary Che Guevara addressed the Organization of Solidarity with the Peoples of Asia, Africa, and Latin America (OSPAAL, also known as the Tricontinental) at their conference in Havana in 1966, his call for "two, three, . . . many Vietnams" was thus amply well understood.[3] Southeast Asia, in short, has played host to some of the most spectacular and significant instances of revolutionary mobilization against colonial rule and imperialism and in support of national independence in all of recent world history.

Benedict Anderson's *Imagined Communities* and Beyond

Against this backdrop, moreover, scholars of Southeast Asian history have produced an impressive body of literature on nationalism and revolution in the region. There have been countless studies of the Philippine, Indonesian, and Vietnamese revolutions, comprising a rich and varied corpus of scholarship encompassing everything from localized "revolutions within the revolution" to the macroperspective of comparative historical sociology. An equally rich stream of research and writing has treated the rise of nationalist consciousness and mobilization across Southeast Asia, covering even putatively uncolonized Siam (later Thailand). Indeed, it is from within Southeast Asian studies that the most influential and illuminating theoretical contribution to the study of nationalism has been produced, namely, Benedict Anderson's brilliant book *Imagined Communities: Reflections on the Origin and Spread of Nationalism*, first published in 1983 against the backdrop of the Third Indochina War and Vietnam's invasion and occupation of Cambodia.[4] Among other things, this book has provided a powerful

---

2. See the various fine essays in Christopher E. Lee, ed., *Making a World after Empire: The Bandung Moment and Its Political Afterlives* (Athens: Ohio University Press, 2010).

3. See Roger Faligot, *Tricontinentale: Quand Che Guevara, Ben Barka, Cabral, Castro et Hô Chi Minh Préparaient la Révolution Mondiale (1964–1968)* (Paris: La Découverte, 2013).

4. Benedict Anderson, *Imagined Communities: Reflections on the Origin and Spread of Nationalism* (London: Verso, 1983).

analytical framework for understanding the rise of nationalist consciousness, not only in Southeast Asia but across the world.

Indeed, Anderson's *Imagined Communities* helps to frame the nationalist revolutions of Southeast Asian history against the backdrop of developments leading to the emergence of nationalist consciousness over the long years of colonial rule in various parts of the region. Colonial rule in Southeast Asia created unified realms of modern state administration whose penetration of society intensified over the course of the nineteenth and early twentieth centuries, thus creating new fields of shared experience, especially for those who joined the expanding ranks of the colonial bureaucracies during this period. The (secular) pilgrimages of those native bureaucrats who circulated across the districts and provinces of the colonies, moreover, were accompanied and extended by the peregrinations of the "native" school pupils and university students who moved from villages to towns to regional entrepôts and colonial capital cities as they were drawn into the circuitries of primary, secondary, and even tertiary education as it evolved to meet the colonial state's needs. As the numbers of these schoolchildren, university students, and bureaucrats continued to swell over the course of the nineteenth and early twentieth centuries in various colonies across Southeast Asia, moreover, they came to speak, read, and write the state vernaculars that the colonial bureaucracies relied on for administrative purposes, but that, thanks to the dynamism of what Anderson calls "print capitalism" soon extended into a broader field of communication, as seen in the emergence of newspapers and novels in the late colonial era. These developments and trends gave rise to more and more Southeast Asians who were socialized within shared administrative, educational, and linguistic fields of experience, and who, in contrast to their counterparts in preceding centuries characterized by loosely structured dynastic realms and cosmopolitan connectedness, could now imagine themselves, as, say, Filipinos, Indonesians, and Vietnamese. As *Imagined Communities* suggests, it was thus thanks to the unintended consequences of colonial-era state formation, penetration, and expansion rather than any shared primordial (e.g., ethnic) identities that Southeast Asians developed identities, attachments, and aspirations associated with nationalism and, in due course, new nation-states.

Anderson's *Imagined Communities* is thus indispensable for explaining crucial features of the revolutions and other struggles leading to independence and the establishment of new nation-states across Southeast Asia. How else to explain the success of the Indonesian Revolusi in simultaneously drawing Acehnese Muslims, Batak Protestants, Balinese Hindus, and West Timorese Catholics into its orbit? How else to explain the establishment and endurance of nation-states whose boundaries coincide so closely with those of colonial territories rather than any precolonial polities in Southeast Asia? Indeed, even those secessionist or national liberation struggles that have challenged the boundaries of established nation-states—and proposed new ones—in the region have done so on the basis of identities, experiences, and imaginings, such as Kachin, Moro, and Papuan, which scholars have traced to distinctive administrative arrangements under colonial rule rather than any more primordial precedents.[5] As for Southeast Asia's three major revolutions, Anderson's account helps to explain how Filipinos, Indonesians, and Vietnamese emerged to think of themselves in such terms and were able to imagine and develop attachments and aspirations to an independent Philippines, Indonesia, and Vietnam.

At the same time, however, Anderson's account of the origin and spread of nationalism in *Imagined Communities* also raises problems and puzzles for our understanding of the putatively nationalist revolutions of Southeast Asian history. If, as Anderson argues, it was only through socialization in colonial bureaucracies and schools, and through literacy and communications in the new state vernaculars that small numbers of men—and even fewer women—were able to imagine themselves as Filipinos, Indonesians, and Vietnamese, then the pool of potential nationalists by the end of the nineteenth century or the middle of the twentieth century was probably too small to make for much nationalist mobilization per se. In recent years, scholarship on these educated, literate, mostly male nationalist elites has emphasized the rarified conditions and dandyish dispositions that distinguished and distanced them from the broad masses of their fellow would-be Filipinos, Indonesians, and Vietnamese.[6] How, then, did these newly nationalist elites manage to mobilize so many—as Anderson argues, far less easily nationalized—peasants and fishermen, workers and artisans in revolutionary struggles?

The conventional response to this conundrum is to correct or to complement Anderson's account of modern, modular, constructed nationalism with empirical research and theoretical arguments drawn from the traditions of history from below, subaltern studies, and the area-specialist literature of Southeast Asian studies. Indeed, such a response is evident not only in Partha Chatterjee's influential

---

5. See Patricio N. Abinales, *Orthodoxy and History in the Muslim-Mindanao Narrative* (Quezon City: Ateneo de Manila University Press, 2011); Gerald A. Finin, *The Making of the Igorot: Contours of a Cordillera Consciousness* (Honolulu: University of Hawai'i Press, 2008); Thomas M. McKenna, *Muslim Rulers and Rebels: Everyday Politics and Armed Separatism in the Southern Philippines* (Berkeley: University of California Press, 1998); Danilyn Rutherford, *Raiding the Land of the Foreigners: The Limits of the Nation on an Indonesian Frontier* (Princeton, NJ: Princeton University Press, 2002); Danilyn Rutherford, *Laughing at Leviathan: Sovereignty and Audience in West Papua* (Chicago: University of Chicago Press, 2012); and Mandy Sadan, *Being and Becoming Kachin: Histories beyond the State in the Borderworlds of Burma* (Oxford: Oxford University Press, 2013).

6. See, for example, Rudolf Mrázek, *Engineers of Happy Land: Technology and Nationalism in a Colony* (Princeton, NJ: Princeton University Press, 2002); Raquel A. G. Reyes, *Love Passion, and Patriotism: Sexuality and the Philippine Propaganda Movement, 1882–1892* (Seattle: University of Washington Press, 2008); and Megan C. Thomas, *Orientalists, Propagandists, and Ilustrados: Filipino Scholarship and the End of Spanish Colonialism* (Minneapolis: University of Minnesota Press, 2012).

critical response to *Imagined Communities*,[7] but in the broader body of historical literature on Southeast Asia, where a stress on the role of indigenous cultures in enabling popular movements dates back to the late 1960s and 1970s, the era of large-scale American military intervention in Indochina. In the case of the Philippine Revolution, for example, we have Reynaldo Ileto's celebrated book *Pasyon and Revolution* (1979), which suggests that peasants' participation in the Philippine Revolution was informed and enabled by distinctively local understandings and practices of folk Catholicism, notions of freedom (*kalayaan*), and forms of brotherhood that were rooted in rural Tagalog society rather than in the Spanish colonial state.[8] In Benedict Anderson's own account of the Indonesian Revolusi in his earlier (1972) classic *Java in a Time of Revolution*, moreover, we likewise find an account of youth (*pemuda*) mobilization inflected and impelled as much by traditional Javanese conceptions of power as by modern experiences of Dutch colonial rule.[9] Finally, in the case of Vietnam, we have a persistent line of argument stressing the endurance and importance of shared consciousness, history, identity, and attachment, as perhaps most clearly and forcefully articulated by Alexander Woodside in his seminal 1976 study *Community and Revolution in Modern Vietnam*: "No amount of statistics, rhetoric, or social science theory can explain the Vietnamese revolution adequately if its properties of acute historical consciousness and cultural pride are insufficiently considered."[10]

But an explanation for these revolutions that combines elite nationalism with this kind of view from below is less than fully satisfying. In descriptive terms, after all, an account of modern, educated, literate, dandyish nationalist elites somehow harnessing the energies of Filipino, Indonesian, and Vietnamese masses with traditional, culturally distinct imaginings and aspirations leaves open a yawning, seemingly unbridgeable gulf of (mis)understandings and (mis)communications. This kind of account thus hardly clarifies matters with regard to the processes and outcomes of revolutionary mobilization. Indeed, one recent study has revealed that the much celebrated success of Việt Minh forces in the decisive siege of Diên Biên Phủ in 1954 owed much to the mobilization of thousands of coolies and foot soldiers drawn not from the ranks of the Vietnamese peasantry but rather from among the upland ethnic minorities of the border areas of western

---

7. Partha Chatterjee, *The Nation and Its Fragments: Colonial and Postcolonial Histories* (Princeton, NJ: Princeton University Press, 1993).

8. Reynaldo Clemeña Ileto, *Pasyon and Revolution: Popular Movements in the Philippines, 1840–1910* (Quezon City: Ateneo de Manila University Press, 1979).

9. Benedict R. O'G. Anderson, *Java in a Time of Revolution: Occupation and Resistance, 1944–1946* (Ithaca, NY: Cornell University Press, 1972).

10. Alexander Woodside, *Community and Revolution in Modern Vietnam* (New York: Houghton Mifflin, 1976), 1.

Tonkin.[11] The broadly construed conceptions and claims of various scholars with regard to peasant consciousness hardly suffice for purposes of understanding how hundreds of thousands, if not millions, were mobilized in the Philippine, Indonesian, and Vietnamese revolutions.

In analytical terms, moreover, this kind of account leaves unexplained, if not unimportant, the variegated timing and trajectory of Southeast Asia's three great "nationalist" revolutions. Why, for example, did the Philippines experience its revolution so much earlier than the rest of the region, but after its defeat show so little in the way of revolutionary mobilization during most of the twentieth century? Why did the Revolusi in Indonesia succeed in winning independence earlier and with far fewer neocolonial holdovers than, say, neighboring Malay(si)a, but suffered from so much internal contestation and conflict within its own ranks? Why did the Vietnamese Revolution prove so strongly solidified and successful, first in winning independence from France through armed struggle and then in the face of direct intervention by the United States? Neither an analysis of colonial state structures, nor an essentialized account of traditional culture, nor a combination of the two would appear to explain the complex pattern of variance observed in revolutionary mobilization in Southeast Asia.

Beyond Nationalism: Cosmopolitan Origins of Revolution

But what if our analysis of the great revolutions of Southeast Asian history should be extended beyond the national boundaries of these new nation-states in the making and beyond elite nationalists, on the one hand, and the deeply ingrained indigenous, or "autonomous,"[12] cultures and traditions of the region, on the other? Scholars working on other areas of the world, after all, have tried to "rescue history from the nation" instead of reproducing the teleological narratives so common to what Anderson calls official nationalism, in which nations emerge through the heroism of nationalists and the preservation or recuperation of authentic, essentialized national identities.[13] Studies of the revolutions that led to national independence in other settings such as the United States and South America, or,

---

11. Christian C. Lentz, *Contested Territory: Điện Biên Phủ and the Making of Northwest Vietnam* (New Haven, CT: Yale University Press, 2019).

12. See the classic article by John R. Smail, "On the Possibility of an Autonomous History of Modern Southeast Asia," *Journal of Southeast Asian History* 2, no. 2 (July 1961): 72–102.

13. See, for example, Prasenjit Duara, *Rescuing History from the Nation: Questioning Narratives of Modern China* (Chicago: University of Chicago Press, 1997), and Steven Kemper, *Rescued from the Nation: Anagarika Dharmapala and the Buddhist World* (Chicago: University of Chicago Press, 2015).

more recently, Algeria and Morocco, have expanded their analytical lenses beyond national(ist) frames,[14] much as the literature on a wide range of other revolutions—English, French, Russian, Chinese, Iranian—has emphasized the importance of international or global context for enabling revolutionary mobilization and shaping its forms and trajectories.[15] So why should we confine our analysis of Southeast Asia's supposedly self-evidently nationalist revolutions to the boundaries of the Philippines, Indonesia, and Vietnam, the ranks of Filipino, Indonesian, and Vietnamese nationalists, and the indigenous cultures and traditions of these nations-in-the-making? Here Benedict Anderson's work beyond *Imagined Communities* has also been instructive, most notably his 2005 book *Under Three Flags: Anarchism and the Anti-Colonial Imagination*, which situates Filipino nationalist icons such as José Rizal, Isabelo de los Reyes, and Mariano Ponce within the transcontinental networks of late nineteenth-century anarchism in an enjoyably Pynchonesque narrative spanning the breadth of East and Southeast Asia, the Americas, and continental Europe. As Anderson noted in the introduction to the book:

> The Scottish Enlightenment was decisive for framing the American anti-colonial insurrection. The Spanish American nationalist independence movements are inseparable from the universalist currents of liberalism and republicanism. In their turn Romanticism, democracy, Idealism, Marxism, anarchism, even, late in the day, fascism were variously understood as globe-stretching and nation-making. Nationalism, that element with the highest valency of all, combined with all these others in different ways and in different times.[16]

Indeed, over the past two decades, a rich, diverse, and growing body of scholarship has begun to suggest the myriad ways we might trace the origins and animating energies of the Philippine, Indonesian, and Vietnamese revolutions to

---

14. See, for example, Jeremy Adelman, *Sovereignty and Revolution in the Iberian Atlantic* (Princeton, NJ: Princeton University Press, 1979); Justin Du Rivage, *Revolution against Empire: Taxes, Politics, and the Origins of American Independence* (New Haven, CT: Yale University Press, 2017); Matthew Connelly, *A Diplomatic Revolution: Algeria's Fight for Independence and the Origins of the Post-Cold War Era* (Oxford: Oxford University Press, 2002); and David Stenner, *Globalizing Morocco: Transnational Activism and the Postcolonial State* (Stanford, CA: Stanford University Press, 2019).

15. See, for example, Robert Brenner, *Merchants and Revolution: Commercial Change, Political Conflict, and London's Overseas Traders, 1550–1653* (Princeton, NJ: Princeton University Press, 1993); Suzanne Desan, Lynn Hunt, and William Max Nelson, eds., *The French Revolution in Global Perspective* (Ithaca, NY: Cornell University Press, 2013); Hamid Dabashi, *Iran without Borders: Towards a Critique of the Postcolonial Nation* (London: Verso, 2016); and Chibli Mallat, *The Renewal of Islamic Law: Muhammad Baqer as-Sadr, Najaf, and the Shi'i International* (Cambridge: Cambridge University Press, 1993).

16. Benedict Anderson, *Under Three Flags: Anarchism and the Anti-Colonial Imagination* (London: Verso, 2005), 1.

forces and dynamics lying beyond the boundaries of the new nation-states that they helped to produce, and, in significant ways, beyond Southeast Asia. First, a number of scholars have followed and fleshed out Anderson's own brief discussion in *Imagined Communities* of the "transcontinental sodalities" connecting the "great sacral cultures," "sacred languages and scripts," and "classical communities" of the premodern, prenationalist era within and beyond the region.[17] Sheldon Pollock, for example, has shown how the first millennium of the so-called Common Era saw much of Southeast Asia become enfolded within what he calls the Sanskrit cosmopolis: the sacral language of Sanskrit emerged as a vehicle for an efflorescence of literary and political expression through which courts in the region produced a common culture and a kind of cosmopolitan community. Even as the cosmopolitanism of this Sanskrit ecumene gave way to processes of vernacularization and localization in what historians term the Early Modern Era, it left important cultural and linguistic traces in many parts of Southeast Asia that endure to this day.[18] Ronit Ricci, moreover, has shown how religious and other texts, literary networks, and practices of reading, learning, and translating spreading as early as the thirteenth century helped to create what she terms an Arabic cosmopolis across the Indian Ocean that came to incorporate much of archipelagic Southeast Asia within its orbit.[19] Over subsequent centuries, alongside the Islamic faith, this Arabic cosmopolis was sustained and strengthened through the circuitries of the Hajj and the evolving, expanding community of Islamic scholars scattered across the region, as historians such as Azyumardi Azra, Michael Laffan, and Eric Tagliacozzo have shown.[20] Meanwhile, the past few decades have seen the production of a steady stream of scholarly research, writing, and debate with regard to the premodern incorporation of what today comprises Vietnam within a broader East Asian Sinosphere of classical Chinese literature, philosophy, and cultural influence.[21] At the same time, the writings of Vicente Rafael have similarly stressed the significance of Christian evangelization, Catholic education, and the linguistic introduction of Spanish and Latin over the sixteenth, seventeenth, eighteenth, and nineteenth centuries for establishing linkages between the Philippine archipelago and the

---

17. See Anderson, *Imagined Communities*, 17–40, especially 20–25.
18. Sheldon Pollock, *The Language of the Gods in the World of Men: Sanskrit, Culture, and Power in Premodern India* (Berkeley: University of California Press, 2006).
19. Ronit Ricci, *Islam Translated: Literature, Conversion, and the Arabic Cosmopolis in Southeast Asia* (Chicago: University of Chicago Press, 2011).
20. Azyumardi Azra, *The Origins of Islamic Reformism in Southeast Asia: Networks of Malay-Indonesian and Middle Eastern 'Ulamā in the Seventeenth and Eighteenth Centuries* (Honolulu: University of Hawai'i Press, 2004); Michael Laffan, *Islamic Nationhood and Colonial Indonesia: The Umma below the Winds* (London: RoutledgeCurzon, 2003); Eric Tagliacozzo, *The Longest Journey: Southeast Asians and the Pilgrimage to Mecca* (Oxford: Oxford University Press, 2013).
21. See, for example, Liam C. Kelley, *Beyond the Bronze Pillars: Envoy Poetry and the Sino-Vietnamese Relationship* (Honolulu: University of Hawai'i Press, 2005).

broader universe of Jesuit science and the post-Enlightenment Republic of Letters.[22]

Second, a rich and growing body of scholarship has stressed how Southeast Asia's deepening integration into the world capitalist economy enhanced and expanded transoceanic and intra-Asian connections and forms of cosmopolitan connectedness within the region, especially from the mid-nineteenth century onward. A group of historians comprised of the late Chrstopher Bayly, Tim Harper, Sunil Amrith, Mark Ravinder Frost, and Su Lin Lewis have collectively constituted a kind of Cambridge School of Asian history that has provided a rich account of the emergence of an interconnected archipelago of cities stretching across Southeast Asia, the Indian subcontinent, and the coast of China during the latter half of the nineteenth and early twentieth centuries.[23] Thanks to the transportation and communications revolutions (e.g., railroads, steamboats, telegraph lines) of the nineteenth century and the extension of Pax Britannica across the Indian Ocean ("a vast British lake") during this period, long-distance trade in bulk goods and large-scale labor migration expanded dramatically at this time, accelerating with the so-called Forward Movement of the British Empire (and, to a lesser extent, its Dutch, French, and American counterparts) at the turn of the twentieth century. These cities—Bombay, Calcutta, Colombo, Rangoon, Singapore, Batavia, Surabaya, Saigon, Manila, Hong Kong, Canton, Amoy, Shanghai—evolved into increasingly vibrant, densely populated, and ethnically diverse cosmopolitan entrepôts, hubs for the extension of market relations and the establishment of market societies in their agrarian hinterlands.

The growth of these cities and their intensifying integration into the world capitalist economy enhanced rather than undermined cosmopolitan communities and connections. The rising waves of mass labor migration and Indian, Chinese, and Arab mercantile diasporic investment washing up on Southeast Asian shores during the Age of Empire created what John Furnivall termed plural societies in which immigrant communities established important and enduring roles.[24] These waves of migration were accompanied by expanding flows of long-distance

---

22. Vicente L. Rafael, *Contracting Colonialism: Translation and Christian Conversion in Tagalog Society under Early Spanish Rule* (Durham, NC: Duke University Press, 1993); Vicente L. Rafael, *The Promise of the Foreign: Nationalism and the Technics of Translation in the Spanish Philippines* (Durham, NC: Duke University Press, 2005).

23. Sunil S. Amrith, *Crossing the Bay of Bengal: The Furies of Nature and the Fortunes of Migrants* (Cambridge, MA: Harvard University Press, 2013); Mark Ravinder Frost, "Globalization and Religious Revival in the Imperial Cities of the Indian Ocean, 1870–1920" (PhD diss., Cambridge University, 2002); Su Lin Lewis, *Cities in Motion: Urban Life and Cosmopolitanism in Southeast Asia, 1920–1940* (Cambridge: Cambridge University Press, 2016); and Tim Harper and Sunil S. Amrith, eds., *Sites of Asian Interaction: Ideas, Networks and Mobility* (Cambridge: Cambridge University Press, 2014).

24. John S. Furnivall, *Colonial Policy and Practice: A Comparative Study of Burma and Netherlands East India* (Cambridge: Cambridge University Press, 1957), 303–306.

travellers, most notably the so-called steamboat *hajjis* making the pilgrimage to Mecca and Medina and the growing numbers of Muslims seeking deeper knowledge of their faith, not only in the Haramayn (the two Holy Cities) of the Hijaz, but at the renowned Islamic university of Al-Azhar in Cairo. These developments helped to strengthen the transregional and transoceanic connections and sense of connectedness of Southeast Asian Muslims, as seen in the growing ranks of Sufi brotherhoods, the increasingly dense network of Islamic schools, the rise of Singapore as a hub for Islamic publishing, and the emergence of regional arcs of intellectual influence such as the Patani School as a source of inspiration for Islamic education across the Malay Peninsula, Sumatra, Borneo, and beyond.[25] Meanwhile, French colonization from the mid-nineteenth century linked Saigon and the expanding rice industry of the Mekong Delta ever more closely to the port cities of the southern coastal provinces of China, even as French railroad construction and other plans for colonization of Indochina pushed northward through Tonkin and Laos toward Guangxi and Yunnan.[26] At the same time, the opening of Philippine ports to foreign trade from the mid-nineteenth century saw the rise to prominence of British, German, and Swiss firms in cities such as Manila, Cebu, and Iloilo, creating new linkages to parts of Europe beyond the colonial metropole.[27]

The era of high colonialism, in short, did not simply see the various colonies of Southeast Asia connected ever more closely to various colonial metropoles, as the deepening incorporation of the region into the circuitries of the global market worked to expand, extend, and enhance the cosmopolitan connections and sense of connectedness of the region vis-à-vis diverse distant sites across the world. Here it is perhaps worth noting that the Spanish conquest of the Philippines in the sixteenth century was financed by merchants from Genoa and Hamburg, and that the Augustinian, Dominican, Franciscan, Jesuit, and Recollect Catholic religious orders, which were so influential in the archipelago over subsequent centuries, were truly transcontinental in their reach.[28] In the Netherlands East Indies, trade flows linked the Outer Islands more closely to Singapore than to Batavia for most of the nineteenth century, and even as this began to change by the turn

---

25. See Laffan, *Islamic Nationhood and Colonial Indonesia*; Tagliacozzo, *The Longest Journey*; and Francis R. Bradley, *Forging Islamic Power and Place: The Legacy of Shaykh Daud bin Abd Allah Al-Fatani in Mecca and Southeast Asia* (Honolulu: University of Hawai'i Press, 2016).

26. Pierre Brocheux and Daniel Hémery, *Indochina: An Ambiguous Colonization, 1858–1954* (Berkeley: University of California Press, 2009), 116–180.

27. Benito J. Legarda Jr., *After the Galleons: Foreign Trade, Economic Change and Entrepreneurship in the Nineteenth-Century Philippines* (Madison: University of Wisconsin Center for Southeast Asian Studies, 1999).

28. Henry Kamen, *Empire: How Spain Became a World Power, 1492–1763* (London: Penguin Books, 2002), 54, 88–89. See also Céline Dauverd, *Imperial Ambition in the Early Modern Mediterranean World: Genoese Merchants and the Spanish Crown* (Cambridge: Cambridge University Press, 2014).

of the twentieth century, the vast plantations of Sumatra and Java saw strong representation of British, Belgian, German, and Swiss capital, even as the Dutch colonial army relied heavily on European recruits from beyond the Netherlands.[29] In a similar vein, the inclusion of Cochinchina, Annam, and Tonkin within the French Empire not only attracted hundreds of thousands of Vietnamese-speaking people into other parts of what became the Union Indochinoise (Indochinese Union, i.e., Cambodia Laos) through the magnetic pull of expanding bureaucracies, railroads, and markets, as Christopher Goscha has shown, but also, by the 1910s and 1920s, drew them into encounters with Algerian immigrants and a diverse range of African intellectuals and activists in Paris and elsewhere in France.[30]

Third, as the studies of the Cambridge School have shown, by the turn of the twentieth century the expanding urban entrepôts and broader market societies of Southeast Asia saw the emergence of modern public spheres, popular cultures, and forms of consciousness and representation that were profoundly cosmopolitan. Alongside their roles in the construction of shared narratives across and within administratively bounded territorial frames and thus in the conception of national imagined communities, new forms of authorship and diverse experiments with newspapers and novels in Southeast Asia opened the growing reading publics of the region to broader and less bounded fields of shared communication and vision and new social imaginaries. Studies of Philippine literature by Francisco Benitez,[31] of Malay-language newspapers and novels by Ahmat Adam, Henk Maier, and James Siegel,[32] of Vietnamese journalism and print culture by Philippe Peycam and Shawn McHale,[33] and of the life and work of the Vietnamese novelist Vũ Trọng Phụng by Peter Zinoman bear testimony to this development.[34] Meanwhile, beyond the spread of what Anderson calls print capitalism,

29. Kees van Dijk, *The Netherlands Indies and the Great War, 1914–1918* (Leiden: KITLV Press, 2007).

30. See Christopher E. Goscha, *Vietnam or Indochina? Contesting Concepts of Space in Vietnamese Nationalism, 1887–1954* (Copenhagen: Nordic Institute of Asian Studies, 1995); and Michael Goebbel, *Anti-Imperial Metropolis: Interwar Paris and the Seeds of Third World Nationalism* (Cambridge: Cambridge University Press, 2015).

31. J. Francisco B. Benitez, "*Awit* and *Syair*: Alternative Subjectivities and Multiple Modernities in Nineteenth-Century Insular Southeast Asia" (PhD diss., University of Wisconsin at Madison, 2004).

32. Ahmat B. Adam, *The Vernacular Press and the Emergence of Modern Indonesian Consciousness (1855–1913)* (Ithaca, NY: Cornell University Southeast Asia Program, 1995); Henk Maier, *We Are Playing Relatives: A Survey of Malay Writing* (Leiden: KITLV Press, 2005); James T. Siegel, *Fetish, Recognition, Revolution* (Princeton, NJ: Princeton University Press, 1997).

33. Philippe M. F. Peycam, *The Birth of Vietnamese Political Journalism: Saigon, 1916–1930* (New York: Columbia University Press, 2012); Shawn Frederick McHale, *Print and Power: Confucianism, Communism, and Buddhism in the Making of Modern Vietnam* (Honolulu: University of Hawai'i Press, 2008).

34. Peter Zinoman, *Vietnamese Colonial Republican: The Political Vision of Vũ Trọng Phụ* (Berkeley: University of California Press, 2014).

cultural and social historians have shown how the forms of popular opera and theater that began to circulate more widely and attract broader audiences during this period—*komedya* in the Philippines, *Komedie Stamboel* in the Netherlands East Indies, *cải lương* in Vietnam—drew on disparate strands of cultural tradition and developed narratives and frames of reference from far beyond the region.[35] Overall, what Vicente Rafael terms "the promise of the foreign" thus played a crucial catalytic role in undermining established hierarchies, senses of identity, and structures of authority, and in opening up new possibilities for imagination, representation, association, and, eventually, revolutionary mobilization.

Fourth, as detailed in this book, these diverse strands of transnational, transcontinental, and transoceanic cosmopolitanism and connectedness helped to provide available mobilizing structures in the Philippines, Indonesia, and Vietnam, as well as sites for solidarity networks and sources of support for revolution making in Southeast Asia from across and beyond the region. After all, it was thanks to the incorporation of the Philippines within both the institutional umbrella of the Catholic Church and the world economy that the Katipunan of 1896 could draw on the rural *cofradías* (confraternities) and the provincial schoolboy networks that Christian evangelization and education had established in the archipelago, and on the infrastructure of newly established Masonic lodges in Manila and its environs to which growing connections to diverse parts of Europe had provided an introduction (see chapter 2). It was likewise thanks to new forms of education, association, and activism introduced by immigrant communities from the Hadhramaut and the southern coastal provinces of China that new forms of popular mobilization began to emerge in the Netherlands East Indies in the 1910s and 1920s, as seen most notably in the rise of the Sarekat Islam (SI) (see chapter 5). It was, moreover, thanks to the expanding infrastructure of Sufi brotherhoods, Islamic schools, and Islamic associational activity, on the one hand, and the early twentieth-century introduction of revolutionary socialist modes of party building and union organizing, on the other, that Islam and communism proved to be such powerful discursive and mobilizational tools during the Revolusi of 1945–1949 (see chapter 7). Similarly, it was thanks to early Vietnamese participation in the Union Intercoloniale (Intercolonial Union), the Parti Communiste Français (French Communist Party), the Comintern, and the Chinese Communist Party in China that Marxism and Leninism were introduced and established so effectively as the basis for revolutionary mobilization in Vietnam (see chapter 9).

---

35. Nicanor G. Tiongson, *Kasaysayan ng Komedya sa Pilipinas: 1766–1982* (Manila: Integrated Research Center, De La Salle University, 1982), 31–38; Matthew I. Cohen, *Komedie Stamboel: Popular Theater in Colonial Indonesia* (Athens: Ohio University Press, 2006); Duane Ernie Hauch, "The Cai Luong Theater of Vietnam, 1915–1970" (PhD diss., Southern Illinois University at Carbondale, 1972).

These mobilizing structures were profoundly cosmopolitan. Filipino revolutionaries enjoyed sympathy and support in various quarters in Europe. The Indonesian Revolusi benefited from concrete forms of assistance from solidarity networks in Singapore and Sydney, Malaysia and Mecca, Canton (Guangzhou), and Cairo. The Vietnamese Revolution drew strength from arms, other matériel, and military advisors provided by their Communist corevolutionaries in neighboring China. But beyond such external backing, the very internal constitutive vehicles of revolution making in the Philippines, Indonesia, and Vietnam were constructed out of models and materials drawn not from the institutional structures of colonial states but from diverse cosmopolitan connections. It was thus largely through the egalitarian premises and promises as well as the distinctive discursive and organizational vehicles of republicanism, Islam, and communism that different kinds of revolutionary brotherhood—and to a much lesser extent, sisterhood—could be invoked and, to varying extents, achieved and sustained in these three revolutions in Southeast Asia.

Fifth and finally, even as deepening incorporation into the world economy and expanding cosmopolitan connectedness provided transnational sources of inspiration and organizational infrastructure for new forms of consciousness, representation, association, and political activism in Southeast Asia, it was only through international conflicts that political opportunities for full-blown revolutionary mobilization emerged in the Philippines, Indonesia, and Vietnam, as detailed in the chapters that follow. Leaving aside the impact of the Seven Years' War, the Napoleonic Wars, and the Wars of Independence in South America, it is obvious that the Cuban War of Independence and then the Spanish-American War were crucial for shaping the onset and trajectory of the Philippine Revolution. As scholars have shown, the Sino-Japanese War, the Russo-Japanese War, and World War I helped to set the stage for the first, foundational phase of popular mobilization in the Netherlands East Indies seen with the rise of the Sarekat Islam.[36] More important, an extensive body of scholarship has shown how World War II, the Japanese occupation period, the Allied Liberation of Southeast Asia, and the onset of the Cold War decisively shaped the course of the Indonesian Revolusi.[37] Historians have similarly shown how World War I, the onset of World War II in Europe in 1939, and the peculiarities of its extension into Indochina in 1940–1945

---

36. See, for example, Takashi Shiraishi, *An Age in Motion: Popular Radicalism in Java, 1912–1926* (Ithaca, NY: Cornell University Press, 1990); Kees Van Dijk, *The Netherlands Indies and the Great War, 1914–1918* (Leiden: KITLV Press, 2007).

37. Benedict R. O'G. Anderson, *Java in a Time of Revolution: Occupation and Resistance, 1944–1946* (Ithaca, NY: Cornell University Press, 1972); Robert J. McMahon, *Colonialism and Cold War: The United States and the Struggle for Indonesian Independence, 1945–1949* (Ithaca, NY: Cornell University Press, 2011).

and Liberation in 1945–1946, combined with the conclusion of the civil war in China to enable the Vietnamese Revolution.[38] Thus, alongside the denationalizing and transnationalizing implications of an emphasis on cosmopolitan origins, efforts at internationalizing the three great revolutions of Southeast Asian history are also worthy of note.

Cosmopolitanisms and Comparisons?

Against this backdrop, this book offers a composite picture of the Philippine, Indonesian, and Vietnamese revolutions that goes beyond both established understandings of these revolutions as nationalist in nature and the various strands of the growing body of literature on the various cosmopolitan connections cited above. The tasks of the book are threefold. First, the book is intended to provide a new descriptive overview of the three major revolutions in Southeast Asian history. In so doing, this work provides a critical counterpoint to those understandings and accounts of these revolutions that, consciously or unconsciously, follow official nationalist narratives in which the rise of national consciousness produces nationalists who make national revolutions. In so doing, the book thus works to undermine efforts to appropriate these revolutions—and the making of these three new nation-states—for the nationalist elites who came to occupy state power in the aftermaths of these revolutions and throughout the postindependence era. By providing alternative narratives, the book suggests ways these revolutions might be understood not only in terms of their victories and their victors but in light of their betrayals and their victims, as the diverse and diverging emancipatory energies that helped to fuel revolutionary mobilization were in various ways absorbed, appropriated, and eviscerated by postrevolutionary (nation-)states.[39]

Second, in the place of a telos of colonial state formation spawning nationalist intelligentsias, nationalist movements, and nationalist revolutions leading to independence for new nation-states across Southeast Asia, the book outlines the arc of an alternative shared trajectory leading to(ward) revolution—and beyond—in the region. This trajectory starts with the emergence and evolution of new social formations up through the early modern era in the Philippine and Indonesian

38. David G. Marr, *Vietnam, 1945: The Quest for Power* (Berkeley: University of California Press, 1997); David G. Marr, *Vietnam: State, War, and Revolution (1945–1946)* (Berkeley: University of California Press, 2013); Stein Tønnesson, *The Vietnamese Revolution of 1945: Roosevelt, Ho Chi Minh, and de Gaulle in a World at War* (London: Sage, 1991); Stein Tønnesson, *Vietnam 1946: How the War Began* (Berkeley: University of California Press, 2011); Qiang Zhai, *China and the Vietnam Wars, 1950–1975* (Chapel Hill: University of North Carolina Press, 2000).

39. On this process in postindependence India, see Srirupa Roy, *Beyond Belief: India and the Politics of Postcolonial Nationalism* (Durham, NC: Duke University Press, 2007).

archipelagos, in parts of what today constitutes Vietnam, and elsewhere across Southeast Asia, social formations constituted by transoceanic trade, waves of long-distance migration, and diverse cosmopolitan currents and connections. With the deepening integration of these areas of Southeast Asia into the world capitalist economy in the latter half of the nineteenth century, moreover, full-blown market societies began to crystallize, giving rise to new social classes, modern public spheres, and diverse new social imaginaries and modes of consciousness, expression, association, and action, most notably in the urban port entrepôts of the region, but also radiating out into their rural hinterlands through the market's expanding circuitries. The cosmopolitanism of these embryonic market societies was evident in the newspapers, novels, and diverse forms of popular theater that sprung up by the turn of the twentieth century and spread across the cities and towns of Luzon and the Visayas, Java and Sumatra, Tonkin, Annam, and Cochinchina, and other parts of Southeast Asia, which hosted growing immigrant communities from the southern provinces of China, the Indian subcontinent, and the Hadramaut region of the Arabian Peninsula.

As suggested most evocatively and instructively in James Siegel's iconoclastic book *Fetish, Recognition, Revolution*, these developments and trends undermined existing social hierarchies and opened up diverse new, modern ways of being, ways of seeing themselves and/in the world, and ways of doing politics among Southeast Asians. The accelerating transoceanic movement of commodities, people, texts, and narratives flowing in and out of the harbors of cities such as Cebu, Surabaya, and Saigon also began to draw more and more Southeast Asians into the orbit of diverse cosmopolitan circuitries and currents that were potentially transgressive—and transformative—of established local authority structures. In different ways in different contexts, republicanism, Islam, and communism provided both an emancipatory, egalitarian ethos and an associational infrastructure for new challenges, not only, or even primarily, against colonial states, but also—and especially—vis-à-vis established authority structures such as the Catholic Church in the Philippines, local aristocracies and European agribusiness empires on Java and Sumatra, and their counterparts in Tonkin, Annam, and Cochinchina. Thanks to the conjunctural opportunities created by international conflicts—the Spanish-American War for the Philippines, World War II for Indonesia and Vietnam—these challenges expanded into full-blown revolutionary insurrections and in one way or another established new state-like structures along variously republican, Islamic, and communist lines. Viewed from this perspective, the provisional, partial victories of these revolutions thus signified not only national independence for the Philippines, Indonesia, and Vietnam, but also—and more important—the establishment and entrenchment of new forms of authority and hierarchy through which to encapsulate and domesticate the diverse energies and aspirations unleashed and at play in the preceding years of social transformation and political upheaval. Thus, instead of the linear telos of the birth, rise, and triumph of the Philippine, Indonesian, or Vietnamese nation, the book suggests a dialectical process of profoundly transnational economic change, social transformation, and political mobilization and institutionalization in the making and remaking of the societies of Southeast Asia over the proverbial *longue durée*.

Third and finally, beyond a new descriptive overview of the trajectories leading to these three revolutions and the making of new nation-states in Southeast Asia, this book is also intended to provide a comparative analysis of the ways diverse cosmopolitan origins, transnational forces, and international conjunctures combined to shape the variegated trajectories of the Philippine, Indonesian, and Vietnamese revolutions. In this regard, the book draws inspiration from scholars working in the tradition of comparative historical sociology, not only those who have analyzed revolutions but also those who have examined the diverging fates of various other great challenges to the status quo in modern society, as exemplified by Robert Wuthnow in his magisterial study, *Communities of Discourse: Ideology and Social Structure in the Reformation, the Enlightenment, and European Socialism*, and Mansoor Moaddel in his seminal book, *Islamic Modernism, Nationalism, and Fundamentalism: Episode and Discourse*.[40]

As in such studies, the three cases chosen from Southeast Asian history are notable not only for their shared commonalities as revolutions but also for their differences. The Philippine Revolution, for example, unfolded nearly a full half century before its Indonesian and Vietnamese counterparts, yet it suffered from greater internal fissures, factionalism, and fragmentation. It led not to the successful establishment of an independent new nation-state, but, after the short-lived Malolos Republic, forced demobilization in the face of violent pacification by the United States and the imposition of a colonial form of limited democracy, with far less revolutionary mobilization accompanying the transition to independence in the early aftermath of World War II than observed in many other parts of Southeast Asia.

The Indonesian Revolusi, by contrast, represented one of the most forceful episodes of revolutionary mobilization leading to independence and the establishment of new nation-states in Southeast Asia in the late 1940s and 1950s. Large-scale mass mobilization and participation in guerrilla warfare unfolded against Dutch colonial forces across much of Java and Sumatra, and elsewhere across the sprawl-

---

    40. Robert Wuthnow, *Communities of Discourse: Ideology and Social Structure in the Reformation, the Enlightenment, and European Socialism* (Cambridge, MA: Harvard University Press, 1989); Mansoor Moaddel, *Islamic Modernism, Nationalism, and Fundamentalism: Episode and Discourse* (Chicago: University of Chicago Press, 2005).

ing archipelago in 1945–1949. The Revolusi eventually achieved the goal of Indonesian independence by the end of 1949, but it did so amidst considerable internal tension and violent conflict, and with notable betrayals and compromises on various sides.

Finally, the Vietnamese Revolution not only achieved independence for the Democratic Republic of Vietnam (DRV) north of the Seventeenth Parallel in 1954 in the face of considerable French resistance and recalcitrance but also (re)unification of the full extent of Vietnam in 1975 after more than a decade of direct US military intervention in Indochina. In its unified leadership, its well-developed (party-)state structures, and its combination of guerrilla and conventional warfare, the Vietnamese Revolution thus stands as the strongest, most successful case of revolution in Southeast Asia. For better and for worse, it provides the most genuinely revolutionary pattern of postindependence social transformation of all the three cases.

Against this backdrop, the pages that follow offer not only a denationalized, transnationalized, and internationalized descriptive account of the Philippine, Indonesian, and Vietnamese revolutions counterposed against nationalized, nationalist, and nation-centered narratives but also an overarching framework for explaining the broad and variegated pattern of revolutionary mobilization across Southeast Asia as a whole. Comparing the Philippine, Indonesian, and Vietnamese revolutions (chapters 1–10), and then concluding by contrasting their emergence and unfolding with less spectacular or successful struggles in what would become Thailand, Malaysia, and Burma, this book suggests a new interpretive perspective and analytical prism through which to understand similarities and differences among the revolutions of the region. Here, following Robert Wuthnow, the emphasis lies in the varying openness and accessibility of different parts of Southeast Asia to different cosmopolitan communities of discourse and transnational bases for revolutionary brotherhood, and their varying vulnerability to international conflicts and other conjunctures enabling revolutionary mobilization.

As signalled in the subtitle of the book, however, the varying openness, accessibility, and susceptibility of different parts of Southeast Asia to what Vicente Rafael calls "the promise of the foreign" did not reflect inherent, enduring differences among the region's diverse cultures but rather the complex and variegated concatenations of accumulated historical sedimentation and social formation that Southeast Asians had fashioned out of successive encounters and interactions with the broader world across and beyond the region over the centuries and decades leading up to these revolutions. Thus, the book is intended to consolidate and clarify the emerging new picture of Southeast Asia that a wide range of innovative and eye-opening recent historical studies has opened up over the past twenty years, and to illuminate the diverse, sometimes desperate, and often doomed efforts of Southeast Asians to undertake revolutionary mobilization and to effect revolutionary transformations of their societies. In this effort, instead of celebrating Southeast Asian nationalists and nationalism and sealing off the region as the exclusive preserve of Southeast Asian studies, this book spotlights the interlopers and also-rans of Southeast Asian history, and suggests the intellectual and political advantages of a more open-ended understanding of the region.

FROM BOHEMIA TO BALINTAWAK

Cosmopolitan Origins of the Philippine Revolution

The Bohemian town of Litoměřice, nestled at the junction of the Elbe and Ohře Rivers some sixty-odd kilometers northwest of Prague in the *pohraničí* (border-lands) of what today comprises the Czech Republic, provides a seemingly unusual, but potentially illuminating, vantage point from which to approach the cosmo-politan dimensions of the Philippine Revolution of the late nineteenth century. Litoměřice, it should be noted, played a prominent role in the development of Czech nationalism over the course of the past two hundred years. Bernhard Bolzano (1781–1848), the mathematician, philosopher, and author of the pioneer-ing 1816 treatise *On the Condition of the Two Nationalities in Bohemia*, was stripped of his post as dean of the Theological Faculty of Charles University in Prague in 1820 on the basis of charges of membership in a secret society said to have been founded by his pupil Michal Josef Fesl, a professor at the Jesuit seminary in Litoměřice. The founding father of Czech linguistics and literature, Josef Jung-mann (1773–1847), moreover, offered the first Czech-language courses at the gymnasium in Litoměřice, and later at the Jesuit seminary in the town, at the turn of the nineteenth century, before writing a series of important books on Czech lit-erature (including the first Czech-German dictionary, a five-volume, 120,000-entry magnum opus) and rising to the position of rector of the University of Prague. Even more important, perhaps, the much loved epic romantic poet Karel Hynek Mácha was buried in a church cemetery in his adopted hometown of Litoměřice in 1836, but, in one of the most famous and moving episodes in Czech history, his grave was exhumed and his remains moved to Prague in May 1938 in the wake of the Anschluss (annexation) of Austria into the Third Reich two months earlier. As German troops prepared to annex the Germanized areas of the Czech *pohraničí* that Hitler called the *Sudetenland*, hundreds of thousands of Czech mourners filled the streets of Prague and streamed past Mácha's coffin as it was installed in the Pantheon of the National Museum in Prague and then interred in the nearby cemetery of the Vyšehrad Castle, in the company of such other Czech national luminaries as the playwright Karel Čapek, the composer Antonín Dvořák, and the writer Jan Neruda.[1]

Yet for the Philippine Revolution, the significance of Litoměřice lies not in its inspirational role in the development of Czech nationalism, but rather as its former identity as Leitmeritz, a town in the Habsburgs' Austro-Hungarian Empire that drew the interest of none other than Dr. José Rizal, the great Filipino novelist and celebrated progenitor of Philippine nationalism. For Leitmeritz served as the home of Ferdinand Blumentritt, allegedly the scion of a Spanish family that departed Manila for Bohemia amidst the expulsion of the Jesuits from the Philippines in the early 1770s, and a local gymnasium teacher and avid student and scholar of Philippine history and society. In 1886, Blumentritt and Rizal embarked on a lengthy and regular correspondence that lasted literally until the eve of Rizal's execution at the hands of the Spanish colonial government in December 1896 amidst the popular uprising in and around Manila that constituted the first phase of the Philippine Revolution. Over the course of the decade leading up to the Philippine Revolution, "Professor" Blumentritt corresponded regularly with Rizal, wrote countless articles and letters on the Philippines, contributed to public debates on the Philippines in various publications in Spain, and engaged in assiduous and at times incendiary defense and promotion of his friend Rizal, assisting in the publication of Rizal's two celebrated novels, *Noli Me Tangere* in 1887 and *El Filibusterismo* in 1891. Against this backdrop, Rizal's visit to Blumentritt's home in Leitmeritz in May 1887 was an event of considerable significance for the two men, as is evident in the deepening warmth and intimacy of their correspondence in its aftermath. Rizal wrote to Blumentritt from the Moravian city of Brünn (Brno) a week later: "Ich bin ja auch Leitmeritzer vom Herzen wie Sie Philippiner" (I am also at heart a Leitmeritzer, just as you are a Filipino).[2]

Despite occasional references to "Dr. Czepelack," a colleague of Blumentritt's whom Rizal had met during his visit to Leitmeritz, Rizal displays no sense of awareness of or affinity with the budding of Czech nationalism in the Bohemia of the nineteenth century; he shows neither sympathy nor a sense of interest. Instead, the solidarities linking Blumentritt and Rizal lay elsewhere. Blumentritt, it

---

1. See Derek Sayer, *The Coasts of Bohemia: A Czech History* (Princeton, NJ: Princeton University Press, 1998), 25–28, 57–60, and 70–73.
2. See Rizal's letter of May 19, 1887, Rizal-Blumentritt Correspondence, José Rizal National Centennial Commission, 1961, 79–81.

should be noted, married off his daughter Dolores not, as he sometimes half-jokingly proposed, to his young friend from the Philippines, but instead to Dr. Karl Pickert, founder and editor of the *Leitmeritzer Zeitung* and a prominent leader and parliamentary representative of the German Liberal Party, which countered the ascendancy of Czech nationalism in the late nineteenth century with the promotion of German culture as a vehicle for intellectual and political progress across the Habsburg Empire.[3] Rizal's visit to Leitmeritz, it is also worth noting, came at the tail end of a year-long stay in Heidelberg and Berlin, during which time he continued and deepened his training in ophthalmology: achieved fluency in the German language; and immersed himself in the cultural, intellectual, and political life of the *bürgertum* (bourgeoisie) of Bismarckian Germany. Among the highlights of Rizal's sojourn was his induction into the Berlin Anthropological Society, at the invitation of its founder and president, the prominent scientist, German politician, and parliamentarian Rudolf Virchow, who had joined forces with Bismarck to champion what Virchow famously called the Kulturkampf ("culture struggle") against the Catholic Church in the realms of German culture, education, and society.

Rizal's visit to Leitmeritz and his correspondence and collaboration with Blumentritt over the last decade of his life thus point to a broader field of experience, inspiration, encouragement, and interlinkages within a set of transcontinental networks of scientists and scholars, liberals and republicans, Freemasons, and other activists and intellectuals stretching across Germany, Bohemia, Belgium, England, and France, and extending into Spain and its far-flung colony in the Philippines. Such connections were built on the cosmopolitan foundations of the Catholic Church, as seen in the transmission to the Philippine archipelago—and the translation into Tagalog—of hagiographic celebrations of the late fourteenth-century martyrdom of Jan Nepomuk, the patron saint and Counter-Reformation icon of Bohemia, by the Jesuits in the mid-eighteenth century.[4] Even today, statues of San Juan Nepomuceno are found in churches across the country and the Nepomucenos rank among the most prominent local political "'dynasties" in the province of Pampanga, just north of Metro Manila.

But even if Rizal's visit to Leitmeritz and relationship with Blumentritt meant so much to him, what was the broader significance for the making of the Philippine Revolution? Rizal's relationship with the Philippine Revolution, after all, was famously ambivalent and ambiguous; he was imprisoned and sent into internal exile in 1892, four years before the outbreak of the revolution, and executed by

---

3. Pieter M. Judson, *Exclusive Revolutionaries: Liberal Politics, Social Experience, and National Identity in the Austrian Empire, 1848–1914* (Ann Arbor: University of Michigan Press, 1996), 167–222.

4. See Howard Louthan, *Converting Bohemia: Force and Persuasion in the Catholic Reformation* (Cambridge: Cambridge University Press, 2009), 277–300.

the Spanish colonial government in December 1896, just a few short months after the revolution had begun to unfold. More broadly, an emphasis on the global peregrinations, transcontinental connections, and cosmopolitan pretensions of Rizal and his compatriots risks an overly (self-)indulgent and admiring focus on small, privileged clusters of effete Filipino intellectuals and flâneurs as they busied themselves in late nineteenth-century belle époque Europe, at the expense of close attention to the broad mass of illiterate, Tagalog- and Ilocano-speaking subalterns—artisans, peasants, and fishermen—back in the Philippines, who provided the foot soldiers of the revolution, and, by many accounts, crucial sources of its ideology and leadership, from its outbreak in mid-1896 in Manila and the provinces of Luzon.

How, then, to connect the likes of Blumentritt in Bohemian Leitmeritz with the Philippine Revolution? The existing body of scholarship on the Philippine Revolution, for all its empirical richness and analytical diversity, provides a coherent narrative account, one whose emplotment follows the nationalist logic so prevalent in the study of Southeast Asian history. On the one hand, the revolution is said to have been led from above by urban—and highly urbane—educated young men[5] familiar from Anderson's *Imagined Communities*, Filipino nationalists who emerged from Spanish colonial schools in the Philippines in the latter half of the nineteenth century and achieved prominence in Madrid and Barcelona, and then in Manila and beyond, as newspaper editors and authors of novels in the late 1880s in what became known as the Propaganda Movement. Literate, educated, well-travelled, and fluent in the colonial lingua franca of Castilian Spanish, this ascendant nationalist intelligentsia was capable of imagining Las Islas Filipinas (the Philippine Islands) not only as an archipelago of great ethnolinguistic, horticultural, and topographical diversity, but as a nation in waiting, populated not simply by populations divided among *indios* (natives), *mestizos*, and *chinos* (Chinese), or by Igorots (upland "pagans") and Moros (Muslims), but more broadly by "Filipinos," a term previously reserved for the small minority of *criollos* (creoles) born of Iberian ancestry within the colony.

These Propagandistas included among their ranks the celebrated novelist José Rizal, the painter Juan Luna, and such activists and writers as Marcelo del Pilar, men whose activities both in the metropole and in the colony helped to inspire a nationalist revolution against Spanish colonial rule. Their ideas and influence were diffused among a wider pool of affluent, educated, Catholic, Spanish-speaking *ilustrados* (educated élites) in Manila, Iloilo, Cebu, and other major urban en-

---

5. On the gender and sexual relations among these early nationalists, see Raquel A. G. Reyes, *Love, Passion and Patriotism: Sexuality and the Philippine Propaganda Movement, 1882–1892* (Seattle: University of Washington Press, 2008).

trepôts across the archipelago, who represented the most educated and enculturated elements among the largely Chinese mestizo class of merchants and landowners in the Spanish colonial Philippines. This nationalist impulse further diffused into the hinterlands, circulating among classically schoolboy networks of local worthies speaking broken Spanish and fluent Tagalog, Ilocano, Ilonggo, or Cebuano, with *provincianos* (provincials) like the Caviteño Emilio Aguinaldo and the Batangueño Miguel Malvar emerging as prominent revolutionary generals amidst the anticolonial upheaval of the late nineteenth century. These Filipino nationalists, in large measure, are credited with the making of the Philippine Revolution.[6]

On the other hand, the Philippine Revolution is also said to have been driven from below by a broader pool of the Filipino masses, by peasants and fishermen across the provinces of the archipelago, and by artisanal laborers in Manila and other port cities. Largely illiterate, unschooled, and unversed in Spanish, these Filipinos-in-the-making were neither readers of the first Filipino novels and newspapers, nor otherwise able, it would appear, to imagine the Philippines as a nation in the sense intended by Benedict Anderson. But they were heirs to a long tradition of millenarian rebellions and everyday forms of resistance over the long centuries of Spanish colonial rule, and their understandings of political legitimacy and social justice were informed and inflected by indigenous understandings of charismatic authority and a moral economy rooted in guarantees of subsistence. Appropriating and reinventing Spanish Catholicism as a distinctly Southeast Asian form of folk Christianity, Tagalog peasants, Ilocano artisans, Ilonggo sugarcane workers, and Cebuano fishermen thus joined the Philippine Revolution not as Filipino nationalists per se, but as representatives of subaltern classes immersed in a culturally distinctive form of popular consciousness and in a counterhegemonic challenge to the existing social order.[7] Hence, the emergence and growth of the revolutionary movement known as the Katipunan (Kataastaasan Kagalanggalang Katipunan ng mga Anak ng Bayan; the Highest and Most Honorable Society of the Sons of the Country) under the leadership of its founder, Andres Bonifacio, and the Katipunan's centrality in the armed uprising that marked the onset of the revolution in 1896.[8] The history of the Philippine Revolution is written as a tale of belated (mis)recognition and a brief merger between these two strands in Philippine society, followed by betrayal and conflict, thus spelling failure

---

6. See, for example, John N. Schumacher, S. J., *The Propaganda Movement, 1880–1895: The Creation of a Filipino Consciousness, the Making of the Revolution* (Quezon City: Ateneo de Manila University Press, 1997).

7. Reynaldo Clemeña Ileto, *Pasyon and Revolution: Popular Movements in the Philippines, 1840–1910* (Quezon City: Ateneo de Manila University Press, 1979).

8. Teodoro A. Agoncillo, *The Revolt of the Masses: The Story of Bonifacio and the Katipunan* (Quezon City: University of the Philippines, 1956).

for the nationalist revolution at the end of the nineteenth century and a deeper fissure within the Filipino nation that has endured to this day.

Yet for all its analytical coherence and empirical richness, this account of the Philippine Revolution leaves important questions essentially unanswered. First of all, and taking the Philippine Revolution on its own terms, how can we explain the mechanisms and processes by which mobilization—and then demobilization—unfolded, linking *ilustrados* such as Rizal to more modestly educated Manileños such as Bonifacio, *provinciano* elites such as Aguinaldo and Malvar, and the broader mass of subaltern Filipinos? Second, and taking a broadly comparative perspective, how can we explain why the Philippine Revolution unfolded so much later than the revolutions of Spanish colonial America, on the one hand, and yet so much earlier than the revolutions in colonial Southeast Asia, on the other? Third and finally, and extending the comparison, how can we square the striking precocity of the Philippine Revolution in the Southeast Asian context with the notable weakness of subsequent revolutionary mobilization a half century later in the heyday of the Indonesian and Vietnamese Revolutions?

As suggested in the pages above and below, the answers to this question lie neither within the Philippines alone, nor solely in the colony's relationship with its metropolitan Spain, nor, more broadly, within the language and logic of nationalism. Instead, as argued throughout this book, the answers to these questions require a mode of comparative analysis that takes into account the international context within which both colony and metropole were embedded, as well as a set of cosmopolitan connections and currents, which impacted on Philippine society in distinctive and decisive ways. Viewing the Philippine Revolution not only as against the later Vietnamese and Indonesian Revolutions, but also in comparison with contemporaneous developments in nearby Siam (later Thailand), this account thus offers a new interpretation of the Philippine Revolution in light of its international context and cosmopolitan origins.

Here it is argued that the Philippine Revolution was enabled and impelled by the integration of the Philippines within the world capitalist economy and by a set of major conflicts in international society, whose consequences were experienced quite differently in the Philippines as compared with other parts of Southeast Asia. Here it is further argued that alongside the social forces and political opportunities generated by world capitalism and global conflicts, the cosmopolitan forces of late nineteenth-century republicanism, liberalism, Freemasonry, and anticlericalism combined with the distinctive cosmopolitan institutions of the Catholic Church itself to provide mobilizing structures and discursive formations for revolutionary brotherhood in the Philippines not available elsewhere in the region. Thus, it is only through a properly denationalized, internationalized, and transnationalized account that the Philippine Revolution can be more fully and fruitfully understood.

The Philippines in the World Capitalist Economy and in International Society

The Philippine Revolution unfolded against the backdrop of dramatic shifts in the archipelago's integration into the world capitalist system and the decisive social changes accompanying this transformation of the Philippine economy. By the turn of the second millennium of the Common Era, the Philippine archipelago had become incorporated into the expanding maritime trading networks that stretched across the Indian Ocean and the South China Sea.[9] Low-volume trade for Chinese porcelains and other foreign luxury goods was sustained over subsequent centuries, with evidence of a dramatic increase by the early 1500s, corresponding with the emergence of more organizationally complex and territorially expansive polities in those regions of the archipelago that were favorably situated for control over this trade.[10]

From the 1560s into the early nineteenth century, moreover, Manila served as a key node in a truly global trading network linking Andalusian cities such as Cádiz and Sevilla, Acapulco and other American ports and the southern coasts of late Ming and early Qing China, the Indian subcontinent, and Japan.[11] Galleons arrived in Manila every year laden with silver from Mexico, departing with cargo holds filled with Asian silks and cotton textiles, spices, and various luxury goods brought into port by Hokkien-speaking *sang-li* (merchants) on junks from Amoy and other coastal towns of Fujian Province and on vessels sailing from the coastal ports of the Indian subcontinent.[12]

Whether understood as a subsidy or as customs duties, the *situado* (the annual apportionment of silver to the authorities in Manila) constituted the underlying

---

9. For background overviews, see Kenneth R. Hall, *A History of Early Southeast Asia: Maritime Trade and Societal Development, 100–1500* (Lanham, MD: Rowman and Littlefield, 2010); Janet L. Abu-Lughod, *Before European Hegemony: The World System A.D. 1250–1350* (Oxford: Oxford University Press, 1989); and Andre Gunder Frank, *ReOrient: Global Economy in the Asian Age* (Berkeley: University of California Press, 1998).

10. Laura Lee Junker, *Raiding, Trading, and Feasting: The Political Economy of Philippine Chiefdoms* (Quezon City: Ateneo de Manila University Press, 2000).

11. See Pierre Chaunu, *Les Philippines et le Pacifique des Ibériques (XVIe, XVIIe, XVIIIe Siècles)* (Paris: S.E.V.P.E.N., 1960), and John J. Tepaske, "New World Silver, Castile and the Philippines 1590–1800," in *Precious Metals in the Medieval and Early Modern Worlds*, ed. John F. Richards (Durham, NC: Carolina Academic Press, 1983), 425–445.

12. William Lytle Schurz, *The Manila Galleon: The Romantic History of the Spanish Galleons Trading between Manila and Acapulco* (New York: E.P. Dutton, 1939).

fiscal basis for colonial rule in the Philippines.[13] Local produce comprised only a miniscule portion of the galleon trade, and there was little economic impetus for the further colonization of the archipelago.[14] The Iberian colonial presence in the Philippines was miniscule, dwarfed by the Hokkien-speaking *sang-li* or *chinos*, whose numbers in the archipelago ran into the tens of thousands by the early seventeenth century. Thus, it is possible to view the Philippines of the late sixteenth, seventeenth, and early eighteenth centuries not (only) as a colony of Spain but (also) as an outpost of a China-centered trading network in the Pacific Ocean.[15]

Yet the emergence and evolution of the galleon trade in Manila was profoundly transformative, both globally and within the Philippine archipelago. As economic historians have long argued, the establishment and entrenchment of the galleon trade enabled and impelled the birth of a world capitalist economy that linked European, American, and Asian ports and their hinterlands for the first time in history.[16] But beyond the role of Manila as the key nodal point for this emerging world economy, the Philippine Islands and their inhabitants played a bigger role that most historians have tended to ignore. The galleon trade, after all, depended heavily on the repair and reconstruction of Spanish galleons in and around Manila Bay, most notably the shipyards of what would become known as the province of Cavite.[17]

Expert *indio* artisans were essential for ship repairs and shipbuilding,[18] as were laborers forced to fell and transport thousands of hardwood trees for hulls, decks, and masts, and to secure hemp for ropes and rigging.[19] Alongside the exploitation of Philippine labor and natural resources came the early prominence of the

13. Josep M. Fradera, *Filipinas, La Colonia Más Peculiar: La Hacienda Pública en la Definición de la Política Colonial, 1762–1868* (Madrid: Consejo Superior de Investigaciones Científicas, 1999), 17–69.

14. Leslie España Bauzon, *Deficit Government: Mexico and the Philippine Situado (1606–1801)* (Tokyo: Centre for East Asian Cultural Studies, 1981).

15. For an argument along these lines, see Katharine Bjork, "The Link That Kept the Philippines Spanish: Mexican Merchant Interests and the Manila Trade, 1571–1815," *Journal of World History* 9, no. 1 (Spring 1998), 25–50.

16. See Dennis O. Flynn and Arturo Giráldez, "Born with a 'Silver Spoon': The Origin of World Trade in 1571," *Journal of World History* 6, no. 2 (Fall 1995): 201–221, and Dennis O. Flynn, "Cycles of Silver: Global Economic Unity through the Mid-Eighteenth Century," *Journal of World History* 13, no. 2 (Fall 2002): 391–427. See also Arturo Giráldez, *The Age of Trade: The Manila Galleon and the Dawn of the Global Economy* (Lanham, MD: Rowman and Littlefield, 2015), and Birgit Tremml-Werner, *Spain, China, and Japan in Manila: 1571–1644: Local Comparisons and Global Connections* (Amsterdam: Amsterdam University Press, 2015).

17. See William J. McCarthy, "The Yards at Cavite: Shipbuilding in the Early Colonial Philippines," *International Journal of Maritime History* 7, no. 2 (December 1995): 149–162.

18. William Henry Scott, "Boat-Building and Seamanship in Classic Philippine Society," *Philippine Studies* 30, no. 3 (1982): 335–376.

19. See Andrew Christian Peterson, "Making the First Global Trade Route: The Southeast Asian Foundations of the Acapulco-Manila Galleon Trade, 1519–1650" (PhD diss., University of Hawai'i at Manoa, 2014), especially, 67–96 and 181–229.

islands' seamen among the ranks of the world's merchant marine: by the late six-teenth century, "the crews of Spain's Pacific galleons were anywhere from 60 to 90% *indio*, often times with only the key administrative positions on board filled by Spaniards."[20] The extent and importance of Philippine labor in the galleon trade can be adduced by the evidence of early transoceanic migration to the Americas by those who became known inas *indios chinos* (Chinese Indians), or simply *chinos*.[21]

But after two centuries of continuity, the position of the Philippines within the Spanish Empire and the world economy began to shift as a consequence of a series of major international conflicts. First, in the aftermath of the Seven Years' War of 1756–1763, the Bourbon king Carlos III (1759–1788) initiated a set of reforms designed to transform the loose, Habsburg-led federation of Iberian realms into a united, centralized, absolutist Spain, while tightening the metro-pole's links to its colonies and other territories overseas, including the Philippines, which had experienced a British invasion and occupation from 1760 through 1762.[22] For the first time, direct sea traffic began to link Manila to Iberian ports, with the 1778 royal decree of *comercio libre* (free trade) facilitating trade between the archipelago and the key Andalusian ports of Cádiz and Sevilla.

New fiscal imperatives stimulated shifts in colonial rule.[23] Spanish governors in the Philippines began to promote the intensification of efforts to settle the pop-ulation of the archipelago in municipalities (*pueblos*) placed under the estab-lished pattern of colonial administration, with local native authorities closely monitored by Spanish Catholic priests. At the same time, new initiatives were un-dertaken to promote a deepening of the economic exploitation of the archipel-ago, with a Real Sociedad Económica de Filipinas (Royal Economic Society of the Philippines) founded by the Spanish governor-general in 1781 and a tobacco monopoly established the same year to stimulate cultivation of the crop by na-tive farmers.[24] The Real Compañía de Filipinas (Royal Company of the Philip-pines) was founded in 1785 to promote commercial links between Spain and the Philippines, enjoying a monopoly on trade with the archipelago through the 1820s that consolidated the position of the metropole at the expense of the previously dominant merchant networks of Spanish America, while reducing Manila's con-nections and central role in the field of intra-Asian trade.[25]

20. Peterson, "Making the First Global Trade Route," 230–274, with passage cited on 266.

21. Edward R. Slack Jr., "The *Chinos* in New Spain: A Corrective Lens for a Distorted Image," *Journal of World History* 20, no. 1 (March 2009): 35–67.

22. John Lynch, *Bourbon Spain, 1700–1808* (Oxford: Basil Blackwell, 1989), 247–421.

23. Fradera, *Filipinas, La Colonia Más Peculiar*, 70–73.

24. Edilberto C. de Jesus, *The Tobacco Monopoly in the Philippines: Bureaucratic Enterprise and Social Change, 1766–1882* (Quezon City: Ateneo de Manila University Press, 1980), 13–70.

25. W. E. Cheong, "The Decline of Manila as the Spanish Entrepôt in the Far East, 1785–1826: Its Impact on the Pattern of Southeast Asian Trade," *Journal of Southeast Asian Studies* 2, no. 2 (Sep-tember 1971): 142–158.

But these shifts in favor of tighter, more exclusive linkages between the Philippines and Spain came undone in the aftermath of the Napoleonic Wars of the early nineteenth century and the struggles for independence in Spanish America that came in their wake. The galleon trade was terminated; the Spanish governor-general in Manila no longer reported to the viceroy of Nueva España ('New Spain') in Mexico City But more important, by the 1830s, the official opening of the Philippines to foreign trade had begun, first in Manila in 1834, extending to Iloilo and Zamboanga in 1855, and with Cebu following suit in 1860. By 1844, the provincial trade monopoly licenses (*indulto de comercio*) enjoyed by Spanish *alcaldes mayors* (provincial governors) were abolished, freeing up interisland commerce from official intervention.[26] British firms operating out of Hong Kong and Guangzhou soon dispatched agents to various Philippine port cities, where they engaged local partners to purchase sugar, abaca, rice, tobacco, and other agricultural commodities, and to sell cotton textiles and small-scale manufactured goods.[27] Trading companies from the United States and various European countries followed suit, with German firms achieving prominence and a second-place position behind their British competitors by the 1880s.[28] With the opening of the Suez Canal in 1869 and Pax Britannica making long-haul shipping cheaper, safer, and speedier, the integration of the Philippines into the world capitalist economy deepened dramatically in the latter half of the nineteenth century.

The resultant export boom stimulated a dramatic social transformation throughout much of the Philippine archipelago. As British, American, German, and Swiss merchants began to arrive in Philippine ports, their diverse stocks of manufactured goods and their demand for local commodities spurred the commercialization of agriculture and the rise of a comprador class of local merchants, moneylenders, and landowners in these entrepôts and their hinterlands. This comprador class in the colonial Philippines was virtually unique in Southeast Asia in terms of its legal status and political potential. As throughout much of the region, trade in the Philippines had long been dominated by "Chinese" immigrants from the southern coastal provinces of the Middle Kingdom, who were residentially and administratively segregated by the colonial authorities, subjected to periodic pogroms and deportations, restricted in terms of dress, residence, and mobility, and heavily taxed. In the Philippines, however, the authorities not only encouraged conversion to Catholicism by these *chino* merchants but also awarded special "mixed" (mestizo) status to the offspring of their unions with "native" (*india*)

26. Benito J. Legarda Jr., *After the Galleons: Foreign Trade, Economic Change and Entrepreneurship in the Nineteenth-Century Philippines* (Quezon City: Ateneo de Manila University Press, 1999).
27. Nicholas Tarling, "Some Aspects of British Trade in the Philippines in the Nineteenth Century," *Journal of History* 11, nos. 3–4 (September–December 1963): 287–327.
28. Wigan Maria Walther Tristan Salazar, "German Economic Involvement in the Philippines, 1871–1918" (PhD thesis, University of London, 2000).

wives, a designation accompanied by release from the onerous taxes and restrictions on mobility, residency, and landownership that had weighed so heavily on their *chino* forefathers.

Armed with the seed capital, commercial contacts and experience accumulated by their *chino* fathers, and the local languages and freedom enjoyed by their *india* mothers, Chinese mestizos fanned out from the port cities of the Philippine archipelago in the mid–late nineteenth century, as sellers of European manufactured goods, purchasers of sugar, tobacco, hemp, and other agricultural commodities, moneylenders, and, increasingly, landowners in the hinterlands. This ascendant class of Chinese mestizo merchants and landowners began to fill the ranks of the *principalia* (local worthies) in rural municipalities around the archipelago, to play an increasingly prominent role in the expanding urban public sphere of the port cities, and to populate the privileged parish schools, *colegios* (secondary schools), and universities of the Philippines (and to a lesser extent, of the Spanish metropole) with their children.[29]

At the same time, the export boom of the latter half of the nineteenth century generated broader demographic and social changes, with the commercialization of agriculture spurring population growth, expansion of urban centers, and increasing marketization, monetization, and density of settlement in the hinterlands of the port cities of the archipelago.[30] By 1857, the Western Visayan entrepôt of Iloilo was an urban center with a population of more than seventy thousand, as large as Chicago, Sydney, Valparaiso, or Caracas at the time.[31] The rise of market society in many areas of the Philippine archipelago, it has been argued, created a growing audience and an increasing demand for popular poetry, music, and theater, and for metrical romances printed as chapbooks, and, in due course, for the newspapers and novels central to Benedict Anderson's account of the rise of nationalism.

In fact, what seems so striking about the late nineteenth-century Philippines is the nature and extent of the cosmopolitanism enabled by the deepening integration of the archipelago within the world economy. The Chinese mestizo merchants and landowners, after all, won their fortunes through partnerships with British, German, Swiss, and American trading firms, rather than as officials of the Spanish colonial state, thus providing a powerful set of counterpoints to the authorities of Manila and Madrid. City streets in Manila, Cebu, and Iloilo prominently featured

---

29. Edgar Wickberg, *The Chinese in Philippine Life, 1850–1898* (New Haven, CT: Yale University, 1965).

30. On the deepening integration of Manila and its hinterland, see Daniel F. Doeppers, *Feeding Manila in Peace and War, 1850–1945* (Madison: University of Wisconsin Press, 2016).

31. Alfred W. McCoy, "Introduction: The Social History of an Archipelago," in *Philippine Social History: Global Trade and Local Transformations*, ed. Alfred W. McCoy and Edilberto C. de Jesus (Quezon City: Ateneo de Manila University Press, 1982), 9.

British banks and German pharmacies, with commodities from diverse corners of the world on sale in market towns across the archipelago. The library of José Rizal famously ranged from Balzac, Hugo, Montesquieu, Renan, and Voltaire, to Heine, Kant, and Schiller, Sophocles and Thucydides, Machiavelli, Shakespeare, and Turgenev.[32]

Beyond the narrow confines of such *ilustrado* circles, moreover, a broader *kosmopolitanisasyon* (cosmpolitanization) was unfolding among the growing population clustered in the archipelago's market towns and cities.[33] This cosmopolitanism of the poor was evident in the diverse points of reference in the popular poems, songs (*awit*, *corrido*), and plays (*comedia* or *komedya*) circulating in major Philippine cities and towns during this period.[34] The most celebrated *awit* of the nineteenth-century Philippines, "Ang Pinagdaanang Buhay ni Florante at ni Laura sa Cahariang Albania," was set in the far-flung kingdom of Albania and features countless references to Greek and Roman mythology.[35] The *komedya* likewise drew on Spanish medieval romances about "Moros y Cristianos" (Muslims and Christians) in distant locations, with "not a single reference to the Philippines, to Filipinos, Chinese, Spaniards, or to local Muslims in the entire range of vernacular dramas." Instead, the *komedya* "conjured a phantasmagoric 'Europe,'" while presenting characters and scenes foreign to the Philippines in a familiar idiom.

> Translation placed European identity in motion, as it were, so that it surfaced in odd ways on colonial stages. Staging *comedia* meant, among other things, bringing both spatial and temporal distances up close. The unknown regions of the Western past now suddenly became accessible to native audiences. As fragments attached to non-European bodies and speech, "Europe" and its past were converted into spectral signposts from which issued a native present.[36]

Among a growing segment of the population, the sociological imagination and frame of reference extended beyond both the Philippine archipelago and "Mother Spain" to the broader world within which the Philippines was profoundly embedded.

---

32. Esteban A. De Ocampo, *Rizal as a Bibliophile* (Manila: Unesco National Commission of the Philippines, 1960), 27.

33. Nicanor G. Tiongson, *Kasaysayan ng Komedya sa Pilipinas: 1766–1982* (Manila: Integrated Research Center, De La Salle University, 1982), 31–38.

34. See J. Francisco B. Benitez, "*Awit* and *Syair*: Alternative Subjectivities and Multiple Modernities in Nineteenth-Century Insular Southeast Asia" (PhD diss., University of Wisconsin at Madison, 2004).

35. Bienvenido L. Lumbera, *Tagalog Poetry, 1570–1898: Tradition and Influences in Its Development* (Quezon City: Ateneo de Manila University Press, 1986), 112–137.

36. Vicente L. Rafael, *The Promise of the Foreign: Nationalism and the Technics of Translation in the Spanish Philippines* (Durham, NC: Duke University Press, 2005), 106–107.

In short, the great global conflicts of the eighteenth and early nineteenth centuries—the Seven Years' War and the Napoleonic Wars—helped to spur the deepening integration of the Philippines within the world capitalist economy and gave rise to a vibrant market society in many parts of the archipelago. Thanks to Spain's increasingly semiperipheral position within the world economy, these processes led not to a tightening of links between colony and metropole, but rather to a broadening of the archipelago's access to diverse flows of commodities and culture emanating from far beyond the Iberian Peninsula, making for a distinctive cosmopolitanism in the port cities and the market towns of their hinterlands. Thanks to Spanish policies encouraging intermarriage between *chinos* and *indias* and according privileged mestizo status to their offspring, moreover, the Philippines of the mid-nineteenth century boasted a comprador class of local merchants, moneylenders, millers, and landowners freed from the problematic pariah status to which their "Chinese" counterparts were consigned elsewhere in Southeast Asia (with the notable exception of nominally independent Siam). This distinctive pattern of class formation, in short, created conditions favorable for social and political upheaval in the late nineteenth century, and combined with the onset of the Cuban Revolution in 1895 and the Spanish-American War of 1898 to set the stage for the Philippine Revolution at the turn of the twentieth century.

Ultramontane Catholicism versus Liberalism, Republicanism, and Freemasonry

Alongside the social forces generated by global capitalism and the political opportunities opened up by interstate wars, late nineteenth-century conflicts between rival cosmopolitan institutions and ideologies also helped to provide the mobilizational and discursive structures that made the Philippine Revolution possible. On the one hand, the institutional imperatives and practices of the Catholic Church provided an underlying infrastructure for Philippine society that, by the nineteenth century, enabled new forms of association and collective action in localities across the archipelago and allowed for communication and collaboration with Catholics halfway across the globe. On the other hand, the quasi-subterranean network of free-thinking intellectuals and Freemasons associated with the Enlightenment of the late seventeenth and eighteenth centuries had, by the mid–late nineteenth century, developed the economic interests, political skills, and social bases required for the promotion of liberalism and republicanism, not only in Western Europe and the Americas but, by the turn of the twentieth century, in the Philippines as well. The late nineteenth-century struggle between ultramontane Catholicism and anticlerical liberalism and republicanism, not only in Restoration Spain but in the late Habsburg Austro-Hungarian Empire, Troisième République France, Bismarckian Prussia, and Risorgimento Italy, served both to enable and to impel the outbreak of the Philippine Revolution in 1896.

If the shifting position of the Philippines within the world capitalist economy established the fiscal parameters for the colonization of the archipelago from the mid-sixteenth century onward, the incorporation of the Philippines within the realms of Roman Catholicism and papal authority determined the administrative and social infrastructure for Spanish colonial rule. The conquest of the Philippines, it is worth recalling, unfolded not only in the century following the consolidation of the Christian Reconquista of the Iberian Peninsula and the establishment of the Inquisition but also in the decades following the (in)famous Council of Trent, amidst the Catholic Counter-Reformation and the restructuring of the institutions of the church.[37] Crucial here was the rise to prominence and revitalization of the religious orders, and their redeployment from areas lost to Protestantism in Europe to the frontiers of Christianity in the New World and beyond. The pioneering role of the newly formed Jesuit order (the Society of Jesus)—the so-called shock troops of the Counter-Reformation—as missionaries in China was perhaps the best known, and most closely studied, example of this broader trend among the mendicant orders of the church.[38]

It is against this backdrop that Habsburg Spain and its territories in Europe, the Americas, and Asia in the sixteenth and seventeenth centuries should be understood. The Spanish monarchy, after all, ruled over not a unified, centralized Spain, but, after the union of Castilla and Aragón with the marriage of Ferdinand and Isabella in 1469, a set of loosely connected realms on the Iberian Peninsula. Even after the Bourbon absolutist reforms in the late eighteenth century, the map of Spain remained "a palimpsest of kingdoms, principalities and provinces, many of them islands adrift in alien territories, where considerable differences (in such elementary matters as weights and measures, terms for money, not to speak of laws, customs, and language) pertained."[39]

But the king known as Carlos I on the Iberian Peninsula was also crowned as the Holy Roman Emperor Karl V in 1519, and successive Castilian monarchs saw themselves as the heirs and successors of the Romans, as the bearers of a divine

37. Ronnie Po-Chia Hsia, *The World of Catholic Renewal, 1540–1770* (Cambridge: Cambridge University Press, 1998).
38. See John W. O'Malley, *The First Jesuits* (Cambridge, MA: Harvard University Press, 1995); Liam Matthew Brockney, *Journey to the East: The Jesuit Mission to China, 1579–1724* (Cambridge, MA: Harvard University Press, 2008), and Florence C. Hsia, *Sojourners in a Strange Land: Jesuits and Their Scientific Missions in Late Imperial China* (Chicago: University of Chicago Press, 2009).
39. Ronald Fraser, *Napoleon's Cursed War: Popular Resistance in the Spanish Peninsular War* (London: Verso, 2008), xv.

mission, and as the creators of a universal empire.[40] Against the backdrop of the Reconquista, a series of papal bulls in the late fifteenth century and early sixteenth century awarded the Spanish monarchy the *patronato real universal*, the right of patronage and presentation to all the major ecclesiastical benefices in both its Iberian territories and in the Americas and Asia, while recognizing its sovereignty over far-flung overseas possessions on the condition of a commitment to evangelization among these newly "discovered" lands.[41] In other words, Madrid won recognition of its rule over the "Kingdoms of the Indies" on the basis of its role as deputized agent of Rome, with the Pope remaining, at least in principle, as the ultimate sovereign of these realms.

Within Spain itself, the Catholic Church remained a powerful institution. The Concordat of 1753 reaffirmed the *patronato real universal* of the Spanish crown, now in Bourbon hands, and the absolutist reforms following the Seven Years' War saw Charles III expelling the Jesuit order from Spain and its possessions. But within Spanish society, the church remained "a state within the state" into the early nineteenth century, "the monarchy's single wealthiest institution, with its own judicial and tax-raising system, the latter generally more efficient than the state's." Through its institutional presence, including the Inquisition, the church "controlled the expression of ideas and personal and social behavior," and its role in education and publishing remained hegemonic well into the nineteenth century, both in Spain and across its overseas territories.[42]

This formative context proved decisive for the nature of Spanish rule in the Philippines, which some of its critics were to deride as a *frailocracía* (rule by friars) and as *La Soberanía Monacal* (Monastic Sovereignty) in the years leading up to the Philippine Revolution.[43] The Augustinian friars accompanying the Basque conquistador Miguel López de Legazpi from Mexico in his conquest of the islands in the 1560s voiced strenuous opposition to Habsburg dominion over the Philippines, and it was only after the 1582 Synod of Manila that Spanish sovereignty in the archipelago was acknowledged by Pope Alexander VI, on the basis of the Habsburg monarchy's service to Rome as an agent of evangelization among the natives of the islands.[44]

---

40. See Anthony Pagden, *Spanish Imperialism and the Political Imagination: Studies in European and Spanish-American Social and Political Theory, 1513–1830* (New Haven, CT: Yale University Press, 1990), and Anthony Pagden, *Lords of All the World: Ideologies of Empire in Spain, Britain and France c. 1500—c. 1800* (New Haven, CT: Yale University Press, 1995), especially 11–62.

41. John H. Elliott, *Imperial Spain, 1469–1716* (New York: St. Martin's Press, 1963), 99–100.

42. Fraser, *Napoleon's Cursed War*, xvii.

43. See, for example, Marcelo H. Del Pilar's 1889 tract, *La Frailocracía Filipina*, translated and published as *The Frailocracy in the Philippines* (Manila: National Historical Institute, 1979).

44. J. Gayo Aragón, O.P., "The Controversy over Justification of Spanish Rule in the Philippines," in *Studies in Philippine Church History*, ed. Gerald H. Anderson (Ithaca, NY: Cornell University Press, 1969), 3–21.

The early years of Spanish rule thus saw the arrival of missionaries from the major religious orders in the archipelago, with the first contingent of Augustinians followed by representatives of the Franciscans (1577), the Jesuits (1581), the Dominicans (1587), and the Augustinian Recollects (1606). King Philip II partitioned the islands among these five orders in 1594 and allowed the "regular" clergy to engage in evangelization across the archipelago before the establishment of episcopates by their "secular" counterparts.[45] Observers in the mid-eighteenth century noted that three-quarters of the parishes in the Philippines were still staffed by "religious" clergy, a condition still obtaining at the end of the nineteenth century; alongside this institutional infrastructure, the religious orders were awarded vast landholdings by the Spanish crown under the system of land grants (*encomiendas*) prevailing in the Kingdoms of the Indies.[46] These so-called friar estates comprised huge tracts of fertile land in and around major port cities like Manila and Cebu and, through complex subleasing arrangements, provided a great source of income and power to the religious orders in the archipelago.[47]

Thus, the limited colonization that unfolded in the Philippines in the two centuries following Legazpi's expeditions to Cebu and Manila was driven and dominated by the institutional imperatives of the Catholic Church, interwoven as it was with the Spanish monarchy and the colonial state. Colonization and evangelization proceeded through *reducción*, the forcible reorganization of mobile *indio* communities into nucleated settlements *bajo de la campana*, that is, within earshot of the church bells. Through *reducción*, the local infrastructure of colonial rule was established: churches were built and municipal plazas constructed around them as town centers, with local authority emanating from the parish priests, who oversaw the election of village headmen (*cabezas de barangay*) and town mayors (*gobernadorcillos*) from among the limited pool of eligible local worthies (*principalia*).[48] In this way, colonization interpellated the native *indios* of the Philippines not only as colonial subjects but as Christian believers, incorporating them not only within the Spanish Empire but within the cosmopolitan realms of Christianity.

Indeed, the *reducción* of the native population into nucleated settlements drew the *indios* into the orbit of the broader discursive and institutional universe of the

45. Horacio de la Costa, S.J., "Episcopal Jurisdiction in the Philippines during the Spanish Regime," in *Studies in Philippine Church History*, ed. Gerald H. Anderson (Ithaca, NY: Cornell University Press, 1969), 44–64.

46. Charles H. Cunningham, "The Ecclesiastical Influence in the Philippines (1565–1850)," *American Journal of Theology* 22, no. 2 (April 1918): 161–162n1.

47. Nicholas P. Cushner, *Landed Estates in the Colonial Philippines* (New Haven, CT: Yale University Southeast Asia Studies, 1976).

48. Vicente L. Rafael, *Contracting Colonialism: Translation and Christian Conversion in Tagalog Society under Early Spanish Rule* (Durham, NC: Duke University Press, 1993), 87–91.

Catholic Church. Attached to local churches were small parish schools, which taught small numbers of native children the Roman alphabet and the rudiments of Castilian Spanish and Latin. In major towns and port cities, a set of Catholic *colegios* sprang up to offer secondary education (and serve as seminaries) to a more limited pool of pupils, even as the Dominicans founded the University of Santo Tomás in Manila in 1611.[49] As this educational system drew increasing numbers of *indios* away from the established indigenous scripts (*baybayin*) of the archipelago and into literacy in the Roman alphabet, in Spanish, and Latin, the religious orders began to promote the circulation of written materials to promote the spread of the Christian faith. The *Doctrina Christiana* was first published in 1593 by the Dominicans in Manila, with the Franciscans, Jesuits, and Augustinians founding their own printing presses in the first decade of the seventeenth century and joining the Dominicans "in turning out grammars, dictionaries, catechism and confession manuals" for native *ladinos* capable of reading and writing in both Spanish and native languages.[50]

In myriad ways, the driving imperative of Christian evangelization in the Philippines thus combined with the deepening integration of the archipelago within the world capitalist economy to generate new forms of shared cultural experience, meaning, practice, and production within an emerging public sphere. As historians of Christianity in the Philippines have noted, the process of evangelization and the maintenance of the church's presence among the *indios* of the archipelago was, as elsewhere in the Catholic world, greatly assisted by the formation and activism of confraternities—sodalities organized among the lay members of a church parish as religious brotherhoods for the faithful.

In the Philippine context, it has been argued, the emergence of *cofradías* can be traced to the post-Reformation policy of direction and deployment "from above," with parish priests forming confraternities among the *principalia* to assist in the evangelization and enforcement of Christian practices among the population at large.[51] In the struggle against the continuing spiritual authority of indigenous healers, sorceresses, and priestesses—the *babaylanes* and *catalonan*—in local society,[52] members of the *cofradías* were tasked with ministering to the sick and dying, by leading Christian prayers, in a practice identified as *magpahesus*,

49. For an overview, see Henry Frederick Fox, "Primary Education in the Philippines, 1565–1863," *Philippine Studies* 13, no. 2 (April 1965): 207–231.

50. Bienvenido L. Lumbera, *Tagalog Poetry, 1570–1898: Tradition and Influences on Its Development* (Quezon City: Ateneo de Manila University Press, 1986), 22.

51. John Bossy, "The Counter-Reformation and the People of Catholic Europe," *Past and Present* 47 (May 1970): 51–70; Hsia, *The World of Catholic Renewal, 1540–1770*, 202–203.

52. Filomeno V. Aguilar Jr., *Clash of Spirits: The History of Power and Sugar Planter Hegemony on a Visayan Island* (Honolulu: University of Hawai'i Press, 1998), and Carolyn Brewer, *Shamanism, Catholicism, and Gender Relations in Colonial Philippines, 1521–1685* (Aldershot: Ashgate, 2004).

inducing the ill and infirmed to invoke the name of Christ in their pleas for deliverance from suffering.[53] But over time, the *cofradías* seem to have come to play a broader set of roles in Philippine society, as elsewhere in the Catholic world:[54]

> Confraternities were aids to expressing penitence, or hopefully earning merit through good works. They could provide spiritual and physical assistance in time of need for members and family. Through festivities they could contribute to spiritual joy—and more mundane fun and entertainment. . . . They were agencies of social-political networking, and peacemaking.[55]

Indeed, at least by the mid-nineteenth century, some *cofradías* had also begun to outgrow their functions in subcontracted evangelization and surveillance of the faithful, to expand beyond the control of parish priests, to develop autonomous linkages across individual parishes, and, in some instances, to evolve into what today would be identified as "intentional communities" under charismatic lay leadership outside the institutional structures of the church. Hence, the considerable scholarly interest in the Cofradía de San José founded by the *donado* (lay brother) Apolonario de la Cruz in the early 1830s, a confraternity that spread across the provinces of Tayabas, Laguna, and Batangas in southern Luzon before establishing a commune that fell to Spanish attack in 1841.[56] Thus, through the institution of religious brotherhood, the Catholic *cofradías* provided a set of local and translocal mobilizing structures that would help to inform, enable, and inspire popular mobilization in the Philippine Revolution at the end of the nineteenth century.

Beyond the *cofradías*, the processes of Catholic evangelization in the Philippines also spurred the development of new forms of artistic and intellectual expression among the population at large. Especially during Holy Week and other major religious holidays, parish priests in the Philippines encouraged the textual elaboration and dramatic enactment of the *pasyon*, religious verses narrating the life, suffering, death, and resurrection of Jesus in the native vernaculars of the archipelago. The chanting, or *pabasa*, of these *pasyon*, it has been argued, allowed

53. John Leddy Phelan, *The Hispanization of the Philippines: Spanish Aims and Filipino Responses, 1565–1700* (Madison: University of Wisconsin Press, 1959), 74–83; René J. Javellana, *Casaysayan nang Pasiong Mahal ni Jesucristong Panginoon Natin na Sucat Ipag-alab nang Puso nang Sinomang Babasa* (Quezon City: Ateneo de Manila University Press, 1988), 12–13.

54. On confraternities in China, for example, see Liam Matthew Brockey, *Journey to the East: The Jesuit Mission to China, 1579–1724* (Cambridge, MA: Harvard University Press, 2007), 329–401.

55. Christopher Black, "Introduction: The Confraternity Context," in *Early Modern Confraternities in Europe and the Americas: International and Interdisciplinary Perspectives*, ed. Christopher Black and Pamela Gravestock (Aldershot: Ashgate, 2006), 2.

56. Ileto, *Pasyon and Revolution*, 29–73.

for the incorporation of indigenous culture and conceptions of spiritual power within the rubric of the versification of the Gospel, the translation of Christianity into terms understandable and appealing to the population of the archipelago, in ways that not only surreptitiously allowed for the survival of native culture and conceptions of legitimate authority but also subtly undermined the authority of Catholic Church and colonial state.[57] In the aftermath of the suppression of Apolonario de la Cruz's Cofradía de San José, it has been noted, parish priests in the Philippines reportedly tried to proscribe the *pabasa*, a move affirmed by the Archbishop of Manila in his call for a formal ban on the practice and a halt to the publication of the *pasyon*.[58]

By the late eighteenth century, moreover, alongside the *pasyon* as published text and the *pabasa* as public practice, there had also emerged a broader realm of artistic production, intellectual discourse, and popular consciousness in the Philippines. As early as the seventeenth century, parish priests had encouraged the staging of local dramas, or *komedya*, during local holidays, and the realm of popular theater expanded and evolved considerably over the course of the last two centuries of Spanish rule in the archipelago.[59] At the same time, as noted above, metrical romances known as *awit* and *corrido* were widely printed and circulated as chapbooks, memorized, and performed in many vernaculars.[60]

The increasing publication of *awit* and the expanding production of *komedya* over the course of the nineteenth century, it has been argued, endowed vernacular literature and theater with unprecedented autonomy and popularity, creating new cultural commodities that circulated among the growing populations in the major port cities of the archipelago and their hinterlands, and gave rise to a new figure in Philippine society, the professional vernacular author. "Part-time scribes, part-time translators, part-time assistants to a priest or government official, or part-time printers or bookbinders," it has been argued, began to appear in and around cities like Manila by the early–mid nineteenth century, catering to the increasing "urbanity and refinement of a Tagalog audience that had grown up in towns and had received some exposure to formal education and economic advancement."[61]

Overall, by the late nineteenth century, the processes of Catholic evangelization had combined with the economic and social transformations generated by

---

57. Ileto, 11–22.

58. John D. Blanco, *Frontier Constitutions: Christianity and Colonial Empire in the Nineteenth-Century Philippines* (Berkeley: University of California Press, 2009), 124.

59. On this trend, see Nicanor G. Tiongson, *Kasaysayan ng Komedya sa Pilipinas: 1766–1982* (Manila: Integrated Research Center, De La Salle University, 1982), 1–95, and Doreen G. Fernandez, *Palabas: Essays on Philippine Theater History* (Quezon City: Ateneo de Manila University Press, 1996).

60. Benitez, "*Awit* and *Syair*," 36–64.

61. Blanco, *Frontier Constitutions*, 55–57.

the deepening incorporation of the Philippines within the world capitalist economy and had facilitated the crystallization of a modern public sphere and new forms of subjectivity and sociality among the population at large that exceeded the control of the church and the colonial state. Among the awkward "excesses" produced by these dynamics of change were new kinds of "organic intellectuals" in Philippine society. Beyond the *ladino* interpreters, scribes, and lay brothers (*donados*) who had assisted the Spanish parish priests in ministering to the faithful from the first decades of evangelization in the archipelago, the Catholic parish schools, *colegios*, and universities of the archipelago also allowed for the training of small but increasingly significant numbers of *indios* and mestizos qualified to serve in the priesthood. While the religious orders did not allow *indios* or mestizos into their ranks, the "secular" hierarchy's need for clergy to staff the parishes necessitated a more open policy toward native priests, with evidence of small numbers of *indios* and mestizos ordained perhaps as early as the mid-seventeenth century, and definitely by the turn of the eighteenth century.[62]

In the aftermath of the Seven Years' War, moreover, Bourbon reforms saw a decisive shift in favor of the "secular" church hierarchy at the expense of the religious orders, as seen in the expulsion of the Jesuits from Spain and its dominions, including the Philippines. This change was evident from the 1770s in the shift away from the practice of allowing the religious orders to staff many parishes with "regular" priests in favor of the promotion of "secular" parishes. By 1810, the numbers of *indio* priests were said to dwarf the regular clergy, with most parishes falling into native hands.

By the mid-nineteenth century, however, this policy had been reversed, with a royal decree in 1826 ordering that all parishes transferred to the secular clergy in the preceding decades should be reverted to the religious orders on the death, removal, or transfer of incumbent priests. In the wake of the revolutions in Spanish America and a series of moves against the church in Spain itself, a new wave of friars came to the Philippines to reclaim parishes for the religious orders, with numbers increasing with the return of the Jesuits to the archipelago in 1859 and the opening of the Suez Canal in 1869.[63] Thus, the *indio* and mestizo priests of the late nineteenth-century Philippines found their earlier ascendancy reversed, their ambitions checked, and their aspirations frustrated by the constraints of church and colonial state policy.

---

62. Luciano P. R. Santiago, *The Hidden Light: The First Filipino Priests* (Quezon City: New Day, 1987). On the religious orders' unwillingness to accept natives into their ranks, see Fr. Rolando V. de la Rosa, O.P., *Beginnings of the Filipino Dominicans: History of the Filipinization of the Religious Orders in the Philippines* (Quezon City: Dominican Province of the Philippines, 1990).

63. Horacio de la Costa, S.J., "The Development of the Native Clergy in the Philippines," in *Studies in Philippine Church History*, ed. Gerald H. Anderson (Ithaca, NY: Cornell University Press, 1969), 65–104.

Meanwhile, the late nineteenth century also witnessed the rise of the so-called *ilustrados* among the ascendant class of Chinese mestizo landowners and merchants in the archipelago, a development enabled by shifts in Catholic education driven by economic and social transformation in the Philippines, by the evolving imperatives of colonial rule in the archipelago, and by contemporaneous trends in Catholic education elsewhere. As noted above, the Jesuits were allowed to return to the Philippines in 1859, and the order, long known for its pioneering role within the church in terms of engagement with modern society and the challenges of medicine and science, was entrusted with a privileged role in educational reform in the archipelago, which was not long in coming.[64] In 1863, a royal decree was proclaimed establishing a new system of Spanish-language schooling in the Philippines, with a full infrastructure of primary, secondary, and tertiary institutions. By the 1870s, nearly four hundred thousand pupils were estimated to be attending primary schools in the Philippines, with more than two thousand said to be enrolled in secondary schools in Manila, Cebu, and Iloilo, and over five hundred in universities.[65]

To meet the demands of this new educational system, the Jesuits were tasked with the training of primary school teachers throughout the archipelago in an Escuela Normal in Manila and were allowed to open a prestigious new secondary school, the Ateneo Municipal in the colonial capital, which later evolved into a Jesuit-run university. Named after the Athenaeum in classical Rome, by the 1880s the Ateneo was offering a form of secondary education that transcended the limits of the scholasticism, theological focus, and Thomism hitherto dominant in the Catholic schools of the archipelago, as elsewhere:

> The Jesuit curriculum for the six-year course leading to the degree of bachelor of arts was considerably tougher than the present [1963] equivalent for high school and college. Besides Christian doctrine, it included Spanish, Latin, Greek and French, world geography and history, the history of Spain and the Philippines, mathematics and the sciences (arithmetic, algebra, geometry, trigonometry, mineralogy, chemistry, physics, botany and zoology), and the classic disciplines of poetry, rhetoric and philosophy.[66]

Even the more conservative Dominicans took steps in a similar direction, opening new faculties of medicine and pharmacy at the University of Santo Tomás in

---

64. See, for example, Mordechai Feingold, ed., *Jesuit Science and the Republic of Letters* (Cambridge, MA: MIT Press, 2003), and Rivka Feldhay, *Galileo and the Church: Political Inquisition or Critical Dialogue?* (Cambridge: Cambridge University Press, 1995).

65. For these figures, see Domingo Abella, "Higher Education in the Philippines to 1863: A Historical Reappraisal," *Philippine Historical Review* 1, no. 1 (1965): 29.

66. Leon Ma. Guerrero, *The First Filipino: A Biography of José Rizal* (Quezon City: Journal Press, 1963), 38.

Manila in 1871, which produced the first native-born doctors, pharmacists, and surgeons with modern training in the Philippines before the end of the decade.[67]

As they expanded the realm of higher education in the humanities and the sciences in the Philippines, it is worth noting, the Jesuits and Dominicans retained the long-established emphasis on instruction in the sacred language of Latin. Latin had always served as the ultimate language of authority in the linguistic hierarchy of the Spanish colonial Philippines:

> Despite the spread of Castilian in Spain, Latin was thought to stand in such close relation to God's own language that it still functioned as the special medium for framing God's laws and for conducting the liturgy of the church. The special status accorded to Latin was inextricably bound to the nature of the message it bore within itself. That Tagalog [and other native tongues of the archipelago] should be organized around the matrix of Latin is a function of the Spanish belief in the proximity of Latin to the spirit of God's Word, a proximity that lent Latin its authority to preside over the vernacular languages.[68]

Beyond the Philippines, moreover, Latin remained, even in the late nineteenth century, the authoritative language of Christian cosmopolitanism. Latin, after all, was retained as the liturgical language of the Catholic Church, the language in which the mass was delivered and the sacraments were administered, throughout this period, and it was also used as the official internal administrative and deliberative language of the church. Among Catholics across the world, moreover, the language was invested with a broader significance, as argued passionately by Joseph de Maistre in a book defending the pope in 1819.

Throughout the world, de Maistre asserted, the shared use of Latin provided "a mysterious bond of immense strength" that helped to forge a brotherhood among Catholics: "Just trace the line where this universal language falls silent: there are the outer limits of European civilization and fraternity."[69] But beyond the Catholic faithful, Latin also served as the key language for the promotion of classical humanism in schools and universities across Europe. Even in Troisième République France, secondary education was in considerable measure focused on Latin, with students in secondary schools devoting one-third to 40 percent of their

---

67. Luciano P. R. Santiago, M.D., "The First Filipino Doctors of Pharmacy (1890–93)," *Philippine Quarterly of Culture and Society* 22, no. 2 (June 1994): 90–102, and Luciano P. R. Santiago, M.D., "The First Filipino Doctors of Medicine and Surgery (1878–97)," *Philippine Quarterly of Culture and Society* 22, no. 2 (June 1994): 103–140.

68. Rafael, *Contracting Colonialism*, 28.

69. Joseph de Maistre, *Du Pape* (Paris: Charpentier, 1841), 133–140, cited in Françoise Waquet, *Latin or the Empire of a Sign: From the Sixteenth to the Twentieth Centuries* (London: Verso, 2001), 64.

time to classical language study in the 1880s and 1890s. In Spain, Latin remained the sole language of instruction at the university level well into the early nineteenth century.[70] Small wonder that the *ilustrado* luminary Dr. José Rizal gave his famous novel (written in Spanish, published in Belgium, soon translated into German) a Latin title—*Noli Me Tangere* (Don't touch me)—which combined with its biblical allusion to be comprehensible among a broad cosmopolitan readership across the Christian world.[71]

While owing their intellectual formation in large measure to the Jesuits and the Dominicans, the *ilustrados* of the late nineteenth-century Philippines were thus—uniquely in the Southeast Asian context—enabled and impelled to circulate among and communicate and collaborate with a diverse range of academics and activists, Freemasons and Freethinkers, republicans and liberals who were pitted against the entrenched interests of the ultramontane Catholic Church in the Philippines as elsewhere in the world. Historians have documented the rise in the late seventeenth and early eighteenth centuries of a quasi-subterranean network of radical Enlightenment thinkers, scholars, and publishers, stretching across Europe, "combining immense reverence for science, and for mathematical logic, with some form of non-providential deism, if not outright materialism and atheism along with unmistakably republican, even democratic tendencies."[72] Radiating out of the major commercial, industrial, and administrative centers of Europe—like Amsterdam, London, Paris, Venice, Naples, Berlin, Vienna, Copenhagen, and Hamburg—the public sphere of this period saw the rise of "new erudite journals, 'universal' libraries, literary clubs, lexicons, and encyclopedias, . . . and generally the new post-1648 Republic of Letters, as well as, more mundanely, newspapers, gentlemen's magazines, tea- and coffee-houses and, after around 1730, also Masonic lodges."[73]

The diffusion of the Enlightenment across Europe during this period was accompanied by the spread of the cosmopolitan networks and associational practices of Freemasonry.[74] Evolving out of the medieval guilds of stonemasons, skilled craftsmen whose trade required literacy, knowledge of geometry and mathematics, and training in architecture and engineering, Masonic lodges

---

70. Waquet, *Latin or the Empire of a Sign*, 13, 25.

71. For an illuminating treatment of the relevant passage in the Gospel of John, see Jean-Luc Nancy, *Noli Me Tangere: On the Raising of the Body* (New York: Fordham University Press, 2008).

72. Jonathan I. Israel, *The Radical Enlightenment: Philosophy and the Making of Modernity, 1650–1750* (Oxford: Oxford University Press, 2001), 12.

73. Israel, *Philosophy and the Making of Modernity, 1650–1750*, 59; see also 119–155.

74. See Margaret C. Jacob, *The Radical Enlightenment: Pantheists, Freemasons and Republicans* (London: Allen and Unwin, 1981); Margaret C. Jacob, *Living the Enlightenment: Freemasonry and Politics in Eighteenth-Century Europe* (Oxford: Oxford University Press, 1991); Margaret C. Jacob, *Strangers Nowhere in the World: The Rise of Cosmopolitanism in Early Modern Europe* (Philadelphia: University of Pennsylvania Press, 2006).

emerged, first in Scotland and later in England by the mid-seventeenth century, as societies with elaborate myths and rituals, and began to attract members of the gentry into their ranks.[75]

> Masonic lodges became places where gentlemen, whether lowly or ti-
> tled, could receive a minimal instruction in mathematics, listen to lec-
> tures in the new science, or make up for what they did not know in
> science by participating in a movement that claimed to be descended
> from the earliest practitioners of applied mathematics—the Masonic
> "architects" who constructed the ancient temples, the medieval cathe-
> drals, and practised the "royal art" or the loyal service of generations of
> English kings.[76]

The lodges grew in number and membership over the course of the eighteenth century, expanding onto the Continent and across the Atlantic, while preserving the distinctive set of practices developed during the formative years of Freemasonry in Scotland and England: elections, majority rule, and representative government. As they spread and grew, the Masonic lodges promoted a distinctive form of sociability that was civic and constitutional in form, freed from the authority of church and crown, and forged in the discourse of the Enlightenment and an avowedly universalist form of horizontal brotherhood.[77] Small wonder that historians have assembled considerable evidence in support of the theory that the Freemasons played important roles in the French and American Revolutions of the late eighteenth century, and that contemporary observers produced elaborate conspiracy theories about the role of the Freemasons in the major conflicts of the nineteenth century as well.[78]

With industrialization, urbanization, and the expansion of the urban public sphere, the threat to the church posed by such forms of revolutionary brotherhood continued to grow. From the French Revolution through the 1848 revolutions across Europe and beyond, the ideas and interests, social forces and everyday practices, nodal points of intellectual production and cosmopolitan networks of associational activity identified with Freemasons, liberals, and republicans were locked in a protracted struggle with the entrenched institutions of church and crown.

---

75. See David Stevenson, *The Origins of Freemasonry: Scotland's Century, 1590–1710* (Cambridge: Cambridge University Press, 1988).

76. Jacob, *Pantheists, Freemasons and Republicans*, 125.

77. Margaret C. Jacob, *Freemasonry and Politics in Eighteenth-Century Europe.*

78. Steven C. Bullock, *Revolutionary Brotherhood: Freemasonry and the Transformation of the American Social Order, 1730–1840* (Chapel Hill: University of North Carolina Press, 1996), and Kenneth Loiselle, *Brotherly Love: Freemasonry and Male Friendship in Enlightenment France* (Ithaca, NY: Cornell University Press, 2014).

By 1870, this struggle had deepened. The Glorious Revolution of 1868 ousted Queen Isabella from the throne in Madrid, leading to several years of turmoil and the brief Republic of 1873–1874; Rome, briefly usurped by Mazzini and the republicans during the Roman Republic of 1848–1849, was captured by Garibaldi's troops in September 1870 amidst the unification of Italy; the Paris Commune of the same year signaled the revival of the anticlerical policies of the French Revolution in the Troisième République; in Berlin, the Lutheran Bismarck was about to embark on his Kulturkampf against the church; in London, a Liberal government was in power, headed by the devout Anglican William Gladstone, who penned a pamphlet on "Vaticanism" in 1874 questioning the loyalties of Britain's Catholic citizens.

Throughout continental Europe, the church was being stripped of its privileged position in education and, in no small measure, of its properties. In Britain and the United States, rising anti-Irish (and in the United States, broader anti-immigrant) sentiment among Protestants had served as the backdrop to a series of anti-Catholic novels over the preceding decades,[79] even as Eugène Sue's famously lurid depiction of Jesuits in his international best seller *Le Juif Errant* (*The Wandering Jew*) reached a wide readership in France, Britain, Spain, and elsewhere.[80]

In the face of this ascendant anticlericalism and anti-Catholicism across Europe and beyond, the church responded with a transcontinental campaign to reassert the authority of Rome, in an effort often identified as "Ultramontanism." The publication of the (in)famous *Syllabus of Errors* in 1864 saw Pope Pius IX issue a bitter public condemnation of liberalism, rationalism, socialism, communism, and Freemasonry, while rejecting calls for the church to "reconcile itself to progress, liberalism, and recent civilization." In 1870, Rome issued a public assertion of the doctrine of papal infallibility.[81] The same years saw a broader campaign to match anticlerical and anti-Catholic views with ultramontane counterpropaganda, as seen in the establishment of the influential Rome-based journal *Civiltà Cattolica* in the wake of the revolutions of 1848 and the founding of a centrally coordinated Catholic news bulletin, *La Correspondance de Genève*, which was run by a shadowy network of wealthy lay activists tagged by some as the Black International.[82] Beyond the emergence of a Catholic press during this

---

79. See Jenny Franchot, *Roads to Rome: The Antebellum Protestant Encounter with Catholicism* (Berkeley: University of California Press, 1994), and Susan M. Griffin, *Anti-Catholicism in Nineteenth-Century Fiction* (Cambridge: Cambridge University Press, 2009).

80. See Berry Palmer Chevasco, *Mysterymania: The Reception of Eugène Sue in Britain, 1838–1860* (Oxford: Peter Lang, 2003), and Elisa Martí-López, *Translation, Imitation, and the Making of the Nineteenth-Century Novel in Spain* (London: Associated University Presses, 2002).

81. For an overview, see Nicholas Atkin and Frank Tallett, *Priests, Prelates and People: A History of European Catholicism since 1750* (London: I.B. Tauris, 2003), 129–194.

82. Emiel Lamberts, ed., *The Black International, 1870–1878: The Holy See and Militant Catholicism in Europe* (Leuven: Leuven University Press, 2002).

period, the final decades of the nineteenth century saw the rise of Catholic youth groups, labor unions, and political parties.[83]

Viewed against this backdrop, the struggles leading up to the Philippine Revolution can thus be understood in terms of what scholars have termed the "Culture Wars" of the late nineteenth century, a transcontinental if not global conflict pitting "anticlerical" scientists, Freemasons, liberals, and republicans against the Catholic Church in its ultramontane incarnation. As one historian has noted: "the culture war was not merely a political civil war of the 'two Frances' or of the 'two Spains.' For, in the eyes of most combatants, this was a European and thus, by the understanding of that time, a global conflict with a prominent transnational dimension,"[84] extending across the world to incorporate the Philippine archipelago within its orbit.

83. Stathis N. Kalyvas, *The Rise of Christian Democracy in Europe* (Ithaca, NY: Cornell University Press, 1996).

84. Wolfram Kaiser, "'Clericalism—that is our enemy!': European Anticlericalism and the Culture Wars," in *Culture Wars: Secular-Catholic Conflict in Nineteenth-Century Europe*, ed. Christopher Clark and Wolfram Kaiser (Cambridge: Cambridge University Press, 2003), 49.

2

MASONERÍA, COFRADÍA, KATIPUNAN

Revolutionary Brotherhoods
in the Philippines, 1896–1901

In the far-flung Philippines, this global culture war was also raging. The latter half of the nineteenth century witnessed increasing tensions between the institutions of the church and the ascendant Chinese mestizo class of landowners, merchants, and their *ilustrado* offspring. In small towns across the archipelago, this trend was evident in the growing frequency of conflicts between parish priests and local worthies. Such conflicts were evident in the rising fractiousness of electoral contests for village-level and municipal government posts, which parish priests had hitherto regulated without much resistance from the local worthies included in the highly restricted electorate, but found increasingly difficult to stagemanage by the late nineteenth century.[1] Meanwhile, in the major cities of the archipelago, the church found its control over the urban public sphere increasingly undermined by the accelerating circulation of goods and ideas, and rising extraecclesiastical accumulation of cultural, financial, and social capital made possible by the inroads of the capitalist market. In Manila, Cebu, Iloilo, and other port cities, the same period saw the crystallization of increasingly heated disputes between Chinese mestizo business interests and the religious orders over urban landholdings, even as the huge "friar estates" in and around Manila were running up against growing tensions over land use vis-à-vis Chinese mestizo landowners and their own tenant farmers (*inquilinos*).[2] The religious orders during these years were

---

1. Greg Bankoff, "Big Fish in Small Ponds: The Exercise of Power in a Nineteenth-Century Philippine Municipality," *Modern Asian Studies* 26, no. 4 (November 1992): 679–700.
2. See, for example, Michael Cullinane, "The Changing Nature of the Cebu Urban Elite in the 19th Century," and Dennis M. Roth, "Church Lands in the Agrarian History of the Tagalog Region,"

standing firm against continuing pressures to open up their ranks to *indio* and mestizo priests, and on the retrocession and retention of parishes once held by native secular clergy.[3] Meanwhile, the advances in education pioneered by the Jesuits and, however grudgingly, implemented by the Dominicans and other orders had encouraged some among the newly educated *ilustrados* to explore the outer limits of acceptable intellectual, cultural, and political expression within and beyond the archipelago, even as continuing economic growth and urbanization allowed an expanding segment of the population to enjoy an unprecedented degree of autonomy from the increasingly attenuated surveillance and control of church curates and censors.

Against this backdrop, the pathways leading up to the Philippine Revolution at the end of the nineteenth century can be recast in terms of the mobilizing and discursive structures of cosmopolitan revolutionary brotherhood—or brotherhoods—forged in the global struggles between the Catholic Church and the anticlerical forces of liberalism, republicanism, and Freemasonry. In late Habsburg Bohemia, as noted above, Rizal, and such key compatriots as Trinidad Pardo de Tavera and Isabelo de los Reyes, found common cause with the humanist scholar Blumentritt, a fellow Catholic liberal working in the shadow of the Jesuits, thousands of miles from Philippine shores.[4]

Rizal's year-long sojourn in Bismarckian Germany also featured many months studying ophthalmology and German language and literature in the Rhenish town of Heidelberg. The site of the oldest university in Germany and the source of the famous "Heidelberg Catechism" of the Protestant Reformation, Heidelberg was a town that had served as home to the famously antiracist anatomist and physiologist Friedrich Tiedemann (1781–1861),[5] played a prominent role in the republican revolution of 1848 in the Rhineland,[6] and served since 1860 as the international headquarters of the openly, indeed avidly, anticlerical Association of Freethinkers.[7]

In Berlin, moreover, Rizal was inducted into the Berlin branch of the German Society for Anthropology, Ethnology, and Prehistory (Berliner Gesellschaft für

in *Philippine Social History: Global Trade and Local Transformations*, ed. Alfred W. McCoy and Edilberto C. de Jesus (Quezon City: Ateneo de Manila University Press, 1982), 251–296, 131–154.

3. John N. Schumacher, S.J., *Revolutionary Clergy: The Filipino Clergy and the Nationalist Movement, 1850–1903* (Quezon City: Ateneo de Manila University Press, 1981), 1–47.

4. For background on the Jesuits in Bohemia, see Louthan, *Converting Bohemia: Force and Persuasion in the Catholic Reformation* (Cambridge: Cambridge University Press, 2009), and Paul Shore, *The Eagle and the Cross: The Jesuits in Late-Baroque Prague* (St. Louis: Institute of Jesuit Sources, 2002). On the broader role of the Jesuits in secondary and tertiary education in the Habsburg Empire, see William Clark, *Academic Charisma and the Origins of the Research University* (Chicago: University of Chicago Press, 2006).

5. Stephen Jay Gould, "The Great Physiologist of Heidelberg," *Natural History*, July 1999, 13–20.

6. Jonathan Sperber, *Rhineland Radicals: The Democratic Movement and the Revolution of 1848–1849* (Princeton, NJ: Princeton University Press, 1991).

7. Jacqueline Lalouette, *La Libre Pensée en France, 1848–1940* (Paris: Albin Michel, 1997).

Anthropologie, Ethnologie und Urgeschichte). This institution not only followed a tradition of republican empiricism stretching back to the Royal Society in the English Civil War but also pioneered a Humboldtian scientific challenge to the classical humanism still entrenched in German schools and society at the time.[8] In joining the society, Rizal became not only immersed in the distinctly Protestant milieu of German intellectual life[9] and the intimate male forms of sociability found in a wider range of associations and clubs so popular among the *bürgertum* of late nineteenth-century Germany,[10] but also personally acquainted with Rudolf Virchow, the society's founder and president. Virchow, the founder and leader of the liberal German Progress Party (Deutschen Fortschrittspartei) in the Reichstag, had championed what he called the Kulturkampf against the Catholic Church in the 1870s, leading to the passage of a raft of legislation curtailing ecclesiastical influence in education and society and imposing secular state control over the church.[11] Thus, in ways no doubt eased and encouraged by their familiarity with diverse foreign commodities and commercial interests in the Philippines of the late nineteenth century, *ilustrados* such as Rizal enjoyed open access, intimate contact, and active encouragement among transnational networks of power, privilege, and prestige across Europe that were counterposed against the Catholic Church and afforded a counterhegemonic cosmopolitan vantage point from which to understand—and attack—the *frailocracía* still so anomalously entrenched in the Philippines.

Crucial to the *ilustrados'* circulation within the circuitries of late nineteenth-century liberal and republican intellectual life and political activism in Europe were the associational linkages and practices of Freemasonry. As historians have shown, Masons and their lodges followed the spread of the British Empire over the course of the nineteenth century,[12] and they were likewise popular among the growing ranks of the German business class;[13] thus, Freemasonry began to

---

8. Woodruff D. Smith, *Politics and the Sciences of Culture in Germany, 1840–1920* (Oxford: Oxford University Press, 1991), and Andrew Zimmerman, *Anthropology and Antihumanism in Imperial Germany* (Chicago: University of Chicago, 1991).

9. Thomas Albert Howard, *Protestant Theology and the Making of the Modern German University* (Oxford: Oxford University Press, 2006).

10. See, for example, James J. Sheehan, *German History, 1770–1866* (Oxford: Clarendon Press, 1989), 793–820, and David Blackbourn and Richard J. Evans, eds., *The German Bourgeoisie: Essays on the Social History of the German Middle Class from the Late Eighteenth to the Early Twentieth Century* (London: Routledge, 1991).

11. On Virchow and the Kulturkampf, see Douglas W. Hatfield, "Kulturkampf: The Relationship of Church and State and the Failure of German Political Reform," *Journal of Church and State* 23, no. 3 (1981): 465–584; David Blackbourn, *Populists and Patricians: Essays in Modern German History* (London: Allen & Unwin, 1987), 143–167; and Michael B. Gross, "Kulturkampf and Unification: German Liberalism and the War against the Jesuits," *Central European History* 30, no. 4 (1997): 545–566.

12. Jessica L. Harland-Jacobs, *Builders of Empire: Freemasonry and British Imperialism, 1717–1927* (Chapel Hill: University of North Carolina Press, 2007).

13. Stefan-Ludwig Hoffman, "Nationalism and the Quest for Moral Universalism: German Freemasonry, 1860–1914," in *The Mechanics of Internationalism: Culture, Society, and Politics from*

wash up on Philippine shores with the opening of the archipelago to foreign trade. Indeed, chroniclers of Freemasonry in the Philippines cite the case of the Basque merchant Jacobo Zóbel, a Mason arrested in 1874 on charges of fomenting rebellion and acting "por una sociedad de agentes alemanes que suponía establecida en Hongkong (for a network of German agents presumed to be based in Hong Kong)."[14] Merchant seamen plying Philippine ports over the years may also have passed on Masonic rituals and imparted more broadly plebeian and egalitarian traditions of association and mobilization,[15] and the famous Italian republican— and Freemason—Giuseppe Garibaldi himself made a number of visits to Manila in the early 1850s during his period of exile following the fall of the 1848–1849 Roman Republic.[16]

But the key pathways connecting the Philippines to the transcontinental circuitries of Freemasonry led through the Spanish cities of Barcelona and Madrid, where *ilustrado* students and sojourners from the Philippines found a measure of sympathy and support among some republican and liberal circles in the late nineteenth century. The Spain of this period was one whose own problematic position within the context of industrializing, modernizing, secularizing, and liberalizing Europe was evident in the abiding tensions and conflicts that divided its own polity and society along shifting but persistently anticlerical versus ultramontane fault lines.[17] Compared with the other metropolitan powers of Southeast Asia—France, Great Britain, the Netherlands—nineteenth-century Spain was a latecomer not only in terms of commercial and industrial capitalism but also in the realm of cultural, intellectual, political, and social change.

The aftermath of the Napoleonic period in Spain saw successive decades of inconclusive struggle between the ascendant forces of liberalism, republicanism, and anticlericalism on the one hand, and the entrenched interests of the monarchy, the landed aristocracy, and the Catholic Church on the other. Forged in the wake of the popular mobilization and social upheaval that arose in response to Napoleon's invasion of the Iberian Peninsula, the Constitution of 1812 abolished the Holy Office of the Inquisition, much to the outrage of the Catholic Church hierarchy.[18] Reversal and retrenchment followed with Ferdinand VII's dissolution

---

the 1840s to the First World War, ed. Martin H. Geyer and Johannes Paulmann (Oxford: Oxford University Press, 2001), 259–284.

14. Teodoro M. Kalaw, *La Masonería Filipina: Su Origen, Desarolla y Vicisitudes Hasta La Época Presente* (Manila: Bureau of Printing, 1920), 16–18.

15. Marcus Rediker, *Between the Devil and the Deep Blue Sea: Merchant Seamen, Pirates and the Anglo-American Maritime World, 1700–1750* (Cambridge: Cambridge University Press, 1987).

16. Pino Fortini, *Giuseppe Garibaldi Marinaio Mercantile (Pagine di Storia Marinara)* (Rome: Carlo Corvo, 1950), 138–144. Many thanks to Lucy Riall for leading the author to this text.

17. Joan Connelly Ullman, "The Warp and Woof of Parliamentary Politics in Spain, 1808–1939: Anticlericalism versus 'Neo Catholicism,'" *European Studies Review* 13, no. 2 (April 1983): 145–176.

18. Ronald Fraser, *Napoleon's Cursed War: Popular Resistance in the Spanish Peninsular War, 1808–1814* (London: Verso, 2008), 450–463.

of the Cortes in 1814, but subsequent decades saw the continuing growth of the urban social forces promoting liberal reforms in Spanish society, at the expense of the interests and powers of the Catholic Church. The 1830s saw the rise of popular anticlerical violence in Spanish cities (the so-called *matanza de los frailes*), followed by the forced closure of monasteries and sale of church properties, affirmed in the Concordat of 1851.[19] During the brief Republic of 1873–1874, moreover, the church's position within republican Spain was drastically reduced:

> In the "republic," the Catholic Church was to be reduced to the level of an ordinary association and shorn of all its privileges. When, in the republican *Cortes* of 1873, [then President] Pi [y Margall] announced that the clergy would be tried in civil courts like any common criminal, he was enthusiastically cheered. Both education and the conduct of policy must be divorced from religious considerations.[20]

But the Restauración of 1874–1875 reversed such changes, in large measure restoring to the church some of its privileges in Spanish education and society, while ushering in a broader period of uneasy political and social stalemate and stability lasting into the twentieth century.[21] The stalemate, embodied in a system of regular, informally regulated alternation between Conservative and Liberal governments known as El Turno Pacífico, failed to resolve the deep fissures in Spanish society, as seen in the continuing skirmishes over educational, economic, and colonial policy during this period.[22] These skirmishes in Spain, enfolded within the wider culture wars of late nineteenth-century Europe, also extended to the Philippines.

Against this backdrop, the years leading up to the Philippine Revolution of 1896 saw the incorporation of the archipelago within the broadly cosmopolitan circuitries of late nineteenth-century liberalism, republicanism, and Freemasonry, both in Spain and in the archipelago. Within the context of Restoration Spain itself, the transcontinental forms of these struggles were apparent in the prominence of Freemasons' lodges in republican circles, and in the controversial influence of the minor German liberal philosopher and Freemason Karl Christian Friedrich Krause (1781–1832) in the universities.[23] A key figure in this

19. See William J. Callahan, *Church, Politics, and Society in Spain, 1750–1874* (Cambridge, MA: Harvard University Press, 1984), 132–135, 159–161, 190–195.

20. C. A. M. Hennessy, *The Federal Republic in Spain: Pi y Margall and the Federal Republican Movement, 1868–74* (Oxford: Clarendon Press, 1962), 76.

21. Frances Lannon, *Privilege, Persecution, and Prophecy: The Catholic Church in Spain, 1875–1975* (Oxford: Clarendon Press, 1987), 119–145.

22. Raymond Carr, *Spain 1808–1939* (Oxford: Clarendon Press, 1966), 348–379.

23. See Pedro Álvarez Lázaro, *La Masonería, Escuela de Formación Del Ciudadano: La Educación Interna de Los Masones Españoles en el Último Tercio de Siglo XIX* (Madrid: Universidad Pontificia Comillas, 1996), 83–88, and Enrique M. Ureña, "Masonería y Pensamiento: Krause," in *La Mason-*

context was Miguel Morayta y Sagrario (1834–1917), a journalist and newspaper editor, university professor, prominent republican politician, and leading Freemason, who even before the 1868 Revolution had called for the representation of Cuba, the Philippines, and Puerto Rico in the Cortes in Madrid. Ousted from his professorial chair in 1884 in the face of charges of anticlerical and Krausisto sympathies, Morayta's cause was championed by progressive university students in Madrid, including the small numbers of *ilustrado* students, such as José Rizal, then in Madrid.[24]

In the years that followed, Morayta—as journalist, publisher, activist, and founder and Grand Master of the Gran Oriente de España (later the Gran Oriente Español) federation of the Freemasonry—worked closely with Rizal and his fellow Propagandistas.[25] Under Morayta's patronage and protection, they published articles in republican newspapers,[26] joined Morayta's Asociación Hispano-Filipina, and formed new Masonic lodges—the overwhelmingly Filipino La Solidaridad and La Revolución in Madrid and Barcelona, respectively.[27] In 1889, it was these *ilustrados* who were the driving force behind the agitation in Spain for reforms in the Philippines and the founding and publishing in Madrid of the famous newspaper of the Propaganda movement, *La Solidaridad*, a publication to which Rizal's dear friend in Bohemian Leitmeritz, Ferdinand Blumentritt, was a regular contributor.[28]

By the early 1890s, moreover, the associational forms and ritual practices identified with Freemasonry had begun to spread across the Philippines, with lodges springing up in and around the expanding port cities and radiating out into the increasingly marketized hinterlands of the archipelago.[29] Recruitment, it seems,

ería en la España del Siglo XIX, ed. J. A. Ferrer Benimeli (Madrid: Consejería de Educación y Cultura, 1987), 589–606.

24. Manuel Sarkisyanz, *Rizal and Republican Spain and Other Rizalist Essays* (Manila: National Historical Institute, 1995), 119–120, 203–215.

25. Maria Asunción Ortiz de Andrés, *Masonería y Democracia en el Siglo XIX: El Gran Oriente Español su Proyección Politico-Social (1888–1896)* (Madrid: Universidad Pontificia Comillas, 1993), especially 142–190.

26. On the republican and liberal press during this period, see David Ortiz Jr., *Paper Liberals: Press and Politics in Restoration Spain* (Westport, CT: Greenwood Press, 2000), and Enrique A. Sanabria, *Republicanism and Anticlerical Nationalism in Spain* (Basingstoke: Palgrave Macmillan, 2009).

27. For details, see Manuel Adán Guanter, "Una logia de Filipinos en Madrid: <<Solidaridad>> nº 53 (1889–1895)," and Pere Sánchez Ferré, "La Masonería Española y el Conflicto Colonial Filipino," in *La Masonería en la España del Siglo XIX*, ed. Benimeli (Madrid: Consejería de Educación y Cultura, 1987), 471–479, 481–496. For a broad overview, see also Kalaw, *La Masonería Filipina*, 20–39, and John N. Schumacher, "Philippine Masonry to 1890," *Asian Studies* 4 (1966): 328–341.

28. John N. Schumacher, S.J., *The Propaganda Movement, 1880–1895: The Creation of a Filipino Consciousness, the Making of the Revolution* (Quezon City: Ateneo de Manila University Press, 1997), 134–146. See also *La Solidaridad*, no. 1 (1889) (Quezon City: University of the Philippines Press, 1967).

29. For an overview, see Susana Cuartero Escobés, *Las Masonería Española en Filipinas: Tomo 1* (Santa Cruz de Tenerife: Ediciones Idea, 2006), 59–154.

was especially intense in urban areas and along the fringes of the vast "friar estates" and the religious orders' other landholdings in and around Manila, such as the neighboring province of Cavite, with more than 35,000 hectares in the hands of the Augustinians, Dominicans, Franciscans, and Recollects.[30] "Constituting a covert public sphere," these lodges "were in constant contact with other lodges in the metropole, effectively bypassing the mediation of the colonial state," Vicente Rafael has noted. "Like the telegraph, Masonic lodges were telecommunicative technologies allowing for discreet transmissions and connections among members across state borders."[31]

Against this backdrop, in 1892 Rizal was among the *ilustrados* of the Propaganda Movement who returned to the Philippines with hopes of promoting reforms in collaboration with the Liberal colonial governor-general in Manila. But the outrage among the religious orders inspired by the dissemination of his novels *Noli Me Tangere* (1887) and *El Filibusterismo* (1891) led to the suppression of his embryonic organization La Liga Filipina and Rizal's arrest and deportation to the distant town of Dapitan on the Zamboanga Peninsula in Mindanao, where he remained in exile until his execution in Manila in December 1896, a series of events described in greater detail below.

Yet during the same years, the newly founded network of Freemasons emerging across the archipelago began to facilitate the creation of new forms of revolutionary brotherhood. Already in the 1880s, activism by *ilustrado* figures such as Marcelo del Pilar had borne fruit in the publication of a short-lived newspaper, the *Diariong Tagalog*, the circulation of a series of bitterly anticlerical pamphlets, and the election of sympathetic *gobernadorcillos* and other local victories over parish priests in municipalities in and around Manila. In 1888, a group of some three hundred prominent worthies, including *gobernadorcillos* and lawyers from in and around the colonial capital, carried to the residence of the governor-general a petition with hundreds of signatures calling for the expulsion of the religious orders from the Philippines. But this initiative provoked a harsh response from the authorities, with the ensuing crackdown forcing Del Pilar to flee into exile in Spain, where he soon published his antifriar tracts, edited *La Solidaridad*, and became a Freemason.[32]

---

30. See Isagani R. Medina, *Cavite before the Revolution, 1571–1896* (Quezon City: University of the Philippines Press, 1994).
31. Vicente L. Rafael, *The Promise of the Foreign: Nationalism and the Technics of Translation in the Spanish Philippines* (Durham, NC: Duke University Press, 2005), 167.
32. Wenceslao Retana, *Cuestiones Filipinas: Avisos y Profecías* (Madrid: 1892), 161–367; Marcelo Hilario Del Pilar, *La Soberanía Monacal en Filipinas* (Manila: Imprenta de Don Juan Atayde, 1898), 143–180; Onofre D. Corpuz, *The Roots of the Filipino Nation Volume II* (Quezon City: AKLAHI Foundation, 1989), 108–144; Schumacher, *The Propaganda Movement*, 105–127.

By the early 1890s, as the limitations on the Propagandistas' success in Barcelona and Madrid had become clear, efforts to mobilize back in the Philippines were resumed, with far-reaching consequences. In 1892, with Rizal's arrest and the suppression of La Liga Filipina, the Kataastaasan Kagalangalang Katipunan ng mga Anak ng Bayan was founded, an organization whose secret rituals and Tagalog discourse drew on both Masonic traditions and those of the *cofradías* in the Philippines, and whose ranks began to swell with new recruits from among students, skilled artisans, shopkeepers, clerks, schoolteachers, and assorted educated worthies of Manila and the neighboring provinces of Luzon. By early 1895, as news of the onset of a large-scale revolutionary insurrection in Cuba reached Philippine shores, the accelerating pace of recruitment by the Freemasons and the Katipunan had drawn into their ranks the likes of Emilio Aguinaldo, mayor (*gobernadorcillo*) of the coastal town of Cavite el Viejo, just south of Manila, the man who would assume leadership of the revolution in 1896–1897 and later emerge as president of the Philippine Republic in 1898–1901.[33]

Viewed against this backdrop, it is clear that the political opportunities and mobilizational and discursive structures of the Philippine Revolution at the turn of the twentieth century were profoundly shaped by international circumstances and cosmopolitan forces at work within and beyond the archipelago. During the Restoration Era, the possibilities for reform in the Philippines waxed and waned in accordance with continuing struggles between conservative and liberal forces in Spain, framed as they were in the terms of the broader culture wars between ultramontane Catholicism and liberalism and republicanism across Europe. Competition and alternation in power between Conservatives and Liberals in Madrid, and pockets of republican influence in the press, universities, and Masonic lodges of Spain combined to produce sympathetic audiences—and signal possibilities for change—in the metropole for forces promoting liberal goals in the colony. Nowhere else in Europe were the conflicts and contradictions within a metropolitan society left so dangerously unresolved and open to cosmopolitan influences from without. Nowhere else in Southeast Asia was the problematic position of the metropole within Europe so deeply embedded within the very fabric of colonial society, and nowhere else in the region were locally rooted social forces and associational forms so tightly linked to broader cosmopolitan currents of revolutionary brotherhood. Such was the backdrop to the onset of the Philippine Revolution in 1896.

---

33. See Emilio Aguinaldo y Famy, "Ang Pagkasapi Ko sa Masoneria at Katipunan," in *Mga Gunita ng Himagsikan* (Manila: National Historical Institute, 1964), 29–34.

Cosmopolitan Forces and International Conjunctures: The Philippine Revolution

Indeed, the central role of cosmopolitan forces and international conjunctures in the making of the Philippine Revolution can be seen not only in the timing of the onset of revolutionary mobilization in its global historical context but also in the very processes by which the revolution erupted, unfolded, and un-raveled in various parts of the Philippine archipelago. To be sure, the revolu-tion was made by Filipinos and with nationalist goals for the Philippines in mind. But the revolution was also enabled by a unique international conjunc-ture, impelled by transcontinental mobilizing structures of revolutionary brotherhood and informed by the cosmopolitan discourses of liberalism and republicanism.

The processes of mobilization in the revolution can be traced back to 1892, when Rizal returned to the Philippines and initiated efforts to organize the Liga Filipina. Controversy over the two novels he had published in Europe—*Noli Me Tangere* (1887) and *El Filibusterismo* (1891)—had earned Rizal the wrath of the religious orders in the Philippines, with vocal demands on the colonial government for his punishment and expressions of concern about his activities. Within three weeks, Rizal was arrested and sent into internal exile in Dapitan on western Mindanao's Zamboanga Peninsula, where he would re-main until his ill-fated return to Manila in August 1896, where (after transport to Barcelona, imprisonment, and summary return), he was executed in De-cember of that year.[34]

But Rizal's initial organizing efforts continued to bear fruit in Manila and in the surrounding provinces over the intervening years. Accounts of the embryonic Liga in 1892 note the prominence of Freemasons among the early participants, whose numbers appear to have been dominated by shopkeepers, bookkeepers, skilled artisans, and clerks, such as Andres Bonifacio, an employee of a German firm in Manila's Chinatown district of Binondo, who also featured as an actor in local *komedya* productions.[35] Here we can see not only the pool of cosmopoli-tan *letrados* (men of learning) in this remote outpost of the global "republic of letters"—Bonifacio's library featuring Rizal's two novels and various issues of *La Solidaridad*, books on the French Revolution and the presidents of the United States, and translations of Eugène Sue's *Le Juif Errant* and Victor Hugo's *Les Misérables*—but also the networks for recruitment and diffusion of revolutionary

---

34. Leon Ma. Guerrero, *The First Filipino: A Biography of José Rizal* (Manila: National Heroes Commission, 1963), 326–341.

35. Guerrero, *The First Filipino*, 329. See also Reynold S. Fajardo, *Dimasalang* (Manila: Supreme Council, 1998), 26–28.

brotherhood provided by transcontinental Masonry.[36] As one account emphasizing Masonic influence has noted:

> As conceived by Rizal, the Liga Filipina would be based on Masonic Practices. . . . Rizal knew that in the 18th and early 19th centuries, many societies which mushroomed in Europe owed much of their success to their adoption of Masonic structures, rituals, procedures and rules of secrecy. Among these societies may be counted the Carbonari, Illuminati, Sublimes Matires Parfaits or Sublime Perfect Masters, Raggi, Lega Nera, Centri, and Guelfi. Indeed the Masonic initiatory ritual, the use of secret recognition signs and passwords, the oaths of secrecy, the binding pledges of mutual assistance, and the adoption by the members of secret names fitted nicely into the needs of secret societies.
>
> Along these lines Rizal wrote the Constitution and By-Laws of the Liga Filipina and gave a copy to Jose Ma. Basa, who had it printed and sent copies to some members of the Comite de Propaganda in Manila.[37]

With Rizal exiled to the remote town of Dapitan on the Zamboanga Peninsula in Mindanao, La Liga Filipina remained embryonic in form and inactive in practice. But organizing efforts in and around Manila continued to evolve. On the one hand, some members of La Liga Filipina, such as the law clerks Apolinario Mabini and Numeriano Adriano, formed the Cuerpo de Compromisarios in late 1894, a small group devoted to raising funds to support continued publication of *La Solidaridad* and the Propagandistas' lobbying efforts in Madrid, to promote reforms of colonial administration in the Philippines. This initiative did not bear much fruit, given the considerable constraints on the group's financial resources and room for political maneuver. By 1895, *La Solidaridad* had ceased publication, and by the end of the following year, some of its leading lights—Rizal, Marcelo del Pilar, Graciano Lopez Jaena—had lost their lives to illness or, in Rizal's case, execution.[38]

On the other hand, with Rizal's arrest and exile to Dapitan, other members of La Liga Filipina devoted themselves to more secretive and subversive activities, with an underground group known as the Kataastaasan Kagalang-galang na Katipunan ng mga Anak ng Bayan emerging under the leadership of Andres Bonifa-

---

36. On Bonifacio's library and the contentious question of his class background, employment, and social status, see Ambeth Ocampo, *Bones of Contention: The Bonifacio Lectures* (Pasig City: Anvil, 2001), 92–93.

37. Reynold S. Fajardo, *The Brethren: Masons in the Struggle for Philippine Independence* (Manila: Enrique L. Locsin and the Grand Lodge of Free and Accepted Masons, 1998), 111.

38. On the Cuerpo de Compromisarios, see Cesar Adib Majul, *Mabini and the Philippine Revolution* (Quezon City: University of the Philippines Press, 1960).

cio and well established in terms of organizational structures by 1894. Using initiation rituals adapted from the Masonic lodges, the clandestine Katipunan drew into its ranks dozens of clerks, artisans, students, and soldiers from Manila and its environs, with recruitment and diffusion greatly facilitated by the networks of Masonic lodges extending from Manila into its hinterlands.[39] Through the assistance of Katipunero printers of the *Diario de Manila*, moreover, the Katipunan managed to circulate some written materials among its members, and, crucially, by 1895 a printing press was purchased along with a limited quantity of paper and type, enabling the publication of hundreds of copies of a single eight-page paper under the title *Kalayaan* (Tagalog for "Freedom") in early 1896. By some accounts, thanks to the publication of *Kalayaan*, Katipunan recruitment dramatically accelerated, with twenty to thirty thousand members reportedly initiated by mid-1896.[40]

Curiously, the *Kalayaan* masthead identified Yokohama, Japan's premier foreign trade hub just south of Tokyo, as the site of publication, perhaps to mislead colonial authorities or to suggest that the cause it represented enjoyed some form of Japanese sponsorship. As suggested by the close coverage of the 1894–1895 Sino-Japanese War in *La Solidaridad* before its closure, politically active Filipino readers took considerable interest in Japan's rising influence and assertiveness in Asia, and, by 1896, awareness that the Treaty of Shimonoseki had ceded to Japan full control over the island of Formosa (today's Taiwan), less than 250 kilometers from Batanes, the northernmost island in the Philippine archipelago.[41] Shifts in world politics, the publisher of *Kalayaan* undoubtedly hoped, would smile on the Katipunan and its cause.

Indeed, even as the cosmopolitan forms of associational activity identified with Freemasonry helped to forge the mobilizing structures of revolutionary brotherhood, events in the distant Caribbean provided an unprecedented if not entirely unexpected international conjuncture for the Philippine Revolution, with events in Cuba proving decisive. Cuba, it is worth recalling, had long intersected with the Philippines' trajectory within the Spanish Empire. Not unlike Manila with its galleon trade, Havana served as a key way station for Spanish trade with continental

---

39. On the importance of Masonic influences on the Katipunan, see Isabelo de los Reyes, *La Sensacional Memoria de Isabelo de los Ryes sobre La Revolución Filipina de 1896–97* (Madrid: Tip. Lit. de J. Corrale, 1899), 70–90. On the sociological bases of Katipunan recruitment, see Jim Richardson's carefully considered piece, "Notes on the Katipunan in Manila, 1892–1896," in *The Light of Liberty: Documents and Studies on the Katipunan, 1892–1897*, ed. Jim Richardson (Quezon City: Ateneo de Manila University Press, 2013), 399–415.

40. For an impressively thorough and insightful discussion of *Kalayaan*, see Richardson, *The Light of Liberty*, 169–174. Richardson's detailed account of *Kalayaan* draws on the full range of available sources in Spanish and Tagalog.

41. See, for example, the various pieces written in *La Solidaridad* by Del Pilar in 1894–1895 in *Escritos de Marcelo H. Del Pilar Tomo II* (Manila: National Library, 1970), 218–225, and 227–251.

South America. At the time of British capture of its forces in 1762 (simultaneous with Manila), Havana was the third largest city in the New World, its population of thirty to forty thousand larger than New York or Boston. But under the Bourbon reforms of the late eighteenth century, Cuba also evolved into a major site for sugar production based on slave labor imported from West Africa. Thus, while the Napoleonic interlude occasioned revolutions by creole patriots throughout much of Spanish America in the 1810s and into the 1820s, in Cuba, the *criollo* planters' fears of a slave uprising (as in nearby Haiti and Saint-Domingue in the 1790s) had deterred them from joining Bolívar in demanding independence from Spain. Belated mobilization in the early-mid 1820s by republicans (many of them Freemasons) calling themselves "Soles y Rayos de Bolívar" inspired *El Libertador* to threaten an invasion of Cuba in 1824 unless Spain agreed to concede independence to continental South America. But the United States government, keen to keep Cuba under Spanish rule and avoid another Haitian-style revolution, pressured Madrid to accept Bolívar's terms, effectively preempting a Cuba Libre. Thus, by the late 1820s, Cuba was left as the core remnant of the Spanish Empire, the richest colony and largest sugar producer in the world, even before the formal opening of Philippine ports to foreign trade and the commercialization of agriculture across the archipelago.[42]

Just as the nineteenth century saw the decoupling of the Philippine economy from the Spanish colonial metropole and the diversification of its trade and investment linkages, so did the same period witness the Cuban economy shift from Spanish control to a position of profound dependency on the United States. By the 1880s, the United States served as the primary source of capital for Cuban sugar plantations, sugar mills, and railroads, and the primary destination for Cuban sugar exports (nearly 95 percent), savings, travelers, and emigrants, with thousands of Cubans working in cigar factories in Florida by the late 1880s and substantial Cuban émigré communities emerging in New York, Boston, and other major American cities.[43]

Against this backdrop, the cause of Cuba Libre enjoyed considerable advantages over the struggle for Philippine independence. Indeed, the Glorious Revolution of 1868 in Spain, which in the Philippines occasioned only a small mutiny at the Spanish naval base in Cavite, helped to inspire a decade-long rebellion across the eastern provinces of Cuba, with rebels calling for freedom from Span-

---

42. Hugh Thomas, *Cuba, or The Pursuit of Freedom* (New York: Da Capo Press, 1998). At mid-century, more than one-third of the population consisted of slaves, and nearly six hundred thousand new slaves arrived between 1816 and 1867, more than all those imported into the United States. See Ada Ferrer, *Insurgent Cuba: Race, Nation, and Revolution, 1868–1898* (Chapel Hill: University of North Carolina Press, 1999), 2.

43. Louis A. Perez Jr., *On Becoming Cuban: Identity, Nationality, and Culture* (Chapel Hill: University of North Carolina Press, 1999), especially 18–55.

ish rule (and annexation by the United States), and the Spanish agreeing to implement reforms in a peace treaty with the rebels signed in 1878. By 1892, moreover, even as Rizal was being bundled off to Dapitan and his Liga Filipina was slipping into inaction and obscurity in Manila, the exiled activist José Martí (1853–1895) was busy founding the Partido Revolucionario Cubano (Cuban Revolutionary Party), recruiting among Cuban émigré cigar factory workers in Key West and Tampa, and mobilizing the remnants of the 1868–1878 Ten Years' War in the nearby Dominican Republic.[44]

By early 1895, against the backdrop of new US legislation imposing steep duties on sugar imports and mounting protests by Cuban sugar planters against the Spanish government's failure to negotiate trade concessions, the Cuban Revolution began to unfold, with a rebellion breaking out in the eastern provinces in February and Martí returning to Cuba in April of that year. Martí died in the fighting a few weeks later, but by early 1896, the insurgency had spread throughout Cuba, with Spanish troops said to be deeply demoralized in the face of this vigorous popular revolt.[45]

The impact of the Cuban Revolution on Spain was devastating. In Catalonia, over half of the textile mills were forced to close due to the interruption of trade with Cuba, but the economic effects were felt throughout the country: "All of Spain, in one fashion or another, suffered from the effects of Antillian war. Taxes increased, food prices rose, rents went up, and unemployment mounted." By mid-1896, "there were few households in Spain untouched by the events in Cuba," an assertion amply supported by statistics: in a country of no more than 16 million, some 200,000 troops had been dispatched to Cuba. "By the summer of 1896, a deep melancholia had settled over the peninsula."[46]

It was thus against the backdrop of deepening crisis in the colonial metropole that incipient organizing efforts by the Katipunan in Manila and its environs began to accelerate and to precipitate the onset of revolution. Strong interest in Cuba dated back to the mid-1880s, when the Propagandistas began to mixed and mingle with their Cuban counterparts in Masonic lodges in Madrid and Barcelona, in some cases establishing deep friendships sustained through transoceanic exchanges of letters and postings of periodicals over the years.[47] Thus, with growing

---

44. Gerald E. Poyo, *"With All, and for the Good of All": The Emergence of Popular Nationalism in the Cuban Communities of the United States, 1848–1898* (Durham, NC: Duke University Press, 1989); Evan Matthew Daniel, "Rolling for the Revolution: A Transnational History of Cuban Cigar Makers in Havana, South Florida, and New York City, 1853–1895" (PhD diss., New School for Social Research, 2010).

45. Louis A. Perez Jr., *Cuba between Empires, 1878–1902* (Pittsburgh: University of Pittsburgh Press, 1983).

46. Perez, *Cuba between Empires*, 83–84.

47. Koichi Hagimoto, *Between Empires: Martí, Rizal, and the Intercolonial Alliance* (Basingstoke: Palgrave Macmillan, 2013), 125–152.

awareness of developments in Cuba and conditions in Spain in 1895 and early 1896, the possibilities for mobilization by the Katipunan began to multiply, and as membership expanded exponentially during these months, so too did the risks of detection by the authorities, along with levels of alarmism about the threat the Katipunan might represent. By May 1896, concerns that the movement may have been compromised combined with the inspiration and opportunity presented by the Cuban Revolution to encourage the Katipunan leadership to explore the possibilities for an insurrection. An emissary was dispatched to Dapitan to obtain Rizal's blessings (which he appears to have withheld). Meanwhile in Manila, Bonifacio and his compatriots succeeded in meeting the captain of a Japanese naval training ship quarantined under Spanish orders in Manila's harbor and in passing on a request for Japanese assistance in the event of an uprising against the colonial government (which was likewise ignored). In late August 1896, the Katipunan was finally betrayed and the extent of its activities revealed to the authorities, forcing Bonifacio and his compatriots to mobilize. Rapidly reconstituting their forces as a poorly equipped revolutionary army, the Katipuneros mobilized on the outskirts of Manila and initiated a set of attacks on Spanish garrisons and arsenals and a series of engagements with Spanish troops, leading to protracted battles around the colonial capital and inspiring a set of simultaneous uprisings in the neighboring provinces as well.[48]

In this first phase of the revolution, the center of gravity soon shifted from Manila, the core citadel of colonial authority and military might, to the province of Cavite, located along the southern coast of Manila Bay. As noted above, the months leading up to August 1896 had seen an accelerated pace of Katipunan recruitment and diffusion in the hinterlands of the colonial capital, which provided a set of mobilizing structures for insurgency as the revolution began. The provinces around Manila were notable not only for the relatively advanced state of commercialization of agriculture by the late nineteenth century but also for their concentration of "friar estates," the vast landholdings of the religious orders, which limited the ascendancy of the Chinese-mestizo mercantile and landowning class and, with the depression of the 1880s and declining commodity prices in the 1890s, led to increasing tensions and conflicts (such a famous dispute in Calamba, Laguna, pitting José Rizal's family against the Dominican hacienda

---

48. Teodoro A. Agoncillo, *The Revolt of the Masses* (Quezon City: University of the Philippines, 1956). On the Japanese connection, see Josefa M. Saniel, *Japan and the Philippines, 1868–1898* (Manila: De La Salle University Press, 1998), 192–195, which is also cited and richly contextualized in Benedict Anderson, *Under Three Flags: Anarchism and the Anti-Colonial Imagination* (London: Verso, 2005), 150–152.

administration).[49] Thus, the Katipunan had drawn into its ranks dozens of local worthies from the provinces of central and southern Luzon: *gobernadorcillos, cabezas de barangay*, and *inquilino* tenants holding leases to tracts of the friar estates.[50] Through these Katipuneros, additional recruits were drawn from among schoolteachers and members of local militias, tenant farmers and other dependents, with old schoolboy networks and family connections helping to staff and structure a hastily improvised and haphazardly armed revolutionary army.[51]

Among all the provinces of central and southern Luzon, Cavite distinguished itself as the most hospitable to revolutionary mobilization. The densely populated northern coastal towns of the province were in close proximity to Manila, with travel to the capital eased and expedited by a regular steamboat ferry service across Manila Bay. This peri-urban status, along with the location of a substantial Spanish naval base in Cavite El Puerto, made Cavite a province that was especially open and accessible to diverse cosmopolitan influences, as seen not only in the ill-fated mutiny at the naval base in 1872 but also in the spectacular growth of Masonic lodges in the early 1890s, second only to Manila in number by the onset of the revolution. At the same time, Cavite played home to the largest agglomeration of friar estates in the Philippines, with the vast, sprawling haciendas of the Augustinians, Dominicans, Franciscans, and Recollects comprising no less than 35,000 hectares and constituting the lion's share of the province's arable land. Thus, the tensions between ultramontane Catholicism, on the one hand, and the currents of liberalism, republicanism, and Freemasonry, on the other, were especially pronounced in this particular Philippine province.[52]

Against this backdrop, mobilization in support of the revolution was especially swift and successful in Cavite. Dozens of local worthies from the province had been inducted into the Katipunan by early–mid 1896, and the local organs of the

---

49. Nicholas P. Cushner, *Landed Estates in the Colonial Philippines* (New Haven, CT: Yale University Council on Southeast Asian Studies, 1976); Dennis Morrow Roth, *The Friar Estates of the Philippines* (Albuquerque: University of New Mexico Press, 1977).

50. For close analyses of this pattern of recruitment across the diverse provinces of Luzon, see, for example, Isagani R. Medina, "Ang Pagsibol at Paglaganap ng Katipunan sa Maynila," and Elsie S. Ramos, "Taga-Bayan Laban sa Taga-Parang sa Tayabas," in *Katipunan: Isang Pambansang Kilusan*, ed. Ferdinand C. Llanes (Quezon City: Trinitas, 1994), 215–228 and 229–239; and Glenn Anthony May, *Battle for Batangas: A Philippine Province at War* (New Haven, CT: Yale University Press, 1991), 36–66.

51. On the importance of the provincial *escuelas de latinidades* as networks for recruitment and mobilization, see Isagani R. Medina, "The Schoolmasters of Cavite in Arms, 1896–1902," in *Ang Kabite sa Gunita: Essays on Cavite and the Philippine Revolution* (Quezon City: University of the Philippines Press, 2001), and Glenn A. May, "Filipino Revolutionaries in the Making: The Old School Tie in Late Nineteenth-Century Batangas," *Bulletin of the American Historical Collection* 9, no. 3 (July–September 1981): 53–64.

52. Soledad Masangkay Borromeo, "El Cadiz Filipino: Colonial Cavite, 1571–1896" (PhD diss., University of California at Berkeley, 1973), especially 63–93.

movement responded promptly to the call to arms in late August of that year, with a series of rapid and largely successful strikes on Spanish military forces in Cavite allowing the revolutionaries to seize control of much of the province over subsequent months and to issue proclamations in the name of a provisional revolutionary government.[53] With revolutionary forces failing to win battles in Manila, Cavite rapidly evolved into the central base of operations for the revolution. By early 1897, the leadership of the Katipunan had been usurped by a former *gobernadorcillo* and Freemason from Cavite El Viejo named Emilio Aguinaldo, who had joined the Katipunan in early 1896, assumed leadership of the movement's local organs in Cavite and enjoyed a growing reputation for his military successes against Spanish forces in the province. In March 1897, a convention held in Cavite elevated Aguinaldo to the presidency of the revolutionary government. Two months later, the now marginalized Bonifacio was executed in the back hills of Cavite on charges of treason to the revolution for his unwillingness to accept the authority of the new government. Meanwhile, the arrival of reinforcements from Spain combined with the internal weaknesses of Aguinaldo's forces to bring the revolution to a halt by the end of 1897. Spanish troops regained control over Cavite over the course of the year, forcing Aguinaldo and his forces to flee north to the province of Bulacan, where emissaries from the Spanish government negotiated with him over the terms of his surrender. By late December 1897, Aguinaldo was en route to exile in Hong Kong, and the first phase of the Philippine Revolution had drawn to a close.

Meanwhile, however, developments in Cuba had continued to unfold in a direction that would soon transform the international context for Spanish rule in the Philippines and provide a new window of political opportunity for the makers of the Philippine Revolution. By the end of 1897, tens of thousands of Spain's troops in Cuba had lost their lives to the revolutionary insurgents or to tropical illnesses of various kinds, the army's numbers were further thinned by desertions, mutinies, and surrenders, and the colonial government's operations were confined to urban centers and occasional forays into the hinterlands. By early 1898, "report of desertions, mutinies, and, with increasing frequency, wholesale surrenders to insurgent forces appeared to announce the imminent collapse of the Spanish army in Cuba."[54] Meanwhile, back in Spain, the situation had further deteriorated:

> The financial burden of 400,000 men in arms and two colonial wars at opposite ends of the world all but totally exhausted the national trea-

---

53. See Isagani R. Medina, ed., *Ilang Talata tungkol sa Paghihimagik nang 1896–97 sinulat ni Carlos Ronquillo y Valdes* (Quezon City: University of the Philippines Press, 1996), 243–443.

54. Perez, *Cuba between Empires*, 80.

sury. Bankruptcy and economic collapse appeared imminent. Spanish credit in the great money markets of Europe plummeted. Spending a million a day on the Cuban conflict, Spain found itself confronted with shrinking sources of credit and a collapsing treasury. In early 1897, Madrid learned that French bankers, on whom Spain had become dependent, had canceled Spanish credit pending a resolution of the Cuban conflict. On Wall Street later that year, Spanish indemnity certificates failed to secure more than eleven cents on the dollar.[55]

In August 1897, Spain's Conservative prime minister, Antonio Cánovas, was assassinated by an Italian anarchist; his successor, the Liberal politician Práxedes Mateo Sagasta, replaced the hard-line commander of the Spanish forces in Cuba with a more moderately inclined officer, who offered an amnesty to the insurgents and other conciliatory gestures.

Against this backdrop of diminishing Spanish capacity and inclination to restore the *status quo ante bellum*, Cuba's wealthy sugar planters began to turn for protection to the same country that supplied them and their families with capital, education, and markets for their produce: the United States. By the onset of the Cuban Revolution, nearly twenty sugar refineries had been built and put into operation by the powerful American Sugar Refining Company, a cartel-like consortium of East Coast sugar refiners known as "The Sugar Trust" that emerged out of the disruption of the American Civil War to dominate the American sugar market and accumulate considerable influence in Washington, DC, especially after the election of the Republican William McKinley to the presidency in 1896.[56] As congressman from Ohio, McKinley had assiduously promoted the interests of the Sugar Trust, most famously in the McKinley Tariff of 1890, which had helped to precipitate the Hawaiian revolution of 1893 and annexation of the territory the following year.[57] As conditions in Cuba for the Trust's interests continued to deteriorate in 1897, McKinley was understandably concerned, and in January of 1898 he dispatched the U.S.S. Maine to Havana to signal American interest and capacity for intervention. With the destruction of the Maine in February, the US Congress introduced resolutions declaring war on Spain, and in March, McKinley presented an ultimatum to Spain and the Cuban rebels, demanding an armistice and offering to purchase Cuba. By late April, with the rebels rejecting the

---

55. Perez, 87.
56. See Alfred S. Eichner, *The Emergence of Oligopoly: Sugar Refining as a Case Study* (Baltimore: Johns Hopkins University Press, 1969), and Luzviminda Bartolome Francisco and Jonathan Shepard Fast, *Conspiracy for Empire: Big Business, Corruption and the Politics of Imperialism in America, 1876–1907* (Quezon City: Foundation for Nationalist Studies, 1985), 1–124.
57. See César J. Ayala, *American Sugar Kingdom: The Plantation Economy of the Spanish Carribean, 1898–1934* (Chapel Hill: University of North Carolina Press, 1999), 52–59.

armistice deal, McKinley ordered a naval blockade of Cuba, precipitating the on-set of the Spanish-American War. In early May 1898, US Navy warships com-manded by Admiral Dewey swiftly defeated the small Spanish naval contingent in Manila Bay, seizing the colonial port's harbor.

Thus, the dramatic expansion of American imperial power at the turn of the twentieth century provided the opening for the second phase of the Philippine Revolution, while presaging its defeat at the hands of US military forces and the onset of American colonial rule in the archipelago. With Dewey's encouragement and assistance, Aguinaldo returned to the Philippines in May 1898, and, in mid-June of that year, declared an independent Republic of the Philippines. By Au-gust 1898, forces pledging loyalty to the revolutionary government had seized control of towns and port cities across Luzon, Bicol, and the Visayas, and its forces were poised on the outskirts of Manila as thousands of American troops arrived to occupy the colonial capital. By January 1899, a congress composed of delegates from forty-one provinces of the archipelago had convened in the town of Malo-los, Bulacan, and promulgated a constitution establishing a republican form of government with an elected legislature and presidency, an array of civil liberties, and provisions for the separation of church and state.[58] Thus, the struggle against ultramontane Catholicism in the Philippines had finally been won.

But the limits of this victory soon became apparent, due to both the external constraints imposed by the United States and the internal contradictions and lim-itations of the revolution itself. Already by August 1898, after all, American troops had begun to occupy Manila, and US officials had begun to distance them-selves from Aguinaldo's forces, derogate the nature of his government, and dampen expectations of recognition and cooperation from Washington, DC. Decem-ber 1898, moreover, saw the signing of the Treaty of Paris, which contained pro-visions for the cession of the Philippines by Spain to the United States. By February 1899, with little sign of American willingness to acknowledge the au-thority of the Malolos Republic or to accept the legitimacy of Philippine inde-pendence, armed hostilities broke out on the outskirts of Manila, and a formal declaration of war was issued by Aguinaldo's government a few months later.[59]

The American response was overwhelming. Tens of thousands of well-armed US troops, hardened by the accumulated experiences and practices of the so-called Indian Wars of the preceding decades, engaged in a massive campaign of consid-erable brutality across the Philippine archipelago, with scorched-earth tactics leav-ing tens of thousands of civilian casualties and subjecting the population at large

---

58. See Teodoro A. Agoncillo, *Malolos: The Crisis of the Republic* (Quezon City: University of the Philippines, 1960).

59. Paul A. Kramer, *The Blood of Government: Race, Empire, the United States, and the Philip-pines* (Chapel Hill: University of North Carolina Press, 2006), 87–111.

to large-scale forced displacement and internment, and untold hardship and suf-fering. By late 1899, the republic's army was forced to abandon conventional combat engagements in favor of guerrilla warfare, with the core leadership re-treating to the northernmost provinces of Luzon under intensive American pres-sure and pursuit. In March 1901, Aguinaldo was captured in a remote area of Isabela Province in northeastern Luzon, and a month later in Manila he issued a formal proclamation of surrender and a pledge of loyalty to the United States gov-ernment in the Philippines. By the end of 1902, most remaining Republican forces had surrendered or fallen to American troops, with the republic abandoned and US colonial rule established in its stead.[60]

Alongside the overwhelming military, logistical, and organizational advantages enjoyed by US forces over the inadequately armed, hastily trained, and poorly sup-plied troops of the Malolos Republic were the internal weaknesses, tensions, and contradictions of the embryonic government and the Revolution it embodied. The Katipunan, it must be recalled, owed much of its organizational structures and early recruitment base to Freemasonry, and as in the Masonic lodges, the Katipu-nan embodied republican and liberal ideas and practices of a cosmopolitan and avowedly universalist nature. The early Katipunan included among its small num-bers modest clerks (*escribientes*), artisans, small shopkeepers, students, and low-ranking soldiers, and, as it expanded its membership over the course of 1896, the broad promise of *kalayaan* (freedom), it has been argued, was couched in demotic Tagalog terms and inflected with references to the *pasyon* and popular understand-ings of folk Catholicism that appealed to the subaltern classes of the archipelago.

But as the Katipunan extended from Manila into its hinterlands, the pro-cesses of recruitment and diffusion drew into the movement local worthies—*gobernadorcillos* and *cabezas de barangay*, landowners, merchants, and money-lenders, and *inquilinos* holding leases to large tracts of the vast estates owned by the religious orders of the Catholic Church—representing the more privileged classes in rural Philippine society at the time. With the onset of the Revolution and the conversion of the Katipunan into a makeshift revolutionary army in 1896–1897, these local worthies mobilized through networks of old school chums, and drew into their ranks scores of family members and dependents, with small-town policemen (*cuadrilleros*) and schoolteachers, tenant farmers and fishermen pro-viding the foot soldiers for a revolutionary army whose commanding officers were overwhelmingly drawn from the *principales* (local worthies) of small-town Lu-zon. When in late 1898 and early 1899 Aguinaldo and his compatriots regrouped and reassembled in Malolos, moreover, the Congress they convened represented

---

60. Stuart Creighton Miller, *"Benevolent Assimilation": The American Conquest of the Philippines, 1899–1903* (New Haven, CT: Yale University Press, 1982); Kramer, *Blood of Government*, 111–158.

the dominant classes of Philippine society that were to survive—and most fully savor—the removal of parish priests from small-town politics and the religious orders from the commanding heights of the economy and the cultural, intellectual, political, and social life of the archipelago. The promise of *kalayaan* thus remained limited by the very nature of the revolution itself.[61]

In this context, alongside the modalities of Freemasonry, other more plebeian and egalitarian forms of brotherhood provided the basis for a revolution within the Revolution, with the associational form of the *cofradía* providing a popular vehicle for subaltern mobilization in many provinces across the archipelago. Even while Aguinaldo's revolutionary government was still finding its footing, the remnants of a Marianist *cofradía* established by the Dominicans, the Guardia de Honor, had mobilized an estimated forty thousand poor peasants and fishermen in the provinces of Pangasinan and La Union, and were soon spreading into other provinces of northern and central Luzon.[62] Thousands more rallied behind other such groups, like the Pansacula brothers in Zambales; the Santa Iglesia in Pampanga, Bulacan, Nueva Ecija, and Tarlac;[63] and the Katipunan de San Cristobal in parts of Batangas, Laguna, Morong, and Tayabas.[64] Even in the inland, upland areas of Aguinaldo's native Cavite, this last *cofradía*, also known as the "Colorum"—from the Latin prayer ending *per omnia saecula saeculorum* (forever and ever)—had spilled over from neighboring Batangas and Laguna to attract thousands of followers.[65] As the Spanish journalist Wenceslao Retana wrote in 1898: "For every Katipunan of 1896, there are now ten such organizations."[66] Reportedly viewed by "los proprietarios" as infected with "las ideas socialista-anarquistas,"[67] these brotherhoods remained at odds with the *principalia*-dominated Malolos Republic from its formation and refused to follow Aguinaldo's surrender in 1901. In Pangasinan, for example:

> municipal officials who failed to secure help from the republican government against the *Guardias* sought American military protection. The *Guardias* employed guerrilla tactics against the American and assaulted

61. See Reynaldo Clemeña Ileto, *Pasyon and Revolution: Popular Movements in the Philippines, 1840–1910* (Quezon City: Ateneo de Manila University Press, 1979), and Milagros C. Guerrero, "Luzon at War: Contradictions in Philippine Society, 1898–1902" (PhD diss., University of Michigan at Ann Arbor, 1977).

62. William Henry Scott, *Ilocano Responses to American Aggression, 1900–1901* (Quezon City: New Day, 1986), 126; Guerrero, "Luzon at War," 185–213.

63. Ileto, *Pasyon and Revolution*, 209–251; Guerrero, "Luzon at War," 175–185.

64. Guerrero, "Luzon at War," 164–215; Ileto, *Pasyon and Revolution*, 75–159.

65. Santiago V. Alvarez, *The Katipunan and the Revolution: Memoirs of a General with the Original Tagalog Text* (Quezon City: Ateneo de Manila University Press, 1992), 207–213, 442–449; Artemio Ricarte Vivora, *Himagsikan Nang Manga Pilipino Laban Sa Kastila* (Yokohama, 1927), 126–131.

66. Cited in Guerrero, "Luzon at War," 168.

67. Cited in Guerrero, 183.

Filipino collaborators. Wealthy and prominent citizens who welcomed the occupation forces seem to have incurred the ire of the *cofrades*. Shortly after General MacArthur's forces were welcomed by the *principalia* in Malasiqui in December 1899, for example, the *Guardias* swept down on the town and killed a number of prominent citizens who had taken part in the gesture.

Young *Guardia* couriers captured by the Americans in early 1900 surrendered lists of landowners marked for assassination so that their property might be distributed among the *cofrades*.[68]

Against this backdrop, the demobilization of the republic's armed forces can be understood not only in terms of defeat and deferral for Filipino nationalist ambitions, but also as a victory of sorts for the liberal and republican aspirations that had animated the Philippine Revolution. For alongside the bloody, brutal "pacification" of the archipelago by US military forces, demobilization was also effected through the rapid establishment of a liberal political infrastructure for American colonial rule. In 1901–1902, elections based on a highly restricted suffrage were held for municipal mayors throughout the archipelago, with those elected given wide discretion over the appointment of local government officials, including municipal police chiefs and treasurers, judges, schoolteachers, and tax collectors. Elections to provincial governorships and a national legislature followed, with the House of Representatives and Senate established in 1916 and a president elected in 1935 under a ten-year Commonwealth in preparation for independence.[69]

With "Filipinization" of local government proceeding from the very first years of American colonial rule under a system of electoral competition based on gradually expanding suffrage, the well-heeled *ilustrados* of Manila and other major port cities, and the broader class of landowners and merchants across the provinces came to enjoy many of the same powers and prerogatives they had aspired to in the final decades of Spanish rule. With American-style separation of church and state, parish priests were removed from their positions of authority in municipal politics, and the religious orders were divested of their vast landholdings and formal powers of control over the cultural, educational, and social life of the archipelago. Dozens of former delegates to the Malolos Republic and former officers in the revolutionary army thus resurfaced as municipal mayors, provincial governors, and congressmen in early colonial elections, with Aguinaldo himself enjoying sufficient political influence in Cavite and elsewhere to manage a

---

68. Guerrero, 209.
69. See the various fine essays in Ruby R. Paredes, ed., *Philippine Colonial Democracy* (New Haven, CT: Yale University Southeast Asia Studies, 1988).

purchase of more than one thousand hectares of former friar lands auctioned by the Bureau of Lands, using generous loans from the government's Philippine National Bank (PNB) that he successfully rolled over until a failed bid for the presidency in 1935 cost him such privileges.[70]

Meanwhile, even as this liberal political order helped to expand and advance the interests of the dominant classes so well represented in positions of leadership in the Propaganda Movement and the government and army of the Malolos Republic, it also served to sublimate and suppress the more popular and egalitarian forms of brotherhood that had helped to inspire and animate the participation of subaltern classes in the revolution. Local leaders of the revolutionary army who refused to follow Aguinaldo into surrender and incorporation into the American regime were derided as bandits and hunted down in remote provincial towns across the archipelago.[71] Efforts to organize workers in Manila were suppressed, as were various other popular political activities deemed to be dangerously "seditious."[72]

By the 1920s, with Philippine sugar enjoying privileged access to the US market and the PNB providing generous loans to friends and family members of the Filipino congressmen who appointed its directors, the leading provincial families succeeded in consolidating their landholdings into vast plantations and moving upstream into processing with the construction of PNB-financed sugar centrals across the archipelago. Under the auspices of a profoundly liberal "colonial democracy," a Filipino landowning oligarchy with embryonic roots in the late nineteenth century began to entrench itself in power, with easy and early access to the colonial state enabling the accumulation of vast concentrations of land, wealth, and political influence unimaginable under Spanish rule.[73] Thus, the early victory for liberalism in the Philippines not only came at the expense of the more egalitarian republican ideals of the Philippine Revolution, but worked to

---

70. John T. Sidel, "Walking in the Shadow of the Big Man: Justiniano Montano and Failed Dynasty Building in Cavite, 1935–1972," in *An Anarchy of Families: State and Family in the Philippines*, ed. Alfred W. McCoy (Madison: University of Wisconsin Center for Southeast Asian Studies, 1993), 109–161.

71. On the Republic of Katagalugan led by Macario Sakay, a former barber, *komedya* actor, and close associate of Bonifacio from Tondo, in southern Luzon in 1902–1906, see Ileto, *Pasyon and Revolution*, 173–197, and May, *Battle for Batangas*, 279–280. Raymond Red's beautifully shot 1993 Tagalog film "Sakay" also evokes something of this strand of the revolution. Meanwhile, on the "pulahanes" in Cebu, see Resil B. Mojares, *The War against the Americans: Resistance and Collaboration in Cebu, 1899–1906* (Quezon City: Ateneo de Manila University Press, 1999), 171–185.

72. See, for example, William Henry Scott, *The Union Obrera Democratica: First Filipino Labor Union* (Quezon City: New Day, 1992), and Reynaldo C. Ileto, "Orators and the Crowd: Philippine Independence Politics, 1910–1914," in *Reappraising an Empire: New Perspectives on Philippine-American History*, ed. Peter W. Stanley (Cambridge, MA: Harvard Studies in American-East Asian Relations, 1984), 85–113.

73. See, for example, John A. Larkin, *Sugar and the Origins of Modern Philippine Society* (Berkeley: University of California Press, 1993), and Michael S. Billig, *Barons, Brokers, and Buyers: The Institutions and Cultures of Philippine Sugar* (Honolulu: University of Hawai'i Press, 2003).

create forms of social inequality and injustice unparalleled elsewhere in Southeast Asia.

Conclusion: Denationalizing, Inter/Transnationalizing the Philippine Revolution

As argued in the pages above, the Philippine Revolution of the late nineteenth century can be most fully understood in light of the international context in which it unfolded and the cosmopolitan mobilizing structures that enabled and impelled the trajectory it followed. To be sure, the Philippine Revolution can be viewed as a nationalist revolution, produced as it was by Filipinos with the goal of an independent Philippine Republic briefly achieved and bitterly defended in the face of overwhelming American military might. But the Philippine Revolution was not only—and not simply—a nationalist revolution, but also a revolution in which a specific kind of international context, a discrete series of international conjunctures, and a particular set of transcontinental, cosmopolitan mobilizational and discursive structures combined, producing processes and outcomes not possible at earlier times in the Philippines or in other places in Southeast Asia at the turn of the twentieth century. The Philippine Revolution, in other words, became imaginable—and, however briefly and partially, realizable—under circumstances and through processes that connected Filipinos at that time to broader currents in world history and allowed them to contribute to the making of world history as well.

As suggested in the preceding pages, the timing of the Philippine Revolution—late relative to South America, early in Southeast Asia—owed less to the nationalizing impact of Spanish colonial state formation than to the cosmopolitanizing consequences of the deepening integration of the Philippine archipelago within the world capitalist economy over the course of the nineteenth century. If the Philippines lacked its creole patriots in the era of Bolívar,[74] by the time of Martí's martyrdom in Cuba the archipelago boasted a growing modern public sphere and an emerging Chinese-mestizo commercial and landowning class whose interests were closely tied to foreign merchant houses and to the circulation of goods, ideas, and people far beyond the Spanish colonial metropole.[75] Nowhere else in Southeast

---

74. See Ruth de Llobet, "Orphans of Empire: Bourbon Reforms, Constitutional Impasse, and the Rise of Filipino Creole Consciousness in an Age of Revolution" (PhD diss., University of Wisconsin at Madison, 2011).

75. For revisionist accounts stressing analogous international circumstances and transnational forces in the making of the early nineteenth-century revolutions that led to independence across Spanish South America, see Jaime E. Rodriguez O., *The Independence of Spanish America* (Cambridge:

Asia was the sociological infrastructure for an 1848-style liberal or republican revolution so fully visible on the horizon.

Nowhere else in Southeast Asia, moreover, were the underlying tensions and conflicts within colonial society so fully and fortuitously interwoven and in sync with the major international and transnational conflicts of the late nineteenth century. For the Philippine Revolution was enabled and constrained not only by Spain's imperial decline and America's imperial rise but also by the culture wars pitting ultramontane Catholicism against Liberalism, Republicanism, and Freemasonry, not only within Spain but across Europe. As the expansion of a modern public sphere and the emergence of a class of Chinese-mestizo merchants and landowners brought increasing tensions and conflicts with the religious orders in the archipelago over the course of the late nineteenth century, Filipinos found themselves politically in tune—and at times personally in touch—with struggles elsewhere. In the promotion of German liberalism against Czech nationalism in Blumentritt's Bohemia, in the post-Kulturkampf settlement of Virchow's Berlin, in Troisième République Paris, in Gladstone's London, and even in Morayta's Madrid and Pi y Margall's Barcelona, among the foreign merchants and in the emerging Masonic lodges of Manila and other Philippine port cities, and in the best-selling novels of Eugène Sue and Victor Hugo in the libraries of both Rizal and Bonifacio, liberalism and republicanism—as discourse and practice—became, in a word, imaginable, at least as much as did an independent Philippine nation.

At the same time, the precocity of the Philippine Revolution in the Southeast Asian context also owed much to the global structures of the Catholic Church. On the one hand, the church had played a fundamental role in the formation of a modern public sphere in the Philippines and in linking the Philippines to the very same cultural, intellectual, and linguistic world of Christianity in which liberal and republican cosmopolitan challenges to the universalist claims of Rome had emerged. The processes of evangelization in the archipelago, after all, had provided an infrastructure of sorts for the public sphere out of which the revolution would arise: a linguistic hierarchy in which Spanish—and Latin—overlay the diverse native vernaculars of the archipelago, an educational system providing schooling and socialization up to the tertiary level, a spatial grid of nucleated settlements organized around church-centered municipal plazas, and an associational life in the sodalities known as the *cofradías*. It was the inclusion of the Philippines within the universe of Catholic worship, discourse and schooling that

Cambridge University Press, 1998); Victor M. Uribe-Uran, "The Birth of a Public Sphere in Latin America during the Age of Revolution," *Comparative Studies in Society and History* 42, no. 2 (April 2000): 425–457; Jeremy Adelman, *Sovereignty and Revolution in the Iberian Atlantic* (Princeton, NJ: Princeton University Press, 2006); and Rafe Blaufarb, "The Western Question: The Geopolitics of Latin American Independence," *American Historical Review* 112, no. 3 (June 2007): 742–763.

allowed the *ilustrados* such easy access to the diverse currents of late nineteenth-century European cultural and intellectual life, that encouraged Rizal to write a novel—in Spanish and with a Latin, biblical title—that outshone those of Benito Pérez Galdós and enabled the likes of Andres Bonifacio to read Hugo, Sue, and books about the French Revolution and the presidents of the United States. No other colony in Southeast Asia at this time saw such a capacity for critical and creative engagement with the "global republic of letters." Blumentritt in the Jesuit seminary town of Litoměřice and Rizal, the graduate of a Jesuit *colegio* and a Dominican university in Manila, were both products of this broad universe of late nineteenth-century Catholicism, their cosmopolitan connectedness owing much to the breadth and depth of the church's mark on the world stretching from Bohemia to the towns and port cities of the Philippines.

On the other hand, the role of the church—or, perhaps, more narrowly, the religious orders—provided an increasingly awkward and untenable institutional fixture amidst the dramatic social transformations of late nineteenth-century Philippine society, opening up unique possibilities for broadly based popular mobilization along decidedly anticlerical lines. These years saw their parish priests increasingly struggling to control local contests for elected municipal posts, their schools trying desperately to square the circle of papal infallibility in an era of modern medicine and science, and their vast landholdings repeatedly pitting them against leaseholders and peasant farmers amidst increasing land pressures and fluctuating commodity prices on the world market. With the church struggling to defend itself in Europe since the time of the French Revolution, and its institutional prerogatives already considerably curtailed and continuously contested in metropolitan Spain, the religious orders' position in the Philippines was increasingly anomalous and unsustainable, as Del Pilar's famously fulminatory anticlerical tracts made amply clear. Not only did late nineteenth-century Philippine society have its own Masonic lodges before Indonesia or Vietnam; the position and role of these lodges was much more subversive in the context of the continuing power of the Catholic Church. In the 1920s, French Freemasons in Saigon published newspapers and promoted "reform" well within the rubric of "*la mission civilisatrice*," much as their Dutch counterparts in Batavia, Semarang, and Surabaya remained in tune with the liberal ethos of the so-called Ethical Policy. In Manila and its hinterlands, by contrast, not only were the Freemasons of the 1890s Filipinos; given the unfulfilled promise of liberal and republican notions of progress the Masons represented in this context, they carried with them the potentialities of revolutionary brotherhood.

Yet the forms that revolutionary brotherhood assumed in the Philippines of the late nineteenth century provided not only the mobilizing structures for the making of the Philippine Revolution but also the seeds of division, demobilization, and defeat. For just as the Masonic forms of recruitment, induction, and organization made for a weak basis of revolutionary mobilization and military discipline, so too did liberal and republican principles of government restrict the capacity of Aguinaldo and his compatriots to contain the proverbial revolution within the Revolution and to channel the subaltern classes' energies into the struggle for an independent republic. As the Katipunan spread across Luzon and into the Visayas in the manner of Masonic lodges, the movement's growth followed the logic of addition rather than multiplication, its membership rolls swelling and its branches increasing in number without any commensurate development of organizational structures to meet the increasing complex task of command, control, and communications for the revolutionary army in the making. The Katipunan, and the revolutionary army and government that it spawned, expanded through networks of extended kinship, friendship, personal dependency, and connection, with factional rivalries haunting and hampering its leadership—and, no doubt, its rank and file—from the outset.

As the revolutionary movement morphed into the embryonic structures of a revolutionary government, moreover, the full implications of its liberal and republican complexion came into view. The narrow class composition of the delegates to the Malolos Congress and the membership of the cabinet placed well-heeled *ilustrados* alongside Aguinaldo's cronies in positions of leadership, even as power at the municipal level was left in the hands of the prerevolutionary *principales.* Elections to the Congress, where they were held, were restricted to men of property, and the vast landholdings of the religious orders were not redistributed among peasant farmers themselves, but rather transferred to the *inquilino* leaseholders instead. Small wonder, then, that the Malolos Republic soon faced not only massive US military intervention but also large-scale popular peasant resistance and rebellions from a welter of scattered *cofradía*-like groups, who challenged the reconstitution of class rule under the liberal republic with subaltern forms of revolutionary brotherhood that Aguinaldo called "the other Katipunan."

Viewed in comparative historical perspective and in the regional context of Southeast Asia, the particular international conjunctures and cosmopolitan forces that enabled and impelled the outbreak Philippine Revolution at the turn of the twentieth century also constrained its trajectory and contained the seeds of its demobilization and defeat. The Philippine Revolution, after all, was a revolution in the tradition of the liberal and republican revolutions of late eighteenth- and nineteenth-century Europe and the Americas, in terms of the mobilizing and discursive structures of revolutionary brotherhood that animated the Katipunan and the Malolos Republic. Nowhere else in Southeast Asia did local circumstances combine with these cosmopolitan crosscurrents to make a republican revolution imaginable, much less realizable at that time. But with the dawning of the twentieth century, a new set of global conflicts and international conjunctures, and new forms of cosmopolitan revolutionary brotherhood, would provide the opportunities and the mobilizational and discursive structures for very different kinds of revolution, as exemplified by the Revolusi in Indonesia of the mid-late 1940s. The next set of chapters thus treats the Indonesian Revolusi in comparative historical perspective, paying close attention to the complexity of the international context and the diversity of cosmopolitan influences that washed up on Indonesian shores, and following Indonesians' multistranded movements as they made their own revolution.

FROM BAKU TO BANDUNG

Cosmopolitan Origins of the
Indonesian Revolution

If the sleepy little town of Litoměřice in late nineteenth-century Bohemia provided an unexpectedly illuminating new point of departure for a reassessment of
the Philippine Revolution, in late 1920 the more economically vibrant and politically volatile Caucasian city of Baku might serve as an equally odd but interesting vantage point for a reevaluation of Indonesia's Revolusi of 1945–1949. As
with late nineteenth-century Litoměřice's cosmopolitan connections to the Philippines, the linkages between Baku and Indonesia were both intimate and instructive, albeit in terms of Islam and communism rather than Catholicism and
republicanism. But here a more extended historical contextualization is required.

By the turn of the twentieth century, Baku was a thriving oil boom town, sup-
plying half the world's oil, and impressing many observers: "equal part Dodge
City, medieval Baghdad, industrial Pittsburgh, and nineteenth-century Paris, fin-
de-siècle Baku was the last great city built before the First World War."[1] Baku's
cosmopolitanism was evident in its leading investors and oil barons, who included
locally rooted Armenians and Jews alongside the Swedish Nobel family, the Royal
Dutch Shell Company, and the Jewish Rothschild dynasty of transcontinental
banking fame.[2] Such cosmopolitanism, moreover, was fully matched in the ranks
of its growing industrial working class, which numbered well over one hundred

---

1. Tom Reiss, *The Orientalist: In Search of a Man Caught between East and West* (London: Chatto
and Windus, 2005), 3–45, at 12.
2. See Robert W. Toff, *The Russian Rockefellers: The Saga of the Nobel Family and the Russian Oil
Industry* (Stanford, CA: Hoover Institution Press, 1976); Niall Ferguson, *The House of Rothschild:
The World's Banker, 1849–1999* (London: Penguin Books, 2000).

thousand laborers and included Russians, Armenians, and Azeris, Dagestanis, and Tatars, Iranians and Turks, and a smattering of Georgians and Jews.[3] "At the beginning of the twentieth century," it has been noted, "Baku was probably the only place in the entire Muslim world, from Morocco to Indonesia, which could claim an authentic industrial proletariat."[4]

Against this backdrop, by the turn of the twentieth century boomtown Baku had emerged as an important hub of modern intellectual activity in the Muslim world. Situated at the crossroads of the Romanov, Ottoman, and Qajar Empires, the Caucasus had evolved over the course of the nineteenth century into a site of exile ("the warm Siberia") for convicted Decembrist officers, Russian Romantic poets (e.g., Pushkin, Lermontov), and agrarian socialist *narodniki*, and a field of activism for *jadidi* Islamic reformist networks stretching from the Crimea to Central Asia and beyond, drawing Baku within the orbit of diverse ideological and intellectual currents.[5] Already in the 1870s, episodic experiments in publishing in Baku had produced a range of periodicals in Russian, Turkish, and Farsi,[6] and with Russia's defeat in the Russo-Japanese War of 1904–1905, the failed Russian Revolution of 1905, and the onset of the Constitutional Revolution in Iran in 1906, Baku's intellectuals began to come into their own. In 1906, a group of Azeri writers, led by Galil Mamed Kuli Zade and Alekper "Hop-Hop" Sabir, commenced publication of the famous satirical journal *Molla Nasreddin*, featuring diverse news articles, fictional pieces, and, most spectacularly, pages of colorful cartoons featuring the eponymous medieval Sufi wiseman-cum-fool who had long served as the buffoon-like protagonist of countless anecdotes and jokes across Muslim Eurasia over the preceding centuries.[7] Using Tbilisi, Tabriz, and Baku as its bases from 1906 to 1917 and 1921 to 1931, *Molla Nasreddin* rapidly evolved into a publication with an avid and extensive readership and circulation far beyond the Caucasus, most notably in Iran, which was said to host half of the journal's subscribers.[8] With Azeri Turkish in Arabic lettering as its primary language but the

3. Ronald Grigor Suny, *The Baku Commune, 1917–1918: Class and Nationality in the Russian Revolution* (Princeton, NJ: Princeton University Press, 1972), 7–14.

4. Alexandre A. Bennigsen and S. Ender Wimbush, *Muslim National Communism in the Soviet Union: A Revolutionary Strategy for the Colonial World* (Chicago: University of Chicago Press, 1979), 10.

5. For context, see Houri Berberian, *Roving Revolutionaries: Armenians and the Connected Revolutions in the Russian, Iranian, and Ottoman Worlds* (Berkeley: University of California Press, 2019).

6. Alexandre Bennigsen andt Chantal Lemercier-Quelquejay, *La Presse et Le Mouvement National chez les Musulmanes de Russie Avant 1920* (Paris: Éditions de L'École des Hautes Études en Sciences Sociales, 1964).

7. Alexandre Bennigsen, "*Mollah Nasreddin* et La Presse Satirique Musulmane de Russie avant 1917," *Cahiers du Monde Russe et Soviétique* 3, no. 3 (July–September 1962): 505–520; M. S. Khartonov, "Mnogoliky Nasreddina," *Dvadtsat' Chetyrye Nasresddina* (Moskva: Glavnaya Redaktsiya Vostochnoi Literatury, 1986), 5–32.

8. Evan Siegel, "The Use of Classical Iranian Literature in Azerbaijani Satire: The Case of Molla Nser od-Din," in *The Middle Eastern Press as a Forum for Literature*, ed. Horst Unbehaun (Frankfurt: Peter Lang, 2004), 231–248.

illustrations comprising half of each issue and captioned in Romanized Turkish as well as Cyrillic Russian, *Molla Nasreddin* carried the potential to appeal to diverse—literate and nonliterate—audiences far from Azeri-speaking areas of the Caucasus and Iran. Yet the journal's appeal lay not only in the medium but also in the message:

> With an acerbic sense of humor and compelling, realist illustrations reminiscent of a Caucasian Honoré Daumier or Toulouse Lautrec, *Molla Nasreddin* attacked the hypocrisy of the Muslim clergy, the colonial policies of the US and European nations towards the rest of the world and the venal corruption of the local elite, while arguing repeatedly and convincingly for Westernization, educational reform and equal rights for women. The magazine was an instant success—selling half its initial print run of 1000 on its first day—and within one month would reach a record-breaking circulation of approximately 5000 on its way to becoming the most influential and perhaps first publication of its kind to be read across the Muslim world, from Morocco to India.[9]

But early twentieth-century Baku was not only a hub of avant-garde intellectual and artistic expression but also a center of revolutionary activism and upheaval. By 1900, activists of the Russian Social Democratic Workers' Party (RSDRP) were organizing cells in Baku, and the city experienced a general strike in July 1903, at the time of the Second RSDRP Congress where Lenin and his comrades—the Bolsheviki (Majority)—split off from the rest of the party. In the remaining years of the decade, strikes in Baku "occurred more often, lasted longer, and [were] on the average more successful than those in any other Russian city," and the city's labor organizations remained predominantly Bolshevik in their affiliations and sympathies, in contrast to the Menshevik (Minority) leanings of their counterparts in neighboring Georgia.[10] The fedora-topped Georgian Bolshevik Josef "Soso" Djugashvili, later known as Stalin, spent much of 1907 to 1910 in Baku, engaged in labor organizing as well as "shakedowns, currency counterfeiting, extortion, bank-robberies, piracy and protection-rackets," and some high-profile kidnappings.[11] After a brief lull from 1910 to 1913, Bolshevik activists succeeded in organizing a set of major strikes and demonstrations in

9. Slavs and Tatars, eds., *Molla Nasreddin: The Magazine That Would've Could've Should've* (Zurich: Christoph Keller Editions, 2011).

10. Suny, *The Baku Commune*, 47. On the Mensheviks in Georgia, see Stephen F. Jones, *Socialism in Georgian Colors: The European Road to Social Democracy, 1883–1917* (Cambridge, MA: Harvard University Press, 2005).

11. See Ronald Grigor Suny, "A Journeyman for the Revolution: Stalin and the Labour Movement in Baku, June 1907—May 1908," *Soviet Studies* 23, no. 3 (January 1972), 373–394, and Simon Sebag Montefiore, *Young Stalin* (London: Weidenfeld and Nicholson, 2007), 160–176.

1914, and again in early 1917 to welcome the February Revolution in Petrograd. But as the Russian Revolution began to unfold in 1917–1918, elections to the Baku *soviet* demonstrated local popular support not only for the Bolsheviki, the Mensheviki, and the Social Revolutionaries but also for such "bourgeois nationalist" parties as the Armenian Revolutionary Federation (Dashnaktsutiun) and the Müsavat (Equality) Party, which claimed to represent the aspirations of the Muslim population of Azerbaijan.

For the Bolsheviki, Müsavat represented an early example of the possibilities and problems associated with transnational forms of revolutionary brotherhood— whether republican or Islamist—linking Muslims to their coreligionists elsewhere across the Muslim world, from Morocco to Indonesia. In 1904, on the eve of the 1905 Revolution, a group of local Bolshevik activists in Baku had begun publishing a periodical—and then founded an organization—called Himmät (Endeavor), which tried to make inroads and extend Bolshevik influence among the Muslim population in the city.[12] In the face of the "Stolypin reaction" of 1906 to 1907, this group essentially disbanded, but some of its leaders fled to Istanbul, where a coup by the Young Turks in 1908 overthrew Sultan Abdulhamid II and entrenched the Committee of Union and Progress (CUP), while others took refuge in neighboring Iran, then in the throes of the constitutional revolution of 1906–1911.

Himmät activists had enjoyed close links with the Organization of Social Democrats (Firqah-yi Ijtima'iyun 'Amiyun), which was founded in Baku in 1905 among immigrant Iranian merchants and workers. Members of this network of Himmät and Social Democrat activists played prominent roles in the formation of a volunteer army of *mujahidin* to defend the revolution in the famous siege of the northern city of Tabriz, in the publication of various periodicals in Tehran, and in the founding of the Democrat Party throughout Iran.[13]

Following British and Russian intervention and the restoration of the monarchy in Tehran in 1911, some of these activists returned to Baku, where they founded the Müsavat (Equality) party the following year, with Muslim unity and independence for Muslim nations rather than socialism as its guiding principles.[14] As the onset of World War I and the tumultuous years leading up to the Russian Revolution saw Russian workers in Baku gravitating toward the various socialist parties and Armenians drawn toward the Dashnaktsutiun, "well-educated

12. Tadeusz Swietochowski, "The Himmät Party: Socialism and the National Question in Russian Azerbaijan, 1904–1920," *Cahiers du Monde Russe et Soviétique* 19, no. 1–2 (January–June 1978): 119–142.

13. Janet Afary, *The Iranian Constitutional Revolution, 1906–1911: Grassroots Democracy, Social Democracy, and the Origins of Feminism* (New York: Columbia University Press, 1996), 81–82, 257–283.

14. Tadeusz Swietochowski, *Russian Azerbaijan, 1905–1920: The Shaping of a National Identity in a Muslim Community* (Cambridge: Cambridge University Press, 1985), 73–75.

professionals from the upper-class echelon of Azerbaijani Turkish society" came to occupy the leadership of Müsavat, while its mass base was recruited from "the poorly-educated Muslim underclass of Baku."[15]

Against this backdrop, the revolution and its early aftermath in Baku demonstrated the possibilities for both communal and international conflict dividing Muslims and non-Muslims along the fault lines of communism and Islam. Müsavat won some 40 percent of the vote in local elections in late 1917, but the Bolsheviks abandoned their tactical alliance with Müsavat and chose to exclude the party from the Baku *soviet*, suspicious as they were of its Pan-Islamic and Pan-Turkic sympathies with the advancing Ottoman army. By December of that year, Baku's Bolsheviki had branded Müsavat as a "counter-revolutionary nationalist organization," and in March 1918 the Bolsheviki stood by while Armenian Dashnak troops conducted a large-scale anti-Muslim pogrom in the city, paving the way for the establishment of a Bolshevik-led Baku Commune over the next several months. In September 1918, Müsavat returned to Baku with backing from the Ottoman "Army of Islam," and soon Azeri militias and Ottoman troops were carrying out anti-Armenian pogroms in retribution for the violence visited on the Muslim population a few months earlier. With the establishment of the short-lived Azerbaijani Democratic Republic (ADR), Müsavat briefly achieved national independence under republican auspices, with a parliament led by Müsavat but representing a wide range of parties elected by universal suffrage. From late 1918 through early 1920, Azerbaijan represented the first and only independent and democratically elected republican government in the Muslim world, its inclusion of women among the electorate preceding the extension of the suffrage in established democracies such as the United Kingdom and the United States.

But with Istanbul facing defeat and Allied occupation, the Allies withholding formal recognition of Azerbaijani independence, and the "White" troops of Denikin's Volunteer Army occupying most of the North Caucasus and fighting to reconstitute the Romanov realms in a centralized, Russified empire, the stage was set for a renewed effort to forge a coalition under the joint banners of communism and Islam in Baku and beyond. By early 1920, local Bolshevik forces were well entrenched in Baku, and even many elements within Müsavat were preparing themselves for the arrival of the Red Army, whose invasion in April of that year marked the end of the ADR and the onset of Sovietization for Azerbaijan.[16] Meanwhile, efforts to promote the revolution in the name of both communism

---

15. Michael B. Smith, "Anatomy of a Rumour: Murder Scandal, the Musavat Party and Narratives of the Russian Revolution in Baku, 1917–20," *Journal of Contemporary History* 36, no. 2 (April 2001): 217–218.

16. The classic account of the complex developments of 1918–1920 remains Firuz Kazemzadeh, *The Struggle for Transcaucasia, 1917–1921* (New York: Philosophical Library, 1951).

and Islam were well under way elsewhere. Already in November 1917, the Bolsheviki had established a Central Commissariat for Muslim Affairs in Inner Russia and Siberia (Muskom), under the People's Commissariat for Nationality Affairs (Narkomnats), headed by the Georgian Bolshevik, Djugashvili, now known as Stalin, to coopt, control, and deploy political activists of variously socialist and nationalist leanings across the Muslim areas of the fallen empire, where the Bolsheviki were weakly represented and the White Army enjoyed initial advantages and attractive power.

Exemplifying these Muslim activists and embodying Bolshevik hopes for their mobilization was the Tatar journalist, intellectual, and activist Mirsaid Sultangaliev, who represented the Bolsheviks within Muskom and served as president of the Central Muslim Military College (Tsentral'naya Musul'manskaya Voennaya Kollegiya). Born the son of an Islamic scholar (*'alim*) in a small Tatar village in Bashkiria,[17] as a young boy Sultangaliev had attended his father's Islamic school (*mektep*), which combined Arabic-language study of the Qur'an and Islamic jurisprudence (*fiqh*) in the classical scholastic tradition with phonetic instruction in Tatar, Russian, arithmetic, geography, and history along the lines promoted by the modernist activists associated with the *jadidi* reformist movement then being developed by Tatar intellectuals in the Volga Basin and Crimea and exported to other Muslim areas of the Romanov Empire.[18] From his *jadidi* Islamic school, Sultangaliev moved on to the elite Russian-Tatar teachers' college in Kazan, and, upon graduation, worked first as a librarian and translator, and, in the wake of the failed 1905 Revolution, as an increasingly prolific and prominent journalist and writer in the Bashkir town of Ufa. By the early 1910s, Sultangaliev had moved to Baku, where he taught at a Tatar school and continued his work as a political activist and public intellectual, collaborating with the Müsavat leader Räsulzadä, freshly returned from exile in Istanbul and Tehran, in the publication of the *Zakavkazkoe Slovo*, while also publishing articles in *Terjuman*, the prominent journal edited by Ismail Bey Gasprinskii, the leading figure in the modernist Muslim *jadidi* movement. Following the February Revolution of 1917, Sultangaliev left Baku to participate in the All-Russia Muslim Congress in Moscow and then to join his close compatriot, Mulla Nur Vakhitov, in founding the Muslim Socialist Committee of Kazan and agitating among the local Tatar population, who remained outside the overwhelmingly Russian ranks of Bolshevik recruitment and mobilization.[19]

---

17. The name Mirsaid—Mirza Sayyid—suggests both membership in an aristocratic lineage and a claim of descent from the Prophet Muhammad.

18. Edward James Lazzerini, "Ismail Bey Gasprinskii and Muslim Modernism in Russia, 1878–1914" (PhD diss., University of Washington, 1973); Adeeb Khalid, *The Politics of Muslim Cultural Reform: Jadidism in Central Asia* (Berkeley: University of California Press, 1998).

19. On the early life and career of Sultangaliev, see Alexandre Bennigsen and Chantal Lemercier-Quelquejay, *Sultan Galiev: Le Père de la Révolution Tiers-Mondiste* (Paris: Fayard, 1986), 57–128.

In Kazan and in two later All-Russia Muslim Congresses in Moscow over the course of 1917, Sultangaliev joined the Bolshevik wing of the RSDRP and began to articulate a vision of revolutionary brotherhood combining communism and Islam. Emphasizing the goals of constructing a national form of socialism in the Muslim world and liberating Muslim colonies from European—including Russian—colonialism and imperialism, Sultangaliev worked to bind Muslim "bourgeois nationalists" to the cause of revolutionary socialism.[20] Under his leadership in Kazan, the Muslim Socialist Committee supported the Bolsheviki in their efforts to consolidate Soviet power, and, with the establishment of the short-lived Tatar-Bashkir Republic in March 1918, he played a leading role in the cooptation and suppression of various "bourgeois nationalist" organizations.[21] More important, within Muskom, and as head of the Central Muslim Military Collegium, Sultangaliev was responsible for mobilizing tens of thousands of Muslim troops for the Red Army and leading a broader propaganda campaign among Muslims in southern Russia, the Caucasus, and Central Asia against the White Army and in support of the Revolution in 1918–1920.

Here the Bolshevik vision of a federal structure within which aspirations for national independence could be accommodated and absorbed, as developed by Lenin and refined and implemented by Stalin and men like Sultangaliev, helped to overcome the initial weakness of the Bolsheviki among the Muslim populations of these regions. In this context, given the strategic significance of Baku the forced incorporation of Azerbaijan and the formation of the Azerbaijan Soviet Socialist Republic in April 1920 were both essential and emblematic of the broader trajectory. By the early-mid 1920s, a formally federal structure of Soviet Socialist Republics had been established throughout the Caucasus and Central Asia, with smaller Autonomous Soviet Socialist Republics within the Russian Soviet Federative Socialist Republic also created to accommodate diverse "nationalities" such as the Bashkirs, Dagestanis, and Tatars in the southern areas of the Russian heartland. To this extent at least, Sultangaliev's vision of "Muslim national communism" had been achieved, albeit with narrowly defined, ethnic "nationalities" presaging fuller encapsulation within a Moscow-centered Soviet state than the broader, more ambitious bases of a "Muslim" identity would have afforded.[22]

It was against this backdrop that in September 1920, a Congress of the Peoples of the East was held in Baku as announced at the Second Congress of the Com-

---

20. Sultangaliev's key articles in the Bolshevik paper *Zhizn' Natsional'nostyei* have been collected and republished in a variety of forms. See, for example, *M. S. Sultan-Galiev: Stat'y* (Oxford: Society for Central Asian Studies, 1984).

21. See Daniel Evan Schafer, "Building Nations and Building States: The Tatar-Bashkir Question in Revolutionary Russia, 1917–1920" (PhD diss., University of Michigan, 1995), 226–277.

22. Alexandre A. Bennigsen and S. Enders Wimbush, *Muslim National Communism in the Soviet Union: A Revolutionary Strategy for the Colonial World* (Chicago: University of Chicago Press, 1979).

munist International (Comintern) in Moscow in July–August of that year.[23] Nearly two thousand delegates congregated in Baku, claiming to represent diverse Peoples of the East from within the former Romanov Empire and the Soviet Union-to-be, as well as Turkey, Iran, and, in smaller numbers, India, China, Korea, and the Arab lands.[24] Comintern Chairman Grigory Zinoviev, a Ukrainian Jew, presided over the Congress and proclaimed its broadly anticolonial and anti-imperialist thrust, asserting that the Comintern "wants brotherly ties with all the peoples of the East," with the "more civilized, more literate, more organized work-ers of the West" providing "wise leadership" to the "peasants of the East."[25] Voicing support for the Kemalist government in Istanbul, but not for its continu-ing claims to the caliphate, Zinoviev rejected what he called "Pan-Islamism" and "Müsavatism," but called for a "holy war" in the East against Western imperialism,[26] a rallying cry repeated many times during the proceedings and re-iterated in the Manifesto issued at its closing. Other delegates spoke more explic-itly about Islam. A Turkmen delegate from Tashkent, identified as Comrade Narbutabekov, for example, called for "the voice of the Muslim working people and the peoples of the East to be heard," arguing that "Muslims will not abandon Soviet power, but this is on condition that the peculiarities of the Eastern peoples be recognized."[27]

In its call for solidarity between the proletariat of the West and the peasantry of the East, and for revolutionary brotherhood bringing Muslims together under the banner of communism, the Congress of the Peoples of the East spoke explic-itly of the fate of the Indonesian archipelago, then under Dutch colonial rule. At the Second Comintern Congress in Moscow in July–August of 1920, the Dutch Comintern agent Henk Sneevliet ("Maring") had spoken at length of the travails and triumphs of the Partai Komunis Indonesia (PKI), including its complex links with an organization known as *Sarekat Islam*, and perhaps some of those attend-ing the Congress of the East in Baku several weeks later recalled the nature and extent of Communist activism and involvement with "Islam" in Java, unparal-leled elsewhere in the East.[28] Although no Indonesian delegates were in atten-dance in Baku in September 1920, the Communist Party of Holland submitted

---

23. Stephen White, "Communism and the East: The Baku Congress, 1920," *Slavic Review* 33, no. 3 (September 1974): 492–514; John Riddell, ed., *To See the Dawn: Baku, 1920—First Congress of the Peoples of the East* (New York: Pathfinder, 1993).

24. A breakdown of the delegates by country of origin is provided in the stenographic notes published after the Congress. *S'yezd Narodov Baku 1–8 Sentyabrya 1920 goda Stenograficheskiye Otchyoty* (Petrograd: Izdatyel'stvo Kommunistichekovo Internatsionala, 1920).

25. *S'yezd Narodov Vostoka*, 35, 38.

26. *S'yezd Narodov Vostoka*, 42–48.

27. *S'yezd Narodov Vostoka*, 87.

28. *The Second Congress of the Communist International Volume 1* (London: New Park, 1977), 150–155.

an appeal to the Congress, which invoked the Communists of the Netherlands
East Indies and their struggle against Dutch capitalism, as well as the "thousands
of Indonesians whom *Sarekat Islam* has united for the common struggle against
the Dutch oppressors." Addressed to "our Indonesian brothers," the appeal called
on them to "join with your oppressed brothers of the East who are also rebelling,
against the British capitalists, the allies of your oppressors."[29] While it is not clear
whether the Dutch Communists' appeal was read out to the delegates, solidarity
with the working peoples of the Indies was expressed in an extravagantly long
speech by a Chechen Communist delegate, Mutushev, which culminated in a reading from the poem "Coffee," penned by the Acmeist poet Sergei Gorodetsky and
recently published in a journal in Baku.[30] The poem, Mutushev explained, depicted a young girl working on a coffee plantation in Java, toiling under the whip
of her overseer, described by Mutushev as British (in tune with the emphasis on
British capitalism and imperialism at the Congress) but in the original as a Dutch-
man, who supervises the packing of the coffee in bales on the pier and its departure for distant, presumably European, shores. Mutushev, surreptitiously
embellishing Gorodetsky's original, concluded the poem, to wild applause from
the delegates:

> That is why, when, in a porcelain cup
> Brewed black coffee, with a golden tint, emits its steam,
> A sea of violent desires rises to the brain,
> The soul suddenly yearns for catastrophe.
> Blow up Europe! Rip away with savage will
> The evil shamelessness of buy-and-sell!
> Whips are not needed for magnolia flowers,
> Guards are not needed for the sun over the sea.[31]

With this poetic flourish, the Congress of the Peoples of the East hailed the people
of the Netherlands East Indies, its proclamations of transnational solidarity among

---

29. *Congress of the Peoples of the East Baku, September 1920: Stenographic Report* (London: New
Park, 1977), 183–186. The Dutch Communists' appeal is translated from a French report of the proceedings of the Baku Congress. It does not appear in the original Russian stenographic notes.

30. After the revolution, Gorodetsky parted ways with fellow Acmeist poet Nikolai Gumilyov,
supporting the Bolsheviks and promoting the revolution in Petrograd, Tbilisi, and Baku. In 1920,
when the poem "Coffee" was published, Gorodetsky was in charge of "artistic agitation and propaganda" in the Transcaucasian section of ROSTA, the Russian Telegraph Agency. See S. I. Mashinsky,
"Sergei Gorodetsky," in *Sergei Gorodetsky: Izbranniye Proizvedeniya Tom 1 Stikhotvoreniya* (Moskva:
Khudozhestvennaya Literatura, 1987), 5–45; Leonid Strakhovsky, "Three Sojourners in the Acmeist Camp: Gergei Gorodetsky, Vladimir Narbut, Mikhail Zenkevich," *Russian Review* 9, no. 2
(April 1950): 131–145; and Harsha Ram, "Modernism on the Periphery: Literary Life in Postrevolutionary Tbilisi," *Kritika: Explorations in Russian and Eurasian History* 5, no. 2 (Spring 2004):
367–382.

31. *S'yezd Narodov Bostoka*, 162–163. Translation by the author. Compare with the original, republished in Mashinsky, *Sergei Gorodetsky*, 344–345.

working peoples and its promise of revolutionary brotherhood among Communist Muslims resonating among the hundreds of thousands mobilizing behind the banners of the Sarekat Islam in parts of Java and Sumatra in the 1910s and early 1920s, and among millions of Indonesians across the archipelago as they waged Revolusi in 1945–1949.[32]

But beyond such poetic expressions of solidarity, how can we connect the Baku of 1920 to the Indonesian Revolution a full quarter century later? The existing body of scholarship on the Indonesian Revolution is rich and diverse, but, as in the case of the Philippine Revolution, it has provided a coherent narrative account along narrowly nationalist lines, with Communists and Islamists largely disavowed, discredited, and depicted as spoilers and saboteurs. On the one hand, the revolution is said to have been led "from above" by urban—and highly urbane—educated young men familiar from Anderson's *Imagined Communities*, a set of Indonesian nationalists who emerged out of Dutch colonial schools in the Netherlands East Indies during the first few decades of the twentieth century and achieved prominence in Batavia, Surabaya, and Semarang, Medan and Padang, as intellectuals and activists, founding organizations and publishing newspaper articles, treatises, and political tracts. Literate, educated, and well travelled within the Indonesian archipelago, this ascendant nationalist intelligentsia began to write, speak, and think in a lingua franca called *Bahasa Indonesia*, and to imagine Indonesia not only as an archipelago of great ethnolinguistic diversity but also as a nation in waiting. These nationalists included among their ranks figures such as Soekarno, Mohammad Hatta, and Sultan Sjahrir, who served as leaders of various nationalist organizations in the 1910s and early 1920s, languished in internal exile in the late 1920s and 1930s, and reemerged in the 1940s to serve as president, vice-president, and prime minister of the Republic of Indonesia. These Indonesian nationalists, in large measure, are credited with the making of the Indonesian Revolution, and in forging a coherent and compelling nation-state that could incorporate the entirety of the vast, sprawling, and highly diverse archipelago under the slogan *Bhinneka Tunggal Ika*, Unity in Diversity.[33]

On the other hand, the Indonesian Revolution is also said to have been driven "from below" by a broader pool of the *pemuda* (youth) representing the broader mass of the Indonesian people, the Rakyat. Mobilized through large-scale civilian and paramilitary training under the rubric of organizations such as the Heiho,

---

32. The poem "Coffee" was reportedly translated into French by the revolutionary writer Henri Barbusse, published in the French Communist daily *L'Humanité*, and retranslated into English and Dutch, thus eventually reaching some readers on Java (Mashinsky, *Sergei Gorodetsky*, 23).

33. George McTurnan Kahin, *Nationalism and Revolution in Indonesia* (Ithaca, NY: Cornell University Press, 1952). See also John D. Legge, *Intellectuals and Nationalism: A Study of the Following Recruited by Sutan Sjahrir in Occupation Jakarta* (Ithaca, NY: Cornell University Southeast Asia Program, 1988).

Seinendan, Jawa Hokokai, and Pembela Tanah Air—Defenders of the Homeland—to help the occupying Japanese forces against an anticipated Allied invasion in 1943–1945, hundreds of thousands of youth on Java and Sumatra provided the rank and file for the Revolusi that followed, staffing the local *lasykar* (militias) that helped to sustain the republic against the Dutch forces. But the *pemuda*, especially on Java were also said to be drawn into revolutionary mobilization through traditional forms of charismatic authority and with distinctly local understandings of power and politics. The *pemuda* thus participated in the Indonesian Revolusi not only with nationalist aspirations in mind, but with local and regional—Javanese, Minangkabau, Acehnese—forms of consciousness and cultural expression inflecting and impelling their actions.[34]

Yet for all its analytical coherence and empirical richness, this account of the Indonesian Revolusi leaves a number of important questions essentially unanswered. First, and taking the Indonesian Revolusi on its own terms, how can we explain the mechanisms and processes by which mobilization unfolded, not only among Republican leaders such as Soekarno and Hatta but in the ranks of *pemuda* and the Indonesian Rakyat as a whole, and through which the connections between revolutionary leaders and foot soldiers were sustained? Second, and taking a broadly comparative perspective, how can we explain why the Indonesian Revolution unfolded when and how it did, and not otherwise? Why did the Revolusi prove to be so messy and manifold in its manifestations, so complicated and compromised in its conclusions, so ambiguous in its implications and impact?

As suggested in the pages above and below, the answers to this question lie neither within the Indonesian archipelago alone, nor solely in the colonial Indies' relationship with the metropolitan Netherlands, nor, more broadly, within the language and logic of "nationalism" in isolation from broader discursive and social formations. Instead, as argued throughout this book, the answers to these questions require a mode of comparative analysis that takes into account the international context within which both colony and metropole were embedded, as well as cosmopolitan currents and connections that impacted on Indonesian society in distinctive—and decisive—ways. Viewing the Indonesian Revolution not only as against the Philippine Revolution that preceded it by nearly a half century but also in comparison with contemporaneous developments in nearby Malaya, Vietnam, and Burma, this account thus offers a new interpretation of the Indonesian Revolution in the light of international context and cosmopolitan connections. Here it is argued that the Indonesian Revolution was enabled and impelled by the deepening integration of the Indonesian archipelago within the world cap-

---

34. Benedict R. O'G. Anderson, *Java in a Time of Revolution: Occupation and Resistance, 1944–1946* (Ithaca, NY: Cornell University Press, 1972).

italist economy and by a set of major international conflicts, whose consequences were experienced quite differently in Indonesia as compared with other parts of Southeast Asia. Here it is further argued that alongside the social forces and political opportunities generated by world capitalism and global conflicts, the cosmopolitan currents of early–mid twentieth-century republicanism, communism, and Islam provided discursive and mobilizational structures for revolutionary brotherhood in Indonesia not available in the same combination or configuration elsewhere in the region. Thus, it is only through a properly denationalized, internationalized, and transnationalized account that the Indonesian Revolution can be more fully and fruitfully understood.

To this end, then, the vantage point of Baku in September 1920 suggests a comparative historical perspective from which to appreciate the importance of both international circumstances and cosmopolitan connections and currents in the making of the Indonesian Revolution. With its cosmopolitan industrial proletariat, unions and strikes, its diverse newspapers and journals, and its Bolshevik and Müsavat activists, Baku foretold the possibilities of organized politics and mass mobilization in the Indonesia of the early–mid twentieth century. If the Philippine Revolution had followed the trajectory of the republican revolutions of the late eighteenth and nineteenth century revolutions of Europe and America, the Indonesian Revolution unfolded in an era in which new imagined communities— the Proletariat (the *'Ummah*)—had come into view and inspired new forms of transnational revolutionary activism. With its tumultuous history of communal violence and military occupation by British, Ottoman, and Soviet troops in 1918–1920 and its transcontinental revolutionary linkages to upheavals in Petrograd and Moscow, Tabriz, Tehran, and Istanbul, moreover, Baku in the early aftermath of World War I also foretold the unprecedented possibilities opened up for the Indonesian Revolution by the dislocations of World War II and by diverse sources of transoceanic solidarity and support from Sydney and Singapore, Aden and Cairo, Moscow and Shanghai, as detailed in the pages that follow. Just as the Philippine Revolution rose and fell in the window of opportunity opened and then closed by the Cuban Revolution and the Spanish-American War, the Indonesian Revolution—and roughly contemporaneous struggles elsewhere in Asia, Africa, and the Middle East—unfolded amidst the global dislocations created by World War II and the onset of the Cold War.

But alongside the revolutionary possibilities, transnational solidarities, and international opportunities symbolized by the experience of Baku in the early aftermath of World War I and by the Congress of the Peoples of the East in September 1920, there were also early signs of the complications, conflicts, and compromises that were to haunt the Indonesian Revolution for years to come. After all, the difficulties of summoning and sustaining revolutionary mobilization in the name of both communism and Islam were already evident in the Second Comintern Congress in July 1920 in Moscow, as seen in one of its resolutions: "A struggle is necessary against Pan-Islamism, the Pan-Asiatic movement and similar currents which try to tie the liberation struggle against European and American imperialism to the strengthening of the power of the Turkish and Japanese imperialism, the nobility, the big landlords, the clergy, etc."[35] Just a few weeks later in the Congress of the East in Baku in September 1920, religion was likewise described by many delegates as an obstacle in the path of socialist revolution, rather than an enabling allied force, and the tensions among and between the communist and non-Communist delegates were scarcely concealed in the stenographic record of the Congress proceedings.

Indeed, these tensions were acutely experienced and expressed among Indonesian revolutionaries in the making, who by the early 1920s had ample experience of the difficulties of sustaining mobilization behind shared Communist and Islamic banners. At the Fourth Comintern Congress in late 1922, an impassioned speech on the subject of Communism and Pan-Islamism was delivered by the exiled Indonesian Communist Party leader Tan Malaka, whose revolutionary activities are discussed at length in the pages that follow:

> Pan-Islamism now means the brotherhood of all Muslim peoples, and the liberation struggle not only of the Arab but also of the Indian, the Javanese and all the oppressed Muslim peoples. This brotherhood means the practical liberation struggle not only against Dutch but also against English, French and Italian capitalism, therefore against world capitalism as a whole. That is what Pan-Islamism now means in Indonesia among the oppressed colonial peoples, according to their secret propaganda— the liberation struggle against the different imperialist powers of the world.
>
> This is a new task for us. Just as we want to support the national struggle, we also want to support the liberation struggle of the very combative, very active 250 million Muslims living under the imperialist powers. Therefore I ask once again: Should we support Pan-Islamism in this sense? So I end my speech.[36]

The official record of the proceedings notes that Tan Malaka's impassioned plea for an alliance between communism and Pan-Islamism was met with "lively applause." But Tan Malaka's memoirs note that after three days of heated debate

---

35. *The Second Congress of the Communist International Volume 1* (London: New Park, 1977), 181.

36. An English translation of the full speech can be found under the title "Tan Malaka: Communism and Pan-Islamism (1922)," at http://www.marxists.org.archive/malaka/1922-Panislamism .html.

following his speech, he was formally prohibited from further contributions to the proceedings,[37] and the official resolutions and theses of the Fourth Comintern Congress, even the "Theses on the Eastern Question," are notably ambiguous on the question of "pan-Islamism" and strikingly silent on the Netherlands East Indies, despite Communist organizational and mobilizational success far greater than achieved anywhere else in the East at that time.[38]

In the subsequent Sovietization of Azerbaijan, moreover, there were also signs of other developments to come for those hoping to combine communism and Islam in revolutionary mobilization. Müsavat activists were imprisoned or forced into exile, the party was branded as counterrevolutionary, and the institutions of Islamic education, worship, and pilgrimage were soon smothered by state control and largely suppressed. By the late 1920s, Stalin's attacks on so-called Sultangalievism had led to the onset of mass purges of the party-state apparatus in various Muslim republics of the USSR, and the large-scale *hujum* (assault) on Islam in Central Asia culminated in the forced unveiling of thousands of Muslim women.[39] In the decades that followed, communism and Islam were pitted against one another as rival forces across the Muslim world, as seen in the early formation of powerful Islamist movements and parties in Iran and Iraq to stem the advancement of Communist mobilizing efforts among the Shi'i Muslim masses in the 1950s.[40] As for Mirsaid Sultangaliev, by late 1920 he was already being marginalized, as seen in his absence at the Baku Congress in 1920; a few years later, he was expelled from the party and arrested for nationalist and Pan-Islamic deviations, leading to nearly two decades in and out of Stalin's gulags before his execution in 1940.[41] With the incorporation of Azerbaijan, Central Asia, and the various autonomous republics of southern Russia and the northern Caucasus within a federalized USSR, Sultangaliev's dreams of revolution under the combined banner of Islam and communism ran their course.

Viewed against the backdrop of Sultangaliev and the 1920 Congress of the Peoples of the East in Baku, the Indonesian Revolution can thus be seen in a new light. First in the late 1910s and early 1920s and again in the late 1940s, Indonesians participated in waves of mass mobilization around the world enabled and

---

37. Tan Malaka, *Dari Penjara ke Penjara, Jilid 1* (Djakarta: Pustaka Murba, 1947), 128.

38. *Resolutions and Theses of the Fourth Congress of the Communist International, Held in Moscow, November 7 to December 3, 1922* (London: The Communist Bookshop, 1923), 53–62.

39. Shoshana Keller, *To Moscow, Not Mecca: The Soviet Campaign against Islam in Central Asia* (Westport, CT: Praeger, 2001); Douglas Northrop, *Veiled Empire: Gender and Power in Stalinist Central Asia* (Ithaca, NY: Cornell University Press, 2004).

40. On Iraq in the 1950s, for example, see Hanna Batatu, *The Old Social Classes and the Revolutionary Movement in Iraq* (London: Saqi Books, 2004), and Chibli Mallat, *The Renewal of Islamic Law: Muhammad Baqer as-Sadr, Najaf, and the Shi'i International* (Cambridge: Cambridge University Press, 1993).

41. Bennigsen and Lemercier-Quelquejay, *Sultan-Galiev*, 191–254.

impelled by the deprivations, disruptions, and dislocations of international conflict on a global scale, with World War I and II paving the way for revolutions in diverse countries across the world. First in the late 1910s and early 1920s, and again in the late 1940s, the languages, networks, organizational tools, and real and imagined solidarities between Islam and communism provided crucial discursive and mobilizational structures through which Indonesians were drawn into revolutionary struggle. But first in the late 1910s and early 1920s and again in the late 1940s, the tensions and conflicts between these two very different forms of cosmopolitan revolutionary brotherhood worked to limit their organizational efficacy and emancipatory potential, presaging demobilization and disappointment with the reconstitution of state authority under republican auspices by the end of the 1940s. First in the late 1910s and early 1920s and again in the late 1940s, the forms of revolutionary brotherhood mobilized in the name of socialism and Islam were diverse and divisive, much as they had been in Baku in September 1920 before the Sovietization of Azerbaijan had run its course, the Stalinization of the Comintern had unfolded, and Sultangalievism had been fully disavowed and destroyed. In these ways, the Indonesian Revolusi, in its coherence and its diversity, its strengths and its weaknesses, and its successes and failures, unfolded in the long shadow of Baku.

The Netherlands East Indies in the World Economy and International Society

Beyond this broad twentieth-century international context, the cosmopolitan connections and currents enabling and impelling the Indonesian Revolution of 1945–1949 can also be traced back, over the proverbial *longue durée*, to the particular mode of incorporation of the Indonesian archipelago within the world capitalist economy and international society. In contrast to the Philippines' absorption within the global orbit of the Roman Catholic Church via the Americas from the sixteenth century, the Indonesian archipelago experienced deepening immersion up through the Early Modern Era within other circuitries of culture and commerce stretching across the Indian Ocean, what scholars have termed Sanskrit and Islamic cosmopolitanisms. In contrast to Manila's brief role as a key link in commodity flows between China, the Americas, and Europe, the islands of the Indonesian archipelago long served as sources of spices and peppers for global markets, and, by the late nineteenth century, parts of Java and Sumatra had evolved into sites for plantation agriculture on a scale unparalleled elsewhere in Southeast Asia. These distinctive features of the Indonesian archipelago's position within the great transformations of global history helped to prefigure possibilities for revolution under international conditions and transnational banners that were very different from those under which the Philippine Revolution had unfolded.

The location of the Indonesian archipelago along the key sea lanes between coastal China and the Indian Subcontinent was crucial. Even before the rise in the mid-seventh century of the sprawling, loosely knit mercantile "empire" known as Śrīvijaya with its hub on the eastern coast of Sumatra, diverse commercial linkages with other parts of Asia were well established and control over maritime trade provided the basis for early state formation among the port polities of the Indonesian archipelago.[42] Beyond economic resources, moreover, maritime linkages also exposed the rulers of these principalities to discursive and institutional forms of legitimate authority already well established in the Indian Subcontinent, which, historians have argued were not simply borrowed wholesale, but rather adapted, translated, and localized over the centuries.[43] As one eminent authority concluded:

> As far as the early trading kingdoms of Indonesia were concerned . . . the rulers of these kingdoms, as a result of growing prosperity and knowledge of the outside world, had become capable of forming independent judgments on the practical advantages of strengthening their institutions of government by means of certain Indian kingship doctrines, a process of borrowing which in time meant that courtly society in Indonesia felt that it was part of, and on equal terms with, the Indian, or "civilized" world. The background to the long story of the "Indianization" of Indonesia, and of other parts of South East Asia, was the gradual enlargement of the field in which the Indian experience was thought to be relevant.[44]

Over the course of the first millennium of the Common Era, court culture in the shifting, loosely structured realms of Sumatra, Java, and other islands of the Indonesian archipelago, it has been argued, became incorporated within what has been termed a Sanskrit Cosmopolis.[45] Stretching across southern Asia, this Sanskrit Cosmopolis cohered and persisted as a shared transregional language of court

---

42. Oliver W. Wolters, *Early Indonesian Commerce: A Study of the Origins of Śrīvijaya* (Ithaca, NY: Cornell University Press, 1967); Jan Wisseman Christie, "Javanese Markets and the Asian Sea Trade Boom of the Tenth to Thirteenth Centuries A.D.," *Journal of the Economic and Social History of the Orient* 41, no. 3 (1998): 344–381.

43. Ian W. Mabbett, "The 'Indianization' of Southeast Asia: Reflections on the Historical Sources," *Journal of Southeast Asian Studies* 8, no. 2 (September 1977): 143–161.

44. Wolters, *Early Indonesian Commerce*, 64.

45. Sheldon Pollock, "The Sanskrit Cosmopolis, 300–1300: Transculturation, Vernacularization, and the Question of Ideology," in *Ideology and Status of Sanskrit: Contributions to the History of the Sanskrit Language*, ed. Jan E. M. Houben (Leiden: E.J. Brill, 1996), 197–247.

culture, literary expression, and religious ritual, a discourse of rulership and a sphere of sacred textual knowledge:

> not just a shared language but a set of shared expressive practices and political representations, which point toward something like an aestheticization of power. If political will—in the form of a declaration of qualification to rule in consequence of history, identity, piety, valor, intelligence, culture, civility, beauty, and an account of what that rule meant in terms of good works and heroic deed—was to be expressed in a public text, it would henceforth and invariably have to be expressed in Sanskrit.[46]

Thus, it has been argued, a traveler around the year 1000 CE "would have seen, from the plain of Kedu in central Java to the basin of Tonlé Sap in Cambodia, from Gangaikondacōlapuram in Tamilnadu to Pravarapura in Kashmir and beyond, imperial polities that had so many features in common they would have seemed to constitute a single culture-power formation."[47] Even today, in the early twenty-first century, traces of Sanskrit are still evident in core conceptual terms in Indonesian such as language (*bahasa*), literature (*sastra*), and religion (*agama*),[48] and over the intervening centuries the two great foundational epic narratives of cosmopolitan Sanskrit culture, the *Mahābhārata* and the *Rāmāyana*, have been continuously reproduced and reworked in local puppet theater (*wayang*) and other forms of popular culture across much of the Indonesian archipelago.[49]

But over the course of the second millennium of the Common Era, as the processes of localization and vernacularization undermined the coherence of this Sanskrit Cosmopolis, the steady strengthening of maritime links across the Indian Ocean and beyond came to incorporate the Indonesian archipelago ever more broadly and deeply within the widening cosmopolitan orbit of Islam. By the thirteenth century, Muslim merchants had developed transoceanic trade routes that stretched from the Arabian Peninsula to the coasts of India and Southeast Asia on the one hand, and from Aden at the mouth of the Red Sea to the Holy Cities of the Hijaz on to the Mediterranean ports of Cairo, Alexandria, Venice, and Genoa, on the other, making the Indian Ocean a vast Muslim lake.[50]

---

46. Sheldon Pollock, *The Language of the Gods in the World of Men: Sanskrit, Culture, and Power in Premodern India* (Berkeley: University of California Press, 2006), 133–134.

47. Pollock, *Language of the Gods*, 256.

48. Russell Jones, ed.) *Loan Words in Indonesian and Malay* (Leiden: KITLV Press, 2007).

49. See, for example, Benedict R. O'G Anderson, *Mythology and the Tolerance of the Javanese* (Ithaca, NY: Cornell Modern Indonesia Project, 1965); Laurie R. Sears, *Shadows of Empire: Colonial Discourse and Javanese Tales* (Durham, NC: Duke University Press, 1996); and Andrew N. Weintraub, *Power Plays: Wayang Golek Puppet Theater of West Java* (Athens: Ohio University Press, 2004).

50. Janet Abu-Lughod, *Before European Hegemony: The World System, A.D. 1250–1350* (Oxford: Oxford University Press, 1989); Roxani Eleni Margariti, *Aden and the Indian Ocean Trade: 150 Years in the Life of a Medieval Arabian Port* (Chapel Hill: University of North Carolina Press, 2007).

> This shift, and the new polities it brought forth, had a singular histori-
> cal result: the creation of a transoceanic "new world" for Islam, sym-
> bolized by a common allegiance to the Shāfi'ī school of Islamic law . . .
> Ultimately stretching from Cape Town on the southern tip of Africa to
> Timor at the limit of the Malay Archipelago, this new world of an en-
> larged Islamic ecumene became a transcultural space that numerous
> Muslims, among them Hadramis from Arabia, traversed and settled in
> with relative ease and great profit, participating in the creation of new
> ports, polities, and even peoples.[51]

Against this backdrop, by the late thirteenth and early fourteenth centuries, rulers and their subjects had converted to the Islamic faith in principalities on the
coasts of Sumatra and Java, with Muslim mercantile communities of diverse origins providing links between the ports of the Indonesian archipelago and distant
centers of Islamic worship, learning, and pilgrimage.[52]

With the rise of the Malacca Sultanate as a key hub for inter-Asian trade in the
mid-fifteenth century, moreover, the power and prestige of Islam began to connect Muslims across the Strait, enabling new kinds of linkages between the islands
of the Indonesian archipelago (as well as the southern Philippines), the Malay Peninsula, and the broader world of Islam through shared religious discourse, schooling, and pilgrimage.[53] Among the itinerant Hadrami and Gujarati merchants were
Islamic scholars (Arabic: 'alim; pl. 'ulama) and Sufi shaykhs, who imparted esoteric
forms of knowledge as they travelled through Indonesian ports, where they often
settled, married into local aristocracies, and enjoyed considerable influence on local
rulers who began to restyle themselves as sultans and rework established notions of
charismatic kingship in tune with emerging new conceptions across the Muslim
world.[54]

Arabic literary networks, it has been argued, through a range of shared texts—
treatises on Islamic law, mysticism, grammar, and ritual; stories, poems, geneal-
ogies, and histories—drew a broad range of authors, readers, listeners, patrons,

---

51. Engseng Ho, *The Graves of Tarim: Genealogy and Mobility across the Indian Ocean* (Berkeley:
University of California Press, 2006), 100.

52. For competing overviews, see Anthony H. Johns, "Sufism as a Category in Indonesian Liter-
ature and History," *Journal of Southeast Asian History* 2, no. 2 (1961): 10–23; Gerardus W. J. Drewes,
"New Light on the Coming of Islam to Indonesia?," *Bijdragen tot de Taal-, Land-, en Volkenkunde*
124, no. 4 (1968): 433–459; Anthony Reid, "Islamization and Christianization in Southeast Asia: The
Critical Phase, 1550–1650," in *Southeast Asia in the Early Modern Era: Trade, Power, and Belief*, ed.
Anthony Reid (Ithaca, NY: Cornell University Press, 1993), 151–179.

53. Jeya Kathirithamby-Wells, "The Islamic City: Melaka to Jogjakarta, c. 1500–1800," *Modern
Asian Studies* 20, no. 2 (1986): 333–351; Luis Filipe Ferreira Reis Thomaz, "The Malay Sultanate of
Melaka," in *Southeast Asia in the Early Modern Era: Trade, Power, and Belief*, ed. Anthony Reid
(Ithaca, NY: Cornell University Press, 1993), 69–90.

54. Thomas Gibson, *Islamic Narrative and Authority in Southeast Asia: From the 16th to the
21st Century* (New York: Palgrave Macmillan, 2007), 27–53.

scribes, and translators across the Indonesian archipelago into the orbit of an Arabic Cosmopolis.[55] Alongside Islamization, immersion within this Arabic Cosmopolis left enduring legacies in the cultures, literatures, and languages of the Indonesian archipelago,[56]as seen in the extraordinary extent of Arabic influence on Malay and what would become Bahasa Indonesia.[57]

Alongside these lasting Islamic linkages across the Indian Ocean came enduring connections between the Indonesian archipelago and the southern coastal provinces of China. Hokkien- and Cantonese-speaking merchants had plied the trade routes from the coastal ports of Fujian and Guangdong to the islands of the archipelago since before the time of Śrīvijaya, and historians have shown how the rise and fall of Śrīvijaya and later Malacca as major commercial empires unfolded in tandem with important developments and trends in Sung (960–1279), Yuan (1271–1368), and Ming (1368–1644) dynasty policies toward foreign trade.[58] Small communities of Hokkien merchants began to settle in the coastal towns of Sumatra from the era of Śrīvijaya, and, by some accounts, the famous voyages of the Yunnanese Muslim eunuch-admiral Zheng He (Cheng Ho) in the early fifteenth century played a crucial role in the development—and, it is worth noting, the Islamization—of the northern coastal (*pasisir*) towns of Java, as did the broader pattern of commerce linking the islands of the Indonesian archipelago to southern China.[59]

Over the course of the "long sixteenth century," moreover, the Ming dynasty's decision to open the city of Guangzhou (Canton) to foreign trade and to license Hokkien-manned junks to depart Fujian's harbors for various Southeast Asian ports engendered a major shift in trade patterns, affecting the Indonesian archipelago and the rest of the world. With the Middle Kingdom claiming from one-quarter to one-third of the world's population, this unprecedented opening of the Chinese market to foreign trade—and, during the same period, the conversion of all duties, taxes, and tributes to silver—stimulated an unprecedented boom in

---

55. Ronit Ricci, *Islam Translated: Literature, Conversion, and the Arabic Cosmopolis of South and Southeast Asia* (Chicago: University of Chicago Press, 2011), especially 245–272.

56. Vladimir I. Braginsky, *The System of Classical Malay Literature* (Leiden: KITLV Press, 1993).

57. Russell Jones, *Arabic Loan-Words in Indonesian: A Check-List of Words of Arabic and Persian Origin in Bahasa Indonesia and Traditional Malay, in the Reformed Spelling* (London: Indonesian Etymological Project, 1978).

58. Oliver W. Wolters, *The Fall of Śrīvijaya in Malay History* (London: Lund Humphries, 1970); Kenneth Hall, *Maritime Trade and State Development in Early Southeast Asia* (Honolulu: University of Hawai'i Press, 1985); Billy K. L. So, *Prosperity, Region, and Institutions in Maritime China: The South Fukien Pattern, 946–1368* (Cambridge, MA: Harvard University Press, 2000), 220–226.

59. Denys Lombard, *Le Carrefour Javanais: Essai d'Histoire Globale II Les Réseaux Asiatiques* (Paris: Éditions de l'École des Hautes Études en Sciences Sociales, 1990); Anthony Reid, "The Rise and Fall of Sino-Javanese Shipping," in *Looking in Odd Mirrors: The Java Sea*, ed. Vincent J. H. Houben, Henk M. J. Maier, and W van der Molen (Leiden: Vakgroep Talen en Culturen van Zuidoost-Azië en Oceanië Rijkuniveriteit te Leiden, 1992), 176–207; Tan Ta Sen, *Cheng Ho and Islam in Southeast Asia* (Singapore: Institute of Southeast Asian Studies, 2009).

global trade. Historians have argued that Chinese demand not only helped to create an "Age of Commerce" in Southeast Asia but also a world capitalist economy,
with Peruvian silver not only flowing from Potosí to Canton and the coastal towns
of Fujian via Manila but fueling long-distance bulk trade in Brazilian and Caribbean sugar, Chinese silks, Indian textiles, and Southeast Asian peppers and spices
in ways that connected Europe, the Americas, and Asia in a unified global trade
market.[60]

In the early sixteenth century, the key commodity chains of global commerce
flowed through a network of ports across South America, Asia, the Indian Ocean,
and Africa under Iberian control. With Felipe II of Spain's assumption of the Portuguese crown in 1581, the Habsburg-controlled network of trade and state finance "literally girdled the globe.

> Its major European centers included Lisbon, Oporto, Medina del
> Campo, Madrid, Seville, Valladolid and Antwerp; in the New World, we
> find them at Pernambuco, Lima, Olinda, Mexico and Cartagena; in Asia
> in Melaka, Macau, Nagasaki, Manila, Goa and Cochin.[61]

Southeast Asia was no exception. Malacca fell into Portuguese hands in 1511 and
the spice trade of the Moluccas a decade later, even as Castilian conquistadores
were making their initial forays in the nearby Philippine archipelago. Thus, small
pockets of the eastern islands of the Indonesian archipelago experienced conversion to Christianity and incorporation into the global circuitries of Roman Catholicism. But by the early seventeenth century, Iberian monarchical mercantilism
had been trumped by the accumulated experience and advantages accruing to the
towns of Holland from early Dutch commercialization, diversification, and intensification of agriculture, long participation in, and increasing domination of,
the Baltic bulk trade (whether in shipbuilding or financial intermediation), and
by the rise of the Verenigde Oost-Indische Compagnie (VOC), the United East
India Company.[62]

The economic success of Holland's trading towns[63] and the emergence of the
Dutch Republic through a long struggle for independence from Habsburg Spanish
over the late sixteenth and early seventeenth centuries combined with the efficiencies

---

60. See, for example, the various essays in Dennis O. Flynn and Arturo Giráldez, *China and the
Birth of Globalization in the 16th Century* (London: Ashgate Variorum, 2010).

61. Sanjay Subrahmanyam, *The Portuguese Empire in Asia, 1500–1700: A Political and Economic
History* (New York: Longman, 1993), 117. See also Charles R. Boxer, *The Portuguese Seaborne Empire, 1415–1825* (Manchester: Carcanet Press, 1991).

62. Immanuel Wallerstein, "Dutch Hegemony in the Seventeenth-Century World-Economy," in
Dutch Capitalism and World Capitalism, ed. Maurice Aymard (Cambridge: Cambridge University
Press, 1982), 93–145.

63. Oscar Gelderblom, *Cities of Commerce: The Institutional Foundations of International Trade
in the Low Countries, 1250–1650* (Princeton, NJ: Princeton University Press, 2015).

of a joint-stock company to give the VOC decisive advantages vis-à-vis its Iberian rivals.[64] "The VOC was a unique politico-commercial institution, and one that could be imitated nowhere else in the world," it has been argued, "because the United Provinces were the world's only federal republic in which a collectivity of town governments, committed to the advancement of trade, industry, and navigation, also wielded great military and naval power."[65] In the decades following its formation in 1602, the VOC achieved rapid expansion in Asia, ousting the Portuguese and entrenching itself in the Moluccas as early as 1605, Batavia on the northwest coast of Java in 1619, and Malacca by 1641, with forts, "factories," and settlements on Ceylon, the Coromandel Coast, and the Cape of Good Hope establishing VOC control over the vast expanse of the Indian Ocean and opening up unimpeded maritime trade from the "East Indies" to the coastal towns of Holland.[66]

Thus, by the early seventeenth century, the Indonesian archipelago was not only deeply integrated into the emerging world capitalist economy but also increasingly incorporated within the transoceanic trade circuitries of the VOC and closely tied to the global entrepôt and financial hub of Amsterdam in the Dutch Golden Age. Thanks to its strategic position within this broader constellation and its location at the crossroads of Indian Ocean and Pacific trade, Batavia emerged as a major emporium in its own right, with diverse European goods, Indian textiles, Moluccan spices, Chinese and Tonkinese silks, and Japanese metals connecting Amsterdam and the VOC's Indian Ocean ports to the Indonesian archipelago and Fujian, Canton, Formosa, and Nagasaki.[67] By the 1680s, with the Tokugawa Shogunate imposing new restrictions on trade in Nagasaki and the Qing dynasty consolidating control over Formosa and liberalizing overseas junk trade of Guangdong and Fujian, the VOC largely abandoned its own Pacific shipping routes and established Batavia as the terminus and hub of its Asian operations, with junks from southern China henceforth servicing the South China Sea sea-lanes north from the Java Sea.[68] Dubbed "the Queen of the Orient," Batavia thus enjoyed a

---

64. Jonathan I. Israel, *Dutch Primacy in World Trade, 1585–1740* (Oxford: Oxford University Press, 1989), 12–37.

65. Israel, *Dutch Primacy in World Trade*, 71.

66. Niels Steensgaard, *The Asian Trade Revolution of the Seventeenth Century: The East India Companies and the Decline of the Caravan Trade* (Chicago: University of Chicago Press, 1973).

67. Leonard Blussé, *Visible Cities: Canton, Nagasaki, and Batavia and the Coming of the Americans* (Cambridge, MA: Harvard University Press, 2008).

68. Leonard Blussé, "No Boats to China: The Dutch East India Company and the Changing Pattern of the China Sea Trade, 1635–1690," *Modern Asian Studies* 30, no. 1 (1996): 51–76; Ronald P. Toby, *State and Diplomacy in Early Modern Japan: Asia in the Development of the Tokugawa Bakufu* (Stanford, CA: Stanford University Press, 1991); Tonio Andrade, *How Taiwan Became Chinese: Dutch, Spanish, and Han Colonization in the Seventeenth Century* (New York: Columbia University Press, 2008); Chin-Keong Ng, *Trade and Society: The Amoy Network on the China Coast, 1683–1725* (Singapore: Singapore University Press, 1983).

central position in intra-Asian trade until the mid-eighteenth century, when British country traders began to undermine the VOC's preeminence in Southeast Asian waters, presaging the bankruptcy and dissolution of the company at the turn of the nineteenth century, on the eve of the Napoleonic Wars. But over the seventeenth and eighteenth centuries, Batavia had already begun to draw the hinterlands of Java and other islands of the Indonesian archipelago within its ambit, its nodal role in VOC commerce and intra-Asian trade attracting ships and sailors, commodities and cultures, political ideas and religious influences from across the Indian Ocean, the Pacific, and beyond.

Compared to the Philippines, the Indonesian archipelago's integration into the emerging world capitalist economy of the seventeenth century was accompanied by incorporation into the orbits of very different forms of cosmopolitanism. In contrast to Manila's linkages via Mexico to the baroque world of the Habsburg Empire and early Counter-Reformation Catholicism, the traffic in and out of Batavia—in goods, people, and knowledge—connected "the Indies" via a network of VOC ports across the Indian Ocean to a predominantly Protestant merchant republic renowned for its central role in global commodity flows and in the spread of modern medicine and science, Enlightenment philosophy, and religious toleration.[69] Historians have emphasized not only the significance of the VOC's operations in the Indies for the Dutch economy and society, with nearly a million people leaving Holland for Asia over the seventeenth and eighteenth centuries, but also their fundamental role in stimulating and sustaining developments in medicine and science, philosophy, and the arts in what is still known as the Dutch Golden Age.[70]

The extension of the VOC's power across the Indonesian archipelago, as elsewhere in Asia, not only facilitated the steady extraction of various commodities for distant markets, but also entailed the violent eviction of diverse peoples from their communities, the forced exile of deposed rulers from their realms, and the criminalization of trading rivals as pirates, creating a vast trade and transportation network of slaves, convicts, political exiles, and other forced migrants connecting the islands of the Indies to Batavia, and Batavia in its turn, to other VOC ports spanning the Indian Ocean and stretching as far south as the Cape of Good Hope.[71] By the late seventeenth century, there were thousands of company- and

---

69. Simon Schama, *The Embarrassment of Riches: An Interpretation of Dutch Culture in the Golden Age* (Berkeley: University of California Press, 1988); Jonathan I. Israel, *Radical Enlightenment: Philosophy and the Making of Modernity, 1650–1750* (Oxford: Oxford University Press, 2001).

70. Harold J. Cook, *Matters of Exchange: Commerce, Medicine, and Science in the Dutch Golden Age* (New Haven, CT: Yale University Press, 2007); Timothy Brook, *Vermeer's Hat: The Seventeenth Century and the Dawn of the Global World* (New York: Bloomsbury Press, 2008).

71. Kerry Ward, *Networks of Empire: Forced Migration in the Dutch East India Company* (Cambridge: Cambridge University Press, 2009).

privately owned slaves in the VOC's settlements across the Indian Ocean, with slaves from Java, Sulawesi, and Bali numbering prominently among them.[72] This network of trade and forced migration overlapped and intersected with the circuitries of Islamic pilgrimage across the Indian Ocean, as perhaps most memorably illustrated by the movements of the Islamic scholar and Sufi adept Shaykh Muhammad Yusuf al-Maqassari (1627–1699) between his native South Sulawesi, Banten, Aceh, the Hijaz, and his periods of forced exile by the VOC in Ceylon (1684–1694) and the Cape of Good Hope (1694–1699).

> As Ceylon was on the pilgrimage route from the archipelago to India, the Haramayn, the rest of the Arabian Peninula, and the Ottoman Empire, the Shaykh had open communication with Muslim pilgrim from all over the Indian Ocean and Dar al Islam. . . . Shaykh Yusuf used his time in Ceylon to write religious works and . . . his presence continued to attract scholars there. The Moghul emperor Aurangzeb was apparently aware of Shaykh Yusuf's presence in Ceylon and ordered the Dutch to provide for his well being.[73]

With the VOC focusing on commerce rather than Christian proselytization, and the company's trade routes and port settlements ringing the Indian Ocean, the deepening integration of "the East Indies" within the world economy of the seventeenth and eighteenth centuries thus facilitated and fuelled the intensifying immersion of the Indonesian archipelago within the broader world of Islam, in stark contrast with the pattern prevailing in the neighboring Philippine islands.

The VOC's apparent indifference and openness vis-à-vis Islam was accompanied by policies of increasing restraint and restriction on the Hokkien merchant communities connecting the Indies, in yet another contrast with the imperatives of evangelization in the early centuries of Catholicism in the Philippines. Prior to the establishment of VOC rule, Hokkien merchants who settled on Java and other islands of the archipelago had assimilated easily into local communities, as seen in their role in Islamization in the fifteenth and sixteenth centuries, and their intermarriage and incorporation into local aristocracies during the same period. But during the eighteenth century, a new pattern of ghettoization emerged in VOC-controlled areas of Java: "Chinese" entry into the Javanese aristocracy was barred by the Dutch and separate residency requirements, legal codes, and administrative practices were imposed on the "Chinese" population on Java. This segregation of Chinese communities and their subordination to a Dutch-appointed *Kapitan Cina*, which enhanced Dutch claims to manpower and tax revenues at

---

72. Markus Vink, "'The World's Oldest Trade': Dutch Slavery and Slave Trade in the Indian Ocean in the Seventeenth Century," *Journal of World History* 14, no. 2 (2003): 131–177.

73. Ward, *Networks of Empire*, 206.

the expense of the Javanese aristocracy, began to harden ethnic boundaries and to create obstacles to movement across them.[74] Moreover, the gradual subordination of the Javanese principalities to Dutch colonial authorities reduced the attractiveness of assimilation—including conversion to Islam—by delinking it from upward social mobility.[75]

Overall, the deepening integration of the Indonesian archipelago into the world economy through the late eighteenth century unfolded in ways that left distinctive and definitive legacies in terms of access and openness to cosmopolitan influences and "transnational" forces. In contrast to the galleon trade in Manila, the absorption of the Indonesian archipelago within the circuitries of global trade not only rendered Batavia an entrepôt but also drew cultivators of Sumatran peppers and Moluccan spices into intensified forms of exploitation. In contrast to the Catholic religious orders' early successes with evangelization in the Philippines, the continuing incorporation of the Indonesian archipelago within the Indian Ocean held the Muslims of the islands within the orbit of transoceanic currents of Islamic worship, learning, and pilgrimage. In contrast to church encouragement of sang-li assimilation through conversion, intermarriage, and creation of the official administrative category of mestizo in the Philippines, the Hokkien merchant communities of the Indonesian archipelago were isolated and identified as foreign, encouraging continued connectedness to China for a pariah entrepreneur minority on the one hand, while presaging their growing estrangement from the Muslim majority on the other. Thus, the distinctive pathways of the Indonesian archipelago's integration into the world capitalist economy in the era of the VOC prefigured deepening immersion within certain circuitries of cosmopolitanism and presaged certain forms of cosmopolitan revolutionary brotherhood that would eventually distinguish the Indonesian Revolusi of 1945–1949 from its Philippine and Vietnamese counterparts.

---

74. On this point, see Mason Hoadley, "Javanese, Peranakan, and Chinese Elites in Cirebon: Changing Ethnic Boundaries," *Journal of Asian Studies* 47, no. 3 (August 1988): 503–518.

75. G. William Skinner, "Creolized Chinese Societies in Southeast Asia," in *Sojourners and Settlers: Histories of Southeast Asia and the Chinese*, ed. Anthony Reid (Sydney: Allen & Unwin, 1996), 66–67.

FROM CULTUURSTELSEL
TO *KOMEDIE STAMBOEL*

The Long Nineteenth Century in the Indies

Just as the Indonesian archipelago's deepening incorporation into the world economy in the era of the VOC through the late eighteenth century expanded its transoceanic connections across the Muslim world and beyond, so too did global economic integration over the course of the nineteenth and early twentieth centuries promote diverse cosmopolitan influences in what came to be known as the Netherlands East Indies. With new forms of exploitation and production for the world market came flows of capital—both corporate and comprador—of variegated European, Arab, and Asian origins. With marketization, proletarianization, and urbanization came new patterns of labor circulation across the archipelago, creating a modern public sphere within which diverse cosmopolitan forms of discourse, sociality, and political action began to emerge and evolve.

Against this backdrop, the early twentieth century in the Netherlands East Indies saw the rise not only of manifold new forms of modernist artistic and intellectual expression reminiscent of the Azeri-Turkish magazine *Molla Nasreddin* briefly described in the preceding chapter but also multiple new initiatives in the realm of political action along lines recalling the Muslim Communist revolutionary aspirations of Mirsaid Sultangaliev also discussed above. As in boomtown Baku in the cosmopolitan crossroads of the Caucasus, immigrants of diverse origins played a prominent role in the rise of new discursive and organizational formations in the Indies, with European, Chinese, and Hadhrami Arab communities most noteworthy in this regard. As in Baku in the era of Ottoman and Romanov imperial demise, Iranian and Russian revolutions, and World War I, external cataclysms and international conflicts—from the Sino-Japanese War of 1894–1995 to the Russo-Japanese War of 1904–1905, the Chinese Revolution of 1911, and World Wars I and II—helped to destabilize social hierarchies and state structures in the Indonesian archipelago over the first half of the twentieth century. As in Baku in the heyday of Ottoman and Persian constitutionalism, Islamic reformism, and Bolshevik agitation, forms of revolutionary brotherhood rooted in republicanism, communism, and Islam provided the basis for revolutionary agitation and mobilization, as seen first in the Sarekat Islam in the 1910s and early 1920s, and then in the Revolusi of 1945–1949.

From the Cultuurstelsel to Corporate Plantation Agriculture: Early Proletarianization

With the bankruptcy and dissolution of the VOC in 1799, the Indonesian archipelago entered a new phase of deepening integration into the world economy. The devastation of the Napoleonic Wars, the loss of foreign trade to the English East India Company, and the secession of Belgium severely weakened the Dutch economy, stimulating new economic initiatives by the Dutch state in the Indies. The late 1820s witnessed the dramatic demonstration and expansion of Dutch coercive power in the Java War against forces under Prince Diponegoro, with victory in 1830 enabling the establishment of a state-run cultivation system (Cultuurstelsel) of forced cultivation of cash crops—coffee, sugar, and indigo—by peasants across much of Java.[1] With the Netherland Trading Company (Nederlandsche Handel Maatchappij) monopolizing export of these commodities and an apparatus of Dutch and Javanese officials elaborated and deployed to organize and enforce the compulsory collections on villages across Java, processes of accelerating land settlement, labor mobilization, population growth, and, it has been argued, immiseration through agricultural involution were set in motion.[2] While the shortcomings and limitations of the cultivation system led to its demise by the end of the 1860s, the four decades of forced commercialization of agriculture

---

1. Peter Carey, *The Power of Prophecy: Prince Dipanagara and the End of an Old Order on Java, 1785–1855* (Leiden: KITLV Press, 2008).
2. See Clifford Geertz, *Agricultural Involution: The Processes of Ecological Change in Indonesia* (Berkeley: University of California Press, 1963); Benjamin White, "'Agricultural Involution' and Its Critics: Twenty Years After," *Bulletin of Concerned Asian Scholars* 15, no. 2 (April–June 1983): 18–31; Cornelis Fasseur, *The Politics of Colonial Exploitation: Java, the Dutch, and the Cultivation System* (Ithaca, NY: Cornell University Southeast Asia Program, 1992); and Robert E. Elson, *Village Java under the Cultivation System, 1830–1870* (Sydney: Allen and Unwin, 1994).

on Java paved the way for the subsequent takeoff of large-scale private plantation agriculture with passage of the Agrarian Law of 1870. By 1900, some 435,000 hectares were leased out to large estates on Java.[3]

Even as the commercialization of agriculture across Java was enabled and accelerated by the initiatives of the Dutch colonial state, the so-called Outer Islands of the Indonesian archipelago experienced a nineteenth-century export boom within the expanding orbit of British free trade. Already in the late eighteenth century, the consolidation of the English East India Company's hold over Bengal after the Battle of Plassey in 1757 and the settlement of the Seven Years' War (1756–1763) had greatly strengthened British control over Asian trade routes.[4] During the Napoleonic Wars, moreover, British military expansion in Asia helped to remake the Indian Ocean into what has famously been described as a British lake: Malacca was taken in 1795, Colombo in 1796, Cape Town in 1806, Aden in 1839, and Hong Kong in 1842, with its brief occupation of Batavia (1811–1816) witnessing an unprecedented extension of Batavia's power across Java.[5] Thanks to steamboats, the opening of the Suez Canal, and Pax Britannica, long-distance maritime commerce became much speedier, safer, and cheaper, dramatically expanding trade links across the Indian Ocean over the nineteenth century.[6] For the Indonesian archipelago, these developments presaged a shift of linkages to the world economy via Singapore, which the British had established as a trading settlement in 1819, and which soon developed into the hub of Southeast Asian commerce under conditions of free trade, especially after the opening of Chinese ports to foreign trade in the Nanjing Treaty following the first Opium War of 1839–1842.[7]

It was not only in the shadow of British global hegemony, but also in the face of Singapore's ascendancy in regional trade that the Netherlands East Indies was constructed as a coherent colonial state over the course of the nineteenth century. Indeed, alongside the cultivation system, the imperative of consolidating and conserving Dutch control over Java also inspired the elaboration of tight restrictions

---

3. Anne Booth, *The Indonesian Economy in the Nineteenth and Twentieth Centuries: A History of Missed Opportunities* (Basingstoke: Macmillan, 1998), 30.

4. The company's assumption of the Bengal *diwani* in 1765 and establishment of Calcutta as its capital in 1772 have often been seen to mark the shift from a North America–centered "first British Empire" to an India-centered "second British Empire." For a more nuanced and comprehensive overview, see P. J. Marshall, *The Making and Unmaking of Empires: Britain, India, and America c. 1750–1783* (Oxford: Oxford University Press, 2005).

5. Peter Carey, *The British in Java, 1811–1816: A Javanese Account* (Oxford: Oxford University Press, 1992).

6. International trade grew twenty-five-fold in 1850–1914; nearly two-thirds of ship tonnage was carried by British vessels. See Michael Pearson, *The Indian Ocean* (London: Routledge, 2008), 191–193.

7. Wong Lin Ken, "The Trade of Singapore, 1819–69," *Journal of the Malayan Branch of the Royal Asiatic Society* 33, no. 4 (192) (December 1960): 5–313.

on the island's trade, with Batavia designated as the sole port of entry for imports and Batavia, Semarang and Surabaya as the only ports for exports, and duties imposed on non-Dutch ships and goods, a "closed economic system" that lasted until liberalization in the 1870s.[8] Beyond Java, Dutch control remained limited in the mid-nineteenth century, confined to the Moluccas, the key West Sumatran port of Padang and its hinterlands (subjected to Cultuurstelsel-style forced coffee cultivation in the 1840s), and roughly a dozen other small settlements scattered across the archipelago, with regular steamship links between Javanese ports and other islands not established until the 1850s. Through the 1860s, Outer Islands trade remained oriented toward Singapore, which together with the free port of Makassar "worked like eastern and western nodes of a vast maritime network around the Java Sea."[9]

By the early 1870s, a marked shift in Dutch policies promoted the extension of colonial state control over the full extent of the Indonesian archipelago while opening the Netherlands East Indies to foreign trade. Military campaigns expanded Dutch rule in Sumatra, Sulawesi, Borneo, and beyond, with the protracted Aceh War (1873–1908) marking consolidation of Dutch sovereignty over the archipelago by the eve of World War I.[10] Economic integration of the Outer Islands and Java from the 1880s was achieved in large measure through the Koninklijke Paketvaart Maatschappij (KPM; Royal Packet Navigation Company), which enjoyed a monopoly on interisland transshipment of mail, official goods, and personnel and expanded its ports of call to more than two hundred in the first two decades of its operations. By the 1920s, the KPM had succeeded in drawing the Outer Islands into the orbit of Java:

> An integrated network of interisland and deep sea shipping focused on the four main deep-sea ports [Batavia, Surabaya, Medan, and Makassar], whose infrastructure and customs procedures were designed to facilitate transshipment. This was supported by a sophisticated financial infrastructure of trading houses, banks and insurance companies. The stranglehold of Singapore over the foreign trade of the Outer Islands was thus broken for all main commodities except rubber.[11]

---

8. Vincent J. H. Houben, "Java in the 19th Century: Consolidation of a Territorial State," in *The Emergence of a National Economy: An Economic History of Indonesia, 1800–2000*, ed. Howard Dick, Vincent J. H. Houben, J. Thomas Lindblad, and Thee Kian Wie (Honolulu: University of Hawai'i Press, 2002), 56–81.

9. J. Thomas Lindblad, "The Outer Islands in the 19th Century: Contest for the Periphery," in *The Emergence of a National Economy*, 82–110, at 94.

10. For a fine overview and analysis, see J. Thomas Lindblad, "Economic Aspects of the Dutch Expansion in Indonesia, 1870–1914," *Modern Asian Studies* 23, no. 1 (1989): 1–24.

11. Howard Dick, "State, Nation-State and National Economy," in *The Emergence of a National Economy*, 23.

In contrast to the Philippines by the time of its revolution, the deepening incorporation of the Indonesian archipelago within the world economy over the course of the nineteenth century entailed advanced forms of exploitation in commercial agriculture, commodity processing, and natural resource exploitation, as well as the elaboration of a modern transportation network, creating a sizeable class of wage laborers. In the Oosthoek ("eastern corner") of East Java, for example, sugar mills were built in the 1830s to mill cane for the Netherlands Trading Company, servicing vast privately owned estates after the demise of the cultivation system in 1870, and delivered refined sugar for export from nearby Surabaya, which had grown into a city of more than one hundred fifty thousand residents by the turn of the twentieth century. Thanks to its naval base, dry dock and ship repair facilities, and railways running to the sugar mills, Surabaya became, in the words of one historian, "an outpost of industrial Europe."

> In this it played a role very similar to other port cities such as Calcutta, Singapore, Hong Kong, and Shanghai and the logic was the same. The needs of defense and the modern steam age, combined with the slowness and unreliability of shipping links with Europe . . . meant that some manufacturing and engineering capability was essential. . . . [A] mill owner could not afford to miss a whole sugar harvest while a vital spare part was ordered and delivered from Holland. Shipowners could not afford a steamer to be laid up for a year.
>
> At the end of the nineteenth century, Surabaya ranked alongside Calcutta, Singapore, Hong Kong, and Shanghai in the application of steam power to modern industry. Surabaya was the workshop of the Netherlands Indies with a heavy industry base supporting sugar milling, railways, and shipping. There was also a limited range of consumer goods industries serving mainly the small European community.[12]

Across much of Java, the jump start provided by the cultivation system produced similar results, such that by 1900 some 435,000 hectares were devoted to plantation agriculture, feeding vast quantities of sugar, coffee, and other commodities into the growing port cities of Batavia, Semarang, and Surabaya for export overseas.

> By 1900 Java was the most technologically modern and integrated economy between Bengal and Japan. The technology of the Industrial Revolution had been applied to a network of transport and communications, to an export-oriented sugar milling industry with giant factories com-

---

12. Howard W. Dick, *Surabaya, City of Work: A Socioeconomic History, 1900–2000* (Athens: Ohio University Center for International Studies, 2002), 261, 253.

manding most of the best land on the island, to irrigation systems, to ancillary metal-working and heavy engineering industries, to the production of some urban middle-class consumer goods such as bread, soft drinks and ice, to construction materials such as bricks and timber to public utilities such as gas and power. Excluding the tiny urban islands of Singapore and Penang, there was nowhere else like it in Southeast Asia.[13]

The construction of a modern infrastructure for intensive export-oriented agricultural production continued apace well into the twentieth century. By 1942, there were 1.3 million hectares of irrigated rice fields, thousands of kilometers of asphalted, and metalled roads, and 5,500 kilometers of railway line on Java.[14]

From the mid-nineteenth century forward, a similarly modern infrastructure was extended to various parts of the other islands of the Indonesian archipelago. By 1900, some 370,000 hectares of land outside Java were held by private estates, with nearly another 480,000 under various kinds of concessions; by the 1920s, there were 500,000 hectares under concession in North Sumatra alone, with private estates across the entirety of the archipelago claiming nearly 3 million hectares of land.[15] Enclaves of concentrated and heavily capitalized production dotted the landscape: a vast plantation belt along the eastern coast of Sumatra, tin mines on the islands of Bangka and Belitung, coal mines in West Sumatra, oil refineries in Borneo, and scattered mines and plantations elsewhere. Most notable was the so-called Deli belt of plantations on the eastern coast of Sumatra:

> By 1930 more than 11,000 Europeans were living on the East Coast, directly or indirectly involved in the estate industry. For the first time, personnel, capital, sites of production, and processing plants drawn from, or situated in, different parts of the Western and colonized worlds were pulled together under single, but notably distinct, corporate structures.[16]

Overall, compared to the Philippines and much of the rest of Southeast Asia at the turn of the twentieth century, the Netherlands East Indies was distinguished by the relatively early emergence of a class of wage laborers concentrated in large-scale

---

13. Dick, "State, Nation-State and National Economy," 17–18.

14. Wim Ravesteijn and Marie-Louise ten Horn-van Nispen, "Engineering an Empire: The Creation of Infrastructural Systems in the Netherlands East Indies, 1800–1950," *Indonesia and the Malay World* 35 (103) (November 2007): 273–292, at 274. See also Wim Ravesteijn and Jan Kop, eds., *For Profit and Prosperity: The Contribution Made by Dutch Engineers to Public Works in Indonesia, 1800–2000* (Leiden: KITLV Press, 2008).

15. Booth, *The Indonesian Economy in the Nineteenth and Twentieth Centuries*, 30, 299.

16. Ann Laura Stoler, *Capitalism and Confrontation in Sumatra's Plantation Belt, 1870–1979* (New Haven, CT: Yale University Press, 1985), 19.

agricultural production and processing and key nodes of modern transport. By 1930, an estimated 300,000 coolie laborers were toiling on the plantations of East Sumatra, and nearly 250,000 more were to be found working on large plantations and mines elsewhere in the Outer Islands.[17] On Java, sizeable concentrations of laborers were likewise to be found, and not only on the plantations: historians have estimated that industrial workers numbered nearly 250,000 by 1942, with an additional 50,000 laboring on the railways, and many thousands more in the harbors of Batavia, Semarang, and Surabaya, and on the steamboats plying interisland and international routes from these ports.[18] With its expanding and increasingly diversified proletariat, the Indonesian archipelago was thus a much more promising site for the revolutionary socialism being practiced and promoted in the Baku of 1920 than much of the rest of Southeast Asia, including the Philippines.

Europeans, "Chinese," and "Arabs": The Internationalization of Capital in the Indies

Alongside early proletarianization, the deepening incorporation of the Indonesian archipelago within the world economy over the late nineteenth century entailed diversified internationalization of the economy and society of the Indies, again much as in the oil-rush boomtown of Baku. While the late nineteenth century saw the consolidation of an integrated Netherlands East Indies in terms of administrative, communications, transportation, and economic linkages, the Indies economy was opened up to non-Dutch trade and investment under Liberal policies from the 1870s onward. By 1920, only 16 percent of Indies exports were destined for the Netherlands (and only 30 percent for Europe as a whole), with 40 percent bound for Asian ports and the remainder shipped to the United States, Egypt, and elsewhere.[19] The Indies were also opened up to foreign capital, as perhaps best seen on the plantation belt of East Sumatra, where Dutch predominance in tobacco was fairly matched by the British in tea, the Americans in rubber, and the French and Belgians in palm oil. Thus, even as the early twentieth

---

17. J. Thomas Lindblad, "New Destinations: Conditions of Coolie Labour Outside East Sumatra, 1910–1938," in *Coolie Labour in Colonial Indonesia: A Study of Labour Relations in the Outer Island, c. 1900–1940*, ed. Vincent J. H. Houben and J. Thomas Lindblad (Wiesbaden: Harrassowitz Verlag, 1999), 79–107l, at 101.
18. John Ingleson, *In Search of Justice: Workers and Unions in Colonial Java, 1908–1926* (Singapore: Oxford University Press, 1986); John Ingleson, "Life and Work in Colonial Cities: Harbour Workers in Java in the 1910s and 1920s," *Modern Asian Studies* 17, no. 3 (1986): 455–476.
19. Booth, *The Indonesian Economy in the Nineteenth and Twentieth Centuries*, 208–209.

century saw the consolidation of Dutch sovereignty and colonial state control over the full extent of the Indies, the archipelago became increasingly internationalized, as seen in the diverse European presence in the islands.

> The Dutch formed the greater part, but people gathered there from all over Europe—most numerous among them the Germans, followed by Belgians, Britons, Swiss, and the French—remained clearly distinguishable. Their share was such that in official parlance the word Dutchman was hardly ever used, preference being given to the term European. . . . Not only did foreign nationals come along with foreign money; for a long time the Dutch at home in Holland had not been very interested in a life in the East. Many employees on the plantations, missionaries, explorers and scholars originated from other European countries.[20]

The international nature of the European presence in the Indies was even evident within the colonial state, as seen in the Royal Netherlands East Indies Army, the Koninklijk Nederlandsch Indisch Leger (KNIL), in which the French poet Arthur Rimbaud was famously, albeit briefly, enlisted in the 1870s.[21] At the turn of the twentieth century, nearly one-fifth of all Europeans in the KNIL came from European countries other than the Netherlands, most notably Germany, Belgium, and Scandinavia.[22] As with its liberal trade policy, Dutch actively encouraged investment in the Indies by a wide range of companies from across Europe, as an insurance policy against threats to Dutch sovereignty in the archipelago in an era of heightening tensions among the Great Powers in Europe and Japan's imperialist expansion.

> The Netherlands Indies was too rich a prize and the investments there of each of the main contestants in the European struggle for power, especially Germany and Great Britain, too valuable for one of them to allow the other to invade and take possession. . . . It was a comforting thought, cherished also by the Dutch government, that for economic and strategic reasons none of the powerful nations would allow a rival to gain control of the Netherlands Indies. As World War I drew closer, foreign economic investments by countries of the Triple Alliance as well as of the Triple Entente over the years had become of such importance that

---

20. Kees van Dijk, *The Netherlands Indies and the Great War, 1914–1918* (Leiden: KITLV Press, 2007), 17.
21. Graham Robb, *Rimbaud* (New York: W.W. Norton, 2000), 278–285.
22. Martin Bossenbroek, "The Living Tools of Empire: The Recruitment of European Soldiers for the Dutch Colonial Army, 1814–1909," *Journal of Imperial and Commonwealth History* 23, no. 1 (1995): 26–53; Gerke Teitler, "The Mixed Company: Fighting Power and Ethnic Relations in the Dutch Colonial Army, 1890–1920," *South East Asia Research* 10, no. 3 (November 2002): 361–374.

the Dutch Minister of the Colonies, Th.B. Pleyte, hoped that should a European war break out this would safeguard the colony from an occupation by one of the belligerents. . . . An unequivocal open-door policy, Pleyte stressed in Parliament as late as 1918, was one of the prerequisites which would allow the Netherlands to remain in the possession of its colony. It would, others argued, also be a reason to have the European Powers oppose a Japanese occupation of the Netherlands Indies.[23]

By the early twentieth century, the internationalization of the Indonesian archipelago's economy was also evident in the increasing prominence and problematic position of diverse diasporic immigrant communities, most notably the so-called Chinese. In contrast to the Philippines, the commercialization of agriculture and extension of market relations in the hinterlands of Java and other islands of the Indies during the nineteenth and early twentieth centuries unfolded through the intermediation of local compradors—immigrant Hokkien-speaking merchants, moneylenders, and rice millers—who were discouraged from assimilation into native society and designated as "foreign orientals."

While trends toward segregation of immigrants from China had already been evident in the VOC era, they accelerated and deepened with the intensification of colonial rule and capitalist penetration in the Indies in the nineteenth and early twentieth centuries. Beginning with the brief British interregnum on Java (1811–1816) during the Napoleonic interlude, the authorities removed residual control over trade routes, markets, and other sources of taxation from the Javanese aristocracy, and auctioned off these and other new revenue farms to the highest bidders, invariably members of the local Hokkien-speaking merchant community. The new opportunities for tax farming and commercial penetration of the Javanese hinterland attracted large numbers of newly arrived immigrants from the southern coastal provinces of China.[24] With the establishment of the cultivation system on Java in 1830, moreover, the Dutch colonial regime introduced new rules "confining the Chinese to designated neighborhoods and severely restricting their movement throughout the island by requiring them to possess short-term travel passes," while granting exemptions to Chinese revenue farmers and their employees, to facilitate the operations of the farms that were so crucial to state revenues.[25]

The consequences of this policy were twofold. On the one hand, through opium and other revenue farms, vast Chinese commercial networks evolved over the

23. Van Dijk, *The Netherlands Indies and the Great War*, 18.

24. Peter Carey, "Changing Javanese Perceptions of the Chinese Communities in Central Java, 1755–1825," *Indonesia* 37 (April 1984): 16.

25. James R. Rush, *Opium to Java: Revenue Farming and Chinese Enterprise in Colonial Indonesia, 1860–1910* (Ithaca, NY: Cornell University Press, 1990), 87.

course of the nineteenth century, with Chinese capital pioneering not only the collection of taxes but the introduction of commodities, the extension of credit, and the expansion of commerce deep into the rural hinterlands of the archipelago. On the other hand, instead of assimilation as in the Philippines during this period, the nineteenth century saw the emergence of a separate community, in which not only new immigrants but locally born (*peranakan*) offspring of mixed immigrant and indigenous parentage were designated as Chinese and, their cultural and linguistic creolization aside, kept in urban ghettos apart from the native population.[26]

With the demise of the cultivation system in the 1870s and the abolition of the opium farm system in the 1890s, this pattern not only survived but deepened, especially on Java. The establishment of a directly state-run *Opium Regie* and the phasing out of other revenue farms at the turn of the century worked to undermine, and in many cases bankrupt, the sprawling commercial empires of the established *peranakan* families. These shifts in state policies coincided with a new wave of immigration from Fujian and Guangdong, nearly tripling the Chinese population of the Indies,[27] with women and non-Hokkien speakers arriving in large numbers for the very first time, producing a growing sense of connectedness to a broader Chinese diaspora in Southeast Asia and awareness of ongoing developments in China.[28] These trends were perhaps most prominently exemplified by the spectacular rise and success of famous tycoons of recent immigrant (*totok* or *singkeh*) stock such as Oei Tiong Ham (1858–1924) and the Guangdong-born Thio Thiau Sat (1840–1916), who married into established *peranakan* families but communicated and circulated among a region-wide network of Chinese merchant families and developed sprawling business empires across Java, Sumatra, Penang, Singapore, and beyond. Even today, Oei Tiong Ham Road and Oei Tiong Ham Park in Singapore and the Cheong Fatt Tze Mansion in Penang testify to the profoundly transregional linkages of Chinese capital in the Indies at the dawn of the twentieth century.[29]

Much as deepening integration into the world economy over the nineteenth century enhanced and enlarged connections among Chinese diasporic communities

---

26. James Rush, "Placing the Chinese in Java on the Eve of the Twentieth Century," *Indonesia* 51 (1991): 17–18.

27. Jamie Mackie, "Towkays and Tycoons: The Chinese in Indonesian Economic Life in the 1920s and 1980s," *Indonesia* 51 (1991): 85.

28. Rush, *Opium to Java*, 243–244.

29. On Oei Tiong Ham and Thio Thiau Siat (alias Cheong Fatt Tze), see Onghokham, "Chinese Capitalism in Dutch Java," *Southeast Asian Studies* 27, no. 2 (September 1989): 156–176; Kunio Yoshihara, ed., *The Oei Tiong Ham Concern: The First Business Empire in Southeast Asia* (Kyoto: Kyoto University Center for Southeast Asian Studies, 1989); and Michael R. Godley, *The Mandarin-Capitalists from Nanyang: Overseas Chinese Enterprise in the Modernization of China, 1893–1911* (Cambridge: Cambridge University Press, 1981).

stretching across the Indonesian archipelago, Singapore and Penang, and the southern coastal Chinese provinces such as Fujian and Guangdong, so too did this internationalization of the economy broaden and tighten linkages among Arab communities across the Indies, other parts of Southeast Asia, and the southern Hadhramaut region of the Arabian Peninsula. As noted in the preceding chapter, Indian Ocean trade and travel over the centuries of the Early Modern Era had brought the Indonesian archipelago within the orbit of Muslim mercantile networks and Islamic scholarly circuits stretching across Southeast Asia, the Indian subcontinent, and the Middle East, with itinerant Hadhramis playing prominent roles first as "religious teachers, Sufis, and court and civic figures," and later as "adventurers, sultans, merchants, diplomats, and landlords."[30] By the late eighteenth century, moreover, these transoceanic peregrinations had led to the rise of small Hadhrami Arab immigrant merchant colonies in port towns such as Palembang, Pekanbaru, and Pontianak, with substantial communities growing in Batavia, Semarang, Surabaya, and other towns—Cirebon, Pekalongan, Tegal—along the northern coastal *pasisir* towns of Java over the course of the nineteenth century. By the turn of the twentieth century, there were Arab quarters in most of the residency capital towns of Java, with over 16,000 Arabs registered in the census of 1893 and over 20,000 across the Indies as a whole.[31] Like their Chinese counterparts, these Arab immigrants and their offspring were identified by the East Indies government as "foreign orientals" (*vreemde oosterlingen*) and confined to urban ghettoes under the colonial pass and quarter system. Just as established *peranakan* Chinese families dominated the ranks of the opium monopoly farmers and *Kapitan Cina*, so too did hereditary *shaykh* enjoy religious authority and *sayyid* (i.e., descendants of the Prophet Muhammad) occupy positions as Dutch-appointed *hoofd* (headmen) in the Arab communities of the Indies.[32] But just as a massive flood of immigration from Fujian and Guangdong in the late nineteenth century gave rise to an ascendant class of *totok* or *singkeh* Chinese tycoons with expanded connections beyond the Indies, so too did contemporaneous streams of new merchant migrants from the Hadhramaut challenge established local hierarchies, while drawing the Arab communities of the archipelago into broader diasporic networks and other circuits stretching across the Indian Ocean and the Muslim world.[33]

---

30. Engseng Ho, *The Graves of Tarim: Genealogy and Mobility across the Indian Ocean* (Berkeley: University of California Press, 2006), 27.

31. Sumit Kumar Mandal, "A History of Arabs in Java under Dutch Rule, 1800–1924" (PhD diss., Columbia University, 1984), 33–34.

32. Sumit Kumar Mandal, "A History of Arabs in Java," 71–82.

33. See, for example, Kazuhiro Arai, "Arabs Who Traversed the Indian Ocean: The History of the al 'Attas Family in Hadramawt and Southeast Asia, c. 1600–1960" (PhD diss., University of Michigan, 2004).

Hadhramis and *Hajjis*, *'Ulamā* and *Shaykh*: Indian Ocean and Jāwī Islam

While these immigrant Hadhrami merchants were smaller in number than their Chinese counterparts and typically more modest in the scale and significance of their business operations, they were immersed not only within transoceanic diasporic networks but also within broader Islamic circuits that began to draw the vast Muslim population of the Indies into their orbit over the course of the late nineteenth century. The initial Islamization of the Indonesian archipelago, after all, had unfolded in the Early Modern Era in the context of expanding travel and trade across the Indian Ocean, and over the seventeenth and eighteenth centuries, the small but steady trickle of pilgrims making the Hajj from these islands had helped to reproduce and reinvigorate connections to centers of Islamic pilgrimage, worship, and learning elsewhere in the Muslim world. A community of Islamic scholars (*'ulamā*) from Southeast Asia—known collectively as the Jāwah—emerged and grew over the years in Mecca, enlisting successive generations of *hajjis* from the region in textual exegesis (*tafsīr*) of the Qur'an and the Hadīth and in Shāfi'ī jurisprudence (*fiqh*).[34] Over the seventeenth and eighteenth centuries, these *'ulamā* and their disciples came to play a leading role in the circulation of Islamic knowledge and discourse and Arabic-language texts and teaching traditions across the Indonesian archipelago and beyond.[35] Over the same years, the annual Hajj season also saw the induction of pilgrims from the Indonesian archipelago and elsewhere in Southeast Asia into Sufi brotherhoods (*ṭarīqa*; pl. *ṭuruq*), initiation into their rituals (*dhikr*, *wird*), and instruction in mystical practices (*taṣawwuf*). Returning *hajjis*, especially those who had earned teaching credentials (*'ijāza*) in this newly acquired esoteric knowledge of Islam, pioneered the recruitment of Muslims across the Indonesian archipelago into Sufi *ṭuruq*, whose diverse strands attracted many adherents into lodges across Java, Sumatra, Sulawesi, and other islands of the Indies.[36] In this way, a distinctly cosmopolitan discursive, textual, and associational infrastructure for Islam emerged and evolved over the seventeenth and eighteenth centuries, drawing pious Muslims across the

---

34. Azyumardi Azra, *The Origins of Economic Reformism in Southeast Asia: Networks of Malay-Indonesian and Middle Eastern 'Ulamā in the Seventeenth and Eighteenth Centuries* (Honolulu: University of Hawai'i Press, 2004).

35. Martin van Bruinessen, "*Pesantren* and *Kitab Kuning*: Continuity and Change in a Tradition of Religious Learning," in *Texts from the Islands: Oral and Written Traditions of Indonesia and the Malay World*, ed. Wolfgang Marschall (Berne: Institut für Ethnologie, 1994), 121–145.

36. Martin van Bruinessen, "The Origins and Development of the Naqshbandi Order in Indonesia," *Der Islam* 67 (1990): 150–179; Martin van Bruinessen, "The Tariqa Khalwatiyya in South Celebes," in *Excursies in Celebes*, ed. Harry A. Poeze and Pim Schoorl (Leiden: KITLVPress, 1991), 251–270; Martin van Bruinessen, *Tarekat Naqsyabandiyah di Indonesia: Survei Historis, Geografis, dan Sosiologis* (Bandung: Mizan, 1992); Martin van Bruinessen, "Origins and Development of the Sufi Orders (tarekat) in Southeast Asia," *Studia Islamika* 1, no. 1 (1994): 1–23.

Indonesian archipelago into circuitries of Islamic authority stretching across Southeast Asia, the Indian Ocean, and beyond.

As scholars have shown, the economic and technological transformations of the nineteenth century helped to broaden, deepen, and transform these connections between Muslims in the Indies and their coreligionists elsewhere. Travellers' lodges, or *pondok* (Arabic: *funduq*) began to evolve into sites of religious instruction for full-time pupils (*santri*), morphing in due course into Islamic boarding schools known variously as *pondok*, *pesantren*, *dayah*, and *surau* across the archipelago.

> The Great Post Road, completed in 1808, and its feeders would be trodden as much by santris moving between the new pondoks as by Dutch overseers inspecting plantations. By the late 1840s, the pondoks located near the main commercial towns became key nodes of intellectual exchange. From here the more advanced students could move on to the larger ports and take advantage of the presence of greater numbers of Arab scholars. Two major destinations in this network were Surabaya, where the Habshi clan was found, and Singapore, the home of 'Abd al-Rahman al-Saqqaf and Salim b. Sumayr, whose primer, the *Safinat al-najah* (The Vessel of Salvation) was popular in the region.[37]

With the intensification and spread of market relations and modern state circuitries on Java and elsewhere in the Indies came increasing travel—seen most dramatically in the construction of railroads—which thickened the flow and widened the arc of religious sojourns and scholarly pursuits across the landscape of Islamic schools and shrines on Java, Sumatra, and elsewhere, as seen in the doubling of the estimated number of Islamic schools and the near-quadrupling of their registered pupils on Java and Madura from 1882 to 1893.[38] With the growth of interisland trade and travel and the rise of the publishing industry, moreover, the dissemination of books and other publications written in *Jawi*—that is, Malay in Arabic script—greatly strengthened the field of shared communication and consciousness among Muslims across the Indies and beyond.[39] Finally, with the invention of the steamboat, the opening of the Suez Canal, and the establishment of Pax Brittanica across the Indian Ocean, sea travel became more affordable,

---

37. Michael Laffan, *The Makings of Indonesian Islam: Orientalism and the Narration of a Sufi Past* (Princeton, NJ: Princeton University Press, 2011), 27. On the origins and evolution of the *funduq*, see Olivia Remie Constable, *Housing the Stranger in the Mediterranean World: Lodging, Trade and Travel in Late Antiquity and the Middle Ages* (Cambridge: Cambridge University Press, 2003).

38. M. C. Ricklefs, *Polarising Javanese Society: Islamic and Other Visions (c. 1830–1930)* (Singapore: National University of Singapore Press, 2007), 70.

39. Martin van Bruinessen, "Kitab Kuning: Books in Arabic Script Used in the Pesantren Milieu," *Bijdragen tot de Taal-, Land- en Volkenkunde* 146, no. 2–3 (1989): 226–269.

rapid, and safe, allowing more and more Muslims from the Indies to make the Hajj or to visit centers of Islamic learning elsewhere in the Muslim world, even as larger numbers of sojourners and settlers from the Hadhramaut arrived on Indonesian shores.[40]

As with Chinese business networks and the broader flows of commodities and capital that sustained them, these expanding circuits of Islamic pilgrimage and schooling transcended the boundaries of the Indies, with the Malay Peninsula, Penang, and, above all, Singapore included within the regional orbit of itinerant *hajjis* and Hadhrami merchants, *'ulamā*, and Sufi *shaykhs*. As noted above, Singapore had long served as an entrepôt for "Outer Island" commerce, attracting thousands of cargo-laden Bugis *prahus* (small sailing boats) from across the Indonesian archipelago. Over the course of the nineteenth century, Singapore emerged as the key regional port of embarkation for the Hajj, with thousands of pilgrims from across the Indonesian and Philippine archipelagos, the Malay Peninsula, and elsewhere boarding steamships for the trip to Mecca each year and many more would-be pilgrims reaching Singapore and remaining there permanently, earning the epithet *Hajji Singapura*. By the 1870s, large-scale migration from Java and Sumatra to the Straits Settlements and the Malay Peninsula were well under way, even as Singapore boasted Southeast Asia's largest and wealthiest Hadhrami merchant community, which served as a key nodal point for diasporic networks of commerce and credit. All in all, Singapore rather than Batavia served as the hub of Islamic life for Indies Muslims, its magnetic pull drawing thousands of aspiring pilgrims and Islamic scholars from across the archipelago.

> Singapore's reputation as a center of Islamic life and learning in the late nineteenth century was widespread, though it rested less on possession of a school of religious thought (or even on particular teachers) than on its position in relation to the pilgrimage and Arab migration, and not least on its role as a publication and distribution center for religious writings. Students from all over the archipelago, wishing to further their studies in doctrine or law, went either to Mecca or to the Strait Settlements, where they met and sat at the feet of itinerant scholars from the Hahdramaut, and from Patani, Aceh, Palembang, and Java—most of whom had themselves studied in Mecca. The city thus stood at the heart of a communications network which fed a constant stream of revivified "orthodox" Muslim thought from the Hejaz into the peninsula and archipelago.[41]

---

40. Christian Snouck Hurgronje, *Mekka in the Latter Half of the Nineteenth Century* (Leiden: Brill, 1970).

41. William Roff, *The Origins of Malay Nationalism* (New Haven, CT: Yale University Press, 1967), 43.

Indeed, by the turn of the twentieth century, Singapore had also come to serve as the hub of the Islamic publishing industry in Southeast Asia, printing a range of Islamic books and periodicals and providing a base for the distribution of religious texts emanating from the Hijaz, Bombay, Cairo, and beyond.[42]

By the turn of the twentieth century, Indies Muslims were thus increasingly immersed within religious, intellectual, and cultural currents that spanned the breadth of the Indian Ocean and the broader Muslim world. The Muslims of the Indies, it has been argued, were enfolded within a region-wide *Jawi* ecumene stretching across the *bilād al-jāwa* to encompass the Malay Peninsula and southern Islamicized areas of the Philippines and Siam, sustained by communication in Arabic-script Malay and circulation among region-wide scholarly networks and Sufi *ṭuruq*.[43] By the finial decades of the nineteenth century, moreover, the experiences of Indies Muslims in the Hijaz as pilgrims, scholars, and Sufi initiates were increasingly matched and arguably overshadowed by the attractive pull of cosmopolitan Cairo, where the famous mosque-university Al-Azhar had long enjoyed fame and prestige as the Muslim world's preeminent institution of Islamic learning, and where the growing numbers of Southeast Asian students had necessitated the construction of a *Jawi* dormitory-cum-study-hall (*riwāq al-jāwa*) by the late 1860s.[44]

With the opening of the Suez Canal in 1859 and the accelerating absorption of Cairo within the British imperial orbit, moreover, the city also emerged as a center for new forms of Islamic reformism, as seen in the teachings and writings of the Persia-born Jamāl ad-Dīn al-Afghānī and his Egyptian disciple Muhammad 'Abduh from the 1870s until the turn of the twentieth century.[45] Operating outside Al-Azhar and traditional structures of Islamic learning, al-Afghānī and 'Abduh worked assiduously to promote modernist forms of education, incorporating individual interpretation and reasoning in the reading of the scriptures, as well as subjects and methods of instruction outside the established practices of Islamic scholasticism. Communicating through study groups, newspaper articles, and public speeches, these reformists transcended existing hierarchies of Islamic authority as they spoke and wrote directly to a broad Muslim audience, whose emergence as a reading public and imagined community—the *'Ummah*—was

42. Ian Proudfoot, "The Print Threshold in Malaysia" (Monash University Centre of Southeast Asian Working Papers, Clayton, Victoria, 1994).

43. Michael Francis Laffan, *Islamic Nationhood and Colonial Indonesia: The Umma below the Winds* (London: RoutledgeCurzon, 2003), 11–36.

44. Laffan, *Islamic Nationhood and Colonial Indonesia*, 114–141.

45. Nikki R. Keddie, *An Islamic Response to Imperialism: Political and Religious Writings of Sayyid Jamāl ad-Dīn "al-Afghānī"* (Berkeley: University of California Press, 1968), 3–97; Albert Hourani, *Arabic Thought in the Liberal Age, 1798–1939* (Cambridge: Cambridge University Press, 1998), 103–160.

crystallizing across the Muslim world amidst the dramatic economic, social, and technological changes of the late nineteenth century.

Although forced into exile in the aftermath of the failed 'Urabi revolt of 1881–1882,[46] al-Afghānī and 'Abduh's reformist writings, teachings, and activities continued to attract and inspire a new generation of Muslim intellectuals emerging outside the entrenched hierarchies of Islamic learning. Across the Ottoman lands, the Indian subcontinent, Central Asia, the Caucasus, and the Crimean Peninsula of southern Russia, and beyond, Islamic reformist initiatives were well under way by the turn of the twentieth century, with Cairo as a key hub of attraction, activity, and information. The year 1908 even saw the short-lived publication in Cairo of an avowedly "sociological, political, progressive-reformist, and literary" Arabic-language newspaper, al-Nahḍa (The Renaissance) under the editorship of the prominent Crimean Tatar Ismail Bey Gasprinskii, the leading light of the Islamic reformist (jadīdī) movement across the Crimea, the Caucasus, and Central Asia, with cartoons from the aforementioned Azeri-Turkish Molla Nasreddin included in its pages, and plans for a "Universal Muslim Congress" discussed in its lead articles.[47]

Along with Alexandria, Cairo boasted an infrastructure—"steamships, a reliable postal system, and a relatively free press—that allowed for the circulation of questions, articles, periodicals, books, and people, coming from many continents,"[48] and this setting enabled more successfully sustained experiments in Islamic newspaper publishing.[49] By 1898, as al-Afghānī lay on his deathbed in Istanbul, Muhammad 'Abduh and his close protégé, the famous Syrian salafi reformist Rashīd Riḍā, had started publishing Al-Manār ("The Beacon" or "The Lighthouse"), a monthly Cairo-based reformist journal that remained in regular circulation through 1936 and, directly and indirectly, reached readers across much of the Muslim world. Combining commentary on the Qur'an by 'Abduh, Islamic legal opinions (fatāwā) by Riḍā, articles on diverse social and political trends across the Muslim world, and correspondence from readers far and wide, Al-Manār drew a growing audience in the bilād al-jāwa within its vast orbit. As scholars have shown, articles treating Dutch colonial rule in the Indies and letters from readers across the Indonesian archipelago appeared with some frequency in the

46. Juan R. I. Cole, Colonialism and Revolution in the Middle East: Social and Cultural Origins of Egypt's 'Urabi Movement (Princeton, NJ: Princeton University Press, 1993).
47. Thomas Kuttner, "Russian Jadīdism and the Islamic World: Ismail Gasprinskii in Cairo—1908," Cahiers du Monde Russe et Soviétique 16, no. 3–4 (July–December 1975): 383–424.
48. Ilham Khuri-Makdisi, The Eastern Mediterranean and the Making of Global Radicalism, 1860–1914 (Berkeley: University of California Press, 2010), 55.
49. Juan R. Cole, "Printing and Urban Islam in the Mediterranean World, 1890–1920," in Modernity and Culture: From the Mediterranean to the Indian Ocean, ed. Leila Farazi Fawaz and Christopher A. Bayly (New York: Columbia University Press, 2002), 344–364.

pages of the journal,[50] and, within a decade, similar journals had begun to spring up in Singapore (*Al-Imām*, 1906–08; *Al-Watan*, 1910), Palembang (*Al-Bashīr*, 1914–15) and Surabaya (*Al-Iqbāl*, 1917–1920), and elsewhere, often reprinting or otherwise making reference to articles, correspondence, and *fatāwā* from *Al-Manār* itself.[51]

Thus by the early twentieth century, Muslims across the Indies were increasingly encouraged and enabled to see themselves and their circumstances as part of a broader world of accelerating change and conflict, with Cairo and a handful of key port cities across the Indian Ocean—from Zanzibar to Aden, Bombay, Singapore, and Surabaya—forming a trans-oceanic chain of increasing labor circulation and social communication. As scholars have shown, the decades spanning the late nineteenth and early twentieth centuries saw the emergence in such cities of a new kind of cosmopolitan, competitive, diversified, and liberalized Islamic "religious economy," with marketization of their hinterlands, expansion of urban populations and public spheres, and revolutions in communication and transportation (printing presses, steamboats, telegraph lines) enabling new forms of religious activity, association, expression, and experience.[52] These trends extended far beyond Islam, as seen in contemporaneous developments among the *Bhadralok* of Calcutta, the Theosophists of Madras, and the 'Protestant Buddhists' of Colombo as they pushed for religious revival, educational reform, and social renewal along lines parallel to ongoing efforts among Muslims in Cairo and Bombay.[53]

The intensification and expansion of British imperialism—and 'free trade'—across the Indian Ocean during the same decades also helped to tighten the connections between the links in this chain, encouraging the rise and spread of grandiose new conceptions of shared identity and aspirations, whether Pan-Islamic or

---

50. Over the years, Rīḍā received requests for *fatāwā* from subscribers in Batavia, Padang, Surabaya, Surakarta, Bonjonegoro, Purworejo, Sambas, and Kupang. See Leor Halevi, *Modern Things on Trial: Islam's Global and Material Reformation in the Age of Rida, 1865–1935* (New York: Columbia University Press, 2019), 57.

51. Mona Abaza, "Southeast Asia and the Middle East: Al-Manar and Islamic Modernity," in *From the Mediterranean to the China Sea*, ed. Claude Guillot, Denys Lombard, and Roderich Ptak, (Wiesbaden: Harrassowitz Verlag, 1998), 93–111; Ahmed Ibrahim Abushouk, "Al-Manār and the Hadhramī Elite in the Malay-Indonesian World: Challenge and Response," *Journal of the Royal Asiatic Society* 17, no. 3 (July 2007): 301–322; Michael Laffan, "'Another Andalusia': Image of Colonial Southeast Asia in Arabic Newspapers," *Journal of Asian Studies* 66, no. 3 (August 2007): 689–722; and Natalie Mobini-Kesheh, "The Arabic Periodicals of the Netherlands East Indies, 1914–1942," *Bijdragen tot de Taal-, Land- en Volkenkunde* 152, no. 2 (1996): 236–256.

52. See, in particular, Nile Green, *Bombay Islam: The Religious Economy of the West Indian Ocean, 1840–1915* (Cambridge: Cambridge University Press, 2011).

53. See Mark Ravinder Frost, "Globalization and Religious Revival in the Imperial Cities of the Indian Ocean Rim, 1870–1920" (PhD thesis, Cambridge University, 2002); and Mark Frost, "'Wider Opportunities': Religious Revival, Nationalist Awakening and the Global Dimension in Colombo, 1870–1920," *Modern Asian Studies* 36, no. 4 (September 2002): 937–967.

Pan-Asian in nature.[54] In the making of this trans-oceanic universe, the role of the British Raj in the Indian subcontinent was crucial, with *sepoy* soldiers and Sikh policemen, Gujarati merchants, Chettiar moneylenders, and Tamil workers pioneering the extension of modern administrative structures and legal systems, market relations, plantation agriculture, and road and railway lines from port towns such as Durban, Nairobi, Rangoon, and Kuala Lumpur into their hinterlands. With hundreds of thousands of immigrant Tamil laborers arriving to work on the rubber plantations and scores of British architects building Mughal-style mosques and palaces across the Malay Peninsula, the neighboring Netherlands East Indies found itself along the fringes of the magnetic force field of this increasingly "Indian" Ocean.[55]

Cosmopolitan *Melayu* Modernity: Newspapers, Novels, and *Komedie Stamboel*

Overall, as seen in the broadening of transregional and transoceanic networks of diasporic and religious circulation, the deepening incorporation of the Indonesian archipelago within the world economy during the late nineteenth and early twentieth centuries saw the intensifying immersion of the Netherlands East Indies within diverse currents of cosmopolitanism. As in the Philippines, the turn of the twentieth century saw the rise of a market society and a modern public sphere in the Indies, within which variegated forms of cosmopolitan culture and discourse circulated and gained currency. With the commercialization of agriculture came dramatic population growth and urbanization, with the major port cities of Java and the other islands of the archipelago expanding manifold and the flows of commodities and communications connecting them ever more closely to their rapidly evolving hinterlands. Massive migratory movement—from countryside to town and city, from Java to Sumatra, and beyond—contributed to the making of what Takashi Shiraishi has memorably termed an Age in Motion.[56]

Accompanying, easing, and accelerating these flows of commodities, information, and people were important new developments in language and discourse,

---

54. Mark Ravinder Frost, "Asia's Maritime Networks and the Colonial Public Sphere, 1840–1920," *New Zealand Journal of Asian Studies* 6, no. 2 (December 2004): 63–94; Mark R. Frost, "That Great Ocean of Idealism: Calcutta, The Tagore Circle and The Idea of Asia, 1900–1920" (Nalanda-Sriwijaya Centre Working Paper Series, Singapore, June 2011).

55. Sugata Bose, *A Hundred Horizons: The Indian Ocean in the Age of Global Empire* (Cambridge, MA: Harvard University Press, 2006); Thomas R. Metcalf, *Imperial Connections: India in the Indian Ocean Arena, 1860–1920* (Berkeley: University of California Press, 2007).

56. Takashi Shiraishi, *An Age in Motion: Popular Radicalism in Java, 1912–1926* (Ithaca, NY: Cornell University Press, 1990).

most notably the rise of Malay as a modern lingua franca for spoken and, crucially, written communication across the Indonesian archipelago. Various forms of the language now known as Malay, or *Melayu*, had been in usage in and around the Indonesian archipelago for centuries, but the late nineteenth and early twentieth centuries saw its accelerating extension and entrenchment as a convenient medium for communication by officials of the expanding Dutch colonial state, as a handy tool for commercial transactions in the Indies' expanding market economy, and as a means of cultural expression in the widening realm of popular entertainment and print media across the archipelago.[57] Freed from the archaicism of the classical Malay of the *Hikayat Hang Tuah*, the aristocratic pretensions of the high (*kromo*) Javanese of the Surakartan and Yogyakartan courts, the colonial state affiliations of Dutch emanating from the Netherlands, and the sacral authority and scholasticism associated with the Arabic of the Qur'an, *Melayu* offered new possibilities for reimagining, reinventing, and rearticulating ideas and identities in a distinctly modern way, unmoored from established fixities and boundaries of location, tradition, and hierarchy.

> By the end of the nineteenth century, a multitude of translations from world literatures began to appear in Melayu. These appeared most often in newspaper as well as in book form. But it was not solely in print that these translations became available. They were also copied by hand and rented out in lending libraries. What is remarkable is that what was translated and what was written in Melayu was so diverse. It includes not only the literature produced at court throughout the archipelago, Persian tales, and Chinese stories but also accounts of the Russo-Japanese war and of local events, including a bank robbery. . . . Batavian newspapers published an epic about Napoleon, Chinese sagas, Persian tales, Sherlock Holmes. . . . Somewhat abruptly, via the medium of the lingua franca, most places in the world began to be felt in the Indies. The messages of the world could speak to anyone and, for a while, it seemed that many did not shrug off what they heard around them with the thought that it was not intended for them. The feeling that there was something to be heard, and no one could know in advance just what it might be, loosened the constrictions imposed by identity.[58]

---

57. John Hoffman, "A Foreign Investment: Indies Malay to 1901," *Indonesia* 27 (April 1979): 65–92; Henk M. J. Maier, "From Heteroglossia to Polyglossia: The Creation of Malay and Dutch in the Indies," *Indonesia* 56 (October 1993): 37–65.

58. James T. Siegel, *Fetish, Recognition, Revolution* (Princeton, NJ: Princeton University Press, 1997), 17–19.

Indeed, the late nineteenth century and the first decade of the twentieth saw the emergence, evolution, and expansion of new forms of written (*Melayu*) expression—newspapers, novels—along with the growth of a (*Melayu*) reading public. From the late 1860s, the interests of Christian missionaries and European printing firms had begun to stimulate experiments with new kinds of Malay-language publications and periodicals, with Eurasian and *peranakan* Chinese editors pioneering a succession of magazines and newspapers in various cities of the Indies over the last three decades of the nineteenth century. As of 1900, more than a dozen newspapers and periodicals were circulating in the Indies, five of them dailies, with a largely Chinese readership. With support from the Dutch colonial government, a fortnightly illustrated magazine titled *Bintang Hindia* (Star of the Indies) was established in 1902 under the editorship of Henri Brousson, a former Dutch colonial army soldier, and Abdul Rivai, a Dutch-educated doctor from West Sumatra. For many readers, it has been argued, the modern cosmopolitanism of *Bintang Hindia* was an "eye-opener":

> The articles and illustrations in the magazine covered a wide range of subjects. There were accounts and pictures of places in Holland and Europe, the Russo-Japanese war, the Dutch military expedition in Boni, and Indies officials, both Dutch and native alike. There were articles on literature, commerce, language-learning, and education in general. Reports and pictures of the Chinese and Arabs in the Indies, especially about their organizations, schools, and material progress, were meant not only to attract support from the two communities but also to urge the Indonesians to emulate their ways in the pursuit of *kemajuan* (progress).[59]

By 1907, *Bintang Hindia* had ceased publication, but a new weekly magazine, *Medan Prijaji*, took its place under the leadership of Tirto Adhi Soerjo, a Dutch-educated former medical student and journalist of Javanese aristocratic background.[60]

Alongside the emergence and evolution of the press, the same decades saw broader shifts in communications and culture that helped to nurture modern forms of consciousness and subjectivity in Indies society. Telegraph lines had been laid across Java from the 1850s, postal services were established in the 1860s, eight railway lines were in operation connecting the fifteen largest cities of Java by the late 1880s, and half a million long-distance telephone calls were being placed through

---

59. Ahmad B. Adam, *The Vernacular Press and the Emergence of Modern Indonesian Consciousness (1855–1913)* (Ithaca, NY: Cornell University Southeast Asia Program, 1995), 105.

60. Pramoedya Ananta Toer, *Sang Pemula, Disertai Karya-Karya Non-Fiksi (Jurnalistik) dan Fiksi (Cerpen/Novel) R.M. Tirto Adhi Soerjo* (Jakarta: Lentera Dipantara, 2003), 40–100.

the island every year by the turn of the twentieth century. The last decades of the nineteenth century witnessed the accelerating spread of photography and phonograph music across the Indonesian archipelago, and wireless radio broadcasts from Holland followed shortly after World War I, with twenty radio stations and more than one hundred thousand registered listeners in the Indies by the early 1940s.[61]

Accompanying these technological transformations were shifts in modes of experience and expression, as seen in contemporaneous trends in Malay-language literature. Scholars have traced subtle shifts in the sense of authorship, agency, and narrative, and voice conveyed in the *syair* (poems) and *cerita* (short stories) of the late nineteenth century, and in the novels that were written and published in the first three decades of the twentieth century as well.[62] Notable in this regard was the depiction of characters circulating in a modern, urban public sphere and transcending (however incompletely and unsuccessfully) the established local confines of family, status hierarchy, and ethnic boundaries, and the unmooring of agency and desire from within the constraints of these "traditional" sources of authority and recognition, as seen in the diverse romantic and sexual adventures and liaisons of the protagonists of these novels.[63]

Beyond the world of literature and the narrow stratum of literate society in the Indies, moreover, the turn of the twentieth century also saw the rise of more popular forms of modern cosmopolitan expression and experience in the growing port cities of the archipelago, as seen most spectacularly in the *Komedie Stamboel*. This itinerant opera owed its roots to Bombay's small, privileged community of Parsis, whose Iranian origins and Zoroastrian faith helped to establish them as key commercial intermediaries and cultural interlocutors for the British Raj, and, by the late nineteenth century, as leading bankers, cotton mill owners, shipping magnates, and industrialists (e.g., Jamsetji Nusserwanji Tata, the founder of today's world-famous Tata Group).[64]

---

61. Suryadi, "The 'Talking Machine' Comes to the Dutch East Indies: The Arrival of Western Media Technology in Southeast Asia," *Bijdragen tot de Taal-, Land- en Volkenkunde* 162, no. 2–3 (2006): 269–305; Karen Strassler, *Refracted Visions: Popular Photography and National Modernity in Java* (Durham, NC: Duke University Press, 2010); Rudolf Mrázek, *Engineers of Happy Land: Technology and Nationalism in a Colony* (Princeton, NJ: Princeton University Press, 2002).

62. J. Francisco B. Benitez, "*Awit* and *Syair*: Alternative Subjectivities and Multiple Modernities in Nineteenth-Century Insular Southeast Asia" (PhD diss., University of Wisconsin at Madison, 2004), 189–268; G. L. Koster, "Making It New in 1884: Lie Him Hok's *Syair Siti Akbari*," *Bijdragen tot de Taal-, Land- en Volkenkunde* 154, no. 1 (1998): 95–115; Kenji Tsuchiya, "Popular Literature and Colonial Society in Late-Nineteenth-Century Java—*Cerita Nyai Dasima*, the Macabre Story of an Englishman's Concubine," *Southeast Asian Studies* 28, no. 4 (March 1991): 467–480.

63. Siegel, *Fetish, Recognition, Revolution*; Tsuyoshi Kato, "Images of Colonial Cities in Early Indonesian Novels," in *Southeast Asia over Three Generations: Essays Presented to Benedict R. O'G. Anderson*, ed. James T. Siegel and Audrey R. Kahin (Ithaca, NY: Cornell University Southeast Asia Program, 2003), 91–123; Henk Maier, *We Are Playing Relatives: A Survey of Malay Writing* (Leiden: KITLV Press, 2004), 157–201.

64. Tanya M. Luhrmann, *The Good Parsi: The Fate of a Colonial Elite in a Postcolonial Society* (Cambridge, MA: Harvard University Press, 1996), 80–99.

By the mid-nineteenth century, members of this highly anglophile, cricket-playing community had established amateur dramatic societies to produce English-language plays and soon expanded into performances for non-Parsi popular audiences on a commercial basis. These performers combined theatrical technology and techniques imported from Europe with scripts in Gujarati and other languages as they began to venture outside Bombay, creating a musical-dramatic repertoire drawing on "Sanskrit epics, Shakespeare, Middle Eastern romances and the Arabian nights, European farce, local legend and history, or the latest adventure novel."[65] By the 1860s, Parsi theater troupes were extending their tours to Rangoon, Malacca, Penang, and Singapore, with reports of appearances in towns in Sumatran in the 1880s, and locally recruited companies sprang up in such cities by the turn of the century to produce performances known as *komedi Parsi, wayang Parsi, komedi Melayu,* and *bangsawan.*[66]

By the turn of the century, Malay-language popular theater troupes inspired by this *komedi Parsi* were circulating and performing regularly in many cities and towns across the Indies, stimulated by the opening of the *Komedie Stamboel* in Surabaya in 1891 and its successes and various spin-offs over the ensuing decade. Combining *peranakan* Chinese entrepreneurship and management, Eurasian ("Indo") direction and acting talent, Javanese ukulele-like *kroncong* musical accompaniment, and Malay scripts of from *The Arabian Nights,* Goethe's *Faust,* and diverse European operas and fairy tales, *Komedie Stamboel* was soon touring to much acclaim across Java and, with somewhat less success, in Medan and Singapore. Its performances and those that followed in its wake drew together diverse audiences in the major towns and cities of fin-de-siècle Java—Batavia, Bogor and Cirebon, Semarang and Tegal, Yogyakarta and Solo, Kediri and Pasuruan, and, of course, Surabaya.[67]

> Itinerant professional troupes with casts and crews of fifty or more visited regularly, performing four- or five-hour tent shows for paying spectators. Diverse audiences attended—drunken European men, middle-income Muslim families, Chinese store owners, prostitutes, sailors and soldiers, Eurasian clerks, and nearly everyone else. Those who could not afford the price of a ticket might listen outside the tent or try to sneak in. Men and women fell madly in love with actors and actresses and lavished gifts and

65. Matthew Isaac Cohen, "On the Origins of the Komedie Stamboel: Popular Culture, Colonial Society, and the Parsi Theatre Movement," *Bijdragen tot de Taal-, Land- en Volkenkunde* 157, no. 2 (2001): 316.

66. Tan Soei Beng, *Bangsawan: A Social and Stylistic History of Popular Malay Opera* (Singapore: Oxford University Press, 1993), 8–72.

67. Matthew Isaac Cohen, *Komedie Stamboel: Popular Theater in Colonial Indonesia, 1891–1903* (Athens: Ohio University Press, 2006).

attention on them. Songs from this theater, known as *lagu stambul*, were sung on the streets, issued as cylinders for music boxes, and incorporated into diverse musical genres. . . . Stories based on *stambul* plays . . . were published regularly in the vernacular press, and professional companies advertised and were reviewed in the Dutch- and Malay-language newspapers. Amateur and semiprofessional groups multiplied, performing scaled-down versions of plays such as *Ali Baba*, *Snow White*, and *Faust* for their amusement and on the streets during communal celebrations such as the Chinese New Year. Ethical aspects of the theater, performers, and spectators were debated. . . . Not everyone was interested in watching *komedi stambul*, but almost everyone had an opinion about it.[68]

Alongside the urbane, cosmopolitan diversity of its origins, actors, and audiences, the *Komedie Stamboel* also embodied and imparted a distinctly modern form of expression and experience. In contrast to the fixity and singularity of the characters and dramas found, for example, in "traditional" Javanese *wayang* (shadow puppet) theater drawn from the *Rāmāyana* and the *Mahābhārata*, the *Komedie Stamboel* engaged in new forms of representation, in both senses of the term.

If a *stambul* troupe put on a Malay version of *The Merchant of Venice*, the actors needed scripts because no one in the cast or audience had any solid idea of who Shylock was, how he should gesture, or what he should say. For one thing, no character in traditional drama had been a Jew or a moneylender. In the event, Shylock could only be played "sociologically," as a representation of intersecting, more or less contemporary, group categories—say, moneylenders, foreign minorities (perhaps *vreemde oosterlingen*), protective fathers of rebellious daughters, etc. The actor had no way to improvise the role, and thus came to depend on a memorized script and the ability to interpret it according to vague standards or social verisimilitude. Shylock "worked" to the extent that his player managed to convince the audience that he was just like, i.e. re-presented (or mechanically reproduced) groups or social types out there in the contemporary real world. In this way the new dramatic forms paralleled the echo effect of the newspaper, conjuring up in the consumer's mind *general categories of similar persons*.[69]

---

68. Cohen, *Komedie Stamboel*, 1–2.
69. Benedict R. O'G. Anderson, "Language, Fantasy, Revolution: Java 1900–1950," in *Making Indonesia: Essays on Modern Indonesia in Honor of George Mc.T Kahin*, ed. Daniel S. Lev and Ruth McVey (Ithaca, NY: Cornell University Southeast Asia Program, 1996), 37.

Thus, as the Indies entered the twentieth century, new and distinctly modern forms of drama were being acted out within transoceanic, cosmopolitan circuits of commerce, communication, and culture and shared structures of feeling, and with increasing excitement and expanding numbers of actors and audiences and bigger performances to be staged in years to come across the Indonesian archipelago.

NEWSPAPERS, RALLIES, STRIKES

The Rise and Fall of Sarekat Islam (SI), 1912–1926

While new and distinctly modern forms of popular operatic theater had begun to circulate to growing acclaim across the Indies over the final decade of the nineteenth century, the early decades of the twentieth century saw major shifts in the public sphere, from experiments in fiction, publishing, and dramatic acting to unprecedented initiatives in associational activity and, in due course, revolutionary political action. Movement among the realms of the imagination, the written page or broadsheet, and political activism became increasingly common. In the 1910s, the pioneering newspaperman Tirto Adhi Soerjo played a prominent role in the founding of the first mass movement in the Indies, the Sarekat Islam (SI),[1] and his fellow journalist and SI activist Marco Kartodikromo wrote several novels, most famously *Student Hijo*, which was first serialized in the daily *Sinar Hindia* in 1918 and then published as a book in 1919.[2] Semaoen, editor in chief of the daily *Sinar Hindia* and Sarekat Islam chairman in Semarang, likewise spent some of his months of imprisonment in 1919 writing a bildungsroman he titled Hikajat Kadiroen, which was published in serialized form in *Sinar Hindia* in 1920 and then issued as a book in 1922 by the Partai Komunis Indonesia (PKI), which Semaoen led until his expulsion from the Indies in 1923.[3] Years later, even as the remnants of the forcibly disbanded Sarekat Islam had lapsed into inactivity

---

1. Pramoedya Ananta Toer, *Sang Pemula, Disertai Karya-Karya Non-Fiksi (Jurnalistik) dan Fiksi (Cerpen/Novel) R.M. Tirto Adhi Soerjo* (Jakarta: Lentera Dipantara, 2003), 134–215.

2. Marco Kartodikromo, *Student Hijo* (Yogyakarta: Yayasan Aksara Indonesia, 2000).

3. Semaoen, Hikajat *Kadiroen: Sebuah Novel* (Yogyakarta: Yayasan Benteng Budaya, 2000). See also Henk M. J. Maier, "Written in the Prison's Light: The Hikajat Kadiroen by Semaoen," *Review of Indonesian and Malaysian Affairs* 30 (Winter–Summer 1996): 1–18.

and the leaders of the PKI—Semaoen, Alimin, Musso, and Darsono—languished in imprisonment in the Boven Digoel colony in West New Guinea or in exile in Moscow, a five-volume popular novel was published in Medan, East Sumatra between 1938 and 1940. Titled *Patjar Merah Indonesia* (The Scarlet Pimpernel of Indonesia), the novel featured a cast of characters readily identifiable from the imprisoned and exiled PKI leadership, restyled and Russified as Semounoff, Ivan Alminsky, Mussotte, and Darsonov. Above all, the novel chronicled the global peregrinations and adventures of the Patjar Merah himself, known as Vichitra in Siam, Tan Min Kha in China, and Ibrahim el Molqa in Palestine, but understood by readers to represent the exiled PKI chairman Tan Malaka, who was expelled from the Indies in 1922 and, following a brief stint in Moscow, spent the remainder of the interwar era engaged in revolutionary activities across Southeast Asia and China, before returning to the Indonesian archipelago in 1942.[4] Thus, even as the leaders of the PKI and other organizations remained imprisoned, exiled, and otherwise immobilized in the Indies of the late interwar era, the promise of revolution remained alive in the imagination of at least some Indonesian authors and readers on the eve of World War II.

Just as the fictional narrative of *Patjar Merah* moved restlessly across Asia, Europe, and the Middle East—Penang, Bangkok, Hong Kong, Colombo, Calcutta; Amsterdam, Paris, Brussels, Moscow; Iran, Palestine—and referred to "Pan-Malay Congresses" in Manila, Calcutta, and Jodhpur, so did the actual trajectories of modern associational activity and revolutionary political action in the Indonesian archipelago unfold in no small measure through empowering transoceanic networks and amidst enabling international circumstances in the early–mid twentieth century. The early 1920s saw a flurry of international congresses sponsored by the Communist International (Comintern), with subsequent Comintern Congresses held in 1924, 1929, and 1935, and a World Islamic Congress assembled in Mecca in 1926 and in Jerusalem in 1931, thus providing prominent points of internationalist reference for the fictional Pan-Malay Congresses treated in *Patjar Merah*.

Furthermore, Eurasian *Indos*, immigrant Hadhrami Arabs, and *peranakan* Chinese played prominent roles in the early experiments with newspaper publishing and popular theater in the Indies at the turn of the twentieth century, and up through the interwar era *peranakan* Chinese authors in particular were also prolific writers of newspapers and novels, making a major contribution to the development of Malay (*Melayu*) as the lingua franca of modern public life and politics

---

4. See Matu Mona, *Pacar Merah Indonesia: Buku Pertama* (Yogyakarta: KITLV, 2001), and Noriaki Oshikawa, "*Patjar Merah* Indonesia and Tan Malaka: A Popular Novel and a Revolutionary Legend," in *Reading Indonesia: Translation of Contemporary Japanese Scholarship on Southeast Asia*, ed. Takashi Shiraishi (Ithaca, NY: Cornell University Southeast Asia Program, 1990), 9–39.

across the Indonesian archipelago.[5] Over the course of the first decades of the twentieth century, moreover, enterprising Europeans and *Indos*, Hadhrami Arabs, and both *totok* and *peranakan* Chinese engaged in unprecedented initiatives in the realm of associational activity, founding modern schools and organizations that challenged established hierarchies of "traditional" education, authority, and identity among these small minority communities defined by the Dutch colonial state as distinctly different from the indigenous population of the Indies.

Furthermore, these putatively foreign forces of cosmopolitan modernism combined with the destabilizing dynamics of marketization, proletarianization, and capital accumulation to produce contagious effects among the broader population of the Indies that could not be fully contained. Over the course of the seventeenth and eighteenth centuries, the VOC had extended its control over Java and other areas of the Indonesian archipelago through (increasingly unequal) alliances and exchanges with the aristocracies of the isles, most notably the Javanese *priyayi*, whose multilayered hierarchy of appanages stretched from exalted sultans to an extended set of *bupati* (regents) and down to a cluster of positions at the village level.[6] With the Dutch state's direct assumption of power on Java in the early nineteenth century and extension and intensification of control over the island in subsequent decades, the *priyayi* were incorporated into an evolving bureaucratic state (*beamtenstaat*) and restyled as "native administrators" (*inlandsch bestuur* or *pangreh praja*) under the Binnenlands Bestuur (Interior Administration Department).

As first the Cultuurstelsel and then private plantation agriculture drew Javanese peasants into production for export, the *priyayi*'s exactions of produce and labor services were progressively reduced even as their established intermediary roles and traditional authority over the native population were gradually subordinated to the logic of a capitalist market and a modern state. By the late nineteenth century, *hoofdenscholen* (chiefs' schools) had been set up to help train the *priyayi* for bureaucratic service, and three branches of the Opleiding School voor Inlandsche Ambtenaren (OSVIA, or Training School for Native Officials) were opened across Java in 1900. With Queen Wilhelmina's proclamation of the Ethical Policy for the Indies in 1901 and the consolidation of Dutch control across the full extent of the Indonesian archipelago, the first decades of the twentieth century saw dramatic expansion of the bureaucracy and of modern secular schools for the training of the *pangreh praja*. In short, these traditional Javanese

---

5. Claudine Salmon, *Le Moment "Sino-Malay" dans la Littérature Indonésienne* (Paris: Association d'Archipel, 1992).

6. Soemarsaid Moertono, *State and Statecraft in Old Java: A Study of the Later Mataram Period, 16th to 19th Centuries* (Ithaca, NY: Cornell Modern Indonesia Project, 1981).

aristocrats and their counterparts elsewhere in the Indies were transformed into a modern bureaucratic elite.[7]

As the commercialization of agriculture unfolded across Java, Sumatra, and the other islands of the Indonesian archipelago, the power and prerogatives of this aristocracy were increasingly complemented, complicated, and compromised by the rise of new social classes rooted in market society rather than the modern state. In contrast to the Philippines, where Chinese-mestizo merchants, moneylenders, and landowners combined capital accumulation with increasing control over local state office (especially under American colonial rule), the rise of traders and tycoons of *peranakan* and *totok* Chinese, Hadhrami Arab, and Javanese, Bugis, and Minangkabau ancestry in the Indies signified the emergence of an alternative basis for social power by the turn of the twentieth century.

In contrast to the British-controlled Federated Malay States, moreover, where the sultans were empowered in positions of authority over the institutions of Islamic education, law, and worship,[8] the aristocrats of the Indies were assiduously encouraged to devote their energies to the reproduction—and reinvention—of court cultures and traditions, especially on Java.[9] With no direct role in economic production or effective authority in religious life, the native aristocracies of the Indies were thus weakly positioned to defend their traditional authority in a rapidly evolving market economy and growing modern public sphere. Indeed, the diminishing force of traditional authority and hierarchy was evident by the turn of the century in the rise of a new generation of privileged, aristocratic youth (*kaum muda*) educated in modern schools—such as Tirto Adhi Soerjo, Marco Kartodikromo, Tan Malaka, and many others—who were attracted to the world of social and political activism rather than positions in the *pangreh praja*.

Against this backdrop, the first decades of the twentieth century saw the emergence and expansion not only of new modes of expression and structures of feeling but also new forms of sociality and solidarity, as seen in the rise of modern associational activity. These new organizations emerged first among the Chinese, Hadhrami Arab, and Eurasian (*Indo*) communities, but by the 1910s they had begun to attract significant numbers of natives into their orbit and to help inspire a new generation of Javanese, Minangkabau, and other activists to engage in unprecedented efforts to mobilize the broad population of the archipelago as a whole. In an era of unparalleled upheaval across the world, these activists drew

---

7. See Heather Sutherland, *The Making of a Bureaucratic Elite: The Colonial Transformation of the Javanese Priyayi* (Singapore: Heinemann, 1979).

8. William R. Roff, *The Origins of Malay Nationalism* (New Haven, CT: Yale University Press, 1967), 11–31, 67–74.

9. John Pemberton, *On the Subject of "Java"* (Ithaca, NY: Cornell University Press, 1994), 28–147.

on cosmopolitan discursive and mobilizational structures of revolutionary brotherhood and solidarity under the banners of republicanism, communism, and Islam, stretching from Cairo and Mecca to Makassar, Singapore and Sydney to Surabaya, Baku and Moscow to Bandung.

As with the Cuban conjuncture in which the Philippine Revolution unfolded in the late nineteenth century, it was only in the context of major international conflicts and conflagrations that early associational activity in the Indies in the first decade of the twentieth century evolved into mass mobilization and large-scale social movement during the 1910s and early 1920s, and into full-blown revolution in the mid-late 1940s. These conflicts included the Sino-Japanese and Russo-Japanese wars around the turn of the century, the overthrow of the Qing, Ottoman, and Romanov dynasties in the 1910s, and, crucially, World War I and World War II. Inspired and empowered by cosmopolitan currents of republicanism, communism, and Islam, and enabled by imperial decline, interimperialist competition, and international conflict across the globe, Indonesians across the archipelago eventually mobilized, with diverse hopes and dreams, in Revolusi.

Shimonoseki, Singapore, Semarang, and Surabaya: The Rise of the Sarekat Islam

The first major international conflict to help set in motion new forms of associational activity and mobilization in the Indies was the Sino-Japanese War of 1894–1895. In the long run, the military success of Meiji troops and the concessions of the Qing government in the 1895 Treaty of Shimonoseki—recognition of Korean independence, Japanese control over Taiwan and the eastern Liaodong Peninsula; the awarding of a huge indemnity and most-favored nation status—marked the beginnings of Japanese imperialism in East Asia, even as the Triple Intervention by Russia, France, and Germany to force the return of the eastern Liaodong Peninsula to the Qing presaged the Russo-Japanese War of 1904–1905 and subsequent conflicts with other imperial powers over control of the region.[10] Beginning with colonization of Taiwan and commercial penetration of Chinese markets from 1895, Japan moved to colonize the Korean Peninsula from 1905, and Manchuria from 1931, moving south into China over the course of the 1930s and occupying much of Southeast Asia in 1942–1945, including the Indonesian archipelago, thus setting the stage for the Revolusi of 1945–1949, as detailed below.

---

10. Sarah C. M. Paine, *The Sino-Japanese War of 1894–1895: Perceptions, Power, and Primacy* (Cambridge: Cambridge University Press, 2003).

In the short run, moreover, the humiliating experience of defeat at the hands of Meiji forces in the war helped to stimulate new initiatives to reform the Qing dynasty and, in due course, to undertake a republican revolution in China. The years immediately following the Sino-Japanese War saw the rise to unprecedented prominence in Beijing of reformist intellectuals such as Kang Youwei and his protégé Liang Qichao, who had both grown up in gentry literati families in the southern coastal province of Guangdong, and whose immersion in classical studies in preparation for civil service examinations was disturbed by their exposure to the urban cosmopolitan milieus of nearby Guangzhou (Canton) and Shanghai, treaty port cities where Western imperial power, market relations, and the modern urban public sphere were most fully developed, and where new forms of knowledge and sources of news were circulating amidst China's ongoing revolution in modern print capitalism.[11] In May 1895, a month after the Treaty of Shimonoseki was signed, Kang and Liang led more than one thousand civil service examination candidates in the submission of a petition to the emperor calling for cancellation of the treaty, reorganization and strengthening of the Qing army, and a broad range of administrative, educational, and social reforms. In the same year, Kang and Liang established the Self-Strengthening Society (Qiangxue Hui), which they used along with a handful of new journals to promote "New Text" Confucianism as well as proposals for constitutional monarchy and modernization along the lines of the Meiji Reformation. In 1898, Kang and Liang succeeded in enlisting support from Emperor Guangxu and in spurring the so-called Hundred Days' Reform, only to find themselves forced into exile in Japan after the conservative palace coup by the Empress Dowager Cixi and the harshly antireformist backlash later that year.[12]

By the turn of the twentieth century, intellectuals such as Kang Youwei and Liang Qichao and other activists were using Japan as a base for promoting the restoration of the emperor and reform of the Qing state on the basis of New Text Confucianism and constitutional monarchy. By 1905, there were as many as twenty thousand Chinese students in Japan on study tours of varying duration under the auspices of Kang and Liang's hosts, the Tō-A Dōbunkai (East Asia Common Culture Society), and alongside this channel of influence, Chinese merchants in Japan helped to fund the publication of journals such as *Xinmin Congbao*

---

11. Xiaobing Tang, *Global Space and the Nationalist Discourse of Modernity: The Historical Thinking of Liang Qichao* (Stanford, CA: Stanford University Press, 1996), 1–2; Joan Judge, *Print and Politics: "Shibao" and the Culture of Reform in Late Qing China* (Stanford, CA: Stanford University Press, 1996), 17–20; Christopher A. Reed, *Gutenberg in Shanghai: Chinese Print Capitalism, 1876–1937* (Honolulu: University of Hawai'i Press, 2004), 3–127.

12. Young-Tsu Wong, "Revisionism Reconsidered: Kang Youwei and the Reform Movement of 1898," *Journal of Asian Studies* 51, no. 3 (August 1992): 513–544; Benjamin A. Elman, *A Cultural History of Civil Examinations in Late Imperial China* (Berkeley: University of California Press, 2000), 585–594.

(New Citizen), filled with articles promoting reforms as well as translations and interpretations of diverse foreign writings, which circulated widely among the growing reading public in major Chinese cities and among Chinese communities across Asia and the Americas.[13] Kang and Liang's efforts also began to bear fruit in China itself with the publication from 1904 of reformist journals such as *Shibao* (Eastern Times) in the French concession—and later out of the Japanese consulate—in the treaty port of Shanghai. The onset of major educational reforms and the abolition of the civil service examination system in the same period produced tens of thousands of new schools and hundreds of thousands of students, many of whom were attracted to calls for reform—and in due course, for revolution,[14] with Japan's victory in the Russo-Japanese War of 1904–1905 and Emperor Guangxu's death in 1908 encouraging radicalization of means and ends.[15]

Indeed, the moderately progressive New Text Confucianism and constitutional reformism advocated by Kang Youwei and Liang Qichao was increasingly complemented and challenged by revolutionary republicanism, as seen in the formation in Japan of the Tongmeng Hui (Chinese Revolutionary Alliance) in 1905. This new movement drew into its ranks Chinese students who had become attracted to the diverse currents of republicanism, anarchism, and socialism during their stay in Japan,[16] as well as disparate elements in the small but growing modern educated segment of society in China and among Chinese communities across Asia and the Americas, as seen most prominently in its official president and ostensible leader, Sun Yat-Sen. Born in 1866, like Kang and Liang, in a rural town in coastal Guangdong Province but into a nongentry family, Sun emigrated at the age of thirteen to Hawai'i, where he boarded at an Anglican preparatory school for four years, graduated with high marks and fluent English, and returned to Guangdong, going on to medical school in Hong Kong in the 1880s. Trained as a doctor, baptized as a Christian, and increasingly critical of the Qing state, Sun tried to find common cause with reformist elements in coastal cities such as Canton, Shanghai, and Tianjin, but abandoned these efforts in the mid-1890s, shifting his energies to revolutionary agitation, conspiracy, fund-raising, and intrigue among Chinese communities in Hawai'i, Hong Kong, London, Penang, San Francisco, Singapore, Tokyo, and Vancouver. From 1905, the Revolutionary Alliance

---

13. Paula Harrell, *Sowing the Seeds of Change: Chinese Students, Japanese Teachers, 1895–1905* (Stanford, CA: Stanford University Press, 1992), 40–60.

14. Judge, *Print and Politics*, 32–53; Elman, *A Cultural History of Civil Examinations*, 594–618; Joseph W. Esherick, *Reform and Revolution in China: The 1911 Revolution in Hunan and Hubei* (Berkeley: University of California Press, 1976).

15. Harold Z. Schiffrin, "The Impact of the War on China," in *The Impact of the Russo-Japanese War*, ed. Rotem Kowner (London: Routledge, 2007), 169–182.

16. Martin Bernal, *Chinese Socialism to 1907* (Ithaca, NY: Cornell University Press, 1976).

was headquartered in Tokyo, with Sun and his fellow republican revolutionaries operating across the Pacific up until the overthrow of the Qing dynasty in the Chinese Revolution of 1911.[17]

Over the course of the first decade of the twentieth century, these diverse currents of reformism and revolutionary republicanism drew into their orbit Cantonese-, Hakka-, Hokkien-, and Teochiu-speaking communities across Asia and the Americas, strengthening communications, modern cosmopolitan sensibilities, and long-distance Chinese nationalism across this vast diaspora. Already in the 1890s reformist intellectuals such as Kang Youwei and Liang Qichao had begun to develop a global perspective on the Qing realms, comparing the Middle Kingdom to the Ottoman Empire and the British Raj in India, and pondering the implications of such diverse developments as the Philippine Revolution and the Boer War at the turn of the twentieth century. Indeed, alongside Kang Youwei's extensive revisionist exegesis of the writings of Confucius, he submitted books on Poland and Turkey to Emperor Guangxu during the 1898 reform period. After 1898, moreover, the vantage point of exile in Tokyo and trips to Penang, Singapore, and as far afield as Hawai'i further expanded the global field of vision within which they situated their hopes and dreams for China, even as the culturally diverse and linguistically divided communities of the diaspora came into focus as part of "the people" of the extended *Chinese* nation.[18] With the rise of Sun Yat-Sen and the Tongmeng Hui, moreover, reformists, revolutionary republicans, and representatives and defenders of the Qing monarchy assiduously cultivated the Chinese diaspora and competed for its recognition and support.[19]

While the effective impact and actual significance of the Chinese diaspora's contribution to the 1911 Revolution may have been limited, the reformist and revolutionary republican organizing efforts of the 1900s had important consequences for the communities of the Chinese diaspora, especially in the Netherlands East Indies. Over the course of the 1890s, reformism and neo-Confucian revivalism were attracting interest in the nearby Straits Settlements, with the New Text interpretation of Confucius in rationalized, reformist terms gaining currency among Chinese merchants and professionals, and new associational activities, Chinese- and Malay-language newspapers and periodicals, and Anglo-Chinese

---

17. Harold Z. Schiffrin, *Sun Yat-sen and the Origins of the Chinese Revolution* (Berkeley: University of California Press, 1968); Marius B. Jansen, *The Japanese and Sun Yat-sen* (Stanford, CA: Stanford University Press, 1970); Marie-Claire Bergère, *Sun Yat-sen* (Stanford, CA: Stanford University Press, 1998), 1–197.

18. On these shifts, see Rebecca E. Karl, *Staging the World: Chinese Nationalism at the Turn of the Twentieth Century* (Durham, NC: Duke University Press, 2002).

19. On Chinese communities in the United States, Canada, and Mexico, see L. Eve Armentrout Ma, *Revolutionaries, Monarchists, and Chinatowns: Chinese Politics in the Americas and the 1911 Revolution* (Honolulu: University of Hawai'i Press, 1990).

schools springing up in Singapore by the turn of the century, with Kang Youwei himself spending six months in Singapore and four months in Penang in 1900.[20]

The same year saw visiting Javanese *peranakan* Chinese intellectuals return from Singapore to publish translations of Confucian texts in Malay, found the Tiong Hoa Hwee Koan (THHK, or Chinese Association) in Batavia, and, from 1901, establish a set of THHK schools in major towns and cities across Java. These schools drew on teachers and teaching methods (e.g., Western-style textbooks) from Chinese schools in Japan, teaching Mandarin Chinese and New Text Confucianism, as well as mathematics, geography, and revealingly, English, a language promising opportunities for further study in Singapore and advantages in the international business world.[21] By 1906, moreover, a branch of the Tongmeng Hui had been founded in Singapore, with further branches established in Penang and Batavia within a year,[22] with revolutionary republicanism spreading through newspapers, other periodicals, and reading clubs in various cities on Java and elsewhere in the Indies in the years leading up to the 1911 Revolution in China.[23]

The development of modern educational institutions, associational activity, and political organizations among the Chinese population of the Indies began to attract recognition and response from various quarters. Kang Youwei himself visited the Indies and in 1903, and in subsequent years representatives of the Qing government also came to inspect the THHK schools on Java, as Beijing rapidly expanded its consular presence across Southeast Asia and, in 1909, proclaimed the extension of its sovereignty to overseas Chinese (*hua qiao*) under the principle of *jus sanguinis*. The Dutch colonial government likewise took notice. By 1899, a few years after the signing of the Treaty of Shimonoseki, the Dutch Parliament had voted to change the legal status of Japanese residents of the Indies from "foreign orientals" (*vreemde oosterlingen*) to that of Europeans, a recognition of Japan's Great Power status affirmed in the proclamation of the Anglo-Japanese Alliance in 1902, "Britain's only formal alliance between the settlement of the Napoleonic Wars in 1915 and the outbreak of World War I in 1914."[24]

---

20. Yen Ching-Hwang, "The Confucian Revival Movement in Singapore and Malaya, 1899–1911," *Journal of Southeast Asian Studies* 7, no. 1 (March 1976): 33–57; Mark Ravinder Frost, "*Emporium in Imperio*: Nanyang Networks and the Straits Chinese in Singapore, 1819–1914," *Journal of Southeast Asian Studies* 36, no. 1 (February 2005): 54–60.

21. Lea E. Williams, *Overseas Chinese Nationalism: The Genesis of the Pan-Chinese Movement in Indonesia, 1900–1916* (Glencoe, IL: Free Press, 1960); Kwee Tek Hoay, *The Origins of the Modern Chinese Movement in Indonesia* (Ithaca, NY: Cornell University Modern Indonesia Project Translation Series, 1969).

22. Yen Ching Hwang, *The Overseas Chinese and the 1911 Revolution with Special Reference to Singapore and Malaya* (Kuala Lumpur: Oxford University Press, 1976).

23. Leo Suryadinata, "The 1911 Revolution and the Chinese in Java: A Preliminary Study," in *The 1911 Revolution: The Chinese in British and Dutch Southeast Asia*, ed. Lee Lai To (Singapore: Heinemann Asia, 1987), 108–124.

24. Paine, *The Sino-Japanese War of 1894–1895*, 7–8.

As in China, the rise of reformist and later revolutionary republican activism among the Chinese communities of the Indies was in considerably stimulated by desires for similar reward and recognition, as the Dutch government understood. Mindful of the ongoing violence visited upon Westerners in China (with the Empress Dowager's blessings) in 1899–1901 during the Boxer Rebellion,[25] the Dutch government was quick to grant permission for the establishment of the THHK and its schools. Over the course of the next decade, moreover, as activity and agitation for change in China mounted among the Indies Chinese, the Dutch government responded by founding Dutch Chinese schools (*Hollandsche Chineesche Scholen*), relaxing restrictions on Chinese movement and commercial activity in the Indies, offering formal (if highly restricted) opportunities for assumption of European legal status, and, in 1910, countering Qing claims on the basis of jus sanguinis by recognizing all Indies-born Chinese as Dutch subjects.[26]

But the rise of reformist and revolutionary republican activism among the Chinese communities of the Indies also generated responses from very different quarters. As noted above, the *peranakan* Chinese communities of the late nineteenth century had creolized Hadhrami Arab counterparts in many cities and towns across the Indies,[27] and by the turn of the twentieth century a new generation of merchants, moneylenders, and modernist Islamic intellectuals were beginning to challenge the established hierarchies of *sayyid* and *shaykh* along lines parallel to those of the THHK. With the opening of the Suez Canal in 1869, Aden had begun to evolve into a major trading entrepôt, with the British expanding their control from their crown settlement into the Hadhrami hinterlands during the 1870s and establishing a protectorate over the realms of the Qu'aytī sultan even as Ottoman forces extended Istanbul's claims over other areas and established links with other rulers of the southern Arabian Peninsula. These developments deepened imperialist penetration of the Hadhramaut, even as the accelerating growth of maritime traffic and trade drew Hadhrami merchants scattered across the Indian Ocean into the orbit of the Islamic reformist currents emanating out of Cairo and Istanbul in the final decades of the nineteenth century.[28]

Against this backdrop, the turn of the twentieth century saw the dawning of the Hadhrami *nahḍa* (awakening or renaissance) in the Indies, as seen in the founding of the Jam'iyyat al-Khayr (Beneficent Society) in 1901, virtually

---

25. Joseph W. Esherick, *The Origins of the Boxer Uprising* (Berkeley: University of California Press, 1987); Paul A. Cohen, *History in Three Keys: The Boxers as Event, Experience, and Myth* (New York: Columbia University Press, 1997).

26. Leo Suryadinata, *Peranakan Chinese Politics in Java* (Singapore: Singapore University Press, 1981), 10–11, 25–28.

27. For a detailed contemporary account, see L. W. C. Van Den Berg, *Le Hadhramout et les Colonies Arabes dans L'Archipel Indien* (Batavia: Imprimerie du Gouvernement, 1886).

28. On these developments, see Ulrike Freitag, *Indian Ocean Migrants and State Formation in Hahdramaut: Reforming the Homeland* (Leiden: Brill, 2003), 38–225.

simultaneously with the formation of the THHK. As with their Chinese counterparts, the emerging Hadhrami reformists of the Indies circulated within transoceanic diasporic networks, with Singapore (and, to a lesser extent, Penang) serving as a regional hub for capital and communications. As with the THHK, moreover, the Jam'iyyat al-Khayr devoted much of its energies to the promotion of modern education, with new schools founded in Batavia, Buitenzorg (Bogor), Palembang, Pekalongan, Solo, and Surabaya during the first decade of the twentieth century.

> The students were divided into graded classes, sat at desks, and used modern textbooks with illustrations (taboo in traditional Islamic schools). They studied arithmetic, geography, Islamic history, and English language, along with Arabic and more traditional Islamic subjects. The underlying philosophy of the schools emphasized the importance of understanding, Arabic language being viewed as the means by which students would be able to read and comprehend the Scriptures for themselves. Apart from formal classes, informal discussions or *majlis* were conducted in which problems of the reform of Islam were discussed, based on articles from the Middle Eastern press including the Egyptian publication *Al-Manār*.[29]

In contrast to the Chinese reformists and revolutionary republicans of the Indies, however, the activists of the Hadhrami *nahḍa* in the Indies of the early twentieth century shared a common faith with the vast majority of the population of the archipelago, and they thus directly assisted in the spread of Islamic reformism among the Muslims of the isles. Indeed, the last decades of the nineteenth century had seen the increasing immersion of Muslims from across the Indies within the orbit of Islamic reformism emanating from Cairo, Istanbul, and Mecca, and by the turn of the century there was growing interest in modern Islamic education in the Indies, especially among the small-scale Muslim merchants of Java and Sumatra. From early on, the Jam'iyyat al-Khayr's schools accepted native pupils into their classrooms, and by the 1910s, modernist Islamic education began to spread among Minangkabau pupils in the Thawalib schools of West Sumatra, and with the founding of Muhammadiyah in Yogyakarta in 1912, in a new network of modernist schools on Java, a trend that would accelerate in subsequent decades.

By the early 1910s, moreover, these experiments in modernist education had begun to expand into new realms of social activism and political action, in tandem with evolving trends across the Muslim world. Over the course of the nine-

---

29. Natalie Mobini-Kesheh, *The Hadrami Awakening, Community and Identity in the Netherlands East Indies, 1900–1942* (Ithaca, NY: Cornell University Southeast Asia Program, 1999), 37.

teenth century, a diverse range of revivalist movements and Sufi *ṭuruq* had provided discursive and mobilizing structures that challenged local aristocracies and countered Dutch efforts to extend their authority across the Indies, from the Wahhabi-inspired Padri War in West Sumatra from the 1810s through the 1840s, to the Budiah sect in Pekalongan in the 1850s, and the Naqshbandiyya ṭarīqa in the 1888 rebellion in Banten.[30] Here there were self-evident parallels with resistance by the Qadiriyah against the French in Algeria in the 1830s and 1840s, Imam Shamil and the Naqshbandiyya-Muridiyya's struggle against Russian imperial rule in the Caucasus from the 1830s through the 1850s, the various *jihād* of West Africa, and mobilization in the name of the Mahdi against the British in Sudan from the 1880s until the turn of the century.[31] The transoceanic scholarly networks and Sufi *turuq* stretching from these remote corners of the Muslim world to Mecca helped to provide discursive and mobilizing structures for disparate movements of Islamic revivalism and resistance to the encroachments of European empire.

By the 1870s, moreover, the Dutch Forward Movement coincided with unprecedented developments in the Ottoman Empire to help promote episodic flirtation with so-called Pan-Islamist mobilization in the Indies, most notably in the northern Sumatran region of Aceh, the westernmost antipode of the archipelago. Beginning in the late eighteenth century, Muslim rulers across Asia—Sultan Tipu of Mysore in the 1780s and 1790s, the Khan of Bukhara in the late 1810s, Yakub Bey in East Turkestan (today's Xinjiang) in the 1820s—had written to the Ottoman sultan in his capacity as caliph of the Muslim world to request assistance in the face of British, Romanov, and Qing imperial encroachments, but the Sublime Porte had consistently refrained from providing assistance.[32] In the aftermath of the Crimean War, however, Istanbul—with active British encouragement—became somewhat more responsive, especially in the Caucasus and Central Asia in an era of Russian expansion into Muslim lands. With the ascension of Sultan Abdulhamid II to the Ottoman throne in 1876, moreover, Ottoman projection of caliphal claims of authority across the Muslim world emerged as both an important aspect of domestic legitimation and a useful bargaining chip vis-à-vis the

---

30. Christine Dobbin, *Islamic Revivalism in a Changing Peasant Economy: Central Sumatra, 1784–1847* (London: Curzon Press, 1983); Jeffrey Hadler, *Muslims and Matriarchs: Cultural Resilience in Indonesia through Jihad and Colonialism* (Ithaca, NY: Cornell University Press, 2008), 17–33; Sartono Kartodirdjo, *Protest Movements in Rural Java: A Study of Agrarian Unrest in the Nineteenth and Twentieth Centuries* (Singapore: Oxford University Press, 1973), 106–141; and Sartono Kartodirdjo, *The Peasants' Revolt of Banten in 1888* (The Hague: Martinus Nijhoff, 1966).

31. For a broad overview, see Marc Gaborieau and Nicole Grandin, "Le Renouveau Confrérique (Fin XVIII Siècle—XIX Siècle)," in *Les Voies D'Allah: Les Ordres Mystiques Dans L'Islam des Origins à Aujourd'hui*, ed. Alexandre Popovic and Gilles Veinstein (Paris: Fayard, 1996), 68–83; John Obert Voll, *Islam: Continuity and Change in the Modern World* (Syracuse, NY: Syracuse University Press, 1994), 84–151.

32. Kemal Karpat, *The Politicization of Islam: Reconstructing Identity, State, Faith, and Community in the Late Ottoman State* (Oxford: Oxford University Press, 2001), 49–67.

major imperial powers, especially Britain, in the face of growing internal and external challenges to Ottoman rule.[33] From the late 1870s, Abdulhamid began to develop an international profile as the spiritual-cum-political leader of the Muslim world, devoting resources to the extension of Islamic education and Islamic law across the Ottoman Empire, demonstrating his largesse as protector of the Holy Cities (*haramayn*) of Mecca and Medina and sponsor of the Hajj,[34] and developing extensive linkages with the Muslim public in British colonial India over the course of his reign.[35] The late nineteenth century likewise saw the extension of linkages between the Ottoman Empire and Muslims of Southeast Asia, with Istanbul establishing consulates in Singapore and Batavia during this period.

Ottoman interest in Southeast Asia, moreover, soon embroiled the Sublime Porte in the protracted Aceh War (1873–1903) in northern Sumatra. In 1850, the sultan of Aceh had dispatched an envoy to Istanbul to request Ottoman protection, and a few years later he demonstrated his loyalty by sending ten thousand Spanish dollars in support of the Ottoman war effort in the Crimea. These tentative diplomatic initiatives soon expanded into more elaborate intrigues, as seen in the machinations of ʿAbd al-Rahman bin Muhammad al-Zahir, a Hadhrami *ʿalim* who had grown up in India, but then settled in Aceh in the 1860s and rose to a position of great influence within the sultan's court. In 1873, as Dutch forces were invading Aceh, al-Zahir travelled to Istanbul as the envoy of the sultan, where he was warmly received by the Ottoman ruler and lionized in the press.[36] Returning via the Hijaz, Singapore, and Penang, al-Zahir attracted considerable official and public attention, and on his arrival in Aceh, he was, by one account, "lionized and received as a representative of the grand Ottoman Caliph, who to the Acehnese was the leader of the only Muslim empire in the modern world."[37] Although al-Zahir returned from Istanbul empty-handed, the attention devoted to his travels—along with apocryphal reports of impending Ottoman intervention—appeared in newspapers and other periodicals in Penang and Singapore, generating considerable interest in the Aceh War.

> The Muslim community of the two British settlements was solidly and actively behind the Atjehnese. Reports on the war were given regularly

---

33. Selim Deringil, "Legitimacy Structures in the Ottoman State: The Reign of Sultan Abdulhamid II (1876–1909)," *International Journal of Middle East Studies* 23, no. 3 (August 1991): 345–359.

34. William Ochsenwald, *The Hijaz Railroad* (Charlottesville: University Press of Virginia, 1980).

35. Azmi Özcan, *Pan-Islamism: Indian Muslims, the Ottomans and Britain, 1877–1924* (Leiden: Brill, 1997).

36. Jan Schmidt, "Pan-Islamism between the Porte, the Hague, and Buitenzorg," in *Through the Legation Window, 1876–1926: Four Essays in Dutch, Dutch-Indian, and Ottoman History*, ed. Jan Schmidt (Istanbul: Nederlands Historisch-Archaeologisch Instituut Te Istanbul, 1992), 58–62.

37. Engseng Ho, "Empire through Diasporic Eyes: A View from the Other Boat," *Comparative Studies in Society and History* 46, no. 2 (April 2004): 220.

after the Friday prayer in many mosques, and the leading partisans would often meet afterwards to discuss what could be done to help. Some Singapore Arabs launched an appeal among their compatriots in the Straits Settlements and Java, which was said to have raised 100,000 Spanish dollars for the Atjehnese cause by the end of 1874. In Penang there was an important colony of Atjehnese, who encouraged their countrymen by relaying optimistic reports of probable overseas support.[38]

While such avowed enthusiasm for the Acehnese cause had faded by 1875, the ascension of Abdulhamid II to the throne the following year helped to nurture sporadic plots and sensationalist rumors of Pan-Islamist support in subsequent years. The stopover of an Ottoman warship in Singapore en route to Japan in 1890 generated a flurry of excitement and intrigue on behalf of the Acehnese cause. Ottoman consuls in Batavia and Singapore also aroused considerable Dutch anxiety and ire at the turn of the century by reportedly encouraging Hadhramis in the Indies to claim European status, as Japanese residents of the isles were granted in 1899.[39]

Thus, by the turn of the twentieth century, if not the reality then "the idea of the Ottomans as the hope of Muslims" had begun to expand the meaning of Islam for Indies Muslims beyond new forms of theological objectification by reformist intellectuals and educators and into its functionalization for social activism and political action on an international stage.[40] Newspapers and periodicals in Cairo and Istanbul, Singapore and Penang, Batavia and Surabaya in the early 1900s began to carry stories bewailing the problematic status of Hadhrami Arab residents of the Indies and lamenting Dutch interference with efforts to raise funds in support of the Ottoman project to build a railway connecting Damascus to the Hijaz.[41] As the Ottoman Empire faced an Italian invasion of Libya in 1911 and Russian- and Greek-backed uprisings by Orthodox Christian forces in Bulgaria, Montenegro, and Serbia in 1912–1913, a wave of sympathy for their Muslim coreligionists was reported in the Indies. "Portraits of the Sultan and his son decorated walls of houses. Donations were readily forthcoming," with a branch of

38. Anthony Reid, "Nineteenth-Century Pan-Islam in Indonesia and Malaysia," *Journal of Asian Studies* 26, no. 3 (February 1967): 275–276.

39. Reid, "Nineteenth-Century Pan-Islam in Indonesia and Malaysia," 278–282; Kees Van Dijk, "Colonial Fears, 1890–1918: Pan-Islamism and the Germano-Indian Plot," in *Transcending Borders: Arabs, Politics, Trade, and Islam in Southeast Asia*, ed. Huub de Jonge and Nico Kaptein (Leiden: KITLV Press, 2002), 53–72.

40. Anthony Reid, "The Ottomans in Southeast Asia" (Asia Research Institute Working Paper Series, Singapore, 2005), 15.

41. Michael Laffan, "'Another Andalusia': Images of Colonial Southeast Asia in Arabic Newspapers," *Journal of Asian Studies* 66, no. 3 (August 2007): 689–722; Sumit Kumar Mandal, "A History of Arabs in Java under Dutch Rule, 1800–1924 (PhD diss., Columbia University, 1984), 137–138.

Al-Hilal Al-Ahmar (the Red Crescent) founded in Batavia in 1912.[42] Thus, even before World War I and the German-backed Ottoman proclamation of *jihād*, powerful social and political overtones had begun to inflect Islam with new significance among the Muslims of the Indies.

It was against this backdrop that the year 1912 witnessed the onset of a dramatic surge in associational activity and political activism in the name of Islam in the Indonesian archipelago. In the Central Javanese city of Yogyakarta, Islamic scholars and Muslim merchants combined to establish an organization called Muhammadiyah, which was devoted to the promotion of modernist education, as seen in the emergence and expansion of new schools (madrasah) under its auspices across Java and Sumatra in subsequent years. Meanwhile, the same year saw the founding of an association called the Sarekat Dagang Islamiyah (Islamic Trade Association) by a group of Hadhrami Arab and Javanese batik merchants in the nearby city of Solo. A revolution had overthrown the Qing dynasty and established a republic in China in October 1911, and in February 1912 celebrations of Chinese New Year in Surabaya had seen rowdy disturbances and defiance of a Dutch ban on the display of republican flags, followed by shop closures by Chinese merchants for several days. In the context of ongoing Chinese commercial expansion with the easing of Dutch restrictions during the preceding decade, these well-publicized events, along with the growing numbers of Chinese cutting their Qing-style queues and adopting Western-style clothing, "were seen by Javanese as a sign not just of Chinese power but also that the Chinese were outside and above the hierarchical Javanese social order."[43]

Such was the immediate setting for the formation of the Sarekat Islam in nearby Solo in 1912. Over the course of the year, a group of Javanese Muslim batik merchants in Solo decided to opt out of a local mutual aid association under Chinese control and to form their own organization, first identified as Rekso Roemekso, a Javanese term for a guard group. After a series of skirmishes with their Chinese rivals and subsequent Dutch police inquiries, the organization was officially registered as the Solo branch of the Sarekat Dagang Islamiyah, or Islamic Trade Association, which a group of Javanese and Arab traders had founded in Buitenzorg (Bogor) in 1909. This original Sarekat Dagang Islamiyah had counted among its founding fathers the prominent journalist Tirto Adhi Soerjo as well as leading Hadhrami worthies, including some educated in Istanbul and active in the local Jam'iyyat al-Khayr, but the association had soon fallen apart in the face of internal fractiousness and official disfavor (as well as insinuations of "Pan-Islamic"

---

42. Kees Van Dijk, *The Netherlands Indies and the Great War, 1914–1918* (Leiden: KITLV Press, 2007), 295–296.

43. Takashi Shiraishi, *An Age in Motion: Popular Radicalism in Java, 1912–1926* (Ithaca, NY: Cornell University Press, 1990), 46.

affiliations), and, even when officially reconstituted as a native-only organization in 1910, failed to develop.[44] In 1912, with Tirto Adhi Soerjo's assistance, the Solo batik merchants of the Rekso Roemekso claimed affiliation with this largely lapsed body on the other side of Java and drew up official statutes committing the Sarekat Islam (SI) to "progress," promotion of commerce, and provision of modern schools. Such grandiose claims notwithstanding, the SI devoted its initial energies to the protection and promotion of its members' commercial interests, as seen in the organization of a series of boycotts against local Chinese firms in 1912 and 1913.

Yet as the SI began to recruit more and more members into its ranks in protection of the batik traders' businesses and in support of the anti-Chinese boycotts, the organization began to evolve into a more broadly based social movement. Thousands of Solo residents joined the SI over the course of 1912 and 1913, and soon the organization was attracting peasants in rural villages and workers on sugar plantations in the hinterlands of Solo, even as the formation of branches in towns and cities across Java created new nuclei for subsequent mobilizing efforts. From mutual aid, security, and boycott activities, moreover, the SI soon began organizing large-scale public rallies, with SI-linked newspapers providing publicity and drawing in an ever broader audience. By early 1913, when the first SI congress was held in Solo, the organization claimed forty-eight branches with a total membership of more than two hundred thousand.[45]

The SI soon spread across Java. Branches were established, typically under the leadership of local *priyayi*, *orang particulier* (educated white-collar private-sector workers), Javanese and Hadhrami merchants, and, in some cases, religious scholars (*kyai*), as seen in Yogyakarta where K. H. Dahlan, the founder of Muhammadiyah, served as SI chairman. Hadhrami and Javanese Muslim merchants backed SI newspapers such as the *Oetoesan Hindia* in Surabaya and similar publications elsewhere to promote the SI, with journalists assuming prominent roles in the movement leadership, most famously Raden Mas Oemar Said Tjokroaminoto, *Oetoesan Hindia* editor in chief and chairman of the Surabaya SI branch. An OSVIA graduate of mixed *priyayi* and *kyai* lineage, Tjokroaminoto enjoyed close ties with leading Dutch officials whose interventions helped to provide protection to local branches and a measure of control over the organization as it expanded across Java.[46]

Under such leadership, the early years of the SI saw reformist aims of promoting Muslim commerce and modern education stressed over more radical goals in SI publications and official proclamations.[47] That said, in towns and villages

---

44. Pramoedya, *Sang Pemula*, 150–163; Mobini-Kesheh, *The Hadrami Awakening*, 42–44.

45. Shiraishi, *An Age in Motion*, 46–50.

46. For accounts and accolades by a diverse range of acquaintances and observers, see Amelz, ed., *H.O.S. Tjokroaminoto: Hidup dan Perdjuangannja* (Djakarta: Bulan Bintang, 1952).

47. Shiraishi, *An Age in Motion*, 48–62.

across Java, SI branches were often involved—or the organization was invoked—in local land and labor disputes and anti-Chinese disturbances of a more rowdy if not radical nature.[48] SI rallies, moreover, drew thousands of Javanese peasants, workers, and other ordinary people (*wong cilik*) into the liminal lived experience of mass mobilization and modern egalitarian brotherhood outside the entrenched structures of aristocratic hierarchy, Chinese capital, and Dutch colonial authority:

> The tone of their speech was militant. Various complaints were openly voiced to the local authorities. Dutch and native administrative officials were sometimes attacked. Native solidarity was appealed to in the name of Islam. And people were told that all the SI members were brothers irrespective of age, rank, and status.[49]

By the time of the second Sarekat Islam congress in mid-1914, on the eve of World War I, the movement claimed more than eighty branches across Java and nearly half a million active members, a movement of impressive proportions. Nothing along these lines was evident anywhere else in Southeast Asia at the time.

War, Ottoman *Jihād*, and Bolshevik Revolution: Radicalization and Retrenchment

With the onset of World War I, moreover, the context for the SI's mobilization was quickly transformed, most notably by the Ottoman proclamation of *jihād* in November 1914. During the preceding century, the accumulated experience of British, French, and Russian intervention and encroachment in North Africa, the Levant, and the Arabian Peninsula, independence struggles by Orthodox Christians in the Balkans, and influx of Muslim refugees from conflicts in the Crimea and the Caucasus had increasingly inflected Ottoman foreign relations with the Great Powers with antagonistic interreligious overtones.[50] During the first decade of the twentieth century, moreover, Germany cultivated close ties with Istanbul, providing training to the Ottoman military and financial backing for an ambitious scheme to build a railway stretching from Berlin to Baghdad.[51]

---

48. See Kartodirdjo, *Protest Movements in Rural Java*, 142–185, and Sartono Kartodirdjo, ed., *Sarekat Islam Lokal* (Jakarta: Arsip Nasional Republik Indonesia, 1975).

49. Shiraishi, *An Age in Motion*, 66.

50. Karpat, *The Politicization of Islam*, 117–307; Mustafa Aksakal, *The Ottoman Road to War in 1914: The Ottoman Empire and the First World War* (Cambridge: Cambridge University Press, 2011).

51. Sean McMeekin, *The Berlin-Baghdad Express: The Ottoman Empire and Germany's Bid for World Power, 1898–1918* (London: Allen Lane, 2010), 7–82.

Against this backdrop, the early months of World War I saw Istanbul eventually opting to side with Germany and Austria, with a series of rulings (*fatāwā*) by leading *'ulama* preceding the mid-November 1914 proclamation by the Sultan-Caliph Abdulhamid II that struggle (*jihād*) against Britain, France, and Russia was an obligation for Muslims across the world.[52] The actual text encompassed all Europeans except Austrians, Hungarians, and Germans, thus leaving open the possibility that governments—and citizens—of neutral European countries such as the Netherlands were legitimate targets. Against this backdrop, Dutch officials began contemplating a ban on the Hajj for Indies Muslims to avoid the contagion of *jihād*, a risky option obviated by wartime disruptions to maritime traffic.[53]

This proclamation of global *jihād* by the Ottoman sultan-caliph combined with intrigues by German intelligence and agitation by Indian revolutionaries to heighten the sense of danger associated with mobilization in the name of Islam in the Netherlands East Indies. Alongside assiduous encouragement of Ottoman assertiveness in the name of Islam, the German government had begun to develop plans before the war to encourage mobilization by Muslim subjects of the British, French, and Russian Empires to supplement German and Austrian military might.[54] Even as German intelligence agents and Ottoman military officers worked to recruit members of the Sanusiyya ṭarīqa in the Libyan desert for an attack on the British in Egypt,[55] more elaborate schemes were developed to encourage uprisings against the British in India and further east. Contact was established with activists of the embryonic Ghadar movement, which in 1913 had founded the Pacific Coast Hindi Association and started publishing the Urdu-language newspaper *Ghadar* (Mutiny) in the San Francisco Bay area, with predominantly Punjabi Sikh immigrant farmers and workers from San Francisco to Vancouver in the Pacific Northwest as their initial audience and constituency for political outreach. In August 1914, upon the outbreak of World War I *Ghadar* broadened its field of activism, declaring in its headlines:

> WANTED: Fearless, courageous soldiers for spreading ghadar in India. Salary: death. Reward: martyrdom. Pension: freedom. Place: the field of India.[56]

52. Mustafa Aksakal, "'Holy War Made in Germany'? Ottoman Origins of the 1914 Jihad," *War in History* 18, no. 2 (April 2011): 184–199.

53. Van Dijk, *The Netherlands Indies and the Great War*, 297–299.

54. C. Snouck Hurgronje, *The Holy War "Made in Germany"* (New York: Putnam, 1915); Fritz Fischer, *Germany's Aims in the First World War* (New York: W.W. Norton & Company, 1967), 120–136.

55. Russell McGuirk, *The Sanusi's Little War: The Amazing Story of a Forgotten Conflict in the Western Desert, 1915–1917* (London: Arabian, 2007).

56. Maia Ramnath, "Two Revolutions: The Ghadar Movement and India's Radical Diaspora, 1913–1918," *Radical History Review* 92 (Spring 2005): 13. For background, see Maia Ramnath, *Haj to Utopia: How the Ghadar Movement Charted Global Radicalism and Attempted to Overthrow the British Empire* (Berkeley: University of California Press, 2011).

With German assistance and funding, elaborate, and ultimately unsuccessful, schemes were launched to smuggle arms via Batavia to coconspirators in India to help launch a large-scale rebellion.[57] Meanwhile, Ghadar activists fanned out across Asia to engage in recruitment efforts among the large numbers of Punjabi Sikh and Muslim troops garrisoned in the various port cities of the British Empire. Agitation and propaganda spread in British army barracks in Shanghai, Hong Kong, Penang, and Rangoon. In early 1915, these efforts bore fruit in a three-day mutiny in Singapore, in which eight British officers were killed.[58]

These events generated considerable interest, excitement, and alarm in the neighboring Netherlands East Indies. As a flood of anti-British pamphlets in Arabic and Malay and a series of Ghadar arms-smuggling plots came to the attention of the Dutch authorities in the Indies, rumors of German conspiracies "involving Arabs, Chinese, and members of the *Sarekat Islam* . . . led to all kind of wild speculations" about plots to overthrow Dutch rule and establish an Islamic state under Ottoman protection.[59] Against this backdrop, the Dutch government enlisted the SI leadership's support for its campaign for a native militia to assist in the defense of the Indies, while establishing an advisory Colonial Council (Volksraad) that would include elected and appointed natives among its members.[60] In short, SI mobilization from within and Ottoman, German, and Indian revolutionary wartime interventions from without combined to inspire moves to coopt and domesticate the diverse popular energies unleashed in Indies society by the mid-1910s.

Meanwhile, however, the economic disruptions and deprivations of World War I helped to stimulate new forms of popular mobilization in the Indies with cosmopolitan connections very different from those linking SI via Singapore to India, Mecca, Cairo, and Istanbul. With the war drastically reducing trade and traffic between the Indies and Europe, export revenues fell, wages stagnated, and import prices rose dramatically, even as the supply of Dutch labor to reinforce and replenish the ranks of plantation clerks and railway workers was likewise interrupted. These wartime conditions helped to enable and impel rapid growth of a labor union movement and dramatic increase of strike activity in the latter half

---

57. Thomas G. Fraser, "Germany and Indian Revolution, 1914–18," *Journal of Contemporary History* 12, no. 2 (April 1977): 255–272. For more on Ghadar-German cooperation and conspiracies, see Tilak Raj Sareen, *Indian Revolutionary Movement Abroad, 1905–1921* (New Delhi: Sterling, 1979), 116–192.

58. Sareen, *Indian Revolutionary Movement Abroad*, 105–111; Kees van Dijk, "Religion and the Undermining of British Rule in South and Southeast Asia during the Great War," in *Islamic Connections: Muslim Societies in South and Southeast Asia*, ed. R. Michael Feener and Terenjit Sevea (Singapore: Institute of Southeast Asian Studies, 2009), 109–133.

59. Van Dijk, *The Netherlands Indies and the Great War*, 325–346; Gerke Teitler, *The Dutch Colonial Army in Transition: The Militia Debate, 1900–1921* (Rotterdam: Erasmus University Rotterdam Comparative Asian Studies Programme, 1980).

60. Van Dijk, *The Netherlands and the Great War*, 255–286.

of the 1910s and into the early 1920s, and to assist in the spread of transoceanic revolutionary socialist and communist currents in the Indies during the same period.[61]

Initial labor-organizing efforts in the Indies first developed among the extensive Eurasian (*Indo*) working class and under the leadership of Eurasian and European activists, most notably E. F. E. Douwes Dekker and Hendricus "Henk" Sneevliet, who, like their *inlandsch* (native) counterparts and sometime collaborators, combined journalism and political activism with considerable flair and success. Born into a family of mixed Dutch, French, German, and Javanese ancestry in the East Javanese sugar mill town of Pasuruan in the late 1870s, Dekker remained in the Indies for his education and, while enjoying European legal status, experienced the social discrimination associated with his mixed parentage. The grandnephew of the famous author "Multatuli" (Eduard Douwes Dekker), whose depiction of the hardships of plantation life on Java in the 1860 novel *Max Havelaar* had gained international acclaim, the young Dekker briefly worked in various menial posts on coffee and sugar plantations in East Java, where he was exposed to working conditions—and Javanese workers—himself. In 1900, however, he and his two brothers joined the small flow of Dutch and *Indo* volunteers leaving the Netherlands and the Indies for South Africa to fight on the side of the Afrikaners in the second Boer War (1899–1902); captured by the British and interned in Colombo, he returned to Batavia upon his release in 1903 and soon found work as a journalist for the Semarang-based newspaper *De Locomotief* and other publications.

Over the course of the next decade, Dekker developed a reputation as a hard-hitting social critic, an advocate of independence for the Indies, and after more than a year of travel across Europe in 1910–1911, a champion of international revolutionary currents, as seen in the global coverage of the bimonthly *Het Tijdschrift* and the daily newspaper *De Expres* he founded in 1911 and 1912. In 1912, moreover, the same year that both Muhammadiyah and Sarekat Islam were established, Dekker joined with prominent Javanese *priyayi* to found the Indische Partij, calling for the Indies to be ruled by the *Indiërs*, a term that encompassed not only *Indos* but natives and Indies-born Chinese. But within a year, this new party's pronouncements and publications—and its promotion of independence—had led to the exile of Dekker and his close collaborators to the Netherlands and the dissolution of the Indische Partij.[62]

It was against this backdrop of abortive early radical activism linking *Indos* and *Inlanders* that the famous Dutch socialist activist and union organizer Henk

---

61. Van Dijk, 353–577.
62. Paul W. van der Veur, *The Lion and the Gadfly: Dutch Colonialism and the Spirit of E.F.E. Douwes Dekker* (Leiden: KITLV Press, 2007), 1–37, 89–267.

Sneevliet arrived in the Indies in 1913. An activist in the small parliamentary Sociaal Democratische Arbeidspartij (SDAP, or Social Democratic Labor Party) in the 1900s, Sneevliet had risen in the ranks to lead the Railway and Tramworkers' Union, then shifted briefly his allegiance to the new revolutionary Sociaal-Democratische Partij (SDP) in 1911 to support striking dockworkers and seamen in Amsterdam and Rotterdam harbors who had joined in an international seamen's strike not backed by the SDAP. But with his union leadership and position in the SDAP compromised by this breach of party discipline and his opportunities for further labor organizing constrained in the tiny Netherlands by the small size of its industrial working class, Sneevliet shifted his energies to the Indies, where the Union of Rail and Tramway Workers (VSTP, or Vereeniging voor Spoor- en Tramweg Personeel) had been founded in 1908, with its headquarters in the booming Javanese city of Semarang.[63]

Combining union-organizing with journalism, Sneevliet soon worked to expand the VSTP from a few hundred Europeans and *Indos* in 1913 into a majority-*inlandsch* union, with more than ninety branches and thirteen thousand members by 1920, and many more workers reading the VSTP's *Melayu* publications, signing its petitions, and participating in its strikes. With concentrations of activists in Semarang, Surabaya, and other key nodes of the railroad system, the VSTP also used the railways to make inroads in the plantation belts in the hinterlands of Java as well as Sumatra, organizing efforts bore fruit in the late 1910s and early 1920s.[64]

Meanwhile, Sneevliet and other activists established the Indische Sociaal-Democratische Vereeniging (ISDV, or Indies Social-Democratic Union) in 1914, which soon began to expand from labor organizing activities into broader forms of social activism and political action. In major cities, VSTP and ISDV activists were soon prominent figures in the SI, challenging the established leadership credentials of the journalists, merchants, *orang particulier*, and *priyayi* who had dominated the movement without serious challenge in the first years of its existence. In its 1916 Congress, this shift was evident in proclamations that the Prophet Muhammad was "the father of Socialism and the pioneer of democracy," "the Socialist par excellence."[65] The trend was most pronounced in Semarang, where the SI expanded more than tenfold from 1916 to 1917 under the chairmanship of the energetic former railway worker, VSTP activist, journalist, and ISDV member, Semaoen.[66]

63. Ruth T. McVey, *The Rise of Indonesian Communism* (Ithaca, NY: Cornell University Press, 1965), 13–17; Fritjof Tichelman, *Henk Sneevliet* (Montreuil: PEC-La Brèche, 1988), 29–42.
64. John Ingleson, "'Bound Hand and Foot': Railway Workers and the 1923 Strike in Java," *Indonesia* 31 (April 1981): 53–60.
65. Van Dijk, *The Netherlands Indies and the Great War*, 483.
66. Soe Hok Gie, *Di Bawah Lentera Merah: Riwayat Sarekat Islam Semarang 1917–1920* (Yogyakarta: Yayasan Bentang Budaya, 1999); Dewi Yuliati, *Semaoen: Pers Bumiputera dan Radikalisasi Sarekat Islam Semarang* (Semarang: Bendera, 2000); Shiraishi, *An Age in Motion*, 98–103.

In late 1917 and early 1918 Semaoen successfully led a series of strikes in the city of Semarang. The first strike was launched by workers in a furniture factory, where about three hundred workers were employed. The success of this strike furnished an example of how to organize unions and strikes. Soon two more work stoppages were called among printers and led by the Semarang SI Labor Group. Both of the strikes also ended successfully. Then strikes were launched by the Singer Sewing Machine Company workers, auto-repair workshop workers, and workers of steamship and *perahu* (prow) transportation. Strikes in Batavia, Surabaya, Bandung, and elsewhere followed, and workers who struck looked to the Semarang SI for guidance. Now trade union movement and strikes came to be seen as an important form of the *pergerakan* (movement). The age of strikes dawned in the Indies and the Semarang SI under Semaoen emerged as a center of the *pergerakan*.[67]

This shift in the direction of labor mobilization, union organizing, and strike activity in the Indies in 1917–1918 coincided with developments around the world to encourage and inspire an escalation of social activism and political action by the SI in the late 1910s and early-mid 1920s. The deprivations, dislocations, and disruptions of World War I had helped to undermine social hierarchies and state structures across much of the world, as seen in the February and October Revolutions of 1917 and the rise of the Bolsheviks to power in Russia. Even as the Armistice of November 1918 drew the war to a close, insurgency and upheaval reigned elsewhere:

> On a line between the borders of France and the Sea of Japan, no old government remained in power. Three great empires, the Habsburg, the Ottoman, and tsarist Russia, had imploded, leaving many of their subject peoples fighting among themselves over nationalism or ideology, or both.
>
> In a Germany bitter and bewildered by the sudden collapse of its army barely a month after their newspapers had proclaimed that the war was won, Berlin, Munich, Hamburg and other cities were torn by revolutionary violence.
>
> Everywhere, in the lands of both victors and vanquished and in the new states scrambling for freedom, the relief of peace was overshadowed by a common fear, the dread of the Red Terror from the east: Bolshevism.[68]

---

67. Shiraishi, *An Age in Motion*, 103.
68. Anthony Read, *The World On Fire: 1919 and the Battle with Bolshevism* (London: Jonathan Cape, 2008), 1.

Indeed, November 1918 saw the onset of the short-lived revolution in Germany, the abdication of Kaiser Wilhelm II, and the proclamation of a republic, with sailors, soldiers, and workers forming soviets and seizing power in cities across the Reich.[69] Socialist revolution had arrived on the very doorstep of the Netherlands, inspiring not only overblown fears but also unrealistic hopes, as seen in SDAP leader Pieter Troelstra's ill-fated rallying call for a Dutch revolution in late 1918.

Revolutionary mobilization under variously socialist, republican, and Islamic banners soon unfolded elsewhere across the world. The year 1919 saw Béla Kun's short-lived Soviet Republic in Hungary, the March First Movement in Korea, the May Fourth Movement in China, and Sa'ad Zaghlul's Wafd Party-led revolution in Egypt.[70] In India, the Khilafat movement initiated the first large-scale mass protests in the cities of the subcontinent in avowed defense of the Ottoman caliph from British intervention in Istanbul, which continued to build up into the ill-fated *hijra* (migration or exodus) to Afghanistan in 1920–1921.[71] Meanwhile, Bolshevik forces fought to claim the Caucasus and Central Asia for the Soviet Revolution, while Comintern leaders intrigued privately and agitated publicly to mobilize committed revolutionary socialists and sympathetic fellow-travellers elsewhere in the Muslim world, as seen in flirtations with the (in)famous "Young Turk" Enver Pasha and the Congress of the Peoples of the East in Baku in September 1920.[72]

In terms of excitement and encouragement, synchronicity and solidarity, this surge of revolutionary mobilization across the globe provided an inspiring backdrop for the SI's escalation of mobilization in the Indies in the early aftermath of World War I. From early 1918, Sneevliet and his comrades had begun agitating and organizing among the lower ranks of the Dutch armed forces along lines familiar from the Bolsheviks' successful strategy in Russia, with hundreds of sailors joining the Bond van Minder Marine-Personeel (Union of Lower-Ranking Naval Personnel) and later the Matrozenbond (Sailors' Union) in Surabaya and other port cities. When a Soldiers' Union was founded in the East Javanese garrison town of Malang in March 1918, three thousand members soon joined. Subsequent months saw a flurry of demonstrations and protest marches by sailors and sol-

---

69. Paul Frolich, *Rosa Luxemburg* (London: Haymarket Books, 2010), 253–283; Arthur J. Ryder, *The German Revolution: A Study of German Socialism in War and Revolt* (Cambridge: Cambridge University Press, 1967), 140–187.

70. Erez Manela, *The Wilsonian Moment: Self-Determination and the International Origins of Anticolonial Nationalism* (Oxford: Oxford University Press, 2007).

71. Gail Minault, *The Khilafat Movement: Religious Symbolism and Political Mobilization in India* (New York: Columbia University Press, 1982); M. Naeem Qureshi, *Pan-Islam in British India: A Study of the Khilafat Movement, 1918–1924* (Leiden: Brill, 1999).

72. Paul Dumont, "L'Axe Moscou-Ankara: Les Relations Turco-Soviétiques de 1919 à 1922," *Cahiers du Monde Russe et Soviétique* 18, no. 3 (July–September 1977): 165–193; Masayuki Yamauchi, *The Green Crescent under the Red Star: Enver Pasha in Soviet Russia, 1919–1922* (Tokyo: Institute for the Study of Languages and Cultures of Asia and Africa, 1991).

diers. In mid-November, less than a week after Troelstra's ill-fated call for a revolution in Den Haag, Sneevliet published an appeal in the ISDV newspaper urging sailors and soldiers to show their solidarity with the SI and the people of the Indies. The authorities in Batavia, fearing Bolshevik-style mutinies, soviets, and uprisings, responded with alacrity, arresting and imprisoning Sneevliet and some of his compatriots and ordering their expulsion from the Indies before the end of the year.[73]

But even with Sneevliet exiled (and Semaoen briefly imprisoned), union organizing and labor mobilization continued to escalate in 1919 and into the early 1920s under the leadership of the newly formed Perserikatan Kommunist di India (PKI). New unions were formed among coach drivers, miners, printers, stevedores, printers, sugar mill workers, and state employees. On sugar and tobacco plantations across Java, newly established unions led strikes for better wages, even as peasant villagers mobilized against the plantation owners in land and labor disputes as well. PKI-affiliated unions spread to the Outer Islands, as seen most dramatically in the 1920 railway strike on the Deli plantation belt in East Sumatra.[74]

This surge in popular mobilization drew on the combined organizational infrastructure, energies, and aspirations associated with communism and Islam, as exemplified by the famous "Islamic Communist" activist Haji Misbach in Solo.[75] A *pesantren*-educated batik trader associated with Muhammadiyah, Misbach joined the SI in the early–mid 1910s and combined editorship of two SI-affiliated publications he founded—*Medan Moeslimin* (1915) and *Islam Bergerak* (1917)—with leadership of a local group of *muballighīn* (preachers), forms of activism that involved him in the organization of peasant strikes on plantations around Solo in 1918 until his arrest and imprisonment in mid-1920. Freed in August 1922, Misbach returned to his Islamic Communist activism, attending SI rallies across Java, establishing a local branch of the PKI in Solo and converting *Islam Bergerak* to *Rakyat Bergerak* amidst a surge of mobilization peaking in a railway strike involving fifty thousand workers across Java in mid-1923.[76]

Yet a backlash against this seemingly dangerous fusion of Islam and communism was not long in coming. The early 1920s saw growing concern among merchants, professionals, and *priyayi* in the SI with regard to the dangers of radicalization and revolutionary socialism within the ranks of the movement. Over the course of 1920 and 1921, these more conservative elements began to work to draw the modernist

73. Van Dijk, *The Netherlands Indies and the Great War*, 558–572, 605–611.

74. Ann Laura Stoler, *Capitalism and Confrontation in Sumatra's Plantation Belt, 1870–1979* (New Haven, CT: Yale University Press, 1985), 62–63.

75. For this broad line of argument, see Shiraishi, *An Age in Motion*, and Hongxuan Lin, "Sickle as Crescent: Islam and Communism in the Netherlands East Indies, 1915–1927," *Studia Islamika* 25, no. 2 (2018): 309–350.

76. For a detailed treatment of Misbach, see Takashi Shiraishi, "Islam and Communism: An Illumination of the People's Movement in Java, 1912–1926" (PhD diss., Cornell University Press, 1986), 223–322, 480–560.

Islam association Muhammadiyah into the SI, and in 1922 Tjokroaminoto joined prominent Muhammadiyah *muballighīn* and the Sudanese Islamic scholar Moehamad Soerkati, leader of the predominantly Hadhrami modernist association Al-Irsyad, in an Al-Islam Congress in the northern Javanese coastal town of Cirebon.[77] Over 1921–1923, moreover, these elements within the SI leadership succeeded in institutionalizing the movement as a Partij Sarekat Islam, and in imposing party discipline such that active PKI members—including the likes of Haji Misbach— were forced out of first the central, and then the local bodies of the new PSI.[78] "Almost totally dependent on the *Muhammadiyah* for its survival both financially and organizationally," the SI thus effectively "transformed itself into a political arm of the *Muhammadiyah*."[79] Even as successive Comintern Congresses saw increasing Bolshevik distance from and disdain toward so-called Pan-Islam and the deepening marginalization of Mirsaid Sultangaliev and his dreams of Muslim national communism, the same years thus saw the dramatic intensification of contradictions and conflicts between communism and Islam in the Indies.

By the mid-1920s, moreover, as the early postwar wave of global revolutionary mobilization began to subside around the world, the PKI's continuing efforts to mobilize workers and peasants in the Indies ran aground in the face of Dutch colonial state repression in the Indies. In 1923, the coordinated railway strike across Java led to arrest and exile for Semaoen, imprisonment of dozens of other VSTP activists, the dismissal of striking workers, the military's assumption of control over the railroad lines, and the imposition of a ban on strikes.[80] Haji Misbach was arrested in early 1924 and exiled until his death in 1926 in the coastal town of Manokwari in Dutch New Guinea (today's West Papua). In 1925, a PKI-led dockworkers' strike in Semarang and Surabaya and other workers' walkouts elsewhere led to another round of arrests and the imposition of additional government restrictions on public gatherings and political activities in the Indies.

Frustrated in the face of increasing constraints on their activities, some elements within the PKI were tempted into ill-advised plans for popular insurrection across the Indies, of which the Dutch colonial secret police were well informed. A series of small-scale uprisings in the Banten region of West Java in late 1926 and West Sumatra in early 1927 provided the occasion for a final crackdown. The rebellions were quickly crushed, and thousands of PKI members were summarily arrested and imprisoned across Java and Sumatra, with more than a thousand top PKI officials relegated to incarceration in the Boven Digoel internment camp in far-flung New Guinea, where they were to remain up until the eve of the Japa-

---

77. On Al-Irsyad, see Mobini-Kesheh, *The Hadrami Awakening*, 52–90.
78. On these developments, see Shiraishi, *An Age in Motion*, 218–238.
79. Shiraishi, 243–244.
80. Ingleson, "'Bound Hand and Foot,'" 62–87.

nese invasion of the Indonesian archipelago in early 1942.[81] Officially banned and effectively banished from public life in the Indies, the PKI and the broader hopes and dreams of socialist revolution it embodied were confined to the fictional adventures of the Patjar Merah and his comrades for readers of the eponymous novels of the late 1930s in the Indies, even as leading Communist exiles such as Semaoen and Tan Malaka continued their activities in exile in Moscow, Shanghai, and elsewhere.

The defeat and demobilization of the SI and the PKI in the mid-1920s coincided with broader disappointments for would-be revolutionaries around the world. Following the formation of the Union of Soviet Socialist Republics in 1922 and the death of Lenin in 1924, the general secretary of the Communist Party of the Soviet Union, Joseph Stalin, had declared the abandonment of world revolution in favor of "socialism in one country." British Communists enthusiastic about the potential trajectory of the General Strike of May 1926 were scorned by Stalin in favor of the accommodationist Trades Union Congress, and the Chinese Communist Party, acquiescing in Stalin's insistence on a "united front from below" with the nationalist Kuomintang Party, saw its activists suppressed by Chiang Kai-Shek's troops in Canton in 1926 and massacred in droves in Shanghai in 1927. Meanwhile, the vehement calls for the preservation—and reinvigoration—of the caliphate seen in the Khilafat movement in India in 1919–1921 and the famous treatise of the Cairo-based *Al-Manār* editor Rashīd Riḍā in 1922 had been dashed by Mustafa Kemal's elimination of the Ottoman sultanate in 1922 and abolition of the caliphate in 1924. Even as British and French proconsuls were stabilizing their hold over the Levantine and Mesopotamian former Ottoman provinces now parcelled out under the mandate system, the forces of London's man Ibn Sa'ud were expanding from the central Najd region of the Arabian Peninsula to seize the Haramayn, capturing Mecca in 1925, claiming the Kingdom of the Hijaz the following year and, with RAF (Royal Air Force) support, consolidating his realm into the Kingdom of Saudi Arabia in 1932. Against this backdrop of retrenchment for Communist and Islamic internationalism, the late 1920s and 1930s were largely years of *rust en orde* (tranquillity and order) in the Netherlands East Indies, requiring another full-blown World War to make possible the Indonesia Revolusi of 1945–1949.

---

81. McVey, *The Rise of Indonesian Communism*, 323–346.

SOEKARNO AND THE PROMISE OF *NASAKOM*

From *Rust en Orde* through the Pacific War, 1926–1945

In 1926, on the eve of the ill-fated PKI-led uprisings in Banten and West Sumatra, an article titled "Nationalism, Religion, and Marxism,"[1] appeared in *Indonesia Muda* (Young Indonesia), the journal of the Algemeine Studieclub (General Study Club) in the exclusive West Javanese Dutch hill-station town of Bandung.[2] The article, which was serialized over three issues of the journal, lamented the conflicts, tensions, and misunderstandings that had come to divide the variously Islamic- and Marxist-oriented leaders of the Sarekat Islam and the broader field of political and social action in the Indies, now described, as the title of the journal indicated, as Indonesia.[3] In style, the article took a decidedly cosmopolitan tack, referring to nationalist leaders such as Mohatma Gandhi and Sun Yat-sen, Islamic activists such as Jamāl ad-Dīn al-Afghānī, Muhammad ʿAbduh, and the Ali brothers of India's Khilafat movement, as well as revolutionary socialist luminaries such as Karl Marx, Friedrich Engels, and the Comintern leader Karl Radek. Yet in substance the argument was a rallying cry for Indonesian nationalism, for "unity which will bring us to the realization of our dreams: a Free Indonesia."[4] Alluding to arguments by French historian Ernest Renan and Austrian socialist Otto Bauer, the article grounded its account of Indonesian nationalism in the shared experience of colonial rule:

---

1. For an English translation, see Soekarno, *Nationalism, Islam and Marxism* (Ithaca, NY: Cornell University Southeast Asia Program, 1970).
2. On Bandung, see Joshua Barker, "The Tattoo and the Fingerprint: Crime and Security in an Indonesian City" (PhD diss., Cornell University, 1999).
3. Robert E. Elson, *The Idea of Indonesia* (Cambridge: Cambridge University Press, 2008), 1–97.
4. Soekarno, *Nationalism, Islam, and Marxism*, 24.

We should not forget that the men who built the Islamic and Marxist movements here in Indonesia, as well as those who guide the Nationalist movement, all share the "desire to live as one," and that, along with the Nationalists, these people feel they are members of "one group, one nation." We must also not forget that all elements in our movement, whether they are Nationalist, Islamic, or Marxist, have shared for hundreds of years a "unity of historical experience." For hundreds of years they have shared a common experience of bondage. We must also not overlook the fact that it is this "unity of historical experience," this common lot, which creates the feeling of "belonging."[5]

After a kaleidoscopic treatment of Nationalism, Islam, and Marxism in Indonesia and across the colonized world, the article concluded with a call for unity:

all Indonesian leaders are aware that only Unity will lead us to Greatness and Independence. . . . It only remains now to create an organization which can realize this Unity; it only remains to look for an organizer who can make himself the Mahatma of this Unity. Does not Mother Indonesia, who has such sons as Umar Said Tjokroaminoto, Tjipto Mangunkusumo and Semaun—does not Mother Indonesia also have a son who can become the Champion of this Unity?[6]

The author of "Nationalism, Islam, and Marxism" was a twenty-five-year old Dutch-educated *ingenieur* named Soekarno, the very same man who would go on to be the "Champion of this Unity," as luminary of the Partai Nasional Indonesia, leading light of Indonesia's independence movement, and first president of the Republic of Indonesia. Born in 1901, Soekarno had grown up in East Java as the son of a schoolteacher of *priyayi* lineage, studied at the Hogere Burger secondary school in Surabaya, and then attended the recently created Technische Hogeschool in Bandung, the pinnacle of modern Dutch-language education in the Indies. Soekarno's high school years in Surabaya coincided with the rise of the Sarekat Islam and the ISDV, and the teenager happened to find lodgings in the city with his father's friend Raden Mas Oemar Said Tjokroaminoto, the famous journalist and SI leader. Through his mentor Tjokroaminoto, the young Soekarno was exposed to a wide range of leading activists of diverse orientations and affiliations, ranging from socialists such as Semaoen and Sneevliet to Islamic reformists such as Haji Agus Salim. Soekarno also met Indische Partij leaders such as Douwes Dekker and Dr. Tjipto Mangoenkoesoemo, who were active in the Boedi Oetomo, a society of Dutch-educated *pangreh praja* and professionals founded

5. Soekarno, 25–26.
6. Soekarno, 38–39.

in 1908,[7] whose youth group—Tri Koro Dharma (Three Noble Objectives), later Jong Java (Young Java)—Soekarno soon joined. He also was evidently attracted to the short-lived antiaristocratic Djawa Dipo movement, which urged the abolition of "high" Javanese (*kromo*) and the use of "low" Javanese (*ngoko*) in public discourse.[8] By the time he arrived in Bandung to begin his tertiary education in Bandung in 1921 at the age of twenty, Soekarno was thus exposed to diverse intellectual currents, immersed in the world of political activism, and experienced in journalism and public oratory.[9]

Against this backdrop, Soekarno's rallying call for unity among Muslims and Marxists and for Indonesian independence in 1926 represented the rise of classically Andersonian nationalism among the bilingual Dutch-educated elite stratum of society in the late colonial Indies. Indeed, the Algemeine Studieclub in Bandung had its counterparts in other major cities across Java, inspired by the Indonesische Studieclub founded by the Dutch-educated Boedi Oetomo luminary Dr. Soetomo in Surabaya in 1924, with students and recent graduates of the leading schools in the Indies predominating among the members. Meanwhile, a similar trend was evident among the small but growing numbers of students from the Indies attending universities in the Netherlands. Already in 1922, such students had renamed the Indische Vereeniging (Indies Association) the Perhimpunan Indonesia (Indonesian Association) to mark their identification with the Indonesian nation-in-waiting, and as they returned to the Indies in subsequent years they joined the Studieclub in various cities, sharing a commitment to Indonesian nationalism that was formalized in 1927 in the founding of the Perserikatan Nasional Indonesia (PNI, or Indonesian National Association) with independence as its openly avowed long-term goal.[10] Thus, much as chronicled in Benedict Anderson's *Imagined Communities*, it was these privileged (and largely *priyayi*) Dutch-educated students in the Netherlands and the key cities of the Netherlands East Indies who first imagined "Indonesia" as a nation and pioneered Indonesia's nationalist movement and struggle for independence from Dutch colonial rule.

But how was the author of the 1926 tract "Nationalism, Islam, and Marxism" able to bring his aspirations for Indonesian unity and for Indonesian national independence to fruition by the end of the 1940s? Soekarno and his fellow found-

---

7. Akira Nagazumi, *The Dawn of Indonesian Nationalism: The Early Years of the Budi Otomo, 1908–1918* (Tokyo: Institute of Developing Economies, 1972).

8. On the Djawa Dipo movement, see Benedict R. O'G. Anderson, "*Sembah-Sumpah*: The Politics of Language and Javanese Culture," in *Language and Power: Exploring Political Cultures in Indonesia*, ed. Benedict R. O'G. Anderson (Ithaca, NY: Cornell University Press, 1990), 215–218.

9. On Soekarno's years in Surabaya, see John D. Legge, *Sukarno: A Political Biography* (Singapore: Archipelago Press, 2003), 61–88.

10. John Ingleson, *Perhimpunan Indonesia and the Indonesian Nationalist Movement, 1923–1928* (Clayton, Victoria: Monash Asia Institute, 1975).

ers of the PNI in 1927, after all, represented only a tiny segment of Indonesian society in terms of their origins, education, and ability to imagine Indonesia as a nation. In 1927, there were less than seventy thousand Indonesians enrolled in Dutch primary schools and fewer than six thousand in Dutch secondary schools, and only 6 percent of the population was said to be literate, a state of affairs that changed little during the 1930s or 1940s.[11] The founders of the PNI consisted of the alumni of exclusive Dutch schools, members of the Studieclub and Perhimpunan Indonesia, and veterans of earlier associations such as the Boedi Oetomo and the Indische Partij, which had been similarly restricted in their membership, appeal, and inclination or ability to engage in mass mobilization. These pioneering nationalists, it has been argued, were essentially flâneurs and dandies, rather than mass activists.[12]

To be sure, Soekarno did reach out to a broader audience through journalism and public rallies, methods already well established during the heyday of the SI, and he and his nationalist compatriots did engage in efforts at organization building during the late 1920s and 1930s. The PNI was renamed the Partai Nasional Indonesia in 1928 and came to claim ten thousand members, and, on its forced dissolution in 1931, a Partai Indonesia (Partindo) soon took its place, doubling its membership within a year. During the late 1920s and 1930s, moreover, a succession of congresses brought together disparate groups in the name of Indonesian nationalist unity, from the 1928 Sumpah Pemuda (Youth Oath) pledging members of Jong Java and Jong Sumatranen Bond and other local youth groups to "one homeland, one nation, one language" (*satu tanah air, satu bangsa, satu bahasa*), up to the Kongres Rakyat Indonesia (Indonesian People's Congress) of 1939, which officially adopted the Indonesian national language, anthem, and flag.

But such proclamations of unity among fractious Dutch-educated intellectuals did not reach the broad audience or entail the active forms of popular participation observed—and experienced—in the late 1910s and early 1920s in the heyday of the SI and the PKI. Soekarno and his compatriots worked to build the PNI into a mass organization in the late 1920s and early 1930s, but their efforts were nipped in the bud by the Dutch authorities. PNI activists trying to organize workers on the Deli plantation belt in East Sumatra were arrested in mid-1929, as was Soekarno and other PNI leaders later the same year. Upon his release in late 1931, Soekarno was met by a large throng of supporters in Bandung and, as he set off by train across Java, by similarly enthusiastic crowds in stops along the way, and, reportedly, six thousand well-wishers on his arrival in Surabaya. But in

---

11. George McTurnan Kahin, *Nationalism and Revolution in Indonesia* (Ithaca, NY: Cornell University Press, 1952), 31, 62.
12. Rudolf Mrázek, *Engineers of Happy Land: Technology and Nationalism in a Colony* (Princeton, NJ: Princeton University Press, 2002), 129–159.

1933, Soekarno was arrested once again and sent into internal exile on the eastern island of Flores. Mohammad Hatta and Sutan Sjahrir, the Dutch-educated, West Sumatra–born leaders of the rival Partai Nasional Indonesia Baru (New Indonesian National Party) were arrested the following year and confined along with the convicted PKI rebels of 1926–1927 in the Boven Digoel internment camp in New Guinea. Although Soekarno was later moved to Bengkulu and Hatta and Sjahrir to the Banda Islands, the Indonesian nationalist movement's leading lights remained in exile for the remainder of the 1930s, even as the embryonic organizations they had established were effectively immobilized and incapacitated. "With most of the radical leaders away or silent, the rest of the era, until the Second World War, was murky, muffled, hopeless, flat, and drab."[13]

If Indonesia's nationalist leaders and nationalist movements were unable to engage in serious organizing efforts and mass mobilization at the beginning of the 1940s, then how was Indonesia's Revolusi brought to fruition in the mid–late 1940s and independence achieved by the end of the decade? As suggested above and substantiated below, much of the answer to this question lies outside the nationalist narrative of nationalists mobilizing a nationalist movement in a nationalist revolution for national independence. As noted above, the mass mobilization of the 1910s and early–mid 1920s under the auspices of the SI and the PKI owed much to the Indonesian archipelago's incorporation within the world economy as a site for large-scale plantation agriculture, its immersion within the cosmopolitan circuitries of the Indian Ocean and the broader Muslim world, and the diverse forms of revolutionary brotherhood associated with republicanism, communism, and Islam circulating across the world during the early decades of the twentieth century. As further noted above, the variegated forms of associational activity and political action that emerged and evolved during the 1910s and early–mid 1920s rose—and fell—as part of a wave of organization building and mass mobilization that stretched from Baku to Bombay, Cairo to Calcutta, Petrograd to Penang, Shanghai to Singapore, and on to Surabaya, Semarang, and elsewhere in the Indies. As treated in the pages that follow, the Indonesian Revolusi of 1945–1949 also drew on the discursive and mobilizing structures of republicanism, communism, and Islam, whose combined energies had helped to produce the unprecedented popular mobilization under the auspices of the SI three decades earlier. But as with the SI and the PKI in the early aftermath of World War I, it would take international conflict among the imperial powers, World War II, and

13. Mrázek, *Engineers of Happy Land*, 150. On Sjahrir and Hatta in exile, moreover, see Rudolf Mrázek, *Sjahrir: Politics and Exile in Indonesia* (Ithaca, NY: Cornell University Southeast Asia Program, 1994), 118–208, and Mavis Rose, *Indonesia Free: A Political Biography of Mohammad Hatta* (Ithaca, NY: Cornell Modern Indonesia Project, 1987), 76–91.

Japanese invasion and occupation of Southeast Asia for the 1920 call from Baku for revolution in the East to resonate with full-blown Revolusi halfway across the world in Indonesia in 1945.

From Exile to Underground:
Communism, 1927–1945

If the late 1920s and 1930s saw the rapid rise and repression-induced fall of nationalist mobilization in the Indonesian archipelago, so did the same years witness apparent quiescence on the part of those forces mobilized in the late 1910s and early-mid 1920s under the banners of Islam and communism. In the wake of the 1926–1927 uprisings, the PKI leadership was confined to the Boven Digoel internment camp in New Guinea and exile in Moscow and elsewhere, even as an official ban on the party, harsh restrictions on union organizing and strike activity, and heightened police surveillance across the archipelago constrained further efforts to mobilize the Indonesian working class.[14] Meanwhile, remnants of the SI, restyled as the Partai Sarekat Islam Indonesia (PSII) in 1929, spent most of the 1930s engaged in a self-conscious withdrawal (*hijra*) from political activism, even as the same years saw continuing, indeed deepening, fractiousness and fragmentation among rival Islamic associations divided by pedagogical and theological differences.[15] Thus, the long, lean years from the failed rebellions of 1926–1927 to the Japanese invasion of early 1942 are often glossed as a period of inactivity and immobilization for communism and Islam in Indonesia, providing little in the way of preparation for the Revolusi to come.

On closer inspection, however, it could be argued that the late interwar era in Indonesia helped to lay the groundwork for communist and Islamic revolution making by sustaining transoceanic connections to diverse sources of real, imagined, and potential solidarity and support across the world, and by maintaining or (re)building discursive and institutional structures for popular mobilization in the name of communism and Islam. As for the PKI, efforts to resurrect the party on Java and Sumatra in the years following the failed rebellions of 1926–1927 were essentially nugatory until the clandestine return to the Indies of party chairman Musso from exile in Moscow in 1935 in the aftermath of the Seventh Congress of the Comintern. Acting in accordance with the Comintern's new "popular front"

---

14. Takashi Shiraishi, *Hantu Digoel: Politik Pengamanan Politik Zaman Kolonial* (Yogyakarta: LKiS, 2001).

15. Robert E. Elson, "Disunity, Distance, Disregard: The Political Failure of Islamism in Late Colonial Indonesia," *Studia Islamika* 16, no. 1 (2009): 1–50.

line advocating cooperation with "bourgeois" and "liberal" forces against fascism and imperialism,[16] Musso worked secretly for months in Surabaya to reconstruct the PKI, drawing on radicalized members of the Persatuan Pemuda Rakyat Indonesia (PPRI, or Indonesian People's Youth Association) and other fellow travellers to help distribute propaganda and form secret cells. But Musso was forced to leave the Indies in 1936 and many of his collaborators were subsequently arrested and exiled to Boven Digoel.[17]

Nonetheless, Musso's short-lived organizing stint in the Indies and the shadowy "Illegal PKI" he constructed in 1935–1936 did leave two lasting legacies of some significance. First, the "Illegal PKI" was notable for its unprecedented recruitment of small numbers of *peranakan* Chinese into its ranks, activists who in a few short years gained control over the recently established Partai Tionghoa Indonesia (Indonesian Chinese Party) and its newspaper, *Sin Tit Po*.[18] Although such recruitment remained limited in numbers and potential impact in the Indies given the small size of the *peranakan* Chinese minority, it carried greater long-term significance in terms of the establishment of linkages among left-wing circuits in the Chinese diaspora stretching across the Indies to Singapore, Penang, and beyond.

Second, the Comintern's "popular front" line pursued by Musso and his comrades in the mid-late 1930s did bear fruit in the PKI's influence within the Gerakan Rakyat Indonesia, (Gerindo, or Indonesian People's Movement), a group formed in 1937 by former members of the dissolved Partindo and other activists who shared a self-consciously socialist and strongly antifascist orientation. Crucially, Gerindo's well developed international orientation led to a prioritization of the struggle against fascism over the pursuit of national independence, opening possibilities for left-wing cooperation with the Dutch authorities that would bear fruit in the years ahead.[19] The participation of PKI cadres in Gerindo, moreover, also intertwined the fate of communism in the Indonesian archipelago with that of a broader range of left-wing organizations, parties, and activists for years to come.[20]

Alongside these internationalist legacies of the late interwar era, other developments and trends helped to sustain the promise of revolutionary socialism on the horizon. Many Indonesian students in the Netherlands during this period,

---

16. E. H. Carr, *The Twilight of the Comintern, 1930–1935* (New York: Pantheon Books, 1982), 403–419.

17. Harry A. Poeze, "The PKI-Muda, 1936–1942," *Kabar Sebarang* 13–14 (1984): 157–176.

18. Leo Suryadinata, *Peranakan Politics in Java, 1917–1942* (Singapore: Singapore University Press, 1981), 166–167.

19. Kahin, *Nationalism and Revolution*, 96.

20. Soe Hok Gie, *Orang-orang di Persimpangan Kiri Jalan: Kisah Pemberontakan Madiun September 1948* (Yogyakarta: Yayasan Bentang Budaya, 1997), 23–28.

after all, had become attracted to the accommodationist SDAP and the Comintern-linked Communistische Partij Holland (known as the Communistische Partij van Nederland, or CPN from 1935), and by the 1930s exiled PKI activists enjoyed considerable sway within the Perhimpunan Indonesia, the Indonesian student organization in the Netherlands.[21] Thanks to students returning to the Indies from Europe,

> Dutch socialist and Communist writing affected virtually the whole of the nationalist intelligentsia of the twenties and thirties. For this reason a *marxisant* vocabulary became the common property of the entire nationalist intelligentsia of those years. The importance of this vocabulary was dual in that it offered a critique of the existing order and suggested a program for its replacement. Because the analysis offered by Marxism was apt and clear, it was taken over wholeheartedly by all important segments of the rising educated elite.[22]

Beyond their role in transmitting Marxist discourse to the Indies during the late 1920s and 1930s, such Indonesian student activists in the Netherlands also engaged in diverse forms of political networking across Europe and Asia. Perhimpunan Indonesia vice president Arnold Mononutu, for example, established links with Indochinese and African anticolonial activists in Paris associated with the Union Intercoloniale, and five Indonesian activists—including Perhimpunan Indonesia chairman Mohammad Hatta and the exiled PKI chairman Semaoen, attended the quietly Comintern-backed[23] Congress against Imperialism in Brussels in 1927.[24]

More important, perhaps, organizing efforts among Indonesian seamen and dockers in the harbor areas of Dutch port cities, dating back to Semaoen's founding of a local branch of the PKI's Sarekat Pegawai Pelabuhan dan Lautan (Dockworkers' and Seamen's Union), appear to have borne fruit.[25] Sailors working for Dutch shipping lines carried PKI communications and propaganda materials back

---

21. Klaas Stutje, "Indonesian Identities Abroad: International Engagement of Colonial Students in the Netherlands, 1908–1931," *BMGN—Low Countries Historical Review* 128, no. 1 (2013): 151–172.

22. Benedict R. O'G. Anderson, "Languages of Indonesian Politics," in *Language and Power: Exploring Political Cultures in Indonesia*, ed. Benedict R. O'G. Anderson (Ithaca, NY: Cornell University Press, 1990), 137.

23. On the role of the Comintern in the League Against Imperialism and the 1927 Congress, see Fredrik Petersson, "'We Are Neither Visionaries Nor Utopian Dreamers': Willi Münzenberg, the League against Imperialism, and the Comintern, 1925–1933" (PhD thesis, Åbo Akademi University, 2013).

24. Klaas Stutje, "To Maintain an Independent Course: Inter-war Indonesian Nationalism and International Communism on a Dutch-European Stage," *Dutch Crossing* 39, no. 3 (November 2015): 198–214.

25. Rianne Kartikasari Sibijanto, "Media of Resistance: A Communication History of the Communist Movement in the Dutch East Indies, 1920–1926" (PhD diss., University of Colorado, 2016), 98–99.

to the Indies on a regular basis,[26] and some such seamen were even enrolled in the Communist University of the Toilers of the East (KUTV) in Moscow,[27] where they mixed and mingled with Vietnamese, Chinese, and other revolutionary activists. Meanwhile, PKI leaders such as Semaoen, Darsono, Musso, and Alimin escaped the fate of their comrades in Boven Digoel and survived the long years following the party's annihilation in 1926–1927 in exile in Moscow and elsewhere as operatives of the Comintern until its dissolution in 1943. Of these exiled PKI leaders, Musso in particular was later destined to play a prominent if problematic role in the Revolusi, as discussed in the pages that follow.

At the same time, as romanticized in the *Patjar Merah* novel serialized in 1938–1940, the iconoclastic former PKI leader Tan Malaka also remained in clandestine international circulation throughout the late interwar period, biding his time in anticipation of the Revolusi to come. Born into an aristocratic Minangkabau family in 1897, Tan Malaka had graduated from Dutch schools in his native West Sumatra and spent six years in the Netherlands during World War I, where he read Marx, Kautsky, and the writings of Dutch leftists and witnessed the short-lived "Troelstra Revolution" of 1918 before returning to the Indies the following year to teach coolie laborers in the Deli plantation belt in East Sumatra. In 1921, he moved to Java and was drawn into the PKI, recruited by Semaoen, first to organize *sekolah rakyat* (people's schools) in Semarang, and, in a matter of months, to replace him as party chairman upon Semaoen's departure for Russia to attend the first Congress of the Toilers of the East. But in early 1922, Tan Malaka was arrested and exiled in the aftermath of a PKI-backed pawnshop workers' strike across Java, returning to the Netherlands (where he was elected to the Dutch Parliament on the CPH [Communist Party of Holland] ticket but then disqualified due to his young age) before proceeding to Moscow for the Fourth Comintern Congress, where, as noted above, he spoke out passionately, if unsuccessfully, in defense of an alliance between communism and Pan-Islamism.[28]

From 1923, Tan Malaka's movements brought him closer to the Indies, even as the distance between his own stance and that of the gradually Stalinized Comintern and the PKI leadership inexorably widened. In late 1923, he was appointed the Comintern representative for Southeast Asia and based in the southern Chinese coastal port city of Canton (Guangzhou), where the Chinese Communist Party was beginning to organize workers into unions with growing

26. See Subijanto, "Media of Resistance," 100–104; Klaas Stutje, "Behind the Banner of Unity: Nationalism and Anticolonialism among Indonesian Students in Europe, 1917–1931" (PhD thesis, University of Amsterdam, 2016), 29; Kris Alexanderson, *Subversive Seas: Anticolonial Networks across the Twentieth-Century Dutch Empire* (Cambridge: Cambridge University Press, 2019), 168–208.

27. Alexanderson, *Subversive Seas*, 178.

28. Harry Poeze, *Tan Malaka: Pergulatan Menuju Republik, 1897–1925* (Jakarta: Pustaka Utama Grafiti, 1988).

success. But over the next few years, as he moved from Canton to Manila to Singapore, Tan Malaka wrote and circulated a series of independently minded tracts in which he called for the PKI to forego narrowly proletarian revolution in favor of a more broadly conceived anti-imperialist coalition of forces, and argued against premature insurrection in favor of organized mass action (*massa actie*) combining strikes, boycotts, legal campaigns, and even parliamentary participation with the development of a disciplined labor union movement and party organization. Thus, when the PKI leadership began to prepare for revolution in 1926, Tan Malaka dispatched a series of harshly critical missives to his comrades in the Indies in a desperate effort to dissuade them from the certain defeat and disaster he foresaw. In the early aftermath of the failed uprisings of 1926–1927, he was thus castigated by former comrades in the PKI and the Comintern for deviating from the party line, demoralizing the party faithful, and disrupting revolutionary developments in the Indies. Subsequent years saw Tan Malaka moving to Bangkok, Hong Kong, Amoy (Xiamen), and Shanghai before returning to Singapore in 1937 and, in early 1942, arriving in the East Sumatran city of Medan.[29]

As he moved from one Asian city to the next to evade Dutch surveillance and avoid arrest by the local authorities in a style amply worthy of *Patjar Merah*, Tan Malaka also engaged in clandestine organizing efforts that did bear fruit, however modestly, back in the Indies, especially in his native region of West Sumatra. While in Bangkok in 1927, Tan Malaka formed the Partai Republik Indonesia (PARI), whose manifesto proudly proclaimed its independence from outside influence or leadership and its indifference in the face of the deepening Stalin–Trotsky schism, while pointedly noting the disastrous consequences of Comintern policy in China and PKI adventurism in Indies from 1926 to 1927. Although PARI was designed to replace the PKI, its modus operandi was confined to clandestine cell formation and propaganda activities among a small circle of committed activist cadres in the Indies.[30]

While Tan Malaka remained in peripatetic exile in Southeast Asia and China, his close comrade Djamaloeddin Tamin, a fellow Minangkabau and former SI and PKI activist, pioneered preliminary PARI organizing efforts in the Indies, most notably in West Sumatra, where the region's two native sons could still draw on a range of close contacts and potential collaborators. As a former student and

29. These movements are evocatively chronicled in parts of the first two volumes of Tan Malaka's 1947 memoirs *Dari Pendjara ke Pendjara*, all three volumes of which have been reissued in Indonesia since 1998 by various obscure publishing houses and also translated into English by Helen Jarvis as *From Jail to Jail* (Athens, OH: Ohio University Monographs in International Studies, 1991). See also Ruth McVey, *The Rise of Indonesian Communism* (Ithaca, NY: Cornell University Press, 1965), 316–346, and Djamaluddin Tamin, "Sedjarah P.K.I." (unpublished manuscript, undated).

30. Helen Jarvis, "Tan Malaka: Revolutionary or Renegade?," *Bulletin of Concerned Asian Scholars* 19, no. 1 (January–March 1987): 47–49.

teacher in the Sumatra Thawalib Islamic schools in West Sumatra, Tamin had a network of fellow Minangkabau migrants and former school chums and students stretching as far as Singapore, Penang, and the peninsular Malay state of Negeri Sembilan. In the aftermath of the failed 1927 rebellion, he was thus able to help activists fleeing Dutch arrest find refuge and employment in nearby Malaya.[31] Tamin "encouraged those who remained in Malaya to become sailors on the trading ships plying the Malacca Strait and the Indonesian archipelago," and in subsequent years he often worked on such vessels himself.[32]

Through these channels, Tamin and other PARI activists managed to smuggle Tan Malaka's writings and other propaganda materials into West Sumatra and elsewhere in the Indies. Thanks to such efforts, Tan Malaka's writings circulated in the late 1920s and 1930s like samizdat among sympathetic activists in various new nationalist organizations, even as the Thawalib and Diniyyah Islamic school networks provided an enduring basis for independent Marxist intellectual activity and episodic organizing efforts in the face of Dutch repression.[33] A group of PARI activists on Java were arrested and exiled to Boven Digoel in 1930, as was Tamin in 1933, but small numbers of PARI activists continued their work well into the late 1930s.

At the same time, fantasies about Tan Malaka and a revival of revolutionary socialism independent of Moscow's control and innocent of anti-Islamic prejudices ascribed to the PKI and the Comintern continued to circulate, as is evident in the *Patjar Merah* novel serialized in 1938–1940 and in Dutch secret police files from this period.[34] As Tan Malaka himself later noted with evident retrospective bemusement in his memoirs, upon his return incognito to Medan in early 1942 he stumbled on copies of *Patjar Merah* and repeatedly encountered rumors that Tan Malaka had arrived back in the Indonesian archipelago.[35] He had been living a dream that was not his alone.

From *Hijra* to *Hizbullah*: Islam, 1927–1942

Meanwhile, the long, lean late-interwar years following the failed 1926–1927 rebellions in the Indies also saw important developments in the realm of Islamic

31. See Kankan Xie, "Estranged Comrades: Global Networks of Indonesian Communism, 1926–1932" (PhD diss., University of California at Berkeley, 2018), 87–89, 127–132, 146–150.

32. Audrey Kahin, *Rebellion to Integration: West Sumatra and the Indonesian Polity* (Amsterdam: Amsterdam University Press, 1999), 63.

33. Hongxuan Lin, "Ummah Yet Proletariat: Islam and Marxism in the Netherlands East Indies and Indonesia, 1915–1959" (PhD diss., University of Washington, 2020), 70–92, 135–136, 169–201.

34. Takashi Shiraishi, "The Phantom World of Digoel," *Indonesia* 61 (April 1996): 93–118.

35. Tan Malaka, *Dari Pendjara ke Pendjara Jilid II* (Jakarta: LPPM Tan Malaka, 2007), 211–223.

educational and associational activity whose long-term significance would also become apparent over the course of the 1940s. As noted above, the early 1910s had seen the formation not only of the SI but also of modernist Islamic associations such as Muhammadiyah and the predominantly Hadhrami Al-Irsyad, and as the SI leadership disentangled and distanced itself from the PKI in the early-mid 1920s, a series of Al-Islam congresses were held in the Indies by the leaders of these increasingly interwoven organizations, with nine such gatherings convened between 1922 and 1932. The early Kongres Al-Islam Hindia helped to set the stage for the formation of delegations to the caliphate congresses in Mecca and Cairo in 1926, for which SI leader Tjokroaminoto and Muhammadiyah's Mas Mansoer were selected to represent the Muslims of the Indies. Although this delegation's participation in the unsuccessful congress in Mecca in May 1926 (and two modernist Sumatran scholars' appearance at the similarly uneventful congress in Cairo a few days later) failed to deliver concrete results of any apparent kind, they did embody and actualize unprecedented efforts to represent the Muslims of the Indies—internationally and within the archipelago—under a single associational rubric, a significant development in the history of Indonesian Islam.[36]

Indeed, these initiatives by modernist Muslim activists soon combined with other developments to generate new forms of associational activity among Islamic scholars (known as *kyai* or *'ulamā*) associated with traditionalist Islamic schools across the Indies. Angered by the claims of Muhammadiyah and SI to represent Indies Muslims and anxious about the implications of the conquest of Holy Cities of the Hijaz by 'Abd al-Azīz ibn Sa'ud and the Wahhābī *ikhwān* for Indies pilgrims adhering to the Shāfi'ī *madhhab* and affiliated with one or another Sufi *ṭarīqa*, a group of prominent Javanese *kyai* joined forces to establish a new "traditionalist" association, known as Nahdlatul Ulama (Arabic: *nahḍat al-'ulamā*; Awakening of the Scholars) in 1926.[37] Originally formed to represent the concerns of established Islamic scholars in the Indies in the international arena, Nahdlatul Ulama dispatched a delegation to Mecca in 1928 that won an audience with Ibn Sa'ud and assurances from the newly crowned king of the Hijaz with regard to the continued freedom of Indies pilgrims to make the Hajj without fear of further Wahhābī persecution.[38]

---

36. Michael Francis Laffan, *Islamic Nationhood and Colonial Indonesia: The Umma below the Winds* (London: RoutledgeCurzon, 2003), 212–214, and Martin van Bruinessen, "Muslims of the Dutch East Indies and the Caliphate Question," *Studia Islamika* 2, no. 3 (1995): 115–140. See also Achile Sékaly, *Le Congrès du Khalifat (Le Caire, 13–19 Mai 1926) et Le Congrès du Monde Musulman (La Mekke, 7 Juin—5 Juillet 1926)* (Paris: Éditions Ernest Leroux, 1926), and Martin S. Kramer, *Islam Assembled: The Advent of the Muslim Congresses* (New York: Columbia University Press, 1986), 86–122.

37. Laffan, *Islamic Nationhood and Colonial Indonesia*, 226–228.

38. Greg Fealy, "Wahab Chasbullah, Traditionalism and the Political Development of Nahdlatul Ulama," in *Nahdlatul Ulama, Traditional Islam and Modernity in Indonesia*, ed. Greg Fealy and Greg Barton (Victoria, Clayton: Monash Asia Institute, 1996), 12–15.

Nahdlatul Ulama's success in this regard combined with the inclusion of prominent Javanese *kyai* among the leadership to draw more and more Islamic schools (*pesantren*) within the orbit of the new association over the remaining years of the late interwar era. Through Nahdlatul Ulama, networks of Islamic scholars—and their students (*santri*)—previously linked by informal webs of scholastic collaboration, intertextuality, and intermarriage were now joined under a more formalized associational rubric, as seen in the annual congresses held from 1926 onward.[39] The formation of Nahdlatul Ulama also attested to—and assisted in—the inexorable opening of the rarefied world of Islamic scholasticism in the Indies to the influences of the modern world in the late 1920s and 1930s. From 1929, for example, the prominent Tebuireng *pesantren* in Jombang, East Java, underwent a dramatic linguistic and pedagogical transformation under Nahdlatul Ulama leadership:

> Henceforth newspapers began to enter the *pesantren*, became known and read by scholars and students there, likewise magazines and books containing general knowledge, written in the Roman alphabet and in the Indonesian language, whereas previously such "progressive" materials were among those worldly items which did not concern religion and the world of religious scholars. The second revivalist revolution was pedagogical. As a headmaster fully empowered over his school, he [Kyai Mohamad Ilyas] began to think of improvements in accordance with the requirements of the times. Thus under his leadership general studies began to enter the school, where previously teachings had been confined to Arabic-language religious books. These general studies consisted of reading and writing in the Roman alphabet, Indonesian language, natural sciences, and Indonesian history, mathematics, all in the Roman alphabet, except for the history of Islam which was still taught in the Arabic alphabet.[40]

If the late 1920s and 1930s saw the emergence of modern forms of educational reform and associational reorganization even among "traditionalist" Islamic scholars, it is unsurprising that the same period witnessed considerable activism and expansion among Islamic "modernist" and "reformist" organizations as well. Muhammadiyah branches grew tenfold between 1923 and 1932 on Java, for example, with membership across the Indies reportedly reaching nearly forty-five

39. A. Farichin Chumaidy, "The Jam'iyyah Nahdlatul 'Ulama: Its Rise and Early Development, 1926–1945" (MA thesis, Institute of Islamic Studies, McGill University, 1976), 64–90.

40. H. Aboebakar, *Sedjarah Hidup K.H. A. Wahid Hasjim dan Karangan Tersiar* (Djakarta: Panitya Buku Peringatan Almarhum K.H.A. Wahid Hasjim, 1957), 85. Translation by the author.

thousand the following year, with the modern Islamic schools affiliated with the association said to number nearly seven hundred by this time and extending to areas of Sumatra, Kalimantan (Borneo), Sulawesi, and elsewhere. This trend continued during the 1930s, with Muhammadiyah branches and schools doubling in number between 1932 and 1937.[41] At the same time, the predominantly Hadhrami modernist association Al-Irsyad continued to expand its branches and schools across the Indies, even as the decidedly puritanical Persatuan Islam (Islamic Union, or Persis) developed from its initial base in Bandung in the early 1920s to establish a small network of schools elsewhere on Java and beyond.[42] Meanwhile, outside Java, other reformist Islamic educational and associational initiatives flourished during the late interwar era, such as the Sumatra Thawalib school network in West Sumatra and the Persatuan Ulama Seluruh Aceh (PUSA or All-Aceh Union of Islamic Scholars) in the northern Sumatran region of Aceh.[43]

These trends in Islamic educational and associational activity during the late interwar era of apparent quiescence left important legacies in terms of the discursive and mobilizational structures associated with Islam. As scholars have noted, the expansion and diversification of Islamic education in the late 1920s and 1930s broadened the ranks of Muslims—especially young Muslim men—who experienced circulation and socialization within milieus outside the established local hierarchies of class, custom, family, and lineage in their home villages. Thus, even as differences in pedagogical approach and theological orientation among these diverse Islamic schools continued to deepen in these years, the *madrasah*, *pesantren*, *pondok*, and *surau* all worked to create and sustain new, supralocal shared experiences, social imaginaries, and schoolboy networks among Islamic students whose overall numbers continued to dwarf those of pupils at the Dutch secular and missionary schools in the Indies at the time. Through these diverse schools and similarly diverse associational activities and publishing ventures, the late interwar era thus saw the expansion of a public sphere of religious discourse in which "Islam" became available for objectification and functionalization for a variety of purposes and projects.[44]

---

41. Alfian, *Muhammadiyah: The Political Behavior of a Muslim Modernist Organization under Dutch Colonialism* (Yogyakarta: Gadjah Mada University Press, 1989), 186–199, 302–314.

42. On Persatuan Islam, see Howard M. Federspiel, *Islam and Ideology in the Emerging Indonesian State: The Persatuan Islam (Persis), 1923 to 1957* (Leiden: Brill, 1997).

43. On the expansion of the Thawalib schools during this period, see, for example, Deliar Noer, *The Modernist Muslim Movement in Indonesia, 1900–1942* (Singapore: Oxford University Press, 1973), 46–56.

44. James T. Siegel, *The Rope of God* (Berkeley: University of California Press, 1969), 98–133; John R. Bowen, *Muslims through Discourse: Religion and Ritual in Gayo Society* (Princeton, NJ: Princeton University Press, 1993), 39–73.

With the expansion and diversification of Islamic educational and associational life in the late interwar era, moreover, came new calls for unity among Muslims and new claims to represent Muslims and Islam in the Indies. In the early–mid 1920s, the dismemberment of the Ottoman Empire, the dismantling of the caliphate, and other important developments across the Muslim world did generate interest, concern, and debate among Islamic activists and a broader Muslim audience in the Indies, as transmitted not only by the rising numbers of pilgrims making the Hajj to Mecca each year but also by the increasingly active and assertive community of students from the Indies at Al Azhar University in Cairo during these years.[45] The writings of the Cairo-based Islamic reformist Rashīd Riḍā on the caliphate in the early 1920s, for example, were widely reproduced, translated, and treated in Islamic publications across the archipelago.[46] As noted above, the caliphate congresses held in Mecca and Cairo in 1926 served as the focus of discussions among modernist activists in Sarekat Islam, Muhammadiyah, and Al-Irsyad, while occasioning the formation of the "traditionalist" association Nahdlatul Ulama in the same year.

As international controversies and conventions concerning Islam faded from view in the early 1930s, moreover, the focus turned to efforts to overcome differences and divisions among Muslims in the Indies. The diverse Islamic associations that had emerged in the 1910s and 1920s found themselves united in a public campaign to oppose the new restrictions on education imposed in 1932 under the Wild Schools Ordinance (De Wilde Scholen Ordonnantie), and the colonial government's withdrawal of the ordinance the following year demonstrated both the political imperative and the potential effectiveness of a united front among Islamic authorities across the Indies.[47] Thus, in 1937, Al-Madjlisul-Islamil-A'laa Indonesia (MIAI, or Supreme Council of Muslims of Indonesia) was formed by leaders of Muhammadiyah, Nahdlatul Ulama, Al-Irsyad, and Sarekat Islam, with additional groups joining and participating in a series of MIAI congresses held in 1938–1941.[48] On the eve of the Japanese occupation of Indonesia, a dense infrastructure for Islamic education and associational life was well established, as were institutional channels for the representation of Islam across the breadth of the archipelago.

---

45. William R. Roff, "Indonesian and Malay Students in Cairo in the 1920s," *Indonesia* 9 (April 1970): 73–87.

46. Laffan, *Islamic Nationhood and Colonial Indonesia*, 202–206. For Riḍā's famous tract, see Henri Laoust, *Le Califat Dans La Doctrine de Rašīd Riḍā: Traduction annotée d'al-Hilāfa au al-Imāma al-'uzmā (Le Califat ou l'Imāma supreme)* (Paris: Librairie d'Amérique et d'Orient, 1986).

47. Noer, *The Modernist Muslim Movement*, 179–183; Taufik Abdullah, *Schools and Politics: The Kaum Muda Movement in West Sumatra (1927–1933)* (Ithaca, NY: Cornell Modern Indonesia Project, 1971), 216–221.

48. Noer, *The Modernist Muslim Movement*, 242–247.

World War II and Japanese Occupation, 1942–1945

The *rust en orde* of the late interwar era in the Indies was interrupted and upended in March 1942 with the arrival of some fifty thousand Japanese troops in the archipelago and the onset of an occupation that would last through August 1945 and set the stage for the Revolusi to come. As noted above, the Dutch government had long been attentive to the rise of Japanese military might and imperial ambitions, dating back to the First Sino-Japanese War of 1894–1895 and growing with the Russo-Japanese War of 1904–1905, Japanese annexation of Korea in 1910, invasion and occupation of Manchuria from 1931, and the onset of the Second Sino-Japanese War in 1937. With German forces occupying the Netherlands from May 1940 and thousands of Japanese troops moving south into Vichy French–controlled Vietnam over the course of the same year, the Dutch government-in-exile shared British and American fears of Japanese designs on the oil reserves and other natural resources of the Indonesian archipelago.

Against this backdrop, the Dutch government-in-exile joined the United States and Great Britain in imposing an embargo on exports to Japan in July 1941, thus denying Japan the access to key raw materials it so desperately coveted, and helping to precipitate the Japanese attack on Pearl Harbor in early December of that year and the invasion of Southeast Asia over the following weeks.[49] By March 1942, interimperialist conflict had finally arrived on the shores of the Indies, with the Dutch government surrendering after little more than a week and Japanese forces occupying and governing the archipelago through August 1945.

While lasting less than three and a half years, the Japanese occupation combined in crucial ways with the legacies of the interwar era to help shape the varying possibilities for mobilization in the name of nationalism, communism, and Islam in the Revolusi that followed in its wake. For the avowed champions of nationalism, such as PNI and Partindo founder Soekarno and PNI Baru leader Mohammad Hatta, these years spelled release from confinement in internal exile, appointment to official advisory bodies by the Japanese authorities, and promises of formal Indonesian independence under "pan-Asian" auspices that had long interested a diverse range of Indonesian intellectuals and activists.[50] Alongside their ostensible role in advising the Japanese authorities and overseeing

---

49. Akira Iriye, *Power and Culture: The Japanese-American War, 1941–1945* (Cambridge, MA: Harvard University Press, 1981), 1–35, and Jonathan Marshall, *To Have and Have Not: Southeast Asian Raw Materials and the Origins of the Pacific War* (Berkeley: University of California Press, 1995).
50. Benedict Anderson, "Japan: The Light of Asia," in *Southeast Asia in World War II: Four Essays*, ed. Josef Silverstein (New Haven, CT: Yale University Council on Southeast Asia Studies, 1966), 13–50; Ethan Mark, "'Asia's' Transwar Lineage: Nationalism, Marxism, and 'Greater Asia' in an Indonesian Inflection," *Journal of Asian Studies* 65, no. 3 (August 2006): 461–493.

administration, Soekarno and his compatriots enjoyed unprecedented public prominence, especially on Java, thanks to Japanese-sponsored speaking tours and regular radio broadcasts, amplified by some fifteen hundred public loud-speakers set up in towns and cities across the island over the course of 1944.[51]

By March 1945, the Body to Consider Efforts in Preparation of Indonesian Independence (Badan Penyeledik Usaha Persiapan Kemerdekaan Indonesia, or BPKI) had convened under Soekarno's leadership, and by July of the same year, the Japanese government had announced the formation of a Committee for the Preparation of Indonesian Independence (Panitia Persiapan Kemerdekaan Indonesia, PPKI), with Soekarno assured that independence would be granted in a matter of weeks.[52] Thus, in a few short years, Soekarno and his nationalist compatriots were catapulted from confinement in internal exile to formal positions of nominal leadership over what would imminently become an ostensibly independent Indonesian nation-state.

On Java, moreover, the brief period of Japanese rule witnessed dramatic government policy changes that helped to expand the discursive and mobilizational infrastructure for Indonesian nationalism beyond the narrow confines of the Dutch-educated interwar nationalist elite. From March 1942, Dutch-language instruction was abolished and *Bahasa Indonesia* was elevated to official status (alongside Japanese) as the language of education and administration, with schools initially taking in unprecedented numbers to help fill a bureaucracy with expanded local participation, given the small numbers of Japanese military and civilian officials on hand to govern Java and the other islands of the archipelago.

From mid-1943, moreover, as the US military offensive in the Pacific began to accelerate, the Japanese authorities began to engage in large-scale efforts in mass mobilization across Java to assist in the war effort and in anticipation of an eventual Allied invasion. Japanese experiments with such mass mobilization included the short-lived Pusat Tenaga Kerja (Putera, or Manpower Center), which drew tens of thousands to its mass rallies; the Seinanden, or Barisan Pemuda (Youth Front), which brought together hundreds of thousands of young villagers from across Java for language training, agricultural work, and physical exercise; the Keibōdan, an auxiliary police force numbering more than one million; and by 1944, the Barisan Pelopor (Pioneer Front) of the Jawa Hōkōkai, an umbrella organization incorporating more than five hundred neighborhood associations (*tonarigumi*) and more than nine million residents across the island by the middle of that year.

Late 1943 also saw the formation of the Tentara Sukarela Pembela Tanah Air (Volunteer Army of the Defenders of the Homeland), known simply as Peta, a

---

51. Aiko Kurasawa, "Propaganda Media on Java under the Japanese, 1942–1945," *Indonesia* 44 (October 1987): 59–116, at 89–90.
52. Legge, *Sukarno*, 173–220.

military force with battalions five to six hundred-strong in each regency (*kabupaten*) across Java, with a combined troop strength of some thirty-seven thousand young men, with an auxiliary force, the Heihō, growing to some twenty-five thousand troops by 1945.[53] Meanwhile in Sumatra, equivalent organizations, such as Giyūgun, BOMPA (Badan Oentoek Membantu Pertahanan Asia), and the Kenkokutai Shinkai, likewise drew tens of thousands of young men from their villages into paramilitary training camps for weeks and months over the course of late 1943, 1944, and early 1945.[54]

Thus, beyond the unanticipated opportunities for accumulating political prominence and power accorded to nationalist leaders such as Soekarno, the Japanese occupation period incorporated unprecedented numbers of villagers on Java and elsewhere into a self-consciously Indonesian public sphere and into forms of supralocal socialization, solidarity, and paramilitary mobilization that would provide a powerful infrastructure for nationalist struggle. Just as decades of military conscription helped to turn peasants into Frenchmen from Bretagne to Provence over the course of the nineteenth century, so too—in dramatically accelerated fashion—did mass mobilization and paramilitary training help to turn peasants into Indonesians from the Oosthoek of Java to Aceh in northernmost Sumatra in 1943–1945.[55] "To youths of all strata who encountered one another" through paramilitary mobilization, "the experience generated that sense of mass power, of fraternal solidarity, of immense possibilities, that lies at the heart of popular nationalism."[56]

But even as the Japanese authorities installed long-exiled Dutch-educated nationalist leaders in positions of formal authority and expanded the orbit of national consciousness during the tumultuous years of occupation, so too did they dramatically enhance the opportunities for mobilization in the name of Islam. After all, like their German counterparts in World War I, Japanese "Pan-Asianists" had long claimed an affinity with Islamic causes, and, over the course of the early twentieth century, Islamic activists across the Muslim world had demonstrated a lively interest in the success of Japan in challenging the hegemony of the European imperial powers.[57]

---

53. Aiko Kurasawa, "Mobilization and Control: A Study of Social Change in Rural Java, 1942–1945" (PhD diss., Cornell University, 1988), 476–530; Shigeru Sato, *War, Nationalism and Peasants: Java under the Japanese Occupation, 1942–1945* (Sydney: Allen & Unwin, 1994), 53–72.

54. Anthony Reid, *The Blood of the People: Revolution and the End of Traditional Rule in Northern Sumatra* (Kuala Lumpur: Oxford University Press, 1979), 118–134.

55. Eugen Weber, *Peasants into Frenchmen: The Modernization of Rural France, 1870–1914* (Stanford, CA: Stanford University Press, 1976), 292–302.

56. Benedict Anderson, *Java in a Time of Revolution: Occupation and Resistance, 1944–1946* (Ithaca, NY: Cornell University Press, 1972), 30.

57. See Cemil Aydin, *The Politics of Anti-Westernism in Asia: Visions of World Order in Pan-Islamic and Pan-Asia Thought* (New York: Columbia University Press, 2007); Michael Laffan, "Tokyo as a Shared Mecca of Modernity: War Echoes in the Colonial Malay World," in *The Impact of the Russo-*

Thus, upon their arrival in the Indies, the Japanese authorities had elevated the recently formed Al-Madjlisul-Islamil-a'laa Indonesia to an officially recognized body and included the chairman of the modernist Islamic association Muhammadiyah, K .H. Mas Mansoer, among the privileged ranks of bodies such as the Central Advisory Board, alongside a handful of Dutch-educated figures such as Soekarno and Hatta. From mid-1943, moreover, the Japanese authorities organized special training (*latihan*) for Islamic scholars across Java, with some fifteen hundred *kyai* convened for a month of lectures, films, and discussion sessions on Japanese culture and history and the regional and international context for the war.[58] In 1944, moreover, the MIAI was replaced by a new body known as Masyumi (Majelis Syuro Muslimin Indonesia, or Indonesian Muslim Consultative Council), with Nahdlatul Ulama founder K. H. Hasyim Ashari as chairman, Muhammadiyah luminary Abdul Kahar Muzakkar as his deputy, and associations such as Muhammadiyah and Nahdlatul Ulama incorporated within its auspices, along with other groups and independent Islamic teachers of diverse pedagogical and theological orientations.[59]

Masyumi provided a new discursive and institutional infrastructure for Islam across Java. Communication was facilitated by regular Masyumi publications such as *Suara Muslimin Indonesia* and the fortnightly *Sinar*, which was issued in romanized Indonesian alongside Javanese and Sundanese in Jawi script, and by the activists of the Badan Propaganda Islam, who spoke regularly at public meetings and on radio broadcasts. Alongside the representation of Masyumi leaders within key advisory bodies of the Japanese administration, moreover, the organization itself served as the basis for the Shumubu or Kantor Urusan Agama (Office of Religious Affairs), with branches in each residency across Java, an apparatus entirely separate from the *priyayi*-staffed *pangreh praja*. From September 1944, moreover, Masyumi was tasked with recruiting young men from Islamic schools across Java into the ranks of a new Islamic paramilitary organization known as Hizbullah (Party of God), with camps in Bogor (West Java) and later Kediri (East Java) providing training for as long as seven months to thousands of Muslim youths in late 1944 and early 1945, and battalions formed in every regency of Java by the summer of 1945.[60] Mean-

Japanese War, ed. Rotem Kowner (London: Routledge, 2007), 219–238; Selçuk Esenbel, "Japan's Global Claim to Asia and the World of Islam: Transnational Nationalism and World Power, 1900–1945," *American Historical Review* 109, no. 4 (October 2004): 1140–1170; and Selçuk Esenbel, "Japan and Islam Policy during the 1930s," in *Turning Points in Japanese History*, ed. Bert Edström (London: RoutledgeCurzon, 2002), 180–214.

58. Kurasawa, "Mobilization and Control," 410–446.

59. Harry J. Benda, *The Crescent and the Rising Sun: Indonesian Islam under the Japanese Occupation, 1942–1945* (The Hague: W. Van Hoeve, 1958), 150–168.

60. Benda, *The Crescent and the Rising Sun*, 178–179; Raden Gatot Mangkupradja, "The Peta and My Relations with the Japanese: A Correction of Sukarno's Autobiography," *Indonesia* 5 (April 1968): 126–128.

while on Sumatra, a parallel process of mobilization in the name of Islam unfolded under Japanese auspices in 1943–1945, as seen in such organizations as the Majelis Agama Islam untuk Bantuan Kemakmuran Asia Timur Raya (Maibkatra, or Islamic Council for the Promotion of the Greater East Asian Co-Prosperity Sphere), the Majelis Islam Tinggi (High Council of Islam), and the paramilitary Sabilillah (The Cause of God). Overall, the brief period of Japanese occupation of the Indonesian archipelago thus helped to expand the discursive and mobilizational structures of Islam and to enhance their independence from other hierarchies of authority.

By contrast with Islam, the Japanese occupation period severely constrained opportunities for organization and mobilization by activists inspired by communism and other strains of revolutionary socialism in the Indonesian archipelago. Unlike neighboring Malaya, for example, where the Malayan Communist Party (MCP) led an armed guerrilla movement known as the Malayan People's Anti-Japanese Army (MPAJA), the prewar PKI was too small and weak to provide the basis for active resistance. Some left-wing activists affiliated with the strongly antifascist Gerindo (Gerakan Rakyat Indonesia) movement of the late 1930s ran a short-lived underground intelligence network funded by the Dutch government in exile under the leadership of Gerindo chairman Amir Sjarifuddin, with Surabaya as the hub of its activities. But Sjarifuddin was arrested and imprisoned in early 1943 and his network was effectively dismantled by the Japanese secret police.[61] Otherwise, on Java, small cells of the "Illegal PKI" appear to have survived in major cities and towns, and among railway workers, eluding Japanese surveillance but remaining largely inactive, even as Tan Malaka and the remnants of his PARI network likewise bided their time without engaging in any organizing activities.[62]

Meanwhile, in late 1944 and early 1945, Japanese naval intelligence officers (based on the 25th Army–controlled Java) established schools in Jakarta and Surabaya and enrolled hundreds of specially selected Indonesian youth, who were "taught to see Indonesia's independence as gaining freedom from the white capitalist and imperialist world," lectured on Marxism and, it appears, otherwise prepared for recruitment into a new clandestine network led by former PKI activists with close connections to Japanese naval intelligence.[63] On Sumatra, some

61. Kahin, *Nationalism and Revolution*, 111–112.

62. Anton Lucas, "The Communist Anti-Fascist Movement in Java," in *Local Opposition and Underground Resistance to the Japanese in Java, 1942–1945*, ed. Anton Lucas (Clayton, Victoria: Monash University Centre of Southeast Asian Studies, 1986), 3–119.

63. Abu Hanifah, *Tales of a Revolution* (Sydney: Angus and Robertson, 1972), 155–156. See also Kahin, *Nationalism and Revolution*, 115–121, and Anderson, *Java in a Time of Revolution*, 44–48. For background on the Japanese Navy and its long-standing conflict with the army over policy and strategy, see Michael A. Barnhart, *Japan Prepares for Total War: The Search for Economic Security, 1919–1941* (Ithaca, NY: Cornell University Press, 1987).

Gerindo activists with backgrounds in the PKI likewise had made contact with Japanese forces in Malaya prior to the March 1942 invasion, and such early assistance had won them influence, access, and, in some cases, official positions under the occupational regime, most notably in the recruitment and training of paramilitary groups such as the Giyūgun and the Kenkokutai Shinkai. Overall, there was no coherent or centralized Communist resistance organization or armed guerrilla movement across the archipelago; the Comintern was dissolved by Moscow in 1943 and transoceanic connections to other Communist parties were disrupted by the war. Only small nodes of residual PKI and PARI networks and new left-wing groupings remained, fragmented and scattered across Java and Sumatra, ready to be reactivated under more auspicious circumstances.

Ironically, however, the Dutch colonial regime's success in suppressing the PKI from the mid-late 1920s onward helped to create an unusual safe haven and site outside Indonesia for renewed political agitation by Communist activists: Australia. In the wake of the Japanese invasion in March 1942, the Dutch government in the Indies sought refuge for its personnel—and, crucially, the Dutch KPM shipping fleet—in Australia, with as many as ten thousand Indonesian merchant seamen, soldiers, civil servants, and medical orderlies in tow. Within a matter of weeks, some two thousand Indonesian seamen had gone on strike, refusing to work for the United States Army shipping armaments and personnel as part of the Allied war effort under conditions far more dangerous and demeaning—and for wages far more modest—than their Australian and Dutch counterparts.[64] Eventually arrested and incarcerated in POW camps on charges of mutiny, these Indonesian seamen's plight attracted the interest of the Communist-affiliated Seamen's Union of Australia, liberal clergymen, and civil libertarians, who campaigned successfully for their release and the renegotiation of their working conditions, and later assisted in the formation of the Indonesian Seamen's Union (Serikat Pelaut Indonesia or SARPELINDO).[65]

By mid-1943, moreover, Dutch ships had also transported to Sydney hundreds of political prisoners from its infamous internment camp in Boven Digoel, New Guinea, with PKI members arrested and imprisoned in the wake of the failed 1926–1927 rebellions heavily overrepresented among their numbers. On arrival in Sydney, these transported prisoners were surreptitiously whisked away by train to isolated internment camps, but not without one prisoner leaving a note describing the internees' plight on a railroad station platform, where it was discov-

---

64. Rupert Lockwood, "The Indonesian Exiles in Australia, 1942–47," *Indonesia* 10 (October 1970): 37–40.
65. For background, see Margo Beasley, *Wharfies: A History of the Waterside Workers' Federation of Australia* (Sydney: Halstead Press, 1996), and Julia Martinez, "'Coolies' to Comrades: Internationalism between Australian and Asian Seamen," in *Labour and Community: Historical Essays*, ed. Raymond Markety (Wollongong: University of Wollongong Press, 2001), 295–312.

ered by a puzzled railway worker and passed on to activists of the Civil Rights League of Australia, who took up their cause. By the end of 1943, a publicity campaign had led the Australian government to order the release of the Indonesian prisoners, and thus over the course of 1944 and early 1945 hundreds of PKI activists and other former political prisoners from Digoel were busy organizing with encouragement and support from Australian Communist comrades and fellow travellers, in anticipation of the approaching end of the war and the opening of new opportunities for a resumption of revolutionary struggle.[66]

Meanwhile, the deprivations and dislocations suffered by the broad mass of the population of the Indonesian archipelago under Japanese occupation undermined existing structures of authority and opened up unprecedented possibilities for revolutionary mobilization. On Java in particular, a harsh system of forced labor conscription known as *rōmusha* was imposed by the Japanese authorities and implemented by the local *pangreh praja*, targeting virtually all healthy men of working age. More than two million coolie laborers were mobilized to work under extremely difficult conditions on major infrastructure projects across Java and nearly three hundred thousand were transported to Sumatra, Borneo, and as far afield as Singapore and Siam to provide manpower for Japanese forces.[67]

Shortages of manpower led to declining agricultural production on Java, even as a system of forced delivery of rice (purchased by a newly formed government agency at very low prices) led to untold hardship for the peasantry.[68] Conditions on Sumatra and elsewhere were similarly dire. By 1945, the fabric of Indonesian society was stretched to a breaking point, as seen in a rash of small-scale uprisings and mutinies in the early months of the year, even as the Japanese authorities began to move toward formal granting of Indonesian independence as Allied forces approached and Japanese defeat drew near.

Thus, as World War II drew to a close, Java, Sumatra, and the other islands of the Indonesian archipelago were brought to the precipice of revolutionary mobilization by disparate forces drawn together by republicanism, communism, and Islam. The late interwar era of *rust en orde* under Dutch rule had seen the defeat and demobilization not only of the PKI and the Sarekat Islam, but also of the various initiatives launched in the late 1920s and early 1930s under the banner of nationalism. Yet the same years also saw the continuation and expansion of Islamic educational and associational activity across the Indies, and under the

66. Rupert Lockwood, *Black Armada* (Sydney: Australasian Book Society, 1975), 14–37; Jan Lingard, *Refugees and Rebels: Indonesian Exiles in Wartime Australia* (North Melbourne: Australian Scholarly, 2008), 61–101.
67. Kurasawa, "Mobilization and Control," 181–274; Sato, *War, Nationalism, and Peasants*, 154–200.
68. Kurasawa, "Mobilization and Control," 118–180; Ben Anderson, "The Problem of Rice," *Indonesia* 2 (October 1966): 77–123.

Japanese occupation unprecedented forms of authority and opportunities for communication and mobilization were afforded to those who claimed to speak in the name of Islam, as seen in the rise of Masyumi and its paramilitary force, Hizbullah. The Japanese occupation years also saw the dramatic reversal of fortunes for champions of republicanism such as Soekarno and Hatta, who reemerged after years in internal exile as figures with unrivalled access to the Indonesian public, through their official positions under the Japanese administration, their regular radio broadcasts and speaking tours, and their roles in formal bodies created to make preparations for Indonesian independence. Meanwhile, the late interwar era and the Japanese occupation period saw a sharp constriction of the available space for mobilization by activists working in the Communist tradition pioneered by the PKI.

Yet the inequities and injustices exacerbated by the Depression of the 1930s and the Japanese occupation of 1942–1945 combined with the deprivations and dislocations of World War II to revive hopes and dreams for social transformation. These aspirations greatly exceeded the discursive and organizational grasp of republican nationalism, on the one hand, and Islam, on the other, as seen in the resurfacing of the long-lost Tan Malaka, first in Sumatra, later in the Banten area of West Java, and finally in the capital city of Jakarta (once known as Batavia). With Japan's surrender in August 1945, the stage was thus set for the onset of a revolution in Indonesia animated by the diverse—and divisive—forces of republicanism, Communism, and Islam.

REPUBLICANISM, COMMUNISM, ISLAM

Revolusi, 1945–1949

Much as events in Cuba had helped both to enable and constrain the Philippine Revolution of 1896–1901, and much as World War I had precipitated revolutionary mobilization of varying success from St. Petersburg and Baku to Berlin, Budapest, and beyond in 1917–1920, so too did the specific circumstances of World War II shape the possibilities for revolution in Indonesia in the mid-1940s. It was the fall of Saipan to US forces in July 1944, after all, that had prompted Japanese prime minister Koiso's proclamation in September of that year that Indonesia would be granted independence "in the near future," given the anticipation of imminent American landings in the Philippines and consequent threats to the sea lanes between Indonesia and Japan. Paramilitary mobilization and training efforts were stepped up in late 1944 and early 1945, and, as noted above, an official body was convened in March 1945 to undertake initial preparations for Indonesian independence.

After consultations during the Potsdam Conference in July 1945, moreover, responsibility for the Netherlands East Indies and French Indochina were suddenly transferred from the South West Pacific Area Command (SWPA) under US general Douglas MacArthur headquartered in Manila to the South East Asia Command (SEAC) under Admiral Lord Louis Mountbatten based in Kandy, Ceylon (Sri Lanka), with the formal shift unfolding on August 15, the very same day Emperor Hirohito announced the surrender of Japan. This decision added half a million square miles of land to the one million already covered by the SEAC, and eighty more million people in addition to the forty-eight million already under its jurisdiction.[1] With British resources and troops already enormously over-stretched, priorities had to be established for the allocation of forces across a region that included former British colonies from India and Ceylon to Burma, Penang, Singapore, the Malay Peninsula, and North Borneo, leading some American commentators to dub the SEAC "Save England's Asian Colonies." In this context, British and other Allied troops were not to arrive in the Indonesian archipelago until the final days of September 1945, with Japanese troops tasked with maintaining order on Java, Sumatra, and elsewhere in the intervening weeks. Thus, the end of World War II presented revolutionaries in Indonesia with a protracted interregnum of severely compromised state sovereignty, a window of unprecedented opportunity for revolution.

Independence, Social Revolutions, and *Diplomasi* versus *Perjuangan*

Indeed, on August 17, 1945, just two days after the announcement of Japan's surrender and the shift of the Indies to Mountbatten's South East Asia Command, Indonesian independence was proclaimed in Jakarta, the news spreading across the breadth of the archipelago over the course of the next few days. Early August had seen the formation by the Japanese authorities of the new Panitia Persiapan Kemerdekaan Indonesia (Committee for the Preparation of Indonesian Independence, or PPKI), with delegates from across the Indonesian archipelago, and Soekarno and Hatta were flown to Saigon on August 8 to confer with high-ranking Japanese officials in advance of a formal announcement. But the Soviet declaration of war on Japan and the American bombing of Hiroshima and Nagasaki the following week undermined plans for a carefully stage-managed proclamation of Indonesian independence under Japanese auspices. On August 15, as rumors of the Japanese surrender began to circulate across Jakarta and beyond, a group of young activists (*pemuda*) approached Soekarno and Hatta and urged them to proclaim independence without further delay or involvement of the Japanese authorities. Soekarno and Hatta refused. The next day, August 16, the two men were roused from their slumbers, told that an imminent uprising jeopardized their safety, removed from their residences, and secretly relocated to the town of Rengasdengklok, some thirty miles outside Jakarta, on the initiative of the same

---

1. Benedict R. O'G. Anderson, *Some Aspects of Indonesian Politics under the Japanese Occupation: 1944–1945* (Ithaca, NY: Cornell Modern Indonesia Project, 1961), 89; Oey Hong Lee, *War and Diplomacy in Indonesia, 1945–1950* (Townsville, Queensland: James Cook University of North Queensland, 1981), 18–19; Christopher Bayly and Tim Harper, *Forgotten Wars: Freedom and Revolution in Southeast Asia* (Cambridge, MA: Harvard University Press, 2007), 159.

activists, who resumed their efforts to convince Soekarno and Hatta, but to no avail. It was only on the intercession of the senior Japanese naval officer on Java, Admiral Maeda, that Soekarno and Hatta were able to return to Jakarta the next day, and, after consultations with senior Japanese army officers, to reconvene the PPKI and, with both Maeda and a group of leading *pemuda* in attendance, to proclaim Indonesian independence on the morning of August 17, 1945. News soon spread across Java, Sumatra, and the other islands of the archipelago, and over the subsequent weeks, local branches of the newly formed Komité Nasional Indonesia Pusat (KNIP, or Central Indonesian National Committee) sprang up across Java, Sumatra, and elsewhere.[2]

This series of events presaged the complex dynamics and multifaceted dimensions of the Revolusi that began to unfold over the remaining months of 1945 and continued until the very end of the decade. On the one hand, the international context provided opportunities and constraints that would in various ways enable and inhibit revolutionary mobilization, and that defined victory in terms of the achievement of national *state* sovereignty. Thus, the Revolusi would involve not only Indonesians and Dutchmen, but Japanese, British, and American military officers, diplomats, and state leaders in key roles as well, and, as Soekarno and Hatta emphasized, *diplomasi* as well as formation of state-like structures, most notably an army, which conformed to the conventions of international society and would win recognition for the republic.

On the other hand, as Tan Malaka stressed, the Revolusi would require revolutionary struggle—*perjuangan*—by social forces mobilized not only in defense of the embryonic Indonesian Republic, but also by hopes and dreams, and forms of revolutionary brotherhood, associated with various strains of republicanism, communism, and Islam. These social forces demanded not only sovereignty for an independent Indonesian nation-state but popular sovereignty, that is, "sovereignty of the People," as seen in the Indonesian slogan *kedaulatan rakyat*. In *perjuangan* extending far beyond the Indonesian archipelago, the diverse and fragmented social forces mobilized by republicanism, communism, and Islam provided the crucial motive energy for the Revolusi, even as their differences and the countervailing, constraining imperative of *diplomasi* and state making would compromise the emancipatory promise of "freedom" that *kemerdekaan* (or simply *merdeka*) signified beyond the narrower meaning of "independence."[3]

---

2. On this series of events, see Benedict Anderson, *Java in a Time of Revolution: Occupation and Resistance, 1944–1946* (Ithaca, NY: Cornell University Press, 1972), 61–84. Note the pronounced left-wing orientation and subsequent affiliation of these young activists, who had been schooled in Marxist analysis and strongly socialized in the schools and dormitories set up by Japanese Naval Intelligence.

3. On this tension between the competing logics of *diplomasi* and *perjuangan*, see Anderson, *Java in a Time of Revolution*, 307–309.

These dynamics were evident in the messy and often bloody series of events that unfolded in late 1945 and 1946, in the first phase of the Indonesian Revolusi. In the weeks following the proclamation of Indonesian independence and in advance of the arrival of British troops in the archipelago, a process of revolutionary mobilization began to emerge, with armed groups surfacing in villages, towns, and cities across Java, Sumatra, and elsewhere to proclaim independence, to assert new forms of authority and, in some areas, to carry out local social revolutions of their own. In many cases, these local *lasykar* (militias) arose out of the ranks of the recently demobilized mass organizations and paramilitary formations recruited and trained by Japanese forces in 1943–1945, with former officers often reassuming commands and local Japanese garrisons and arsenals raided for weapons and ammunition. By late September 1945, the formation of such organized groups had combined with broader popular mobilization to lead to seizures of power in cities such as Surabaya, Semarang, Bandung, Malang, and Solo, with the Japanese authorities typically ceding what vestigial control they had retained in the face of large crowds carrying sharpened bamboo spears and other improvised weapons.[4]

October 1945 witnessed the arrival of British troops on Java and Sumatra and their forcible assumption of control over major urban centers, most famously in Surabaya, but beyond the major cities of the archipelago the Revolusi continued to unfold in late 1945 and well into 1946. Throughout much of the "Three Regions" (Tiga Daerah) of Brebes, Pemalang, and Tegal in the northern Central Javanese residency of Pekalongan, for example, local revolutionary groups mobilized as branches of the Komité Nasional Indonesia (KNI) to force out the local *pangreh praja* over the course of October 1945, with impromptu viva voce elections leading to the installation of local *kyai*, schoolteachers, former Sarekat Islam activists, and gangsters in their stead. These local *revolusi sosial* began in rural villages, taking village-level officials and Chinese-owned shops and rice mills as their initial targets, and soon shifted upward to district- and regency-level offices in the towns and cities of the Tiga Daerah.[5] A parallel process unfolded in the Banten region of West Java, with local officials from the village level up to *bupati* variously arrested, murdered, or forced into flight and replaced by local *kyai* elevated by popular acclamation, and a People's Council (Dewan Rakyat) formed by revolutionaries to impose order throughout the residency.[6]

---

4. George McTurnan Kahin, *Nationalism and Revolution in Indonesia* (Ithaca, NY: Cornell University Press, 1952), 134–146; Anderson, *Java in a Time of Revolution*, 125–166.

5. Anton Lucas, *One Soul One Struggle: Region and Revolution in Indonesia* (Sydney: Allen and Unwin, 1991), 103–189.

6. Michael C. Williams, *Communism, Religion, and Revolt in Banten* (Athens: Ohio University Center for International Studies, 1990), 275–309; Else Ensering, "Banten in Times of Revolution," *Archipel* 50 (1995): 131–164.

Meanwhile in northernmost Sumatra, Acehnese 'ulama and activists of the modernist Islamic association PUSA began to assemble in October and November 1945 and to rally behind the call for jihād. By early 1946, local revolutionary forces began to launch violent attacks on the local aristocrats (uleëbelang), oust them from local offices, and elect PUSA-linked 'ulama to serve in their stead throughout much of Aceh.[7] A similar series of events unfolded in East Sumatra in March 1946, as armed revolutionary bands attacked, forcibly evicted, arrested, or violently eliminated local sultans and rajahs, even as revolutionary lasykar seized lands across the vast Deli plantation belt for redistribution among workers and peasants.[8] In villages and towns elsewhere in Java and Sumatra, countless other small-scale revolusi sosial erupted in late 1945 and early 1946, with groups of armed revolutionaries engaging in autonomous acts to oust local aristocratic authorities and establish popular sovereignty (kedaulatan rakyat), with the term mendaulat acquiring currency in connection with

> the deposition, humiliation, kidnapping, or murder of hated officials or other representatives of authority. . . . In the wake of such daulat actions, improvised local governments were often formed under the loose control of the social revolutionaries, typically heterogeneous clusters of religious, military, and pemuda [youth] elements, frequently bearing romantic traditional or radical names.[9]

Islam and Communism: Organizational Infrastructure, International Support, 1945–1946

While these revolusi sosial were carried out against local aristocracies by locally recruited and mobilized revolutionary groups drawing on distinctly local grievances, memories, networks, and traditions, they depended heavily on communism and Islam in their discursive and mobilizational structures, and on cosmopolitan forms of revolutionary brotherhood stretching far beyond the Indonesian archipelago. Although local bandits and gangsters figured prominently

---

7. Anthony Reid, The Blood of the People: Revolution and the End of Traditional Rule in Northern Sumatra (Kuala Lumpur: Oxford University Press, 1979), 192–211.

8. H. Mohammed Said, "What Was the 'Social Revolution of 1946' in East Sumatra?," Indonesia 15 (April 1973): 145–186; Michael van Langenberg, "East Sumatra: Accommodating an Indonesia Nation within a Sumatran Residency," in Regional Dynamics of the Indonesian Revolution, ed. Audrey R. Kahin (Honolulu: University of Hawai'i Press, 1985), 113–144; Ann Laura Stoler, "Working the Revolution: Plantation Laborers and the People's Militia in North Sumatra," Journal of Asian Studies 47, no. 2 (May 1998): 227–247.

9. Anderson, Java in a Time of Revolution, 334–335.

among the leaders of the *lasykar* that spearheaded the *revolusi sosial* of late 1945 and early 1946, Islamic schools and Communist networks of prewar vintage provided an underlying infrastructure for revolutionary mobilization across Java and Sumatra.[10] The *lasykar* drew not only on solidarities developed during the accelerated paramilitary mobilization drives of the Japanese occupation but also on Islamic schools; Islamic associations such as Muhammadiyah, Nahdlatul Ulama (NU), and PUSA; and the Islamic militias Hizbullah and Sabilillah affiliated with Masyumi.[11]

These Islamic school networks and associations also provided supralocal structures of authority, as seen in the predominance of *kyai* and *'ulama* among the *bupati* and other local officials elected by acclamation in the wake of these local *revolusi sosial*.[12] Thus, the various calls for *jihad fi sabilillah* (Arabic: struggle in the cause of God), including *fātāwa* issued by NU and repeated appeals by Masyumi, linked the discursive frame and claims of Islam to a well-grounded infrastructure for mobilization in the name of the faith.[13]

At the same time, Communist networks variously rooted in the VSTP and the Sarekat Rakyat of the 1910s and 1920s, Tan Malaka's PARI of the late 1920s and 1930s, and the "Illegal PKI" and Gerindo of the late 1930s and early 1940s also provided a basis for recruitment and leadership in local revolutionary mobilization in many cases.[14] Tan Malaka himself had spent much of the Japanese occupation period working in a Mitsubishi-operated coal mine in Banten, and he evidently developed a local network that emerged as a prominent element of the *lasykar* mobilizations in the region in late 1945.[15] In East Sumatra, members of Gerindo, including some with PKI backgrounds, had risen to positions of prominence within the Japanese-run administration in 1943–1945 and played leading roles in reassembling many ex-Giyūgun officers and their troops in armed *lasykar* in late 1945, with long dormant PKI organizing networks soon revived among the workers on the Deli plantation belt.[16] Together and separately, the associational networks and egalitarian, universalist languages of Islam and communism

---

10. See, for example, Robert Cribb, *Gangsters and Revolutionaries: The Jakarta People's Militia and the Indonesian Revolution, 1945–1949* (Honolulu: University of Hawai'i Press, 1991).

11. Kevin W. Fogg, *Indonesia's Islamic Revolution* (Cambridge: Cambridge University Press, 2020), 66–78.

12. See the various overviews and regional studies cited in notes 5–8 above. See also John R. W. Smail, *Bandung in the Early Revolution, 1945–1946: A Study in the Social History of the Indonesian Revolution* (Ithaca, NY: Cornell Modern Indonesia Project, 1964), and David Charles Anderson, "Military Politics in East Java: A Study of the Origins and Development of the Armed Forces in East Java between 1945–1948" (PhD thesis, School of Oriental and African Studies, University of London, 1976).

13. Fogg, *Indonesia's Islamic Revolution*, 49–65. On NU's *resolusi Jihad*, see K. H. Saifuddin Zuhri, *Berangkat Dari Pesantren* (Jakarta: Gunung Agung, 1987), 254.

14. On the "Tiga Daerah" region of northern Central Java, for example, see Lucas, *One Soul One Struggle*, 55–65.

15. Williams, *Communism, Religion, and Revolt in Banten*, 283–289, 291–292.

16. Reid, *The Blood of the People*, 173–174.

provided mobilizational and discursive infrastructures for the overthrow of local aristocracies and the advancement of local *revolusi sosial.*

In late 1945 and 1946, moreover, the cosmopolitanism of communism and Islam combined with international circumstances and transnational solidarities to provide critical assistance to the Revolusi from locations outside the Indonesian archipelago, ranging from Australia to Penang, Singapore, and beyond. In Australia, PKI activists from among the former Boven Digoel internees had founded a New Indonesian Association (Sarekat Indonesia Baru) and coordinated with Indonesian sailors in various ports to establish SARPELINDO, the Indonesian Seamen's Union, which was affiliated with the Australian Seamen's Union, in late 1944. By mid-1945, these activists had worked with sympathetic Australians to set up Indonesian Independence Committees as well as an Australia-Indonesia Association, whose members included liberal intellectuals, clergymen, women's activists, and labor union leaders. It was against this backdrop that July 1945 saw the Labor government in Canberra reject a Dutch plan to use Australia as a base for the training and transportation of one hundred thousand troops to assist in reclaiming the Netherlands East Indies, as well as preparations for further resistance to the restoration of Dutch rule.[17]

In the aftermath of the proclamation of Indonesian independence in Jakarta, revolutionary activists in Australia immediately began to mobilize. By September 1945, with the full support of the Communist Party of Australia, the Waterside Workers' Federation, the Seamen's Union of Australia, and the 250,000-strong New South Wales Trades and Labour Council, Indonesian seamen had launched a dockside strike and imposed a "black ban" on Dutch ships and other vessels designated for use in transport of troops and supplies to the Indies. In Brisbane, Melbourne, Sydney, and Fremantle harbors, Indonesian crewmen deserted their ships and Australian longshoremen refused to load cargo, even as Indonesian soldiers in KNIL units stationed in various Dutch camps in Australia led a wave of small-scale mutinies against their Dutch commanders.[18] Dutch efforts to overcome the black ban by importing Indian seamen were foiled by the assiduous efforts of pro-Indonesian activists from the Indian Seamen's Union of Australia, who agitated among the ranks of the would-be strikebreakers and convinced them to join in the strike.[19] The militant Chinese Seamen's Union also gave its support.[20]

---

17. Jan Lingard, *Refugees and Rebels: Indonesian Exiles in Wartime Australia* (North Melbourne: Australian Scholarly, 2008), 103–122.

18. Rupert Lockwood, *Black Armada* (Sydney: Australasian Book Society, 1975); Lingard, *Refugees and Rebels*, 143–160.

19. Heather Goodall, "Port Politics: Indian Seamen, Australian Unions and Indonesian Independence, 1945–47," *Labour History* 94 (May 2008): 43–68.

20. Drew Cottle, "Forgotten Foreign Militants: The Chinese Seamen's Union in Australia 1942–1946," in *A Few Rough Reds: Stories of Rank and File Organising*, ed. Hal Alexander and Phil Griffiths,

Thanks to the coordinated efforts of Indonesian, Australian, Indian, and Chinese seamen, stevedores, and other supportive laborers and activists, the strike persisted into July 1946, and was later resumed in 1947 and 1948. All in all, the strike prevented more than 550 Indonesia-bound ships from embarking from Australian ports:

> Thirty-six merchant and troop ships, 21 Dutch vessels of war, two British troop ships, three Australian Navy vessels, two tankers and 35 smaller ocean-going oil-carrying crafts, and 450 power and dumb barges, lighters and surf-landing craft, essential to stevedoring in Indonesian ports without wharves, in shallow estuaries, rivers and canals. Among Dutch cargoes held by boycott on Australian wharves and warehouses were munitions, uniforms, foodstuffs, over 1,000 motor-trucks, cement, canvas and other items of military value.[21]

The impact on Dutch efforts to reestablish control over the Indies in 1945–1946 was considerable:

> The Netherlands armed forces, despite the bridgeheads won for them in Java by the British, had no chance of immediate or effective offensives against the Republic without the 450 barges, lighters and surf-boats and the fuel transport craft held in the hammerlock of the Australian boycott. . . . Without power and dumb barges the Dutch could not handle war cargoes, except at Batavia and a few other points, and could not use canal and streams to penetrate inland and prevent consolidation of Republican bases.[22]

Meanwhile, linkages to Singapore and Penang produced additional forms of external support for the Revolusi. In October 1945, Indonesian workers in Singapore formed the Persatuan Kaum Buruh Indonesia (Indonesian Labor Association) in affiliation with the Communist-controlled General Labour Union, and these activists soon launched their own waterfront work stoppages to prevent the departure of vessels laden with troops or materials to assist the Dutch in restoring colonial rule across the Indonesian archipelago.[23] More important, late 1945 and early 1946 saw the establishment of trade linkages between areas of Sumatra under the control of revolutionary *lasykar*, on the one hand, and Singapore and

---

(Canberra: Australian Society for the Study of Labour History, 2003), 136–151; Lockwood, *Black Armada*, 168–170.

21. Rupert Lockwood, "The Indonesian Exiles in Australia, 1942–47," *Indonesia* 10 (October 1970): 52.

22. Lockwood, *Black Armada*, 294–295.

23. Yong Mun Cheong, *The Indonesian Revolution and the Singapore Connection* (Singapore: National University of Singapore Press, 2003), 28–32.

Penang, on the other. Dutch intelligence reports tracking flows of rubber from *lasykar*-controlled plantations in East Sumatra estimated that some 30,000 tons worth nearly 11 million Straits dollars were shipped in February–April 1946 alone, with well over one hundred million dollars' worth of plantation produce transported by November of that year.[24] The export of Sumatran rubber, palm oil, sisal, and other commodities helped to pay for the purchase of huge quantities of "rifles, machine guns, revolvers, grenades, ammunition, motor vehicles, uniforms, helmets, boots and other military equipment from Malaya/Singapore."[25] Such trade with Singapore in support of the Revolusi extended via Palembang to *pasisir* ports such as Cirebon and Tegal on the north coast of Java, and Probolinggo on the Oosthoek along the Madura Strait, with exports of Javanese plantation produce similarly matched by imports of weapons and other war matériel.[26] Working closely with various revolutionary authorities in Java and Sumatra, prewar networks of political activists, Islamic schools, and "Chinese" businessmen extending across the Indonesian archipelago to Singapore and Penang played a key role in facilitating this trade.[27]

Beyond Southeast Asia, transoceanic Islamic connections provided important bases for solidarity with and support for the Revolusi. Such connections extended as far as Mecca, where as many as four thousand Southeast Asian Muslims congregated during the Hajj season of 1945, and Cairo, the global hub of Islamic reformism, the vibrant center of Arab nationalism, and, thanks to the Suez Canal, a major gateway for international maritime trade.[28] Indonesian students in Cairo and their counterparts in Baghdad and Mecca organized in support of the Revolusi and waged a protracted campaign in the media to draw attention to the ongoing struggle in the Indonesian archipelago.[29] Thanks to their efforts, Arabic newspapers carried statements in support of the Revolusi and news stories about developments in Indonesia, Radio Cairo played "Indonesia Raya" and other songs and speeches in support of the Republik, and governments were successfully lobbied to win the Arab League's official recognition of the Republik in

24. Reid, *The Blood of the People*, 220.

25. Michael van Langenberg, "National Revolution in North Sumatra: Sumatera Timur and Tapanuli, 1942–1950" (PhD thesis, University of Sydney, 1976), 528, 732–734; Audrey R. Kahin, *Rebellion to Integration: West Sumatra and the Indonesian Polity* (Amsterdam: Amsterdam University Press, 1999), 148–151.

26. Robert Cribb, "Opium and the Indonesian Revolution," *Modern Asian Studies* 22, no. 4 (1988): 710.

27. Twang Peck Yang, *The Chinese Business Élite in Indonesia and the Transition to Independence, 1940–1950* (Kuala Lumpur: Oxford University Press, 1998), 195–253.

28. Valeska Huber, *Channelling Mobilities: Migration and Globalisation in the Suez Canal Region and Beyond, 1869–1914* (Cambridge: Cambridge University Press, 2013).

29. For background on Indonesian students in Cairo, see Michael Laffan, "An Indonesian Community in Cairo: Continuity and Change in a Cosmopolitan Islamic Milieu," *Indonesia* 77 (April 2004): 1–26.

November 1946.[30] These efforts also led Al-Azhar, the oldest and most prestigious center of Islamic scholarship in the Muslim world, to issue a *fatwa* in October 1946 to declare pilgrimage traffic to Mecca on Dutch ships to be *haram* (i.e., proscribed according to Islamic law), a ruling that was widely disseminated during the Hajj season in 1947 and eventually helped to overcome the initial hesitation (and Dutch counterpressures) delaying official recognition of the Republik by the Kingdom of Saudi Arabia.[31]

Thanks to transoceanic Islamic solidarity, such efforts on behalf of the Revolusi by Indonesian students in Cairo also bore fruit in concrete terms paralleling those of their Communist counterparts in Australia. The early postwar years in Egypt saw increasing labor activism and political mobilization, building up to the strike wave of September 1947 through April 1948, with nationalist, Communist, and Islamist organizers establishing strong linkages to different unions across the country.[32] In the harbors of the key ports of the Suez Canal, the dockworkers' unions were largely affiliated with the Muslim Brothers (Al-Ikhwān ul-Muslimīn), who had emerged in 1928 in the mid-canal city of Ismailia and expanded their influence along the waterway northward to Port Said and southward to Suez.[33] Thanks to Indonesian and Ikhwān activists, the passage through the Suez Canal of a Dutch warship carrying two thousand troops to provide reinforcements for the first Dutch "Police Action" against the Republik in July 1947 occasioned mass mobilization in support of the Revolusi:

> On 9 August 1947, the ship *Volendam* arrived at Port Said. Thousands of local residents and workers gathered in the harbor and dozens of motorboats circled the opening of the waterway, blocking the motorboats owned by foreign companies that were trying to bring food and water to the ship. These motorboats were filled with militant workers, especially those from the Muslim Brothers carrying Indonesian flags and pictures of King Farouk.[34]

A local journalistic account of what followed is worth citing in full:

---

30. Kevin W. Fogg, "Islam in Indonesia's Foreign Policy, 1945–1949," *Al-Jāmiah: Journal of Islamic Studies* 53, no. 2 (2015): 303–335. See also Muhammad Zein Hassan, *Diplomasi Revolusi di Luar Negeri (Perjoangan Pemuda/Mahasiswa Indonesia di Timur Tengah)* (Jakarta: Bulan Bintang, 1980).

31. Hassan, *Diplomasi Revolusi di Luar Negeri*, 169–171.

32. Joel Beinin and Zachary Lockman, *Workers on the Nile: Nationalism, Communism, Islam, and the Egyptian Working Class, 1882–1954* (Princeton, NJ: Princeton University Press, 1987), 330–362.

33. Beinin and Lockman, *Workers on the Nile*, 384–388. On the founding and early years of the Muslim Brothers, see Richard P. Mitchell, *The Society of the Muslim Brothers* (Oxford: Oxford University Press, 1969), and Brynjar Lia, *The Society of the Muslim Brothers in Egypt: The Rise of an Islamic Mass Movement, 1928–1942* (Reading: Ithaca Press, 2006).

34. Hassan, *Diplomasi Revolusi di Luar Negeri*, 234. Translation by the author.

The protesters chased the motorboats trying to bring water and food to the ship and forced them back to the harbor. After half an hour, the ship docked and a motorboat carrying water and food, tightly guarded by twenty armed policemen, came alongside the ship. On board was Mr. Blackfield, Honorary Consul of the Netherlands, an Englishman who served as director of a company handling Dutch ship traffic in the harbor.

The motorboats filled with Egyptian workers chased after this motorboat and some of the workers managed to jump on board. They attacked the crew, seized control of the steering wheel, and turned the boat around, kicking off the crewmen when they tried to retake the helm. The consul would have been badly beaten up if the deputy harbormaster and police chief had not arrived at the last minute.

Mr. Blackfield threatened to have the Dutch government protest the humiliating treatment he had experienced and the protesters' shouts of verbal abuse against the Dutch. He also threatened to take unilateral action together with the two thousand Dutch soldiers on the ship to seize control of the harbor if ordered was not immediately restored.

Mahmud Sabit Bey, the deputy police chief of the Suez Canal, who had come on board the motorboat, tried to assuage Mr. Blackfield while explaining to him that the people's anger he had witnessed was really a manifestation of the flood of sympathy they felt for their brothers in faith. All day and all night, the newspapers and radio broadcasts reported news of Dutch aggression against the Muslim people of Indonesia. They didn't mean to insult or hurt the consul. The police had managed to save him from the danger he had needlessly created for himself. He was also warned not to make baseless accusations to the Egyptian police.[35]

In the end, as an Indonesian activist noted:

The ship left Port Said at midnight with a police motorboat escort, but without receiving food or water. It was only in the harbor of Ismailia, which was entirely controlled by the English, that the ship received proper provisioning. In the harbor of Suez, still accompanied by police motorboats, the ship was met by thousands of workers and the general public with shouts of *Merdeka!* accompanied by the waving of Indonesian flags and hostile shouts of abuse. Along the full length of the canal, from Port Said to Suez, the ship was shadowed by hundreds of *pemuda.*

---

35. Hassan, 234–235. Translation by the author.

> Thereafter, every Dutch ship that passed through the Suez Canal experienced the same treatment.[36]

Thus, in very concrete and crucial ways, the linkages, networks, and solidarities of communism and Islam stretching across and beyond the Indonesian archipelago helped to provide sources of sustenance for the Revolusi and to compromise and complicate its enemies' counterrevolutionary efforts.

Diplomasi and *Perjuangan*, Recognition and Revolution

Yet the surge of revolutionary mobilization unfolding across Java and Sumatra in late 1945 and well into 1946 with such strong support from Communist and Islamic networks and such demonstrations of solidarity from beyond the archipelago soon ran up against considerable external constraints and internal conflicts.[37] On the one hand, with the arrival of British troops in October 1945 came the imperative of establishing *kedaulatan rakyat* (popular sovereignty) across the Indonesian archipelago and winning international recognition for such sovereignty as the Dutch government began to reassert its claims to the Netherlands East Indies and to attempt to restore colonial rule. This imperative was accompanied by related exigencies, such as the elaboration of a form of government—and governance—whose authority would be externally acknowledged and accepted.

On the other hand, with the mobilization of local *lasykar* in the weeks following the Japanese surrender and the unfolding of small-scale social revolutions in parts of Java and Sumatra during subsequent months came the challenge of controlling and channelling the popular energies and aspirations unleashed by the violent onset of the Revolusi. Given the vast extent of the Indonesian archipelago and its variegated ethnic, linguistic, and religious landscape, the dangers of centrifugal anomie, incoherence, and anarchy within the Revolusi remained quite pronounced. As a recent study of the revolutionary mobilization among the ethnic Karo areas of upland northern Sumatra concluded:

> Popular violence was, at one time or another, directed against local officials who had cooperated with the Japanese or the Dutch; village moneylenders, entrepreneurs, and wealthy landowners; lowland refugees and political prisoners, including those who were ethnically Karo; support-

---

36. Hassan, 235–236. Translation by the author.
37. The following discussion of these constraints and conflicts draws heavily from the analysis provided in Anderson, *Java in a Time of Revolution*, perhaps articulated most clearly and concisely on pp. 307–309.

ers of left- or right-wing political organizations or members of rival fighting units; and those who signalled, intentionally or not, some perceived affinity with the Dutch. But in a broad sense, repolusi [*sic*] stood not for a specific moment or event but for a condition of pervasive fear and indiscriminate violence, in which *anyone* could become a victim. . . .

When Karo men and women began to imagine independence in 1945, they did so in ways that had little, if anything, to do with "Indonesia" as a historically given national entity or even a conceptually useful political object. The kind of community they imagined in stories of mobilization, aspiration, and even revolutionary violence had to do with more intimate forms of comradeship, equality, and social justice.[38]

Even in and around Jakarta, the multiplicity of *lasykar* made for a similarly expansive understanding and experience of *kedaulatan rakyat* and an equally immense challenge for the establishment of revolutionary state power:

Their numbers ran into the hundreds and they ranged from the quasi-military BKR (*Badan Keamanan Rakyat,* or People's Security Bodies), moderately well-armed and dominated by former members of the Jakarta PETA, to small and evanescent clusters of young people of both sexes, armed, if at all, with bamboo spears. They formed, typically, around existing social nuclei in local bosses, religious leaders, ethnic associations, semi-skilled labor groups, school groups, neighborhood associations and the many youth groups set up by the Japanese, and they drew on the increased organizational experiences and political mobilization which people had gained during the Japanese period. Only a few, however, had definite political affiliation beyond their nationalism. What they had in common was a fervent desire to share the state of mind that was the Republic. The idea of the Republic and the idea of independence were inextricably intertwined; to act as a free Indonesian was to embody the Republic and the way to demonstrate one's acceptance of the Republic was to act and to exult in the freedom to act.[39]

In the face of these external constraints and internal challenges, the embryonic and embattled Republik Indonesia moved quickly to establish recognizable institutions of republican, representative government through which to absorb

---

38. Mary Margaret Steedley, *Rifle Reports: A Story of Indonesian Independence* (Berkeley: University of California Press, 2013), 61, 319.

39. Robert Cribb, *Gangsters and Revolutionaries: The Jakarta People's Militia and the Indonesian Revolution, 1945–1949* (Honolulu: University of Hawai'i Press, 1991), 62.

and appropriate for itself the popular energies and aspirations embodied in the slogan *kedaulatan rakyat*. Within days of the proclamation of independence in August 1945, the Committee for the Preparation of Indonesian Independence (Panitia Persiapan Kemerdekaan Indonesia, or PPKI) in Jakarta had elected Soekarno as president and Hatta as vice president and promulgated a constitution. By the end of the month, a cabinet was formed, filled almost entirely by men who, like Soekarno and Hatta, had occupied senior positions under the Japanese administration. With the dissolution of the PPKI, moreover, the Komité Nasional Indonesia Pusat (KNIP, or Central Indonesian National Committee) was constituted in late August 1945 as an advisory body, with more than one hundred members drawn from diverse regions, religions, and realms of public life across the Indonesian archipelago, and provincial-level counterpart KNIs were established during the following months. Meanwhile, the same weeks saw the formal establishment of a Badan Keamanan Rakyat (People's Security Body, or BKR), which morphed into the Tentara Keamanan Rakyat (People's Security Army, or TKR) in October 1945; the Tentara Rakyat Indonesia (Indonesian People's Army, or TRI) in January 1946; and finally, the Tentara Nasional Indonesia (Indonesian National Army, or TNI) in August 1947.[40]

By October 1945, moreover, the landings of British forces prompted the leadership of the Republik in Jakarta to move further to enhance its credibility as a representative, responsible, and respectable government. The KNIP was converted from a purely advisory body into a quasi-legislative body sharing authority with the president until a proper parliament could be elected and convened. A smaller Working Group (Badan Pekerja, or BP-KNIP) was also formed under the leadership of Sutan Sjahrir, the prominent political activist of the late interwar era whose years of internment in Boven Digoel in the 1930s and subsequent leadership of underground resistance to the Japanese occupation had earned him impeccable credentials—domestically and internationally—sorely lacking among Soekarno, Hatta, and the members of their appointed cabinet. The same month also saw the publication of Sjahrir's pamphlet *Perjuangan Kita* (Our Struggle), a manifesto that denounced the xenophobic and demagogic *nasionalisme* of the likes of Hitler and called for an Indonesian Revolusi informed by liberal internationalism and democratic socialism, focused against "bureaucratic feudalism" while amenable to compromise with global capital.[41] Meanwhile, October 1945 also witnessed not only the formal reconstitution of the Badan Keamanan Rakyat as the Tentara Keamanan Rakyat (TKR, or People's Security Army) but also the recruitment of

---

40. Anderson, *Java in a Time of Revolution*, 85–166.
41. Rudolf Mrázek, *Sjahrir: Politics and Exile in Indonesia* (Ithaca, NY: Cornell University Southeast Asia Program, 1994), 269–283.

former officers of the Dutch colonial army, the KNIL, to senior positions in the new military formation, most notably the high-ranking and highly respected Urip Sumoharjo as TKR chief of staff.

By November 1945, moreover, in the wake of the violence in Surabaya and the onset of local social revolutions elsewhere, the republican government in Jakarta took crucial steps to establish its linkages to the diverse popular energies and aspirations mobilized in localities across Java, Sumatra, and elsewhere in the Indonesian archipelago. Under Sjahrir's leadership, the BP-KNIP suggested that political parties be freely established and that cabinet ministers be made responsible to the pseudoparliamentary KNIP rather than just the president, a proposal that was quickly accepted and acted on, as seen in the dismissal of the cabinet and formation of a new one headed by Sjahrir in mid-November 1945. Against this backdrop, November 1945 saw the formation of a multitude of political parties and other organizations in Jakarta and elsewhere across the Indonesian archipelago, with the three main forces of nationalism, Islam, and communism represented along the lines Soekarno presaged and promoted in his 1927 call for an alliance of *Nasionalisme, Agama* (religion), and *Komunisme* (*NASAKOM*). First, a new Partai Nasional Indonesia (PNI) was constituted in November 1945 out of the remnants of its various predecessor parties of the 1920s and 1930s, drawing into its orbit not only older intellectuals and activists but also civil servants, professionals, and members of local aristocracies aligned with the Republik, in other words a party closely identified not only with Soekarno but with the embryonic national *state*.[42] Second, Masyumi (Majelis Syuro Muslimin Indonesia, or Council of Indonesian Muslim Associations) was similarly reconstituted in November 1945, drawing on the infrastructure established under the Japanese administration and including all its constituent associations, including Muhammadiyah and Nahdlatul Ulama (NU), thus representing the sprawling networks of both modernist and traditionalist Islamic schools across the archipelago.[43]

Third and finally, the Partai Komunis Indonesia (PKI) officially reemerged out of obscurity in November 1945, albeit without the built-in advantages of the PNI and Masyumi from the Japanese period, and instead with its activists depleted and divided by nearly two decades of repression, recriminations, and relocations after the failed rebellions of 1926–1927. Alongside the formal reemergence of the PKI, November thus saw the formation of a new Partai Buruh Indonesia (Indonesian Labor Party, or PBI) and Pesindo (Pemuda Sosialis Indonesia, or Indonesian

---

42. Anthony Reid, *The Indonesian National Revolution, 1945–1950* (Victoria: Longman, 1974), 85–86.

43. Fogg, *Indonesia's Islamic Revolution*, 141–155.

Socialist Youth), followed shortly thereafter by the establishment of the Partai Sosialis in December 1945 as a fusion of two short-lived separate socialist parties formed the preceding month. All of these organizations counted numerous former PKI activists and fellow travellers in their ranks and among their leaders.[44]

It was thus with a noncollaborationist prime minister, a professional army leadership, and a seemingly more presentable cabinet and pseudoparliamentary KNIP that the Republik began to engage in both external *diplomasi* and internal *perjuangan* in late 1945 and early 1946. But the results were decidedly limited. By the end of November 1945, Surabaya had fallen under Allied control, as had other major cities on Java and Sumatra, and the restoration of Dutch control over virtually all of the eastern half of the archipelago had been realized. By the end of the year, the arrival and assertiveness of Dutch troops in Jakarta made the security of the Republican leadership so untenable that in early 1946 the capital of the Republik was relocated to the central Javanese city of Yogyakarta, where the headquarters of the Tentara Keamanan Rakyat (People's Security Army), now renamed the Tentara Rakyat Indonesia (Indonesian People's Army), had been established. Against this backdrop, negotiations brokered by the British government between the Republik and the Dutch government proceeded in early 1946 from a position of republican weakness, with Prime Minister Sjahrir soon signalling his willingness to concede to Dutch proposals for the absorption of the Java-based Republik within a federal United States of Indonesia still associated with the Netherlands.

The Republik similarly remained fragile vis-à-vis the diverse popular energies and aspirations mobilized in revolutionary struggle. Sjahrir's cabinet, after all, was filled with university-educated, Dutch-speaking intellectuals, with Christians overrepresented and no prominent representative of Islamic associations among its members. The various political parties that sprang up in late 1945, moreover, appeared to be "little more than clusters of small personal cliques originating in the politics of the prewar period, without "any organized base among the masses, even in the urban areas."[45] The incipient efforts of the new army leadership to create a professional military under a unified command likewise seemed to carry little prospect for immediate success given the highly localized and personalized forms of leadership, recruitment, and sourcing of arms and ammunition.[46]

44. Harry Poeze, *Tan Malaka, Gerakan Kiri, dan Revolusi Indonesia Jilid 1: Agustus 1945–Maret 1946* (Jakarta: KITLV Jakarta/Yayasan Obor Indonesia, 2008), 151–154.

45. Anderson, *Java in a Time of Revolution*, 230.

46. Selo Soemardjan, "Bureaucratic Organization in a Time of Revolution," *Administrative Science Quarterly* 2, no. 2 (September 1957): 182–199, especially 189–193.

Revolutions within the Revolusi, 1946–1947

Against this backdrop, the fate of the Revolusi over 1945–1949 depended heavily both on forces other than those narrowly defined by nationalism and by factors beyond the boundaries of the Indonesian nation-in-waiting. As already evident in the role of left-wing *pemuda* in forcing Soekarno and Hatta to proclaim Indonesian independence in August 1945, the rather disorganized and divided set of forces rooted in the partially reconstituted remnants of the PKI were to play a crucial role in articulating popular energies, organizing mass mobilization, and exerting pressure for continued *perjuangan* and against overly conciliatory *diplomasi* with the Dutch government. As already foreshadowed in discussions among Truman, Churchill, and Stalin in Potsdam in July 1945 about the liberation of Southeast Asia, moreover, the international constellation of cooperation and conflict among the Great Powers—and, in particular, the onset of the Cold War—was also destined to prove decisive in the contestation between the Republik and the Netherlands over their competing claims of sovereignty over the Indonesian archipelago. Thus, from within and without, the real and imagined possibilities represented by communism shaped the overall trajectory and ultimate outcome of the Revolusi in important ways.

The centrality of communism to the fate of the Revolusi was clear from the outset. Early 1946, for example, witnessed the mounting of a major challenge to the Republik from within, a "revolution within the Revolution" led by none other than Tan Malaka, the long-exiled former PKI leader who had returned to Indonesia in early 1942, remained incognito throughout the Japanese occupation period, and then resurfaced in Jakarta in August to reveal his identity and resume a role among those caught up in the onset of the Revolusi.[47] While maintaining a discreet distance from the republican government as it emerged and evolved in August–November 1945, Tan Malaka reappeared in early December 1945 with the publication of a pamphlet titled *Muslihat* (Strategy), which countered the Republican leadership's call for a conciliatory approach to the Dutch with a call for armed guerrilla warfare and sustained popular resistance.[48] In early January 1946, moreover, he spoke at a large public meeting held in the town of Purwokerto in Central Java, where he urged the creation of a popular front uniting socialists, religious

---

47. Tan Malaka, *Dari Pendjara ke Pendjara Jilid II* (Jakarta: LPPM Tan Malaka, 2007), 197–323. For an English translation of the original (1947 or 1948) Indonesian text by Helen Jarvis, see Tan Malaka, *From Jail to Jail* (Athens: Ohio University Center for International Studies, 1991), 2:119–196.

48. Tan Malaka, *Moeslihat* (Jogjakarta: Badan Oesaha Penerbitan Nasional Indonesia, 1945), republished as Tan Malaka, *Muslihat, Politik dan Rencana Ekonomi Berjuang* (Yogyakarta: Penerbit Narasi, 2014).

believers, and nationalists behind the slogan *Merdeka Seratus Persen* (100 Percent Freedom) and a Minimum Program requiring the departure of all foreign troops from the Indonesian archipelago, the formation of a people's government and a people's army, and nationalization of plantations and industrial enterprises.

A second public meeting several days later in the Central Javanese city of Solo attracted representatives from a diverse range of organizations and parties and occasioned the formation of a popular front under the banner of Persatuan Perjuangan (Struggle Union), with Tan Malaka soon joined by figures from Pesindo, Partai Sosialis, PBI, PKI, and various other organizations including Masyumi and the army, thus posing a major challenge to the republican government. In mid-February 1946, the Persatuan Perjuangan organized a massive demonstration in Yogyakarta, and within a few short weeks Prime Minister Sjahrir had tendered his resignation and a new Persatuan Perjuangan–based cabinet with Tan Malaka as its leader seemed to be in the cards. The broad-based revolutionary mobilization encompassing Islam and communism advocated by Tan Malaka so earnestly but unsuccessfully at the Fourth Comintern Congress in Moscow in 1922 now finally appeared to be coming to fruition.[49]

But the divisions between and among the parties and organizations representing Islam on the one hand and various shades of socialism and communism on the other were too great to overcome the built-in impediments to this kind of commitment to *perjuangan*. March 1946 saw Sjahrir's reinstatement as prime minister and the formation of a new cabinet in which Masyumi was more strongly represented alongside Sjahrir's Partai Sosialis, signalling its abandonment of Persatuan Perjuangan. At the same time, the inclusion in the cabinet of Pesindo founder Amir Sjarifuddin as defense minister and API (Angkatan Pemuda Indonesia, or Indonesian Youth Generation) Wikana as minister of state for youth affairs signalled the defection of these popular organizations from Persatuan Perjuangan, evidencing the continuing divisiveness of Tan Malaka's leadership and internal divisions on the Left. By the end of March 1946, Tan Malaka and his closest comrades had been arrested and imprisoned by the republican government, and Sjahrir had resumed negotiations with the Dutch government, offering important new concessions behind the scenes.

Against this backdrop, by November 1946, with all British forces now departed from the Indonesian archipelago and tens of thousands of Dutch troops occupying Jakarta and other major Indonesian cities, a reconsolidated republican government firmly recommitted to *diplomasi* over *perjuangan* had signed an agreement with the Netherlands extending a ceasefire and incorporating the Republik on

---

49. See Anderson, *Java in a Time of Revolution*, 269–295; Poeze, *Gerakan Kiri, Tan Malaka, dan Revolusi Indonesia Jilid 1*, 207–335.

Java, Madura, and Sumatra within an otherwise effectively Dutch-controlled United States of Indonesia, which would be subsumed within a Netherlands–Indonesian Union alongside Suriname and the Netherlands Antilles. Plantations and other enterprises would be restored to their prewar Dutch owners, and private property would otherwise be guaranteed.[50] The Republik had committed itself to something far short of the "100 Percent Merdeka" called for by Tan Malaka.

Indeed, the November 1946 Linggadjati Agreement presaged a dramatic narrowing of the possibilities for the Revolusi under Soekarno and Sjahrir's *diplomasi*-focused strategy for the Republik. Over the following months, the Dutch strengthened their control over major cities on Java and Sumatra, maintained an economic blockade on the Republik, and established a set of puppet states in eastern Indonesia, Kalimantan (Borneo), and the Pasundan area of West Java. Republican protests against the Dutch interpretation and implementation of the Linggadjati Agreement generated little positive response, as seen in the Dutch Parliament's ratification of a considerably restricted version of the accord. By June 1947, mounting dissatisfaction within the Republik had percolated up into the government itself, with increasingly vehement condemnation of Sjahrir's policies forcing his resignation by the end of the month. In late July 1947, moreover, a so-called police action involving some one hundred thousand troops saw a Dutch military campaign on Java leading to the reduction of the Republik to parts of Central and East Java and economically marginal areas of Sumatra. With Dutch control over major ports, interisland shipping routes, the railways, and the plantation belts of Java and Sumatra, as well as the remaining areas of Borneo and eastern Indonesia, *diplomasi*, it was clear, had led only to a drastic diminution of the Republik and the Revolusi.[51]

Against this backdrop, the remaining months of 1947 saw the belated rise to power within the Republik of the so-called Sayap Kiri (Left-Wing) forces under the leadership of Amir Sjarifuddin, the former Gerindo chairman, resistance leader, and Pesindo founder who had served continuously as minister of defense in Sjahrir's cabinets since November 1945. Sjarifuddin had joined forces with Sjahrir in the formation of a new cabinet in November 1945 and in a fused Partai Sosialis in December of that year, but his affiliations and orientation had long been more left-leaning, as seen in his key role in the formation of the Sayap Kiri coalition in late 1946, consisting of the Partai Sosialis, the PKI, the Partai Buruh

---

50. On the significance of provisions for the restoration of Dutch plantations and other European-owned properties to their prewar owners, see John Orval Sutter, "Indonesianisasi: A Historical Survey of the Role of Politics in the Institutions of a Changing Economy from the Second World War to the Eve of the General Elections (1940–1955)" (PhD diss, Cornell University, 1959), 456–457.

51. See Oey Hong Lee, *War and Diplomacy in Indonesia, 1945–50* (Townsville: James Cook University of North Queensland Committee of South-Easts Asian Studies, 1981), 145.

Indonesia (PBI), Pesindo, the labor federation SOBSI (Sentral Organisasi Buruh Seluruh Indonesia; the All-Indonesian Central of Workers' Organizations), and the Barisan Tani Indonesia (BTI, or Indonesian Peasants' League).[52]

With rising Sayap Kiri criticism of the Sjahrir-led government during early–mid 1947, Sjarifuddin was a natural choice as new prime minister. The new cabinet he formed in early July 1947 drew members from the PNI, the left wing of the Partai Sosialis, the PBI, and the PKI, as well as the small new Partai Sarekat Islam Indonesia (PSII), which had split off from Masyumi and traced its roots back to an earlier incarnation that championed noncooperation vis-à-vis the Dutch colonial government in the 1930s.[53] No less than fifteen of the thirty-five seats in the cabinet were in the hands of Sayap Kiri–affiliated organizations and parties.

Under Amir Sjarifuddin, moreover, the Sayap Kiri was also positioned to strengthen control over the newly renamed Tentara Nasional Indonesia (Indonesian National Army, or TNI). From the outset of his tenure as defense minister since November 1945, Sjarifuddin had worked continuously against the efforts of the ex-KNIL officers and their allies to "professionalize" the military structures of the Republik, pushing instead for a more self-consciously politicized form of armed mobilization. Sjarifuddin had been instrumental in encouraging the formation in November 1945 of Pesindo, Indonesian Socialist Youth (Pemuda Sosialis Indonesia), the most broadly based coalition of youth groups, whose affiliated local left-wing *lasykar* he continued to patronize during 1946 and 1947.[54] A Biro Perjuangan (Struggle Bureau) was established to integrate the *lasykar* into the army, and in early 1946, Sjarifuddin created an Education Staff (Staf Pendidikan Politik Tentara, or Pepolit) within the army devoted to instilling ideological and political education among its officers and rank and file, and subsequent months saw moves to appoint "political officers" (*opsir politik*) to each of the army's divisional commands, in a clear echo of Trotsky's placement of Political Commissars within the Red Army during the Civil War.[55] As a senior army commander noted, the Biro Perjuangan

> increasingly developed into a second army, whose members numbered far more than the TRI and were generally more suited to struggle than the army. They were not constrained by the official diplomacy of the gov-

---

52. On the Sayap Kiri, see Harry Poeze, *Tan Malaka, Gerakan Kiri, dan Revolusi Indonesia Jilid 2: Maret 1946—Maret 1947* (Jakarta: KITLV-Jakarta/Yayasan Obor Indonesia, 2008), 269–271.

53. On the inclusion of the PSII, see Kevin W. Fogg, "The Missing Minister of Religion and the PSII: A Contextual Biography of K.H. Ahmad Azhary," *Studia Islamika* 20, no. 1 (2013): 35–57.

54. Anderson, *Java in a Time of Revolution*, 253–260.

55. See Anderson, *Java in a Time of Revolution*, 250–252, 370–371, and Djenderal Abdul Haris Nasution, *Tentara Nasional Indonesia I* (Djakarta: Seruling Masa, 1970), 280–283. For a Pepolit insider's account, see also Hersri Setiawan, *Negera Madiun? Kesaksian Soemarsono Pelaku Perjuangan* (Jakarta: Forum Studi Perubahan dan Peradaban, 2002), 85–86.

ernment. They struggled simultaneously in the military and political fields. They really had the form and content signified by the term "total people's defense," which had become the motto of Minister Amir Sjarifuddin at that time.[56]

In the wake of the Dutch "police action" of July 1947, moreover, Sjarifuddin established a formal auxiliary organization to the Tentara Nasional Indonesia, the TNI Masyarakat (Society's TNI), absorbing the Biro Perjuangan and assuming autonomous control over appointment of the commanders of reconstituted local *lasykar*.[57] Thus, by the end of 1947 the Republik and its army appeared to be increasingly "red" in its organizational composition and ideological complexion, even as events in Europe and elsewhere marked the onset of the so-called Cold War.

Revolutions within the Revolusi, 1948–1949

It was against this backdrop that the US government became increasingly concerned about the radicalization of the Revolusi in Indonesia and began to take steps to intervene. With former prime minister Sjahrir calling for international intervention in the wake of the Dutch "police action" and enlisting Jawaharlal Nehru, prime minister of the newly independent India, to raise the issue before the United Nations Security Council, the United States belatedly offered itself as a potential mediator between the Indonesians and the Dutch government, albeit without officially recognizing the Republik Indonesia. Encircled, embattled, and economically exhausted by the Dutch blockade, the Republik was highly susceptible to external pressures, as was the Netherlands, given its heavy reliance on US Marshall Plan funds for postwar reconstruction and economic recovery. Through its representative on the UN's Good Offices Committee, the United States pressured both the Indonesians and the Dutch into new negotiations, resulting in an accord signed in January 1948 aboard the *U.S.S. Renville*, which anchored in Jakarta bay. The Renville Agreement, as it came to be known, entailed a full cease-fire throughout the Indonesian archipelago, the withdrawal of Republican troops from Dutch-controlled territory, the restoration of plantations and other property to prewar Dutch owners, and the effective reduction of the Republik to areas of Central and East Java, the Banten region of West Java, and the interior of Sumatra. The agreement further entailed a Dutch commitment to hold plebiscites

---

56. Nasution, *Tentara Nasional Indonesia I*, 309. Translation by the author.
57. Kahin, *Nationalism and Revolution*, 261.

to determine popular preferences for the Republik Indonesia or separate states to form a federal United States of Indonesia to be subsumed within a Netherlands Union, as per the Linggadjati Agreement of November 1946.[58]

The bitter disappointment and further diminution of the Republik marked by the signing of the Renville Agreement in January 1948 undermined the credibility of Amir Sjarifuddin's leadership, enabling his removal from power and the onset of an escalating conflict between republicanism, communism, and Islam in Indonesia. With US encouragement, Masyumi withdrew its support from Sjarifuddin and worked with the PNI to form a new cabinet purged of Sayap Kiri influence under the premiership of Mohammad Hatta, whose conservatism and Islamic piety marked a dramatic departure from his predecessor. Hatta's new government committed itself not only to the implementation of the Renville Agreement but also to the "rationalization" of the TNI, which entailed large-scale demobilization of *lasykar* and diminution of the army to a smaller, more professional fighting force.[59] Thus, January 1948 marked the inception of a counterrevolutionary movement, with disappointing capitulation on the diplomatic front coupled with a dramatic constriction of the political power and prerogatives of the Left.

Over the course of 1948, this conservative movement unfolded, provoking countermobilization from the Left and pushing the Revolusi toward closure amidst the deepening of the Cold War. February 1948 saw Sjarifuddin restyling himself as the leading critic of the Republik, rejecting the implementation of the very Renville Agreement he had signed as prime minister, and reconstituting the Sayap Kiri as an oppositional Front Demokrasi Rakyat (FDR), or People's Democratic Front. In response, former prime minister Sjahrir and other like-minded liberals broke with Sjarifuddin and formed a new Partai Sosialis Indonesia, which allied itself with the Hatta government. Over subsequent months, as Hatta proceeded with "rationalization" of the army and adherence to the Renville Agreement in the face of persistent Dutch foot-dragging and increasingly flagrant violations of the accord, Sjarifuddin and the FDR responded with published attacks in the press and mass protests in the streets of Yogyakarta and other towns and cities held by the Republik.[60]

---

58. On US involvement leading up to the signing of the Renville Agreement, see Robert J. McMahon, *Colonialism and Cold War: The United States and the Struggle for Indonesian Independence, 1945–49* (Ithaca, NY: Cornell University Press, 1981), 206–210.

59. For a detailed army insiders' account of "reorganization and rationalization" (reorganisasi dan rasionalisasi), see Djenderal Abdul Haris Nasution, *Tentara Nasional Indonesia 2* (Djakarta: Seruling Masa, 1968), 123–272, and Himawan Soetanto, *Perintah Presiden Soekarno: "Rebut Kembali Madiun . . .": Siliwangi Menumpas Pemberontakan PKI/Moeso 1948* (Jakarta: Pustaka Sinar Harapan, 1994), 60–68.

60. Soe Hok Gie, *Orang-Orang di Persimpangan Kiri Jalan: Kisah Pemberontakan Madiun September 1948* (Yogyakarta: Yayasan Bentang Budaya, 1977), 161–200; Ann Swift, *The Road to Madiun:*

May and June 1948, moreover, saw escalating tensions between the FDR and the Republik in the face of polarizing pressures from without and within. In May 1948, the Soviet Union announced that it had reached agreement with an Indonesian representative in Prague, PKI Politburo member Suripno, for the official recognition of the Republik and the inauguration of diplomatic relations between the USSR and the Indonesian government. This announcement provoked angry protests from the Netherlands, opposition by the United States, and awkward expressions of disavowal and disapproval by the Hatta government, which recalled Suripno from Prague and renounced any interest in establishing formal ties with the Soviet Union. This series of events served to strengthen the FDR's critique of the Hatta government's commitment to the Revolusi while sowing Republican suspicions of links between the Soviet Union and the FDR.[61]

Meanwhile, growing popular discontent with the Republik began to surface in new forms, enabled and encouraged by the shift of Sayap Kiri–affiliated parties, unions, and other organizations from support for the government to open opposition under the banner of the FDR. In May 1948, worsening labor conditions on a Republik-controlled complex of cotton plantations and textile mills outside Solo had led the PKI-controlled plantation workers' union SARBUPRI (Sarekat Buruh Perkebunan Republik Indonesia) to abandon its previous policy of restraint in favor of demonstrations and strike action. The month of June saw a broadening of the confrontation, with the PKI's labor federation SOBSI weighing in on behalf of the workers, and various FDR-affiliated organizations and newspapers joining the fray. By July 1948, there were armed clashes between strikebreakers and members of Hizbullah, the Masyumi-linked *lasykar*, on the one hand, and SARBUPRI strikers and armed Pesindo units, on the other, before TNI intervention and government arbitration belatedly resolved the strike.[62]

But August and September 1948 saw further escalation of this process of political polarization to the point of open conflict, enabled if not impelled by developments and trends halfway around the world. A year earlier, in September 1947, the founding conference of the Cominform as a new federation of Communist parties to replace the defunct Comintern, had seen its Soviet chairman, Andrei Zhdanov, articulating the "two camp" theory of irreconcilable conflict between

The Indonesian Communist Uprising of 1948 (Ithaca, NY: Cornell Modern Indonesia Project, 1989), 17–26; Harry A. Poeze, *Tan Malaka, Gerakan Kiri, dan Revolusi Indonesia Jilid 3: Maret 1947—Agustus 1948* (Jakarta: KITLV-Jakarta/Yayasan Obor Indonesia, 2010), 47–140.

61. For a detailed account of this series of events based on Soviet documents, see Larisa M. Efimova, *Stalin i Indoneziya: Politika SSSR v Otnoshenii Indonezii v 1945–1953 godakh: Nyeizvestniye Stranitsi* (Moskva: MGIMO, 2004), 59–68.

62. Poeze, *Tan Malaka, Gerakan Kiri, dan Revolusi Indonesia Jilid 3*, 140–148; Soe Hok Gie, *Orang-Orang di Persimpangan Kiri Jalan*, 200–206. For background, see Jafar Suryomenggolo, *Organising under the Revolution: Unions and the State in Java, 1945–48* (Kyoto: Kyoto University Press, 2013).

an "imperialist" bloc led by the United States and a "democratic" bloc led by the Soviet Union. By February 1948, Communist control over Czechoslovakia had been consolidated, a second Cominform congress had been held, and a Soviet-backed youth conference in Calcutta had begun to bring word of the new Zhdanov Line to Communist parties across Asia.[63] In Burma, Malaya, the Philippines, and Vietnam, Communist parties were engaged in armed insurrection, even as victory for the Communists in the civil war in China loomed on the horizon.

Against the backdrop of these developments, longtime PKI activist Musso ended his many years in exile in the Soviet Union and began his return to Indonesia after consultations with CPSU (Communist Party of the Soviet Union) officials in Moscow. In March 1948, Musso arrived in Prague, where he met with Suripno and Paul de Groot, the chairman of the Communist Party of the Netherlands, whom he reportedly convinced to abandon the CPN's (Communist Party of the Netherlands) ambivalence with regard to Indonesian independence.[64] Upon his arrival in Indonesia in mid-August 1948, Musso launched a campaign to reorient the PKI and the broader course of the Revolusi, winning PKI Politburo endorsement of a resolution calling for a "New Path for the Indonesian Republic" (*Jalan Baru untuk Republik Indonesia*). This New Path entailed the abandonment of the PKI's previous strategy of maintaining a low profile within the Republik, acceding to a conciliatory approach to the Dutch and embedding party cadres within different parties and organizations without openly demonstrating the PKI's real strength or solidity. Instead, Musso argued, the PKI should repudiate the Linggajati and Renville agreements, recognize the USSR and rally behind the Soviet-led "democratic" bloc of the Zhdanov Line, reject the Hatta government as illegitimate, and reorganize the forces of the Sayap Kiri/FDR into a tightly organized, PKI-led coalition to seize control of the Revolusi.

By the end of August, less than three weeks since his return to Indonesia, Musso had assumed the post of general secretary of the PKI, achieved the merger of the Partai Sosialis and the Partai Buruh Indonesia (PBI) with the PKI and the dissolution of the FDR, and organized a wave of PKI rallies in areas controlled by the Republik. Leading figures from the Sayap Kiri and FDR—including, most famously, former prime minister and longtime defense minister Amir Sjarifuddin—enthusiastically endorsed these moves, accepted senior positions in

---

63. Ruth T. McVey, *The Calcutta Conference and the Southeast Asian Uprisings* (Ithaca, NY: Cornell Modern Indonesia Project, 1958); Efimova, *Stalin i Indoneziya*, 69–92; Larisa Efimova, "Did the Soviet Union Instruct Southeast Asian Communists to Revolt? New Russian Evidence on the Calcutta Youth Conference of February 1948," *Journal of Southeast Asian Studies* 40, no. 3 (October 2009): 449–469.

64. On the question of Soviet "instructions" to Musso, see Ruth T. McVey, *The Soviet View of the Indonesian Revolution* (Ithaca, NY: Cornell Modern Indonesia Project, 1957); Efimova, *Stalin i Indoneziya*, 93–121; and Larisa M. Efimova, "Who Gave Instructions to the Indonesian Communist Leader Musso in 1948?," *Indonesia and the Malay World* 31, no. 90 (July 2003): 171–189.

a new PKI Politburo, and openly asserted that they had long been underground PKI members themselves. In early September, Musso and his comrades launched a tour of PKI strongholds in Central and East Java, holding large-scale mass rallies before audiences of thousands in open defiance of the Republican leadership, even as calls were made on the PNI and Masyumi to join with the PKI in a National Front government.[65] The enthusiasm with which Musso's arrival and ambitious initiative were met across the broad ranks of the Left thus clearly reflected not only the international conjuncture but local conditions propitious to a "New Path."[66]

But instead of incorporating the PKI in the alliance of republicanism, Islam, and communism embodied in Soekarno's 1927 slogan *NASAKOM* and in the proposed tripartite PNI-Masyumi-PKI-led government, the Republik and its army responded with violence. Mid-September 1948 saw attacks by the TNI's Siliwangi Division, recently relocated from West Java under the Renville Agreement, on units of the leftist *lasykar* organization Pesindo and allied local military forces in the Central Javanese city of Solo, which had long been a bastion of independence and opposition vis-à-vis the Republik with its capital in nearby Yogyakarta. Forces affiliated with Pesindo and allied with the PKI fled Solo and other cities within the Republik and began to regroup in the nearby East Javanese town of Madiun, which was notable as a railroad hub, a stronghold for the PKI-controlled labor organization SOBSI, and the site of the Sayap Kiri's "Marx House" for the indoctrination and organization of its cadres. But the excitement generated by Musso's "New Path" was not matched by organizational solidity or armed strength, and defections and desertions left the PKI with too few troops to defend themselves in Madiun. By the end of September 1948, scattered remnants of what official anti-Communist historiography later described and derided as the "Madiun rebellion" faced capture and imprisonment in the hinterlands of East and Central Java; smaller-scale uprisings in other towns of the Republik had been fully suppressed; and throughout the Republik, the PKI and allied organizations were disarmed and dozens of their leaders subjected to disciplinary proceedings and detention. The Communist "revolution within the Revolution" had been defeated.[67]

Ironically, yet instructively, it was in fact the defeat of Communist revolution that enabled the ostensible final victory of the Revolusi in the sense of the

65. Soe Hok Gie, *Orang-Orang di Persimpangan Kiri Jalan*, 211–225; Swift, *The Road to Madiun*, 51–67.

66. On this point, see Soerjono and Ben Anderson, "On Musso's Return," *Indonesia* 29 (April 1980): 59–90.

67. David Charles Anderson, "The Military Aspects of the Madiun Affair," *Indonesia* 21 (April 1976): 1–63; Soe Hok Gie, *Orang-Orang di Persimpangan Kiri Jalan*, 225–267; Swift, *The Road to Madiun*, 67–80.

successful establishment of the Republik Indonesia and a belated transition to independence. Emboldened by the evident internal weakness of the Republik, the Dutch government launched a second "police action" in December 1948, an aggressive and intensive military campaign that culminated in the capture of Yogyakarta and seizure of Soekarno, Hatta, and much of the cabinet. But even as Dutch forces gained control over the cities and towns of the rump areas of the Republik in Central and East Java, the scorched-earth tactics of the retreating Indonesian armed forces foreshadowed the prospect of protracted armed guerrilla warfare and other forms of resistance that would render impossible the restoration of *rust en orde* across the Indonesian archipelago.[68] Crucially, the reestablishment of control over the plantation belts of Java and Sumatra was complicated and fatally compromised by the entrenchment of the PKI's plantation labor federation SARBUPRI as well as the opportunities for continuing sabotage, subterfuge, and myriad other forms of everyday resistance. This reality was already evident after the "First Police Action" of mid-1947, which reportedly left at least half of all estates subjected to scorched-earth tactics (*dibumihanguskan*); when, after the "Second Police Action" of December 1948,

> most of the remaining estates and industries were occupied by the Dutch, the figuratively inflamed atmosphere often became a reality, as workers and farmers took to the hills in guerrilla warfare and returned to apply the torch. Business managers, especially in the relatively isolated estates, had to maintain their own armed guards, who as often as not defected to the guerrillas along with their arms. Where it could be done with impunity, squatting on estates increased. As tension eased slightly in 1949, some estates in East Sumatra arranged to give their laborers 1500 square meters of land apiece in which to raise their own vegetables. Some workers, feeling that earlier actions in staking out estate lands for themselves had been thus ratified, proceeded to expand over even more land, and to plant rice (which had been forbidden).[69]

At the same time, the violent defeat and defanging of the PKI had strengthened the anti-Communist credentials of the Republik Indonesia in the eyes of the US government. American interests were not well served by the possible implosion of the Republik and the opportunities thus created for a reconstituted PKI, or by the Dutch government's stubbornly and shortsightedly military approach.

---

68. P. M. H. Groen, "Dutch Armed Forces and the Decolonization of Indonesia: The Second Police Action (1948–1949), A Pandora's Box," *War and Society* 4, no. 1 (May 1986): 79–104.

69. Sutter, "Indonesianisasi," 619–620, 621. On the Deli plantation belt in East Sumatra, see Ann Laura Stoler, *Capitalism and Confrontation in Sumatra's Plantation Belt, 1870–1979* (Ann Arbor: University of Michigan Press, 1985), 113–121.

Nor were American interests well served by the outcry in the United Nations against Dutch military actions that openly flouted the Linggajati and Renville agreements, thus discrediting efforts to depict the United States as an honest broker and sympathetic supporter of self-determination in Indonesia and elsewhere across Asia, Africa, and the Middle East, rather than the leader of the "imperialist camp" as depicted in Zhdanov's Line. Thus, by January 1949 the US government had suspended Marshall Plan assistance to the Netherlands allocated for the Indonesian archipelago and sponsored a unanimous United Nations Security Council resolution calling on the Dutch to release the Republican leadership, resume negotiations on the basis of previous agreements, refrain from further military action, and relinquish claims to sovereignty to a United States of Indonesia by July 1950. Over subsequent months, moves afoot in the Truman administration, in Congress, and in the American media made clear that Dutch recalcitrance would be met with a full suspension of US assistance to the Netherlands.[70]

Meanwhile, the mounting challenges and claims to leadership of the Revolusi launched in the name of communism over the course of 1948 were mirrored in parallel forms of mobilization in the name of Islam, whose persistence and escalation in 1949 helped to push the Republik and the Dutch to reach a final agreement for a stage-managed decolonization of the Indonesian archipelago and the formation of an independent new Indonesian nation-state. As noted above, many of the local *lasykar* that emerged in late 1945 and early 1946 in various parts of the Indonesian archipelago were distinctly Islamic in their leadership, organizational structures, discursive practices, and aspirations, as seen in their continuing self-identification with terms such as Hizbullah (the Party of God) and Sabilillah (the Cause of God), which the Japanese administration had used for Islamic paramilitary formations. It was in no small measure in recognition of the strength and significance of the political and military infrastructure of Islam that Masyumi had been accorded such a prominent place in successive cabinets by Sjahrir during his tenure as prime minister of the Republik from November 1945 through June 1947. After all, many observers identified Masyumi as the largest of all the political parties, and it drew on the extensive school and associational networks of both Nahdlatul Ulama and Muhammadiyah, as well as other Islamic educational groups. But under Amir Sjarifuddin's period in office, the entrenchment of the Sayap Kiri's parties in government and the advantages and allocations of resources accorded to Pesindo-linked and other left-wing *lasykar* had alienated many Islamic activists, Hizbullah and Sabilillah *lasykar* leaders, and their followers, some of whom remained embittered about the last-minute removal of

70. See Robert J. McMahon, *Colonialism and Cold War: The United States and the Struggle for Indonesian Independence, 1945–49* (Ithaca, NY: Cornell University Press, 1981), 218–293.

key phrases promising the implementation of Islamic law from the constitution promulgated by the Republik in August 1945.[71]

The continuing autonomy and antipathy of Islamic forces vis-à-vis the Republik became pronounced in West Java under the leadership of Sekarmaji Marijan Kartosuwiryo, an established Islamic activist with a long history of militant commitment to Islamist causes. In the late 1920s, Kartosuwiryo had served as Surabaya branch leader of the Jong Islamieten Bond (Islamic Youth Association) and as Sarekat Islam leader Tjokroaminoto's private secretary, and then in the 1930s as party secretary of the Partai Sarekat Islam Indonesia (PSII), before abandoning the PSII in 1940 due to its cooperation with non-Islamic parties and setting up a splinter group in West Java, along with a special training center for its cadres. Kartosuwiryo's prominence was recognized in his appointment as a Masyumi delegate to the KNIP in 1946–1947, and when the PSII broke off from Masyumi to join the new government of Amir Sjarifuddin in July 1947, he was even offered the post of deputy minister of defense, which he declined in favor of an assignment as Masyumi regional commissioner for West Java. Subsequent months saw him asserting increasing independence from Masyumi and from the left-leaning Sjarifuddin government, creating local Defense Councils of the Islamic Community (Dewan Pertahanan Ummat Islam) that incorporated Hizbullah and Sabilillah forces under his leadership and operated with increasing effectiveness against the Dutch and autonomy vis-à-vis the TNI.[72]

With the signing of the Renville Agreement in January 1948, the retreat of TNI troops from West Java across the so-called Van Mook Line into the rump area of the Republik in parts of Central and East Java, and the Republik's de facto recognition of Dutch authority in West Java, Kartosuwiryo's authority—and ambitions—further expanded. By some estimates, as many as four thousand armed Hizbullah and Sabilillah troops remained in West Java, without competition or constraints from the TNI. Kartosuwiryo rallied local Islamic networks together under a Majelis Umat Islam (Council of the Islamic Community), which was designed to serve as a provisional government in West Java, with Kartosuwiryo as its "imam" and a close associate as leader of a Tentara Islam Indonesia (Islamic Army of Indonesia, or TII). Over the course of 1948, this government began to morph into a

---

71. Robert E. Elson, "Another Look at the Jakarta Charter Controversy of 1945," *Indonesia* 88 (October 2009): 105–130.

72. On the evolution of Kartosuwiryo's Islamic activism and thinking from the 1920s through 1947, see Chiara Formichi, *Islam and the Making of the Nation: Kartosuwiryo and Political Islam in 20th Century Indonesia* (Leiden: KITLV Press, 2012), 15–108. See also Pinardi, *Sekarmadji Mardijan Kartosuwirjo* (Djakarta: PT Badan Penerbit Aryaguna, 1964), 20–33; Hiroo Horikoshi, "The Dar ul-Islam Movement in West Java (1948–62): An Experience in the Historical Process," *Indonesia* 20 (October 1975): 59–86; and S. Soebardi, "Kartosuwirjo and the Darul Islam Rebellion in Indonesia," *Journal of Southeast Asian Studies* 14, no. 1 (March 1983): 109–133.

self-proclaimed Negara Islam (Islamic State), whose effective authority extended across large swathes of West Java.[73]

As with the showdown between the Hatta government and the PKI in Madiun in September 1948, this challenge to the Republik's claims to leadership of the Revolusi in the name of Islam escalated into frontal violence in 1949. When TNI troops were deployed to West Java in response to the second Dutch "police action" of December 1948, they found themselves ambushed or otherwise outmaneuvered by units of the TII. Over the course of 1949, as negotiations between the Republik and the Dutch government resumed, TNI troops in West Java reached informal "live and let live" arrangements with Dutch troops before retreating once again to Central Java after a ceasefire was agreed on in May of that year. But the troops of the TII were said to number as many as fifteen thousand men, with the Negara Islam Indonesia enjoying effective control over large swathes of West Java and operating as an aggressive guerrilla force against Dutch forces and their local "puppet"-state collaborators. By August 1949, as representatives of the Republik and the Dutch government were meeting in The Hague to negotiate the transfer of sovereignty, Kartosuwiryo had proclaimed an Islamic State of Indonesia (Negara Islam Indonesia) as an alternative claimant to the leadership of the Revolusi.[74]

It was thus against the backdrop of the onset of the Cold War, the escalating conflict between republicanism, communism, and Islam, and the eventual violent defeat of the Communist "revolution within the Revolution" that the formal transition to an independent Republic of Indonesia was ultimately effected. Acceding to pressures from the United States and elsewhere, the Netherlands agreed to a ceasefire agreement in May 1949 and, in the Round Table Agreement in The Hague in August of the same year, to a transfer of sovereignty to the Republic of the United States of Indonesia four months later. By the dawning of 1950, the Republic of Indonesia was an independent nation-state. But the terms of the agreement helped to reinforce the fragile authority of local aristocracies in many areas of the Indonesian archipelago, to restore plantations and other large-scale enterprises to Dutch and other European owners from the prewar period, and to restrict the role of Islam in the exercise of state power. Thus, even as a Republik Indonesia achieved independence on the eve of 1950, the diverse Communist and Islamist hopes and dreams of "100 Percent Merdeka" that had provided such crucial energies for the Revolusi remained dashed or at least deferred.

---

73. On these developments, see Robert E. Elson and Chiara Formichi, "Why Did Kartosuwiryo Start Shooting? An Account of Dutch-Republican-Islamic Forces Interaction in West Java, 1945–49," *Journal of Southeast Asian Studies* 42, no. 3 (October 2011): 466–468.

74. Formichi, *Islam and the Making of the Nation*, 109–144.

Conclusions: Republicanism versus Communism versus Islam?

As detailed and demonstrated in the previous pages, the Indonesian Revolution was not simply a struggle by Indonesian nationalists for Indonesian independence, a struggle that can be fully understood within a national(ist) framework for analysis. As with the Philippine Revolution at the turn of the twentieth century, the onset, unfolding, and immediate outcome of the Indonesian Revolusi of 1945–1949 were profoundly shaped by developments and trends in the international realm, most notably rivalries and conflicts among the Great Powers. World War II, the Japanese occupation and its large-scale paramilitary training programs, and the Allies' phased liberation of Southeast Asia enabled and impelled not only the proclamation of Indonesian independence in August 1945 but also an irruption of mass mobilization previously unseen if not unimaginable in parts of the Indonesian archipelago. The onset of the Cold War, real and imagined Soviet influence, and very concrete and consequential forms of US intervention further determined the trajectory and terminus of the Revolusi over the course of 1948 and 1949. The involvement of the United Nations, the interest and assistance manifested by India and the Arab League, and the insurrections and independence struggles elsewhere in Southeast Asia provided crucial "mood music" for the negotiations between the Republik and the Dutch government—and the ultimate settlement of the terms of independence—brokered (if not imposed) by the United States. *Diplomasi*, in the end, proved as decisive as *perjuangan*.

As with the Philippine Revolution, moreover, the underlying discursive and mobilizational infrastructures of the Revolusi in the mid-twentieth century were profoundly shaped by the enduring legacies of the Indonesian archipelago's deepening immersion within transoceanic currents of global commerce and cosmopolitan culture over the *longue durée*. These diverse legacies were seen in Islamic schools, associations, and linkages stretching across Java, Sumatra, other islands of the archipelago, extending to Singapore, Penang, the Malay Peninsula, and southern Siam, and connecting Indonesian Muslims to Mecca, Cairo, and other centers of Islamic intellectual and political activism. They were also seen in a highly industrialized and concentrated agro-export economy, with vast plantation belts and huge pools of wage laborers on Java and Sumatra connected via extensive railway networks and port cities such as Medan, Semarang, and Surabaya to international commodities markets. By the turn of the twentieth century, an emerging market society and a modern public sphere in the towns and cities of the archipelago brought new experiments in popular culture, print capitalism, and political activism that bore the hallmarks of diverse cosmopolitan influences, as seen in the *Komedie Stamboel*, myriad newspapers and novels, the Vereeniging voor Spoor-en Tramweg Personeel (VSTP), the Tiong Hoa Hwee Koan (THHK), Al Irsyad, and Muhammadiyah. Small wonder that it was in the major port city of Surabaya that the first dramatic surge of mass mobilization in the Revolusi unfolded in the protracted violent battle with British troops in late October and November 1945.[75]

Furthermore, as with the Freemasons and religious confraternities in the making of the Katipunan and the Philippine Revolution, the very institutional bases and egalitarian promises of revolutionary brotherhood undergirding the Indonesian Revolusi were profoundly cosmopolitan rather than national or nationalist in their origins and orientations. On the one hand, the accumulated infrastructure of autonomous Islamic educational networks and associational activities, the established authority of Islamic discourse, and the extensive linkages and imagined and expressed solidarities connecting Indonesian Muslims to their coreligionists in Cairo and Mecca provided a rubric not only for imagining and actualizing an independent Indonesian nation-state but also for undertaking *revolusi sosial* against local aristocracies in various parts of the archipelago. On the other hand, the attractive power of the language of Marxism, the organizational potential of labor unions and Leninist party structures, and the internationalist promise of communism served to inspire diverse forms and factions of struggle, not only for *Merdeka* in the sense of formal Indonesian independence but also against feudalism, capitalism, and imperialism. Small wonder that Masyumi and the various parties of the Sayap Kiri played such important roles in the making—and unmaking—of the Republik. Without Islam and communism, nationalism would not have sufficed for purposes of winning Indonesian independence.

Furthermore, as with the Philippine Revolution at the turn of the twentieth century, the international conjuncture in the early aftermath of World War II combined with the idiosyncratic constellation of cosmopolitan legacies and linkages enabling revolutionary mobilization in the Indonesian archipelago to determine the Revolusi's specific trajectory and immediate outcome. In contrast to the assimilated Chinese mestizo merchants and landowners and their struggle for liberalism against the Catholic Church in the Philippines of the late nineteenth century, the segregation of immigrants from China in the Netherlands East Indies prefigured forms of Chinese mobilization—educational reform, associational innovation, support for the Revolution of 1911 in China, and demands for new freedoms and privileges—that helped to stimulate other responses from among the archipelago's broader population, as seen in the rise of the Sarekat Islam. Thus, unlike the Filipino landowners and local worthies, merchants, and Masons who

---

75. William H. Frederick, *Visions and Heat: The Making of the Indonesian Revolution* (Athens: Ohio University Press, 1988).

formed the Katipunan, the batik merchants, journalists, Islamic scholars, and left-wing labor activists who led the Sarekat Islam in the late 1910s and early–mid 1920s were not fighting against Dutch bureaucrats, local aristocrats, Chinese tax farmers, and European plantation owners for the full liberalization of the market economy and the public sphere but for other aims and aspirations instead.

Finally, as with the Philippine Revolution, the international circumstances of the early postwar, Cold War era and the local constellation of cosmopolitan legacies and linkages combined not only to enable revolutionary mobilization in the Indonesian archipelago but also to complicate, compromise, and constrain it, engendering multiple revolutions within the Revolution and undermining the Revolusi's revolutionary promise(s) as a whole. On the one hand, the Revolusi's overall trajectory and immediate outcome was determined by the persistent divides among the cosmopolitan currents of communism and Islam, emanating as they did from very different sources of intellectual and political power and embodying very different institutions and social forces across the Indonesian archipelago. In the early years of the Sarekat Islam, it had been possible for pious Muslims, and even Islamic intellectuals and activists such as Haji Misbach, to embrace Karl Marx's writings and imagine themselves as Communists,[76] and it was thus with some real basis in lived experience and local knowledge that Tan Malaka had tried to convince his Comintern comrades that "Pan-Islam" could and should be an ally in socialist revolutionary struggles against imperialism. But since the break between the "Red" and "White" factions of the Sarekat Islam in the early 1920s, communism and Islam essentially remained at odds or were otherwise unable to join their combined energies in a fused form of *perjuangan*, which rendered them both separately susceptible to cooptation, domestication, and encapsulation within the secular republican state, as seen in the shifting party composition of successive cabinets during the Revolusi.[77]

On the other hand, the Revolusi's overall trajectory and immediate outcome was also determined by diffidence, disorganization, and divisions within the ranks of both Communist and Islamist forces. Communism in the embryonic and embattled Republik Indonesia, after all, was represented across a disparate set of Sayap Kiri parties and other organizations by activists with widely divergent wartime experiences in Indonesia, the Netherlands, and Australia, and with varying degrees of confidence in the prospects for achieving a socialist revolution under

---

76. On Misbach in particular and this broader point in general, see Takashi Shiraishi, *An Age in Motion: Popular Radicalism in Java, 1912–1926* (Ithaca, NY: Cornell University Press, 1990), 127–165, 249–298.

77. But for a close, careful, and creative analysis of continuing efforts and opportunities for the advancement of "Islamic communism" after 1927 and through the Revolusi, especially in West Sumatra, see Hongxuan Lin, "Ummah Yet Proletariat: Islam and Marxism in the Netherlands East Indies and Indonesia, 1915–1959" (PhD diss., University of Washington, 2020), 131–317.

the rubric of the Revolusi. Differences among these activists were accompanied by deeper division and distrust regarding the supposed adventurist (*avonturir*) and Trotskyist Tan Malaka, whose vehement insistence on *perjuangan* contrasted with the far more accommodating emphasis on *diplomasi* of those who publicly styled themselves as socialists. The belated effort to unify and embolden Communist forces behind the banner of the PKI and seize control of the Revolusi in 1948 came only after the Sayap Kiri had been removed from its position within the cabinet and the TNI, and thus relieved of responsibility for implementing the Renville Agreement, leaving them isolated and in danger of extirpation.

Meanwhile, Islam was represented in the Republik through Masyumi, an umbrella organization-cum-party incorporating the very different Islamic associations Muhammadiyah and Nahdlatul Ulama and their affiliated school networks. Among the party leaders and within the ranks of the local *lasykar* identified with Masyumi circulated widely divergent views regarding the proper place of Islam in the constitution and the Republik, and regarding the very beliefs and practices associated with the faith. As the Revolusi unfolded, moreover, the autonomy of Islamic *lasykar* outside Republican areas enabled the attenuation of Masyumi control and capacity for appropriating and encapsulating the discursive and organizational power of Islam within the Republik, as seen in West Java under the leadership of Kartosuwiryo.

The Revolusi's immediate outcome was thus not only independence for the new nation-state of Indonesia but also the successful subordination of communism and Islam to the republicanism of Soekarno and Hatta's Republik Indonesia along the lines suggested decades earlier in Soekarno's call for *NASAKOM*. From 1950, a reconstituted PKI, Masyumi, and, after its secession in 1952, Nahdlatul Ulama occupied seats in Parliament and Soekarno's cabinet as junior partners in an independent Indonesia where foreign ownership of the commanding heights of the economy, secular institutions of education and governmentality, and the authority of local aristocracies were being reestablished under republican auspices. Over the course of the first two decades of independence, the egalitarian promises and emancipatory potentialities of communism and Islam continued to provide bases for articulating resentment and organizing resistance to the compromises and constraints imposed on the Republik by the terms of decolonization, prompting a succession of countervailing shifts in the direction of more exclusionary politics, authoritarianism, and militarism. In this sense, the conflicts among republicanism, communism, and Islam extended in various forms beyond the transition to independence and the establishment of a new nation-state; indeed, they continued to shape Indonesian politics for many years after the ostensible end of the Revolusi. As Ben Anderson noted in 1972:

The revolution never became more than a "national revolution"; it ended in 1949, when the Dutch transferred legal sovereignty over the archipelago to Indonesian hands, and Sukarno moved into the palace where governors-general had ruled for generations. What it might have been can only be glimpsed in the short-lived, isolated social revolutions in the provinces, and in the memories of some of its survivors. Long after Indonesian sovereignty was recognized by the world, the search for 100 per cent merdeka was to continue and was to remain sentenced to disappointment. But the hopes are still with us.[78]

---

78. Anderson, *Java in a Time of Revolution*, 409.

FROM GUANGZHOU, PORTO NOVO, AND ANTANANARIVO TOWARD ĐIỆN BIÊN PHỦ

If the Bohemian town of Litoměřice provided an odd but illuminating point of departure for a reconsideration of the Philippine Revolution, and the Caucasian oil–boom city of Baku offered an equally unusual but instructive springboard for a reinterpretation of the Indonesian Revolusi, then the southern Chinese coastal metropolis of Guangzhou suggests itself as a patently obvious and potentially interesting vantage point from which the Vietnamese Revolution can be resituated and revisited. Guangzhou (or Canton), after all, served for centuries as a major hub for maritime trade in ways that included or otherwise impacted on various parts of the territory stretching from the Tonkin Gulf and the Red River plain to the Mekong River Delta that today comprises Vietnam. Such lineages and linkages can be dated at least as far back as the consolidation of the Han dynasty, its southward expansion, and conquest and absorption in 111 BCE of the autonomous realm of "Southern Yue" (Nan Yue) with its capital Panyu located in today's Guangzhou and a breadth encompassing the area (later the Tang imperial circuit) that came to be known as Lingnan (South of the Pass) along the southeastern coastal rim of China, including the modern Chinese provinces of Guangdong and Guangxi, as well as the Red River plain.[1]

Under the Han, two great port cities emerged and expanded, Guangzhou at the mouth of the Pearl River Delta, and Jiaozhi, located near the mouth of the

---

1. Charles Holcombe, "Early Imperial China's Deep South: The Viet Regions through Tang Times," *Tang Studies* 15–16 (1997–1998): 125–156.

Red River Delta, east of what today comprises Hà Nội.[2] Of the two port cities, Jiaozhi served as regional capital and was initially larger and more important, thanks to the greater agricultural productivity and population density of the Red River plain at the time as well as Jiaozhi's evolution into the premier trading hub of the South Sea trade for the duration of the Han period and as late as the era of the Northern and Southern Dynasties (420–589 CE).[3] But by the inception of the Tang dynasty in 618 CE, Guangzhou had long been administratively separated from Jiaozhou and had begun to outstrip Jiaozhi as a hub for international maritime trade, thanks to improvements in ship-building technology enabling eastward shifts in shipping routes[4] and the increasing accessibility and integration of its vast and expanding hinterlands, rendering it especially attractive to Arab, Persian, and Indian traders from across the Indian Ocean.[5]

The early commercial centrality and cosmopolitanism of Guangzhou helped to set the stage for its subsequent reemergence as a major node in international maritime trade in the late seventeenth century under the Qing and its official designation as China's sole port for foreign trade from 1757 to 1842.[6] By the end of the eighteenth century, Guangzhou (or "Canton") had emerged as the key port of entry to China for the English East India Company and the hub for the tea trade.[7] But the seventeenth and eighteenth centuries also saw the dramatic expansion of trade, financial, and migratory linkages between Guangzhou and Southeast Asia, most notably with ports in the Mekong Delta such as Cancao (today's Hà Tiên).[8] Over the latter half of the nineteenth century, moreover, the inclusion of Guangzhou among the treaty ports forcibly opened up to foreign trade combined with the dramatic expansion of wet rice cultivation for export in the Mekong Delta and elsewhere in what was emerging as French colonial Indochina to deepen these linkages, as detailed in the pages that follow. It is thus against the backdrop of deep historical lineages and linkages that

---

2. Li Tana, "Jaiozhi (Giao Chi) in the Han Period Tongking Gulf," in *The Tongking Gulf through History*, ed. Nola Cooke, Li Tana, and James A. Anderson (Philadelphia: University of Pennsylvania Press, 2011), 39–66.

3. Wang Gungwu, "The Nanhai Trade: A Study of the Early History of Chinese Trade in the South China Sea," *Journal of the Malaysian Branch of the Royal Asiatic Society* 31, no. 182 (June 1958): 3–135.

4. Catherine Churchman, *The People between Two Rivers: The Rise and Fall of a Bronze Drum Culture, 200–750 CE* (Lanham, MD: Rowman and Littlefield, 2016), 55–56.

5. Claudine Salmon, "Les Persans à L'Extrémité Orientale de la Route Maritime (II A.E.—XVII siècle)," *Archipel* 68 (2004): 23–58.

6. Paul A. Van Dyke, *The Canton Trade: Life and Enterprise on the China Coast, 1700–1845* (Hong Kong: Hong Kong University Press, 2005). For background, see Robert B. Marks, *Tigers, Rice, Silk, and Silt: Environment and Economy in Late Imperial South China* (Cambridge: Cambridge University Press, 1998).

7. Kirti N. Chaudhuri, *The Trading World of Asia and the English East India Company, 1660–1760* (Cambridge: Cambridge University Press, 2006).

8. Li Tana and Paul A. Van Dyke, "Canton, Cancao, and Cochinchina: New Data and New Light on Eighteenth-Century Canton and the Nanyang," *Chinese Southern Diaspora Studies* 1 (2007): 10–28.

Guangzhou's significance for the Vietnamese Revolution can be appreciated and understood.

In fact, during the first decades of the twentieth century, Guangzhou became—like Baku—a hub for diverse forms of revolutionary activity. Thanks to Guangzhou's early and extensive commercial development and the emergence and expansion of its local commercial elite, the city was a prominent site for republican revolutionary activity, as seen in the failed Canton uprising of 1895, Sun Yat-sen's own Cantonese roots and recruitment efforts, and the participation of local businessmen and bankers among the urban reformist elite that played such an important role in the 1911 Revolution that overthrew the Qing dynasty and established the Chinese Republic.[9] By the early–mid 1920s, moreover, Guangzhou had come to serve as the capital for Sun Yat-sen's nationalist government until his death in 1925, and it was on the outskirts of Guangzhou that the famous Whampoa Academy was established, with the help of Soviet assistance and instructors, to train military officers for what became the Northern Expedition of 1926–1928 through which the Kuomintang succeeded in unifying China.[10] For Nationalist Kuomintang leaders Sun Yat-sen and Chiang Kai-shek aspiring to reunify China, end the unequal treaties with imperial powers, and modernize the nation, Guangzhou was nothing less than the "cradle of the revolution."[11]

On the other hand, Guangzhou served not only as the site for Soviet and Comintern officials' consultations with Sun Yat-sen on the restructuring of the Kuomintang along Leninist lines and contributions to military training at the Whampoa Academy but also as a launching pad for revolutionary socialist mobilization in China.[12] The Canton-Hong Kong Strike of 1925–1926, for example, witnessed unprecedented working-class mobilization against the imperial powers.[13] The short-lived and ill-fated Canton Commune in December 1927 served as a landmark moment in the Chinese Communist Party (CCP)'s history, as it suffered violent purges at the hands of the Kuomintang amidst the breakdown of the united front between the two parties.[14]

---

9. See Harold Z. Schiffrin, *Sun Yat-sen and the Origins of the Chinese Revolution* (Berkeley: University of California Press, 1968), 56–97, and Marie-Claire Bergère, *Sun Yat-sen* (Stanford, CA: Stanford University press, 1998), especially 55–59, and 184–189. See also Michael Tsin, *Nation, Governance, and Modernity in China: Canton, 1900–1927* (Stanford, CA: Stanford University Press, 1999).

10. See Richard Brian Landis, "Institutional Trends at the Whampoa Military School: 1924–1926" (PhD diss., University of Washington, 1969), and Richard Eugene Gillespie, "Whampoa and the Nanking Decade (1924–1936)" (PhD diss., American University, 1971).

11. C. Martin Wilbur, *The Nationalist Revolution in China, 1923–1928* (Cambridge: Cambridge University Press, 1983), 1.

12. C. Martin Wilbur and Julie Lien-ying How, *Missionaries of Revolution: Soviet Advisers and Nationalist China, 1920–1927* (Cambridge, MA: Harvard University Press, 1989).

13. Ming K. Chan, "Labor and Empire: The Chinese Labor Movement in the Canton Delta, 1895–1927" (PhD diss., Stanford University, 1975), 308–356.

14. Bernard S. Thomas, *"Proletarian Hegemony" in the Chinese Revolution and the Canton Commune of 1927* (Ann Arbor: University of Michigan Center for Chinese Studies, 1975).

Against this backdrop, Guangzhou was destined to play a much more decisive and much more direct role in the making of the Vietnamese Revolution as compared with that of Litoměřice for the Philippine Revolution, or even Baku for the Indonesian Revolusi. It was in Guangzhou in 1912, in the early aftermath of the Chinese Revolution that overthrew the Qing dynasty that the early Vietnamese revolutionary Phan Bội Châu founded the Việt Nam Quang Phục Hội (Vietnam Restoration Society) in self-conscious emulation of Sun Yat-sen's Tongmenghui, thus shifting from a monarchical to a republican vision of an independent Vietnam.[15] Over the following decade and on until his arrest in Shanghai and forced return in French custody to Hà Nội in 1925, Phan and his compatriots relied heavily on Guangzhou as a key node in an embryonic clandestine network of revolutionary activists extending from southern China to Hong Kong, Singapore, and from Bangkok across Siam and along the Mekong into French colonial Indochina.[16]

From 1925 into 1927, moreover, Guangzhou served as a base for Nguyễn Ái Quốc, the Comintern agent who came to be known as Hồ Chí Minh. It was in Guangzhou that he founded the Việt Nam Thanh Niên Cách Mệnh Đồng Chí Hội, or Vietnamese Revolutionary Youth League (usually abbreviated and referred to as Thanh Niên), the first Marxist-Leninist organization to operate in Vietnam. Drawing on remnants of Phan Bội Châu's network, Kuomintang and Chinese Communist Party linkages, and access to the Whampoa Military Academy, Thanh Niên succeeded in using Guangzhou as a base for new kinds of revolutionary activism in 1925–1927. With French repression of student strikes in Tonkin, Annam, and Cochinchina sending a wave of disaffected secondary school pupils into brief exile in Guangzhou,[17] Thanh Niên was able to recruit and train a few hundred new revolutionary activists during these years and to reinsert them back into Vietnamese society before the violent breakdown of the united front and the Kuomintang repression of the CCP forced Nguyễn Ái Quốc to relocate to Shanghai and then on to Moscow.[18] The remnants of Thanh Niên provided the foun-

---

15. For background, see Vĩnh Sính, ed., *Phan Bội Châu and the Đông Du Movement* (New Haven, CT: Yale University Council on Southeast Asia, 1988), and Vĩnh Sính and Nicholas Wickenden, trans., *Overturned Chariot: The Autobiography of Phan- Bội-Châu* (Honolulu: University of Hawai'i Press, 1999).

16. David G. Marr, *Vietnamese Anticolonialism, 1885–1925* (Berkeley: University of California Press, 1971), 212–248; Christopher E. Goscha, *Thailand and the Southeast Asian Networks of the Vietnamese Revolution, 1885–1954* (Richmond: Curzon, 1999), 28–49.

17. See Gail Paradise Kelly, "Franco-Vietnamese Schools, 1918 to 1938" (PhD diss., University of Wisconsin at Madison, 1975), 296–327, and Micheline R. Lessard, "Tradition for Rebellion: Vietnamese Students and Teachers and Anticolonial Resistance, 1888–1931" (PhD diss., Cornell University, 1995), 198–268.

18. William J. Duiker, "The Revolutionary Youth League: Cradle of Communism in Vietnam," *China Quarterly* 51 (July–September 1972): 475–499; Huỳnh Kim Khánh, *Vietnamese Communism, 1925–1945* (Ithaca, NY: Cornell University Press, 1982), 63–89.

dations for subsequent revolutionary organizing within and beyond Vietnam during subsequent decades, even as broader developments and trends in China continued to spill over into Vietnam in ways that proved decisive for the Vietnamese Revolution, as detailed in the pages that follow.

But if Guangzhou provides a fairly familiar vantage point from which to acknowledge the oft-noted and amply well documented importance of China for the Vietnamese Revolution, then what about the relevance of such far-flung and seemingly obscure African cities as Porto Novo and Antananarivo? Here, as described at length in the pages that follow, Paris suggests itself as the obvious partner to Guangzhou in terms of the diverse points of influence and interlinkage for Vietnamese revolutionaries such as Nguyễn Ái Quốc (alias Hồ Chí Minh), ranging from the French Communist Party to the diverse African and Antillean activists with whom he founded the Union Intercoloniale and the magazine *Le Paria* in the early 1920s in open defiance and vehement denunciation of colonial rule across the full breadth of the French Empire and beyond.[19] But if Paris, the cosmopolitan modern capital of the late nineteenth and early twentieth centuries par excellence, briefly served as a point of contact, comradeship, and collaboration for Vietnamese and other anticolonial activists, it was in such French African colonies as Dahomey (now Benin) and Madagascar where the foundations for these intercolonial solidarities were rooted and where the fate of these interconnected anticolonial struggles would be resolved. After all, it was not only on the pages of Hồ Chí Minh's famous 1925 tract *Le Procès de la Colonisation Française* (French Colonialism on Trial) that exploitation of the workers and peasants of Dahomey and Madagascar figured alongside that of the subaltern classes of colonial Indochina,[20] and it was not only in close collaboration with prominent activists such as the Dahomeyan Louis Hunkanrin and the Malagasy Jean Ralaimongo in the early 1920s that the Vietnamese Revolution intersected with African struggles. From the shared experiences of African soldiers and Indochinese laborers in France in World War I and its early aftermath to the significance of African troops in French efforts to reestablish colonial rule in Indochina after World War II, and the sudden irruption of mobilization in Madagascar in 1947, Africans—and, as some historians have suggested, African-Americans in 1965–1973—were destined to play seemingly small but still subtly supportive roles in the making of the Vietnamese Revolution, as argued in the pages that follow.

But if earlier chapters' linking of Bohemia to Balintawak and Baku to Bandung drew readers' attention to the consequences of various cosmopolitan influences

19. Brent Hayes Edwards, "Shadow of Shadows," *Positions: East Asia Cultures Critique* 11, no. 1 (Spring 2003): 11–49.

20. Alain Ruscio, ed., *Ho Chi Minh: Le Procès de la Colonisation Française et Autres Textes de Jeunesse* (Paris: Les Temps des Cerises, 2012).

and transnational networks for enabling mobilization in the opening salvos of the Philippine and Indonesian revolutions, the allusion in this chapter's title to the famously decisive 1954 battle of Điện Biên Phủ alludes to yet another dimension of the Vietnamese Revolution that distinguishes it from those treated in the pages above. After all, unlike the 1896 skirmishes in the Manila suburb of Balintawak or the 1945 violence in the West Javanese city of Bandung, the battle of Điện Biên Phủ in 1954 unfolded in the westernmost province of Tonkin, just ten kilometers from the border with Laos and in a valley overwhelmingly populated by Thai and, to a lesser extent, Khu, Mu, Hmong, or Lao, peasants unable to speak the Vietnamese language and otherwise essentially unincorporated within the educational and institutional circuitries of the emerging Vietnamese nation-state. Thus, in contrast to Balintawak and Bandung, the battle of Điện Biên Phủ serves as a signifier of both the more impressive military trajectory of the Vietnamese Revolution as compared with its Philippine and Indonesian counterparts, and, crucially, the broader ethnic, institutional, and geographical context of Indochina within which the Vietnamese revolutionary struggle was embedded.

As spelled out in the pages that follow, this revisiting—and retriangulating—of the Vietnamese Revolution from the combined vantage points of Guangzhou, Porto Novo and Antananarivo, and Điện Biên Phủ provides an alternative to the established body of scholarly literature in which Vietnamese nationalism is privileged as the primary ends and means of revolutionary mobilization. In the memorable words of one eminent historian:

> No amount of statistics, rhetoric, or social science theory can explain the Vietnamese Revolution if its properties of acute historical consciousness and cultural pride are insufficiently considered. These properties were not so much destroyed as psychologically enlarged by the shock of French colonialism.[21]

Instead of a Vietnamese Revolution whose greater vigor and more impressive victories are attributable to an Andersonian intelligentsia more systematically socialized in a shared educational tradition and a population with a more broadly and deeply felt sense of homogenous ethnic identity and historical consciousness than their Filipino and Indonesian counterparts, a properly denationalized, internationalized, and transnationalized account suggests an alternative basis for comparative analysis. The greater strengths and successes of the Vietnamese Revolution, it is argued, should be understood in light of the specific enabling circumstances provided by Vietnam's proximity to China and its position both

---

21. Alexander B. Woodside, *Community and Revolution in Modern Vietnam* (Boston: Houghton Mifflin, 1976), 2.

within the full ambit of the French colonial empire and within French colonial Indochina. As in the Philippine and Indonesian archipelagos, the history of the territory today known as Vietnam is one in which commerce and cosmopolitan culture provided the bases for the formation of a succession of states and societies over the centuries up into what historians term the Early Modern Era. As in the Philippine and Indonesian archipelagos, moreover, the late nineteenth century and early twentieth century witnessed the deepening incorporation of what came to be known as Tonkin, Annam, and Cochinchina into the world economy and the emergence and expansion of market societies and modern public spheres in which diverse cosmopolitan influences and diasporic communities took root. Finally, as in the Philippines and Indonesia, the myriad possibilities for new forms of consciousness, association, and organization opened up by economic and social change combined with international conflicts to set the stage for revolutionary mobilization in Vietnam in the mid-twentieth century. Compared with the Philippines and Indonesia, however, the legacies of early cosmopolitan culture, the modalities of Vietnam's integration into the world economy, and the position of Vietnam within the French Empire and vis-à-vis neighboring China, Laos, and Cambodia enabled a Vietnamese revolution notable for its greater solidity, strength, stamina, and, judged in its own terms, success, as treated in the pages that follow.

Sinographic Cosmopolitanism and Maritime Commerce into the Early Modern Era

As with the Philippine and Indonesian revolutions, some of the crucial cosmopolitan linkages enabling the Vietnamese Revolution can be traced back, over the proverbial *longue durée*, to the particular ways the territory today identified as Vietnam and its peoples were immersed within circuitries of cosmopolitan culture and commerce over the centuries stretching from the Bronze Age to the Early Modern Era. In contrast to the Philippine archipelago's absorption within the global orbit of the Roman Catholic Church from the sixteenth century and the Indonesian archipelago's earlier incorporation within the Indian Ocean ambit of Sanskrit and Islamic cosmopolitanisms, the realms stretching from the Red River plain south along the coast to the Mekong River Delta experienced a complex history of intensive immersion and interaction within a "Sinosphere" in which what some scholars term "Sinographic cosmopolitanism" was coupled with a succession of wars, occupations, expulsions, and the ebb and flow of recurring waves of migration and maritime commerce over much of the past two millennia. Indeed, over the centuries, the very making and unmaking of polities and societies in what came to be Vietnam was intimately intertwined with the making of China. This distinctive feature of Vietnam's position within the great transformations of global history helped to prefigure possibilities for revolution under international conditions—and transnational constellations—different from those under which the Philippine and Indonesian revolutions unfolded.

The location of what today comprises Vietnam on the southern periphery of what today comprises China was crucial. As briefly noted above, from 111 BCE the Han dynasty's southward expansion and conquest extended across what today constitute Guangdong and Guangxi Provinces into the Red River plain and further south to what today is the central Vietnamese city of Hué. By the first century of the Common Era, the forcible incorporation of the Red River plain into the Han dynastic realm had initiated the formation of a new class of local rulers, whose origins, official positions, and education linked them to China:

> Over several centuries, a number of leading Chinese clans established family interests in Tongking and gradually settled into, helped modify, and were finally absorbed into the social, economic, and political environment in northern Vietnam. The ultimate result of this process was the emergence of a ruling Sino-Vietnamese elite.[22]

Through the Tang period (618–907 CE), the Red River plain continued, with few interruptions, to remain within the imperial circuits of the Middle Kingdom, albeit with real attenuation and recurring oscillations in the nature and extent of central control. In the early Tang years, the Protectorate of An Nam (Pacified South) replaced the Jiaozhou Commandery as the formal jurisdiction for the territory, a designation that lasted into the early tenth century, when the disintegration of the Tang dynasty and the transition to the Song dynasty (960–1127) based in northern China enabled the emergence of the independent state of Đại Việt.[23]

Although the Sinicization of this region under Chinese imperial sovereignty over the first millennium of the Common Era seemingly remained confined to the ranks of ruling local state-based elites, there is evidence that its impact was broader, deeper, and more significant for the making of Vietnamese society over subsequent centuries. Overall, the long centuries from the Han to the Tang periods saw successive waves of immigration and sustained exposure to forms of education, religion, administration, and socialization imported from China in the Red River plain and beyond. These early centuries left lasting legacies of commu-

---

22. See Jennifer Holmgren, *Chinese Colonisation of Northern Vietnam: Administrative Geography and Political Development in the Tongking Delta, First to Sixth Centuries A.D.* (Canberra: Australian National University Press, 1980), 172.

23. For useful overviews, see Charles Holcombe, *The Genesis of East Asia, 221 B.C.—A.D. 907* (Honolulu: University of Hawai'i Press, 2001), 146–164, and Keith J. Taylor, *A History of the Vietnamese* (Cambridge: Cambridge University Press, 2013), 14–50.

nication and interaction between and among those who were considered "civilized subjects" of the realm and those "barbaric" peoples incompletely absorbed within the imperial administrative system and dominant culture.[24]

These legacies have been most evident in terms of language. Today as much as 75 percent of the modern Vietnamese lexicon is estimated to be of Chinese origin, with the bulk of Sinitic loan words traced by linguists to bilingual contact over more than a thousand years, between speakers of Old Chinese, Middle Chinese, and, more important under the Tang, Late Middle Chinese, on the one hand, and the local speakers of Proto-Viet-Muong, on the other.[25] The extent of Hán-Việt influence in the Vietnamese lexicon far exceeds the "bejeweling" of the language with a stratum of neologisms and prestige loan words to include "such a vast number of basic Chinese loanwords" as to indicate "a form of contact that was far more intimate, and far more pervasive."[26] The Chinese language spoken, however, was not an imported northern dialect, but rather a home-grown Annamese Middle Chinese, whose speakers shifted to Proto-Viet-Muong over the centuries following the end of Chinese imperial control, creating through their import of Chinese words and structures a hybrid form of Proto-Viet Muong that came to enjoy cultural and social prestige.[27]

From the eleventh century, state formation and social change unfolded over the centuries in fits and starts in various regions of the territory that today comprises Vietnam. A dynastic state identified as Đại Việt established itself with its capital in Thăng Long (today's Hà Nội) in the eleventh century under the Lý (1009–1225), and by the thirteenth century under the Trần (1225–1400) the growth of trade following the reunification of China under the Song dynasty (960–1279) had helped to stimulate rising economic prosperity and expanding political power in the coastal area of the Red River Delta. The evolution of coastal commercial forces in twelfth- and thirteenth-century Đại Việt involved new waves of immigration from southern China and the establishment of the Chinese examination system as a socializing rubric for the recruitment and selection of local state officeholders. Rooted in coastal commercial networks, these scholars of classical Chinese texts, including scions of immigrant Chinese literati families of recent vintage, helped to spearhead the increasing economic and political integration of the Red River plain during this period.[28]

24. Michael Churchman, "Before Chinese and Vietnamese in the Red River Plain: The Han-Tang Period," *Chinese Southern Diaspora Studies* 4 (2010): 25–37.

25. See John Duong Phan, "Lacquered Words: The Evolution of Vietnamese under Sinitic Influences from the 1st Century BCE to the 17th Century CE" (PhD diss., Cornell University, 2013).

26. John Duong Phan, "Re-Imagining 'Annam': A New Analysis of Sino-Viet-Muong Linguistic Contact," *Chinese Southern Diaspora Studies* 4 (2010): 9.

27. Duong Phan, "Re-Imagining 'Annam,'" 14–15.

28. John K. Whitmore, "The Rise of the Coast: Trade, State and Culture in Early Đại Việt," *Journal of Southeast Asian Studies* 37, no. 1 (February 2006): 103–122; Momoki Shiro, "Dai Viet

Subsequent developments further strengthened Sinographic cosmopolitanism in the Đại Việt realm. The brief Ming occupation (1407–1427) saw the founding of dozens of new schools, mostly in the Red River Delta and around the capital, enabling the establishment of a new system of triennial examinations for scholars steeped in classical Chinese texts and the recruitment of successive cohorts of neo-Confucian literati into state service. With seventy thousand men sufficiently schooled to take the exams by the turn of the sixteenth century, this "new, neo-Confucian indoctrinated elite" served as "cultural brokers at home in both village and capital" and as "role models and moral exemplars at the same time as they . . . watch[ed] over cultural orthodoxy in Đại Việt's more than seven thousand Vietnamese villages."[29]

For these literati, Đại Việt was the Southern Country, with the Northern Country ruled by the Ming: "Vietnamese elites engaged in a southern kind of self-representation, positing themselves and their country as inheritors and preservers of the classical culture that they shared with what they called the Northern Country, while still rooted in their southern land. While seeming to confirm the centrality of China by sharing classical 'Chinese' culture, Vietnamese governments and elites were actually decentering the Chinese world by positing a cultural hub beyond the borders of the Chinese state."[30] For these literati, Đại Việt constituted a "domain of manifest civility" akin to that found in China,[31] and with their immersion in classical Chinese texts came a set of proclivities and practices conducive to the strengthening of state power, most obviously through the production and accumulation of new forms of (written) knowledge.[32]

These developments and trends combined with the twenty-year period of Chinese reconquest and reincorporation of the Red River plain (1407–1427) in the tumultuous early years of the Ming dynasty (1368–1644) to set the stage for subsequent state formation and expansion under the Lê dynasty. The defeat of the Ming armies proved decisive: "With the increasingly centralized government, greatly expanded revenues, more advanced military technology and freedom from

---

and the South China Sea Trade from the 10th to the 15th Century," *Crossroads* 12, no. 1 (1998): 1–34.

29. Nola Cooke, "Nineteenth-Century Vietnamese Confucianization in Historical Perspective: Evidence from the Palace Examinations (1463–1883)," *Journal of Southeast Asian Studies* 25, no. 2 (September 1994): 270–312, at 280.

30. Kathlene Baldanza, *Ming China and Vietnam: Negotiating Borders in Early Modern Asia* (Cambridge: Cambridge University Press, 2016), 6.

31. Liam C. Kelley, *Beyond the Bronze Pillars: Envoy Poetry and the Sino-Vietnamese Relationship* (Honolulu: University of Hawai'i Press, 2005), 37. See also Liam Kelley, "Vietnam as a 'Domain of Manifest Civility' (Văn Hiến chi Bang)," *Journal of Southeast Asian Studies* 34, no. 1 (February 2003): 63–76.

32. See John K. Whitmore, "Literati Culture and Integration in Dai Viet, c. 1430–c. 1840," *Modern Asian Studies* 31, no. 3 (July 1997): 665–687, and John K. Whitmore, "Paperwork: The Rise of the New Literati and Ministerial Power and the Effort toward Legibility in Đại Việt," in *Southeast Asia in the Fifteenth Century: The China Factor*, ed. Geoff Wade and Sun Laichen (Singapore: NUS Press, 2010), 104–125.

Chinese threats, Đại Việt imposed firm control over its neighboring areas on a scale that had never been seen in its history."[33] But by the mid-seventeenth century, dynastic transition and turmoil in China combined with a broader recession in international commerce to reduce the externally derived revenues facilitating if not fueling Đại Việt state formation. Although Đại Việt's victories over the kingdom of Champa in what today comprises central Vietnam enabled extension of its control over South China Sea trade flows in the region, the topography of the series of riverine valleys lining the narrow lowland belt between the coastline and the Annamite mountain range from the Red River plain to the Mekong River Delta constrained the possibilities for sustained southward state building by Đại Việt. Indeed, the Lê dynasty faced serious challenges in the early–mid sixteenth century, and by the turn of the seventeenth century, Đại Việt had disintegrated as a coherent realm, with the Red River plain under the effective control of the influential Trịnh clan, while what today comprises central Vietnam was in the hands of the Nguyễn clan.[34]

From the early seventeenth century through the mid-nineteenth century, new patterns of international commerce and processes of institutional change began to unfold far south of the Red River plain and the Tonkin Gulf, with new forces of economic development and political dynamism emerging outside Đại Việt.[35] Enabled by the military technologies and institutional transformations inherited from the Ming occupation,[36] the Nguyễn established their rule in the former lands of Champa, a loosely structured maritime state within the orbit of the Sanskrit Cosmopolis that had experienced a period of efflorescence in the tenth and eleventh centuries before its gradual eclipse and eventual evisceration by Đại Việt in the late fifteenth century.[37]

Here by the seventeenth century, a new commercial hub emerged in the coastal town of Hội An, at the mouth of the Thu Bồn River, the biggest waterway between the Red River plain to the north and the Mekong Delta to the south, with tributaries extending deep into the highlands as far as today's border with Laos.[38] Crucial to the emergence and evolution of Hội An as a major port was its large

33. Li Tana, "The Ming Factor and the Emergence of the Việt in the 15th Century," in *Southeast Asia in the Fifteenth Century*, 92.

34. See Nola Cooke, "Regionalism and the Nature of Nguyen Rule in Seventeenth-Century Dang Trong (Cochinchina)," *Journal of Southeast Asian Studies* 29, no. 1 (March 1998): 122–161.

35. See Li Tana, "An Alternative Vietnam? The Nguyen Kingdom in the Seventeenth and Eighteenth Centuries," *Journal of Southeast Asian Studies* 29, no. 1 (March 1998): 111–121.

36. Sun Laichen, "Chinese Gunpowder Technology and Đại Việt, ca. 1390–1497," in *Việt Nam: Borderless Histories*, ed. Nhung Tuyet Tran and Anthony Reid (Madison: University of Wisconsin Press, 2006), 72–120.

37. See Kenneth R. Hall, *Maritime Trade and State Development in Early Southeast Asia* (Honolulu: University of Hawaii Press, 1985), 178–193.

38. See Charles J. Wheeler, "Cross-Cultural Trade and Trans-Regional Networks in the Port of Hoi An" (PhD diss., Yale University, 2001).

community of so-called Ming Loyalists (Minh Hương), itinerant traders and immigrants from the southern coast of China during the preceding centuries whose numbers were enhanced by refugees fleeing the Qing after the upheaval of 1644, and who served as crucial intermediaries in the growing trade with ports such as Guangzhou and Nagasaki.[39] Thanks to rising revenues from the expanding maritime commerce mediated by Minh Hương merchants in Hội An, the Nguyễn state was strengthened against its Trịnh rivals to the north and fiscally sustained as it extended its control southward into the Mekong Delta.

> The state consolidated its control over key regional markets, where Chinese merchants were already established, and products under court monopoly like aromatic woods and precious metals. The military secured the integration of new conquests with other regions in Dang Trong, by establishing posts along the coastal highway and at key overland passes. Security of travel encouraged the increased flow of male Vietnamese migrants from northern regions into native population centers of the southern frontier, which stimulated interregional trade within Dang Trong. Population, commerce, and trade grew in coastal port centers and these centers shipped their growing exports to Hoi An.[40]

Indeed, over the course of the seventeenth and eighteenth centuries, the "water frontier" of the Mekong Delta emerged as a new hub for maritime commerce, as Chinese junks, British country traders, and other Asian and European mercantile interests established and expanded trade links with ports along the vast coastline stretching south from Hội An to the Mekong Delta and west along the Gulf of Siam and south to the Malay Peninsula.[41] In particular, these ports became the major focus of Guangzhou's junk trade, attracting 85 to 90 percent of all the Cantonese junks sailing annually between Guangzhou and Southeast Asia by the 1760s.[42] As in Hội An, immigrants from the southern coastal provinces of China played a key role in the settlement of the Mekong Delta and in the establishment of new ports paying taxes or tribute to the Nguyễn state with its capital in Phú Xuân (present-day Huế). But compared with Hội An, the new ports of the Me-

39. Charles Wheeler, "Interests, Institutions, and Identity: Strategic Adaptation and the Ethno-evolution of *Minh Hương* (Central Vietnam), 16th–19th Centuries," *Itinerario* 39, no. 1 (April 2015): 141–166.

40. Wheeler, "Cross-Cultural Trade and Trans-Regional Networks," 174.

41. On the thriving port of Hà Tiên, for example, see Li Tana and Paul A. Van Dyke, "Canton, Cancao, and Cochinchina: New Data and New Light on Eighteenth-Century Canton and the Nanyang," *Chinese Southern Diaspora Studies* 1 (2007): 10–28. See also Li Tana, "The Eighteenth-Century Mekong Delta and Its World of Water Frontier," in *Việt Nam: Borderless Histories*, ed. Nhung Tuyet Tran and Anthony Reid (Madison: University of Wisconsin Press, 2006), 147–162.

42. Li Tana, "The Water Frontier: An Introduction," in *Water Frontier: Commerce and the Chinese in the Lower Mekong Region, 1750–1880*, ed. Nola Cooke and Li Tana (Lanham, MD: Rowman and Littlefield, 2004), 9.

kong Delta were distinguished by their access to much more extensive and fertile hinterlands, extending up the Mekong and deep into what today comprises Cambodia, providing the basis for unprecedented rice exports to Guangzhou, Xiamen, Singapore, and elsewhere.[43] The forested areas of the Delta also provided timber for a growing shipbuilding industry, enabling the construction and sale of hundreds, indeed thousands, of Chinese junks for use in the expanding rice trade by the mid-eighteenth century.[44]

While driven by accelerating demographic growth and increasing dependency on rice imports in the Pearl River Delta and elsewhere in the southern coastal provinces of China,[45] these developments of the "Chinese century"[46] in the Mekong Delta had transformative consequences for the making of state and society in the territory that today comprises Vietnam. By the mid-eighteenth century, the Nguyễn state had extended its administered territory across the breadth of the Mekong Delta,[47] exploiting the fruits of expanding overseas trade as the fiscal basis for state making during a period of escalating competition and conflict—and territorial consolidation and centralization—across mainland Southeast Asia.[48] In its growing ambition and aggression, the Nguyễn state clearly overextended itself, as seen in recurring conflicts with Siamese forces and rising tax demands on the ethnically diverse and geographically dispersed populations of the lowland plains, coastline, and upland areas of its expanding realm, which eventually provoked a large-scale uprising, the Tây Sơn rebellion, that lasted more than thirty years (1771–1802) and engulfed the full breadth of the territory stretching from the Mekong Delta to the Red River plain and the border of Guangxi Province in China, including the realm of Đại Việt long ruled by the Trịnh clan.[49]

But as the Nguyễn retreated to the Gia Định area around what came to be Sài Gòn and regrouped, the revenues from control over the rice trade in the Mekong Delta and the access to the resources of its unparalleled hinterlands allowed for the recruitment of a diverse group of soldiers and sailors, the launching of well-equipped military assaults by land and sea, and, eventually by 1802, the

43. Anthony Reid, "Chinese Trade and Southeast Asian Economic Expansion in the Later Eighteenth and Early Nineteenth Centuries: An Overview," in *Water Frontier*, 21–34.

44. Li Tana, "Ships and Shipbuilding in the Mekong Delta, c. 1750–1840," in *Water Frontier*, 119–135.

45. Marks, *Tigers, Rice, Silk, and Silt*, 277–308.

46. Leonard Blussé, "Chinese Century: The Eighteenth Century in the South China Region," *Archipel* 58 (1999) 107–129. See also Carl A. Trocki, "Chinese Pioneering in Eighteenth-Century Southeast Asia," in *The Last Stand of Asian Autonomies: Responses to Modernity in the Diverse States of Southeast Asia and Korea, 1750–1900*, ed. Anthony Reid (Basingstoke: Macmillan, 1997), 83–101.

47. Li Tana, *Nguyễn Cochinchina: Southern Vietnam in the Seventeenth and Eighteenth Centuries* (Ithaca, NY: Cornell University Southeast Asia Program, 1998).

48. Victor Lieberman, *Strange Parallels: Southeast Asia in Global Context, c. 800–1830*, vol. 1, *Integration on the Mainland* (Cambridge: Cambridge University Press, 2003), 338–456.

49. George Dutton, *The Tây Sơn Uprising: Society and Rebellion in Eighteenth-Century Vietnam* (Honolulu: University of Hawai'i Press, 2006), 34–36. See also Tana, *Nguyễn Cochinchina*, 141–144.

unprecedented unification of the full breadth of the territory that today comprises Vietnam.[50] Manpower, elephants, rice, tax revenues, and timber for the construction of ships in the Nguyễn navy were sources from the Khmer-speaking areas of the Mekong Delta and up into what today comprises Cambodia.[51] It was the resources of the Mekong Delta and its hinterlands that enabled the Nguyễn to secure the assistance of Siamese troops, Portuguese mercenaries, and French ships and naval officers who proved so crucial for the gradual defeat of the Tây Sơn forces over 1787–1802.[52]

It was thus in considerable measure thanks to Cantonese trade, Chinese settlers, merchants, and peasants, and Khmer rice cultivators that a new kind of Nguyễn state emerged at the turn of the nineteenth century, setting the stage for a new kind of Vietnamese society that stretched from the Red River plain to the Mekong Delta. Based in its capital in Huế, the Nguyễn state was far more centralized and successfully institutionalized than its predecessors, especially after the administrative reforms of 1832 under the reign of Minh Mạng (1820–1841). Nguyễn expansion also extended into Cambodia, with an expedition of thirty thousand troops in 1813 overseeing the establishment of a new capital in Phnom Penh, and canal construction in the Mekong Delta during the following decade enabling easy access for Nguyễn warships.[53] By 1834, Phnom Penh had become a "Vietnamese city": "The market sold only Vietnamese food; rice and other foodstuffs were for the most part imported from Vietnam," and when members of the court were summoned for consultations with Nguyễn officials, they "had to put on Vietnamese bureaucratic costumes, and spoke what appears to have been a form of pidgin Vietnamese."[54] Although Siamese intervention in the 1840s drastically reduced Nguyễn influence and intervention in Cambodia, a steady process of "Vietnamization" continued to unfold in the ethnically diverse Mekong Delta, with the forcible imposition of Vietnamese language, dress, and customs.[55]

---

50. "Besides French, Spaniards, British, Lao and Chinese soldiers, Siamese troops, Khmer, Malays, and Chams participated in Nguyễn Phúc Ánh's military operations. Chinese pirates and hill minorities were also members of his forces." Choi Byung Wook, *Southern Vietnam under the Reign of Minh Mang (1820–1841): Central Policies and Local Responses* (Ithaca, NY: Cornell University Southeast Asia Program, 2004), 33. See also Wynn Wilcox, "Transnationalism and Multiethnicity in the Early Nguyễn Ánh Gia Long Period," in *Việt Nam: Borderless Histories*, 194–216.

51. Wilcox, "Transnationalism and Multiethnicity," 35.

52. Frédéric Mantienne, "The Transfer of Western Military Technology to Vietnam in the Late Eighteenth and Early Nineteenth Centuries: The Case of the Nguyễn," *Journal of Southeast Asian Studies* 34, no. 3 (October 2003): 519–534, especially 530–532.

53. David P. Chandler, "Cambodia before the French: Politics in a Tributary Kingdom, 1794–1848" (PhD diss., University of Michigan, 1973), 90–91, 103. See also David Biggs, "Problematic Progress: Reading Environmental and Social Change in the Mekong Delta," *Journal of Southeast Asian Studies* 34, no. 1 (February 2003): 77–96, at 86–88.

54. Biggs, "Problematic Progress," 128–129.

55. Choi Byung Wook, "Vietnamisation of Southern Vietnam during the First Half of the Nineteenth Century," *Asian Ethnicity* 4, no. 1 (February 2003): 47–65.

This "Vietnamization" drew on legacies of Sinographic cosmopolitanism appropriated by the Nguyễn state through its revival and restrengthening of the civil service examination system that had first developed under the Lê dynasty in Đại Việt in the fifteenth century. Under Minh Mạng in particular, the imperative of consolidating power over the sprawling territory of the Nguyễn realm encouraged reliance on established institutions for cooptation and control of regional and local elites far from the imperial capital in Huế.[56] In the 1830s, new schools were established for these purposes at the provincial, prefecture, and district levels, and the full triennial examination system was revived, including the higher, metropolitan level that awarded the most prestigious titles to successful candidates.[57] Through the examination system and the schools that sprung up to support it, the neo-Confucian core curriculum, "the Four Books and the Five Classics," provided the basis for socialization of Vietnamese men into the "Sinographic cosmopolitanism" that had largely survived in the northern Red River heartland of Đại Việt but had never really taken hold in the Nguyễn realm to the south, much less the ethnically diverse frontier zone of the Mekong Delta before the nineteenth century.[58]

> The whole examination system was a process of professional acculturation, of social and cultural change, for the individual Vietnamese student. He had to prove that he excelled, not merely in writing Chinese-style poetry but also in wearing specific types of clothing and in conforming to specific behavioral demands, like those associated with the proper Chinese-style methods of bowing, meditating, and using honorific words in encounters with equals and superiors. The higher his place became on the social and occupational scale as a result of the examinations, the more rigidly his behavioral patterns were prescribed for him. . . .
>
> This progressive cultural sinicization of the Vietnamese scholar as he rose through the examination system, together with the strong personal relationships he eventually developed with his examiners and with other students, bound him socially, intellectually, and emotionally to the values and interests of the bureaucratic ruling class.[59]

---

56. Nola Cooke, "The Composition of the Nineteenth-Century Political Elite of Pre-Colonial Nguyen Vietnam (1802–1883)," *Modern Asian Studies* 29, no. 4 (October 1995): 741–764, especially 762.

57. Wook, *Southern Vietnam under the Reign of Minh Mang (1820–1841)*, 115–128.

58. Nola Cooke, "Nineteenth-Century Vietnamese Confucianization in Historical Perspective: Evidence from the Palace Examinations (463–1883)," *Journal of Southeast Asian Studies* 25, no. 2 (September 1994): 270–312.

59. Alexander Barton Woodside, *Vietnam and the Chinese Model: A Comparative Study of Vietnamese and Chinese Government in the First Half of the Nineteenth Century* (Cambridge, MA: Harvard University Press, 1988), 199–200.

Indeed, this Sinographic cosmopolitanism was distinctive—and different from its Catholic and Islamic counterparts in the Philippine and Indonesian archipelagos—in its full subordination to the logic of state power and the project of state formation, prefiguring particular problems and possibilities for revolution making in Vietnamese society in the twentieth century when state support for this discursive tradition was eventually withdrawn.

Overall, as in the Philippine and Indonesian archipelagos, the emergence, evolution, and expansion of a "Vietnamese" state and society during the centuries of the Early Modern Era (1350–1850) unfolded in large measure in response to forces emanating from outside the realm of "Vietnam" and "the Vietnamese." On the one hand, the great transformations under way in China, especially in its southern coastal provinces, spilled over into the lands that today comprise Vietnam through successive waves of invasion, migration, and commercial integration, spurring a series of phases of state formation that eventually crystallized in a single unified realm. On the other hand, the intensifying interactions between the port polities of the Vietnamese coastline and their ethnically diverse hinterlands extending inland (and in some places, upland) far into present-day Cambodia and Laos provided the material resources and manpower for the making of a "Vietnamese" state and society. From the mid-nineteenth century through World War II, these key externally driven dynamics were reinforced by developments unfolding under the rubric of French colonial Indochina in ways that profoundly enabled the making of the Vietnamese Revolution.

Commercialization, Indochinese Integration, New Cosmopolitanism, 1850–1940

If the emergence, evolution, and expansion of Vietnamese society up into the Early Modern Era was enabled and impelled by maritime commerce, military occupations, and migratory movements emanating from China, so was its integration and internal transformation further facilitated and fuelled by external stimuli and by deepening incorporation into the regional and global circuitries of the world capitalist economy from the mid-nineteenth century through the onset of World War II. Thus, the period usually glossed as "the French colonial era" can also be understood as one in which the commercialization of agriculture and the creation of a market society unfolded in tandem with broadening and tightening linkages to the southern provinces of China, the upland interior regions, the "Indochinese" protectorates of Cambodia and Laos, and, as suggested above, French imperial outposts as far away as Madagascar and Dahomey (today's Benin). Against this backdrop, the late nineteenth and early twentieth centuries encouraged the emergence and efflorescence of new forms of modern cosmopolitanism in the Vietnamese territories of Cochinchina, Annam, and Tonkin, as seen in popular theater, literature, intellectual activity, and the political realm.

The immediate driver of change was French military conquest and the onset of colonization from the late 1850s into the mid-1880s. Beginning with an attack on Đà Nẵng by a small force of French and Spanish troops in 1858 and escalating with the seizure of Sài Gòn the following year, the French-led military campaign was ostensibly precipitated by growing concern about official persecution of Catholics at the hands of the Nguyễn, beginning under Emperor Minh Mạng in the 1820s and 1830s, and persisting under his successors Thiệu Trị (1841–1847) and Tự Đức (1848–1883).[60] By this time, an estimated eighty thousand Catholics were living in the Mekong Delta and as many as four hundred thousand elsewhere across the Nguyễn realm, reflecting the success of proselytization by the Société des Missions Étrangères de Paris (Society of Foreign Missions of Paris) during the preceding centuries.[61]

The religious imperative had been invoked decades earlier as a justification for foreign intervention at the time of the Tây Sơn rebellion in the late eighteenth century. The missionary Pierre Pigneau de Béhaine (1741–1799) assiduously sought assistance for the embattled Nguyễn prince Nguyễn Ánh, first from the Dominicans in Manila and Macao, and then from Louis XI, who promised military assistance in exchange for exclusive French trading rights in the Treaty of Versailles, which was signed in 1787 on the eve of the French Revolution but not implemented during subsequent years. In the end, Pigneau himself raised funds to purchase arms, ammunition, and warships, and recruited French soldiers, sailors, and officers who played a role in the defeat of the Tây Sơn and the restoration of the Nguyễn at the turn of the nineteenth century.[62]

In contrast to the lack of follow-through on the part of the Ancien Régime, the Deuxième Empire under Napoleon III (1852–1870) was one of dramatically increasing trade, expanding naval power, and aggressive liberal "free trade imperialism," as seen in French investment in the construction of the Suez Canal (1858–1869) and sustained interest in East Asia in the decades following the Opium Wars in China (1839–1842, 1856–1860). By 1862, French military conquest had forced the formal cession of Sài Gòn and the southern provinces of the Mekong Delta by the Nguyễn emperor, with a French protectorate established

---

60. Jacob Ramsay, *Mandarins and Martyrs: The Church and the Nguyen Dynasty in Early Nineteenth-Century Vietnam* (Stanford, CA: Stanford University Press, 2008).

61. Alain Forest, *Les Missionaires Français au Tonkin et au Siam (XVIIᵉ-XVIIIᵉ Siècles): Analyse Comparée d'un Relatif Succès et d'un Total Échec* (Paris: L'Harmattan, 1998).

62. Frédéric Mantienne, *Pierre Pigneaux: Evêque d'Adran et Mandarin de Cochinchine (1741–1799)* (Paris: Les Indes Savantes, 2012).

over Cambodia in 1863 and the remaining provinces of the Mekong Delta occupied by French forces by 1867.[63] By 1874, a second treaty won formal recognition of French sovereignty over the entire Mekong Delta and the full breadth of the region identified as Cochinchina, as well as the opening of the Red River and the ports of Hà Nội and Hải Phòng to French commerce. By 1885, a French protectorate had been established over the Nguyễn court in Huế and the territories that became known as Annam and Tonkin in what today comprise central and northern Vietnam, respectively, with Tonkin's borders with the Chinese provinces of Guangxi and Yunnan recognized by the Qing court at the end of the Sino-French War of 1884–1885. Thus, even as the avowed concern for fellow Catholics seen in the Deuxième Empire was replaced by the official anticlericalism of the Troisième République after 1870,[64] the commercial interests of Lyon, Bordeaux, Marseille, and Paris, the growing ambitions of the French Navy, and the strategic imperative of gaining access to China sustained the forward movement of French imperialism from the Mekong Delta upriver and inland into Cambodia, northward along the Vietnamese coast to the Gulf of Tonkin, and inland along the Red River toward the Chinese province of Yunnan in the final decades of the nineteenth century.[65]

French conquest and colonization precipitated the onset of economic and demographic processes across Cochinchina, Annam, and Tonkin roughly parallel to those unfolding across many areas of the Philippine and Indonesian archipelago during the latter half of the nineteenth century and the early twentieth century: the expansion and intensification of commercialized agricultural production, the acceleration of population growth, and new waves of migration on a massive scale accompanying deepening incorporation into the world economy. The impact was most obvious in Cochinchina, where French establishment of free trade, massive investment in canal construction and land reclamation in the Mekong Delta, and the awarding of 600,000 hectares in land concessions helped to stimulate a dramatic expansion in rice cultivation.[66] Land planted to rice grew from an estimated 500,000 acres in 1870 to 4.1 million acres on the eve of World War I; demographic growth saw the population rising from an estimated 1.2

---

63. Thi Thanh Nguyễn, "The French Conquest of Cochinchina, 1858–1862" (PhD diss., Cornell University, 1992).

64. J. P. Daughton, *An Empire Divided, Religion, Republicanism, and the Making of French Colonialism, 1880–1914* (Oxford: Oxford University Press, 2006).

65. See Milton E. Osborne, *River Road to China: The Mekong River Expedition, 1866–1873* (London: Allen & Unwin, 1975); Michael P. M. Finch, *A Progressive Occupation? The Gallieni-Lyautey Method and Colonial Pacification in Tonkin and Madagascar, 1885–1900* (Oxford: Oxford University Press, 2013).

66. See John Louis Bassford, "Land Development Policy in Cochinchina under the French (1865–1925)" (PhD diss., University of Hawaii, 1984), and David Biggs, *Quagmire: Nation-Building and Nature in the Mekong Delta* (Seattle: University of Washington Press, 2010), 23–51, 70–90.

million in 1867 to 3.0 million in 1910, and 4.6 million in 1936. Rice exports boomed, from an average of 55,000 tons per annum in the early 1860s to nearly 800,000 tons per annum in the early 1910s, and 1.7 million tons per annum by the mid-1930s.[67] From a sparsely settled "frontier" region, the Mekong Delta and the broader region of Cochinchina was rapidly transformed into a densely populated export production and processing zone.

Meanwhile, previously established regions of concentrated settlement in coastal and lowland Tonkin and Annam likewise experienced dramatic economic and demographic transformation as French rule deepened their incorporation into the world economy. French land concessions totaling 100,000 hectares in Tonkin and 168,000 hectares in Annam combined with rising taxes and "free trade" to stimulate an intensification and expansion of rice cultivation and accelerated population growth, spelling Javanese-style agricultural involution, especially in Tonkin. By the early 1930s, the population of Tonkin had swelled to an estimated 6.5 million, with a density of 430 people per square kilometer, which was unmatched across Southeast Asia, and a landscape increasingly subdivided into ever tinier parcels of more and more intensively cultivated rice land. As of 1932, more than 60 percent of Tonkinese smallholders owned parcels of less than 0.36 hectares, and more than 90 percent owned parcels of less than 1.8 hectares. Rising pressures on the land produced increasing landlessness, indebtedness, and immiseration, encroachment on villages' communal lands, and large-scale labor migration, with an estimated 50,000 Tonkinese peasants leaving the Red River Delta each year by the 1930s for the coal mines of Tonkin, the rubber plantations of Annam and Cochinchina, major cities such as Hà Nội, Hải Phòng, and Sài Gòn, and other destinations.[68]

In some measure, these dramatic economic and demographic trends and transformations across Cochinchina, Annam, and Tonkin gave rise not only to a market society but also to a *Vietnamese* society whose unprecedented integration was enabled by both a capitalist market and a colonial state. Villages and villagers once only loosely incorporated within dynastic realms through the institution of the classical Chinese-style civil service examinations were now more intensively and intimately drawn into the orbit of Hà Nội, Hải Phòng, and Sài Gòn through market circuitries; modern road, rail, and steamboat links; the administrative grid of the colonial bureaucracy; an expanding network of primary and secondary schools; and the accompanying spread of the field of "print capitalism" in the

67. See Norman G. Owen, "The Rice Industry of Mainland Southeast Asia, 1850–1914," *Journal of the Siam Society* 59, no. 2 (January 1971): 75–143, and Guy Gran, "Vietnam and the Capitalist Road to Modernity: Village Cochinchina, 1880–1940" (PhD diss., University of Wisconsin at Madison, 1975), 63.

68. Pierre Gourou, *Les Paysans du Delta Tonkinois: Étude de Géographie Humaine* (Paris: Mouton, 1965), 197, 213–217, 356–357.

romanized Vietnamese writing system known as *quốc ngữ*. Circulation and communication within this increasingly unified realm made it more and more possible for more and more migrant laborers, school graduates, colonial civil servants, railroad and steamboat passengers, and newspaper readers to begin to imagine themselves as fellow Vietnamese. Demographic growth, rising landlessness, and increasing migration also saw increasing numbers of lowland Vietnamese speakers moving in unprecedented numbers into highland areas and border regions of Annam and Tonkin, enabling and impelling a process of ethnolinguistic Vietnamese internal colonization of the full extent of the territory today known as Vietnam.[69]

At the same time, however, the economic and demographic trends and transformations unfolding across Cochinchina, Tonkin, and Annam over the latter half of the nineteenth century and the first four decades of the twentieth century had other important consequences accompanying and exceeding those associated with Vietnamese (proto-) nationalization. First, the deepening incorporation of Cochinchina, Tonkin, and Annam into the world economy was accompanied by tightening commercial, infrastructural, and financial integration with southern China, most notably Guangzhou (or Canton) and its hinterland in the coastal province of Guangdong. The ports of Sài Gòn and Hải Phòng, it is worth noting, attracted considerable French interest as potential commercial hubs and points of access to southern China rivaling British Hong Kong, especially after the forced evacuation of French forces from Zhoushan (Chusan) Island, across from the Chinese port city of Ningpo, in Zhejiang Province, south of Shanghai, following the signing of the treaties ending the Second Opium (or Arrow) War in 1860. French exploration of the Mekong and the Red River from the late 1860s through the mid-1880s had likewise been undertaken with an eye to commercial penetration of the southern inland provinces of the vast Qing realm.

With the establishment of the Banque de l'Indochine in 1875 by a consortium of French banks and companies based in Paris, Lyon, Marseille, and Strasbourg, a vehicle emerged for French investment in southern China, challenging the hegemonic position of British banks in the region.[70] While serving as the issuing bank of the French colonial state in Indochina, the Banque de l'Indochine began to work with major French shipping lines such as the Marseille-based Messageries Maritimes to expand trade along routes connecting French, Vietnamese, and

---

69. Andrew Hardy, *Red Hills: Migrants and the State in the Highlands of Vietnam* (Copenhagen: Nordic Institute of Asian Studies, 2003), 69–116.

70. Yasuo Gonjo, *Banque Coloniale ou Banque d'Affaires: La Banque de l'Indochine sous la IIIe République* (Paris: Comité pour l'Histoire Économique et Financière de la France, 1993), 30–37. See also Marc Meuleau, *Des Pionniers en Extrême-Orient: Histoire de la Banque de l'Indochine (1875–1975)* (Paris: Fayard, 1990), especially 32–59 on the founding of the bank, and 179–251 on its expansion into southern China.

Chinese ports from the 1880s onward,[71] while joining a consortium of French banks and major railway firms to fund a railroad line connecting Tonkin to Yunnan Province in the early 1900s.[72] By 1895, a succession of treaties and trade conventions had not only formally established the borders between Indochina and the Qing realm but also forcibly opened southern Chinese coastal ports and inland provinces to French commerce, mining concessions, and railroad construction. Thanks to its beachhead in Indochina, the position of French banks and companies as junior partners to British capital in East Asia was established by the turn of the twentieth century, as seen in the opening of new Banque de l'Indochine offices in Hankou, Guangzhou, and Chongqing and its participation in British-led consortia funding large-scale railroad construction and other major ventures across the Qing realms.[73]

The integration of Cochinchina, Annam, and Tonkin within this broader French strategy and surge of investment in late Qing China extended beyond the realm of finance to encompass trade flows as well. Exports of rice from Sài Gòn found their way to diverse markets across Southeast Asia and beyond, but with Hong Kong and other southern coastal Chinese ports as primary destinations consistently claiming the largest share of overall value and volume, from the 1880s through the 1930s.[74] As Chinese peasants in the Pearl River Delta converted more and more land from rice cultivation to mulberry tree embankment and fishpond-based sericulture to meet rising demand from Lyonnais merchants desperate for new supplies of raw silk after the devastation of the silkworm epidemic (la pébrine) in mid-nineteenth century France, rice imported from Sài Gòn (and to a lesser extent, Hải Phòng) helped to compensate for the increasing shortfall in paddy cultivation in the hinterlands of Guangzhou.[75] Thus, the making of a market society across Cochinchina, Annam, and Tonkin unfolded in lockstep with broader economic transformations in the neighboring coastal provinces of southern China.

71. Marie-François Berneron-Couvenhes, *Les Messageries Maritimes: L'Essor d'une Grande Compagnie de Navigation Française, 1851–1894* (Paris: Presses de l'Université Paris-Sorbonne, 2007), 131–134, 223–227.

72. Rang Ri Park-Barjot, "Le Patronat Français des Travaux Publics et les Réseaux Ferroviaires dans l'Empire Français: L'Exemple du Chemin de Fer du Yunnan (1898–1913)," in *L'Esprit Économique Imperial (1830–1970): Groupes de Pression et Réseaux du Patronat Colonial en France et dans l'Empire*, ed. Hubert Bonin, Catherine Hodeir, and Jean-François-Klein (Paris: Société Française d'Histoire des Outre-Mers, 2008), 653–670.

73. Evan W. Edwards, "The Origins of British Financial Co-operation with France in China, 1903–6," *English Historical Review* 86, no. 339 (April 1971): 284–317. Robert S. Lee, *France and the Exploitation of China, 1885–1901: A Study in Economic Imperialism* (Oxford: Oxford University Press, 1989), 110–137, 141–173.

74. Kham Vorapeth, *Commerce et Colonisation en Indochine (1860–1945): Les Maisons de Commerce Françaises, Un Siècle d'Aventure Humaine* (Paris: Les Indes Savantes, 2004), 563–564, 571–575.

75. Marks, *Tigers, Rice, Silk, and Silt*, 117–120, 181–183; Julia Martinez, "Chinese Rice Trade and Shipping from the North Vietnamese Port of Hải Phòng," *Chinese Southern Diaspora Studies* 1 (2007): 82–96.

Deepening economic integration, moreover, entailed expanding circulation not only of commodities but also of labor and capital. On the one hand, the expanding steamboat traffic on the shipping lanes between Sài Gòn (and to a lesser extent, Hải Phòng), Hong Kong, Guangzhou, and other Chinese ports drew thousands of sailors from Tonkin, Annam, and Cochinchina into maritime employment and travel in the South China Sea and elsewhere, thus vastly expanding their horizons beyond the shores of Vietnam.[76] On the other hand, the proximity and primacy of the southern Chinese market for Indochinese rice and other export products encouraged a dramatic increase in immigration and investment from Guangzhou and its hinterlands in the late nineteenth and early twentieth centuries, prefiguring a position for Chinese capital within the emerging Vietnamese economy and society arguably even more prominent—and potentially problematic—than that observed in the Philippine and Indonesian archipelagos during the same period. As hundreds of thousands of Chinese immigrants arrived in Cochinchina, Annam, and Tonkin during these decades, they came to assume control over the milling and marketing of rice and other key commodities, to capture the lucrative revenue farms not reserved for French companies, and to dominate the ranks of the moneylenders and merchants who served as the intermediaries in the expanding circuitries of the emerging Vietnamese economy.[77] French insistence on registration, taxation, and juridical cantonment of these immigrants in *congrégations* and other colonial regulations combined with ease and frequency of steamboat traffic to and from southern Chinese ports to inhibit assimilation into Vietnamese society.[78]

Overall, this formative period in the making of an integrated Vietnamese market society across Cochinchina, Annam, and Tonkin unfolded in a specific regional and international context and thus in a particular fashion rather different from that observed in the Philippine and Indonesian archipelagos. The establishment of French colonial rule was accompanied, enabled and impelled, and arguably overshadowed by deepening economic integration with southern China and economic colonization by both French and Chinese capital. In this context, the Vietnamese market society that had begun to crystallize by the turn of the twen-

---

76. Berneron-Couvenhes, *Les Messageries Maritimes*, 480–490; Kimloan Vu-Hill, *Coolies into Rebels: Impact of World War I on French Indochina* (Paris: Les Indes Savantes, 2011), 121–122.

77. Gerard Sasges, *Imperial Intoxication: Alcohol and the Making of Colonial Indochina* (Honolulu: University of Hawai'i Press, 2017); Gerard Sasges, "Scaling the Commanding Heights: The Colonial Conglomerates and the Changing Political Economy of French Indochina," *Modern Asian Studies* 49, no. 5 (September 2015): 1485–1525; Chantal Descours-Gatin, *Quand L'Opium Finançait La Colonisation en Indochine: L'Élaboration de la Régie Générale de l'Opium (1860–1914)* (Paris: Éditions L'Harmattan, 1992).

78. Tracy C. Barrett, "Transnational Webs: Overseas Chinese Economic and Political Networks in Colonial Vietnam, 1870–1945" (PhD diss., Cornell University, 2007); Trung Vu Nguyen, "Marginalizing Practices: Bureaucracy, Ethnography and Becoming Chinese in Colonial Vietnam" (PhD diss., University of Wisconsin at Madison, 2009).

tieth century was one in which Vietnamese capital formation was severely constrained, as was the emergence of a protonational(ist) bourgeoisie, even along the
relatively modest lines witnessed in Java and Sumatra in the heyday of the Sarekat
Islam.[79]

Meanwhile, alongside the enormous impact and enduring importance of *Chinese* context, connections, and economic control, the making of Vietnamese society was also marked by its simultaneous extension and integration within
Indochina. French canal construction and land reclamation in the Mekong Delta
greatly facilitated steamboat travel up the Mekong River and the extension of Sài
Gòn's hinterland into the rice-growing villages of Cambodia. By the early twentieth century, as demographic pressures continued to build up in Tonkin and Annam, and as commercialization of agriculture and French colonization penetrated
further inland and upriver into the western reaches of Indochina, thousands of
Vietnamese migrated to Laos and Cambodia, as plantation laborers, railroad workers, peasant settlers, fishermen, petty traders, and colonial civil servants.[80] By the
late 1930s, more than 190,000 migrants from Tonkin, Annam, and Cochinchina
were estimated to be living in Cambodia, where they constituted more than
60 percent of the population of Phnom Penh and a high proportion of the residents of other conurbations in the territory; another 27,000 were estimated to be
residing in Laos, where they occupied a majority of local bureaucratic posts and
outnumbered Laotians in the capital of Vientiane and other towns.[81] Patterns of
Vietnamese mercantile activity and migration in the late nineteenth and early
twentieth centuries also extended beyond French colonial Indochina, spilling over
into neighboring Siam (later Thailand), where thousands of Vietnamese émigrés
settled in Bangkok and other towns, especially in northeast provinces adjacent to
Laos and along the Gulf of Siam.[82]

At the same time, such patterns of movement extended far beyond Southeast Asia to enable an even broader and more cosmopolitan set of contacts,

79. Pierre Brocheux, *Une Histoire Économique du Viet Nam 1850–2007: La Palanche et Le Ca-
mion* (Paris: Les Indes Savantes, 2009), 121–128, especially 125–126. For the Vietnamese counterpart
to Sarekat Islam, see Micheline Lessard, "'*Organisons-Nous!*': Racial Antagonism and Vietnamese
Economic Nationalism in the Early Twentieth Century," *French Colonial History* 8 (2007): 171–201.

80. For an illuminating overview, see Christopher E. Goscha, *Vietnam or Indochina? Contesting
Concepts of Space in Vietnamese Nationalism, 1887–1954* (Copenhagen: Nordic Institute of Asian
Studies, 1995), 13–46.

81. Alain Forest, *Le Cambodge et la Colonisation Française: Histoire d'une Colonisation sans
Heurts* (Paris: Éditions L'Harmattan, 1980), 446; Margaret Slocomb, *An Economic History of Cambodia in the Twentieth Century* (Singapore: National University of Singapore Press, 2010), 47; Pierre
Brocheux and Daniel Hémery, *Indochina: An Ambiguous Colonization, 1858–1954* (Berkeley: University of California Press, 2009), 262; Christopher E. Goscha, *Thailand and the Southeast Asian Networks of the Vietnamese Revolution, 1885–1854* (Copenhagen: Nordic Institute of Asian Studies,
1999), 27; Søren Ivarsson, *Creating Laos: The Making of a Lao Space between Indochina and Siam,
1960–1945* (Copenhagen: Nordic Institute of Asian Studies, 2008), 101.

82. Goscha, *Thailand and Southeast Asian Networks*, 14–23.

communications, and connections across the vast expanse of the French colonial empire and beyond. World War I served as a catalyst thanks to heavy French reliance on and recruitment of African and Asian soldiers and laborers during the conflict. French troops included more than 170,000 soldiers from Algeria, 60,000 from Tunisia, 40,000 from Madagascar, 37,000 from Morocco, and nearly 50,000 from Indochina, overwhelmingly from Annam and Tonkin. More than 220,000 workers from Asia and Africa were recruited to work in munitions factories, administrative services, road works, and other private and public ventures, with 48,000 imported from Indochina and the remainder drawn from various French colonies in Africa.[83] By one estimate, the total number of Asian and African colonial troops and workers transported to Europe during the war came to 900,000,[84] plus well over 150,000 Chinese coolie laborers.[85] While deployment of these African and Asian soldiers and workers was highly regimented and restrictive in terms of wages, working conditions, and mobility, some Indochinese troops and laborers enjoyed considerable opportunities for mixing and mingling with their counterparts from elsewhere across the French Empire and for immersion within the more broadly multicultural milieu of the "French" working class, with its sizeable pockets of recent Spanish and Italian immigration, most notably in the "gateway" port city of Marseille and in certain *arrondissements* and *fauborgs* of Paris.[86] The end of the war saw immediate demobilization and unceremonious repatriation of these Asian and African soldiers and workers, but small numbers stayed on to work and to study, supplemented by a small but steady flow of Vietnamese students over subsequent decades.[87] Thus, by the early decades of the twentieth century the transcontinental and transoceanic ambit of circulation, communications, and connections for tens of thousands of Vietnamese speakers extended far beyond the boundaries of Cochinchina, Annam, Tonkin, and the broader expanse of Indochina to encompass diverse parts of Asia, Africa, and Europe.

Against this backdrop, by the 1920s the growth of Sài Gòn, Hà Nội, Hải Phòng, and other cities and towns accompanying the commercialization of agriculture

---

83. Kimloan Thi Vu Hill, "A Westward Journey, An Enlightened Path: Vietnamese Linh Tho, 1915–1930" (PhD diss., University of Oregon, 2001), 28–29, 41.

84. Claude Liauzu, *Aux Origines des Tiers-Mondismes: Colonisés et Anticolonialistes en France (1919–1939)* (Paris: Éditions L'Harmattan, 1982), 100.

85. Marilyn A. Levine, *The Found Generation: Chinese Communists in Europe during the Twenties* (Seattle: University of Washington Press, 1993), 65–66.

86. Kimloan Hill, "Strangers in a Foreign Land: Vietnamese Soldiers and Workers in France during World War I," in *Việt Nam: Borderless Histories*, ed. Nhung Tuyet Tran and Anthony Reid (Madison: University of Wisconsin Press, 2006), 256–289. See also Tyler Stovall, "Colour-blind France? Colonial Workers during the First World War," *Race and Class* 35, no. 2 (1993): 35–55.

87. Scott McConnell, *Leftward Journey: The Education of Vietnamese Students in France, 1919–1939* (New Brunswick, NJ: Transaction, 1989); Erica J. Peters, "Resistance, Rivalries, and Restaurants: Vietnamese Workers in Interwar France," *Journal of Vietnamese Studies* 2, no. 1 (Winter 2002): 109–143.

and the evolution of an increasingly integrated market society across Cochinchina, Tonkin, and Annam had enabled the emergence not only of a shared field of Vietnamese national imagining and identity but also of new forms of cosmopolitan modern consciousness and representation in the urban public sphere and beyond.[88] With the abolition of the Chinese-style civil service examination system in the 1910s[89] came the evisceration of the system of schooling in classical Chinese philosophy and literature, the eclipse of Sinographic cosmopolitanism, and the establishment in its place of institutions of modern education in French and, crucially, Vietnamese in the romanized script known as *quốc ngữ*,[90] which had been invented by Portuguese missionaries in the seventeenth century[91] but remained largely unused until its rediscovery and redeployment in the 1860s and its gradual development over subsequent decades by the embryonic French colonial regime.[92] As enrollment in these schools increased to encompass hundreds of thousands of new pupils during the interwar era,[93] literacy in *quốc ngữ* expanded, incorporating an estimated 1.8 million speakers and readers of the Vietnamese language (roughly 10 percent of the population) by the eve of World War II.[94] Mass literacy in *quốc ngữ* enabled and impelled the rise of new forms of print culture, as seen in the proliferation of newspapers, magazines, and other periodicals in the 1920s and 1930s.[95]

These publications reflected and reproduced a distinctly modern form of cosmopolitan consciousness, especially in urban settings notable for their sizeable Chinese, European, and Indian populations and for technological and cultural fixtures linking them to other cities and societies across the world. A single Sài Gòn or Hà Nội newspaper page in the 1920s or 1930s might feature, for example, "advertisements for sausages, trains and diamonds among announcements

---

88. On Tonkin, for example, see Nguyên Văn Ký, *La Société Vietnamienne face à la Modernité: Le Tonkin de la Fin du XIXᵉ Siècle à la Seconde Guerre Mondiale* (Paris: LHarmattan, 1995).

89. Emmanuel Poisson, *Mandarins et Subalternes au Nord du Viêt Nam: Une Bureaucratie à l'Épreuve (1820–1918)* (Paris: Maisonneuve et Larose, 2004).

90. Gail Paradise Kelly, "Franco-Vietnamese Schools, 1918 to 1938" (PhD diss., University of Wisconsin at Madison, 1975).

91. Roland Jacques, "Le Portugal et La Romanisation de la Langue Vietnamienne: Faut-il réécrire l'Histoire?," *Revue Française d'Histoire d'Outre-Mer* 85, no. 318 (1998): 21–54.

92. John DeFrancis, *Colonialism and Language Policy in Viet Nam* (The Hague: Mouton, 1977), 71–219.

93. Enrollment rose from 125,000 students in 1920 to more than 287,000 in 1938. Kelly, "Franco Vietnamese Schools," 76a–77c. See also Trần Thị Phương Hoa, "From Liberally-Organized to Centralized Schools: Education in Tonkin, 1885–1927," *Journal of Vietnamese Studies* 8, no. 3 (2013): 27–70.

94. David Marr, *Vietnamese Tradition on Trial, 1920–1945* (Berkeley: University of California Press, 1981), 34.

95. Shawn Frederick McHale, *Print and Power: Confucianism, Communism, and Buddhism in the Making of Modern Vietnam* (Honolulu: University of Hawai'i Press, 2004), 17–27; Philippe M. F. Peycam, *The Birth of Vietnamese Political Journalism: Saigon 1916–1930* (New York: Columbia University Press, 2012).

of ship timetables, essays on colonial life and commentaries on the role of women in the family."[96] The "backward" village chief Lý Toét spoofed in the cartoon series produced in the Hà Nội weekly *Phong Hóa* published by the self-consciously modernist Self-Strengthening Literary Group in the 1930s repeatedly—and to great comic effect—encountered modern technologies (trains, telegraphs, telephones, photographs, automobiles), clothing (swimwear), urban sights (traffic police booths, public toilets), and habits (shopping, sports) to highlight the novelty of the lived experience of modernity in the age of mechanical reproduction, in a manner reminiscent of the Baku-based *Molla Nasreddin* cartoon serial discussed previously.[97] Thus, in contrast to their literate counterparts in earlier generations, readers of *quốc ngữ* newspapers "saw a particularistic world of nations rather than a universalistic world in which the distinctions made between people had to do with their ability to acquire, understand and be well versed in various classical Chinese ideologies."[98]

The novels and nonfiction reportage produced during the 1920s and 1930s further attested to the emergence of new forms of modern consciousness and representation in Vietnam during this period.[99] Notable here was the "autoethnography" of personal testimony and investigative journalism (*phóng sự*) exemplified by Vũ Trọng Phụng's celebrated accounts of prostitution and venereal disease and the plight of domestic servants in Hà Nội[100] and the "industry of marrying Europeans" in a village in nearby Bắc Ninh province[101] as well as his hilarious 1936 satirical novel, *Dumb Luck*, about the improbable social ascendancy and uproarious sexual adventures of "Red-Haired Xuân" from street urchin to ball boy at a Hà Nội tennis club to a celebrated and sartorially resplendent "doctor," champion of social and religious reform, and public media sensation.[102]

Through such novels and new forms of reportage, a distinctly modern sense of authorship emerged, with the signature incorporation of the first-person pro-

96. Wynn Wilcox, "Women, Westernization and the Origins of Modern Vietnamese Theater," *Journal of Southeast Asian Studies* 37, no. 2 (2006): 205–224, at 205.

97. George Dutton, "Lý Toét in the City: Coming to Terms with the Modern in 1930s Vietnam," *Journal of Vietnamese Studies* 2, no. 1 (2007): 80–108.

98. Wilcox, "Women, Westernization and the Origins of Modern Vietnamese Theater," 209.

99. John C. Schafer and Thế Uyên, "The Novel Emerges in Cochinchina," *Journal of Asian Studies* 52, no. 4 (November 1993), 854–884.

100. Shaun Kingsley Malarney, introduction to *Lục Xì: Prostitution and Venereal Disease in Colonial Hanoi*, by Vũ Trọng Phụng (Honolulu: University of Hawai'i Press, 2011), 1–41; Vũ Trọng Phụng, "Household Servants," in *The Light of the Capital: Three Modern Vietnamese Classics*, ed. Greg Lockhart and Monique Lockhart (Kuala Lumpur: Oxford University Press, 1996), 121–156; Peter Zinoman, *Vietnamese Colonial Republican: The Political Vision of Vũ Trọng Phụng* (Berkeley: University of California Press, 2014).

101. Vũ Trọng Phụng, *The Industry of Marrying Europeans* (Ithaca, NY: Cornell University Southeast Asia Program, 2006).

102. Peter Zinoman, ed., *Dumb Luck: A Novel by Vũ Trọng Phụng* (Ann Arbor: University of Michigan Press, 2002).

noun *tôi* "as the articulation of an individual's autonomy, interior depth, psyche, and self-consciousness."[103] At the same time, these publications represented and reproduced new notions of "society" through their depictions of diverse sociological types, ranging from rickshaw drivers, street peddlers, and prostitutes to civil servants, police officers, Buddhist monks, and wealthy landlords, plantation owners, and businessmen.[104] As against established hierarchical notions of family and village community, an "expanded social vision emphasized democratic, lateral linkages between people beyond the old communal categories" and "produced new ideas of the 'individual', 'individual freedom,' and much else, including free-floating points of view."[105] The field of vision also extended beyond Vietnamese society, as seen perhaps most famously in Nhất Linh's semifictional account "Going to France," which was serialized in a popular Hà Nội journal in 1935–1936.

Similar trends were evident in the realm of popular entertainment, most notably in the new style of musical theater known as *cải lương* that emerged in the first decades of the twentieth century, in a manner reminiscent of the *komedya* of the 1880s and 1890s in the Philippines and the *Komedie Stamboel* of fin de siècle Java. By the 1920s and 1930s, "almost every town with a population of ten thousand or more people had a *cải lương* troupe in residence."[106] While drawing on established forms of popular/folk musical theater (*hát chèo*) and Chinese-style opera (*hát tuồng*), *cải lương* introduced innovations in both form and content.[107] During the interwar era, Western instruments such as the piano were incorporated into Vietnamese orchestras, as were Western-style melodies such as French *chansons à la mode* (increasingly set to Vietnamese lyrics) and contemporary subject matter drawn from Western plays or, by the 1930s, films and radio.[108] *Cải lương* combined these Western influences with those accompanying the flow of immigration from Guangdong, as seen in extensive borrowings from Cantonese operas, with the Chinese stories and melodies incorporated while dialogue and lyrics were reworked for Vietnamese audiences.[109]

---

103. Ben Tran, *Post-Mandarin: Masculinity and Aesthetic Modernity in Colonial Vietnam* (New York: Fordham University Press, 2017), 87.

104. On the emergence of the concept of "society" (*xã hội*) in early twentieth-century Vietnam, see George Dutton, "'Society' and Struggle in the Early Twentieth Century: The Vietnamese Neologistic Project and French Colonialism," *Modern Asian Studies* 49, no. 6 (November 2015): 1994–2021.

105. Greg and Monique Lockhart, "Broken Journey: Nhất Linh's 'Going to France,'" *East Asian History* 8 (December 1994): 73–134, especially 85.

106. Duane Ernie Hauch, "The Cai Luong Theater of Vietnam, 1915–1970" (PhD diss., Southern Illinois University, 1972), 3.

107. Jason Gibbs, "Spoken Theater, La Scène Tonkinoise, and the First Modern Vietnamese Songs," *Asian Music* 31, no. 1 (Fall–Winter 1999–2000): 1–33.

108. Jason Gibbs, "The West's Songs, Our Songs: The Introduction and Adaptation of Popular Song in Vietnam before 1940," *Asian Music* 34, no. 1 (Fall–Winter 2003–2004): 57–83. On the "radio craze" of the 1930s, see Erich DeWald, "Taking to the Waves: Vietnamese Society around the Radio in the 1930s," *Modern Asian Studies* 46, no. 1 (January 2012): 143–165.

109. Hauch, "The Cai Luong Theater of Vietnam," 33–36.

Whether in novels or reportage, *cải lương* or radio dramas, these new forms of representation both celebrated the emancipatory implications of modernity and suggested the bases for sociopolitical critique, most notably with regard to gender relations and sexuality. On the one hand, some of the writers associated with the Self-Strengthening Literary Group authored love stories and novellas that affirmed the ideal of romantic love as the product of individual free choice liberated from the conventions and constraints of the Confucian family, most notably arranged marriages.[110] As in the literature published in the wake of the 1919 May Fourth Movement in neighboring China, the freedom to choose one's marriage partner was portrayed as a fundamental right of individuals as autonomous moral agents, with "free love" represented "as a battle between tradition and modernity, East and West, feudalism and enlightenment, hypocrisy and authenticity, old and young."[111] On the other hand, as articulated most famously and forcefully in the writings of Vũ Trọng Phụng, the libidinous energies unleashed by the marketization and modernization of Vietnamese society were shown to circulate not so much in line with "free love" as in accordance with the machinations of capitalist exploitation, individual self-interest, and social inequalities and injustices, as seen in his attention to prostitution, venereal disease, masturbation, rape, and forced marriages for money.[112] The seemingly open-ended possibilities for social intercourse and (self-)invention associated with modernity were variously understood as emancipation or existential abyss.

Overall, the final decades of the nineteenth century and the first four decades of the twentieth century witnessed dramatic transformation of Cochinchina, Annam, and Tonkin under the auspices of French colonial rule. With the expansion of land clearance and settlement and cultivation of rice for export in the Mekong Delta, and accelerated marketization and monetization, intensified population growth, and agricultural involution in the Red River Delta and elsewhere, a market society emerged that prefigured the possibilities for the national integration of Vietnam or possibly even Indochina. By the eve of World War II, as the rail links of the Transindochinois (the North–South railway) were now connected across Tonkin, Annam, and Cochinchina and belatedly extended across Cambodia and, in a more limited fashion, Laos, some 17 million passengers were in movement every year, even as flows of rice and other commodities, and the circulation of currency and capital, tightened—and broadened—the links between town and country, and between cities such as Sài Gòn, Hà Nội, and Hải Phòng

---

110. Tran, *Post-Mandarin*, 66–84. See also Cao Thị Như Quýnh and John C. Schafer, "From Verse Narrative to Novel: The Development of Prose Fiction in Vietnam," *Journal of Asian Studies* 47, no. 4 (November 1988): 756–777.

111. Haiyan Lee, *Revolution of the Heart: A Genealogy of Love in China, 1900–1950* (Stanford, CA: Stanford University Press, 2007), 5, 96.

112. Zinoman, *Vietnamese Colonial Republican*, 131–155.

and their rural hinterlands.[113] But the market society that had crystallized by the interwar era in what today comprises Vietnam was one whose territorial, economic, cultural, and intellectual boundaries were porous and permeable, with Vietnamese rice cultivators, rubber plantation laborers, coal miners, stevedores, steamboat deckhands, and soldiers drawn into the orbit of the world capitalist economy and immersed within cosmopolitan currents of modern communications and culture circulating through *quốc ngữ* newspapers and novels, radio dramas, films, and *cải lương* performances that incorporated diverse Asian and European referents within the shared field of experience and imagination of Vietnamese readers, listeners, and viewers.

With the demise of Sinographic cosmopolitanism accompanying the French colonial state's abolition of the civil service examinations and the emergence of new forms of modern consciousness and representation in the urban public sphere and beyond came new possibilities for modern political association and action, including prospects for revolutionary mobilization on the horizon. Much as in the 1880s and the early–mid-1890s in the Philippines and as in the 1910s and 1920s in the Indonesian archipelago, these possibilities were enabled and constrained by specific features of the Vietnamese sociological landscape in the interwar era, most notably the uprooting of Sinographic cosmopolitanism from its role in the reproduction of the state and the social order and the overwhelming predominance of French and Chinese capital in the market economy. Much as in 1896 in the Philippines and 1945 in Indonesia, however, the prospects for revolutionary mobilization were profoundly determined not only by cosmopolitan intellectual and ideological currents but also by international circumstances beyond the shores of the Vietnamese coastline, by interimperial competition and conflicts in Europe and Asia, and by developments and trends in neighboring China, as detailed in the pages that follow.

---

113. David Wilson Del Testa, "Paint the Trains Red: Labor, Nationalism, and the Railroads in French Colonial Indochina, 1898–1945" (PhD diss., University of California at Davis, 2001), 90.

FROM CẦN VƯƠNG TO VIỆT-NAM DUY-TÂN HỘI TO THANH NIÊN

While the emergence of a distinctly and coherently Vietnamese society during the first two millennia of the Common Era was in crucial ways enabled if not impelled by influences, interactions, and waves of immigration emanating from the southern coastal provinces of neighboring China, the prospects for revolution in Vietnam were further enfolded within and intertwined with the fate of French imperialism as it was extended across Africa and Asia in the final decades of the nineteenth century, entrenched over the first four decades of the twentieth century, and upended in the early aftermath of World War II. The colonization of Indochina in the late nineteenth century, after all, was undertaken by soldiers and civil servants (most famously army generals Joseph-Simon Gallieni and Hubert Lyautey) whose careers progressed through the "pacification" of territories as varied as Niger, Tonkin, and Madagascar, and included postings as diverse and distant as the islands of Réunion in the Indian Ocean and Martinique in the Caribbean West Indies.[1]

More important, French naval strategists in the 1870s and 1880s established Indochina alongside Tunisia and Madagascar as key pillars of imperial policy under the Troisième République.[2] Britain had supported French naval advances

---

1. Michael P. M. Finch, *A Progressive Occupation? The Gallieni-Lyautey Method and Colonial Pacification in Tonkin and Madagascar, 1885–1900* (Oxford: Oxford University Press, 2013); Paul Rabinow, *French Modern: Norms and Forms of the Social Environment* (Chicago: University of Chicago Press, 1995), 105–125, 142–151, 157–165, 278–319.

2. See, for example, Théophile Bilbaut, *Le Canal de Suez et les Intérêts Internationaux, la Cochinchine Française et le Royaume de Cambodge* (Paris: Chalamel Ainé, 1870).

in Indochina through coal supplies and coaling stations, shipbuilding and repairs in the 1850s and 1860s, but entente shifted to a resumption of rivalry during the remaining decades of the nineteenth century.[3] While Tunisia served to match British naval bases in Gibraltar and Malta and to ensure a French naval presence along the Mediterranean route to India via the Suez Canal, and Madagascar likewise enabled the projection of French naval power around the Cape of Good Hope and into the Indian Ocean, Indochina played an even more crucial role vis-à-vis Britain during the fin de siècle period of heightened Anglo-French rivalry preceding the signing of the Entente Cordiale of 1904.[4] As one senior French naval strategist argued in 1885: "Without the establishment of our dominance on the Indochinese peninsula and the creation of a naval base in Saigon, the vast depths of the Indian Ocean and the South China Sea, where almost all the riches of the British Empire are found along with more than half of its commercial fleet, would remain completely closed to our warships, which would be unable to operate or to counter the key strategic positions of Singapore and Hong Kong, or to intercept British ships along the direct route between England and India."[5]

Over subsequent decades, moreover, the Indochinese economy became increasingly integrated not only with the French metropole—and with commercial interests in Bordeaux, Lyon, and Marseille[6] as well as *haute finance* centered in Paris—but also with the broader ambit of French imperial interests across Asia and Africa. As noted in the preceding chapter, the *mise en valeur*—and the profitability—of Indochina rested largely on exports of Cochinchinese, Cambodian, and, to a lesser extent, Tonkinese rice to Guangzhou, Hong Kong, Singapore, and other Asian ports, and on the use of Indochina as a base for investment in, and transport and commercial access to, southern China. But the capital accumulated in

3. On the 1850s and 1860s, see James R. Fichter, "British Infrastructure and French Empire: Anglo-French Steam Interdependency in Asian Waters, c. 1852–1870," *Britain and the World* 5, no. 2 (2012): 183–203, and James R. Fichter, "Imperial Interdependence on France's Maritime Periphery: France and Coal in Ceylon, Singapore, and Hong Kong," in *British and French Colonialism in Asia, Africa, and the Middle East*, ed. James R. Fichter (Cambridge: Cambridge University Press, 2019), 151–179.

4. Paul Ollendorff, ed., *Les Colonies Nécessaires: Tunisie, Tonkin, Madagascar par Un Marin* (Paris, 1885), 33–34, 57–88. The anonymous author is said to have been either Admiral Alexandre Louis François Peyron, who served as minister of the navy in 1883–1885, or Admiral Charles-Eugène Galiber, who succeeded Peyron in 1885–1886. See Theodore Ropp, *The Development of a Modern Navy: French Naval Policy, 1871–1904* (Annapolis, MD: Naval Institute Press, 1987), 152–153.

5. Ropp, *The Development of a Modern Navy*, 34–35. Translation by the author.

6. See Étienne Denis, *Bordeaux et la Cochinchine sous la Restauration et le Second Empire* (Paris: Delmas, 1965); Jean-François Klein, *Un Lyonnais en Extrême-Orient: Ulysse Pila Vice-Rois de l'Indochine (1837–1909)* (Lyon: Éditions Lyonnaises d'Art et d'Histoire, 1994); and Marie-Françoise Berneron-Couvenhes, *Les Messageries Maritimes: L'Essor d'une Grande Compagnie de Navigation Française, 1851–1914* (Paris: Presses de l'Université Paris-Sorbonne, 2007).

Indochina and (on an even greater scale) in China by the Banque de l'Indochine, and by the consortium of French banks that established and owned it, not only accrued to Parisian, Lyonnais, and other French shareholders, but also became available for reinvestment elsewhere across the French Empire. Thus, even as the Banque de l'Indochine financed the establishment and expansion of rubber plantations in Cochinchina and Cambodia, coal mines in Tonkin, and railroad lines across Indochina and southern China, it also directly and indirectly funded other key investments in French colonies across Africa. For example, companies in which the Banque de l'Indochine had invested and held equity pioneered the cultivation, processing, and export of palm oil and rubber cultivation in Côte d'Ivoire in the 1910s as well as investments in agriculture, mining, water, and electricity in Madagascar in the 1920s.[7]

Thus, beyond the lingering legacies of centuries of immersion within the orbit of Sinographic cosmopolitanism, the late nineteenth century and early decades of the twentieth century not only incorporated Cochinchina, Annam, and Tonkin within a broader Indochina and within a regional economy whose center of gravity lay in southern China but also within the broader transoceanic and transcontinental circuitries of the world economy and the international order, with important implications for the prospects for revolutionary mobilization. On the one hand, the fate of Indochina was, from the outset, intertwined not only with that of the vast expanse of the French Empire but also with the broader field of interimperial rivalries among the Great Powers, from the heyday of Pax Britannica in the nineteenth century to Japan's ill-fated Greater East Asia Co-Prosperity Sphere in the mid-twentieth century and US military intervention during the Cold War era.

On the other hand, the deepening incorporation of Cochinchina, Annam, and Tonkin within Indochina, economic interdependence with southern China, and integration within the French Empire opened up and expanded new channels of circulation and communication for revolutionary mobilization. The steamboats and ocean liners of the Messageries Maritimes and other French shipping companies connected Vietnamese revolutionaries not only to sympathizers and solidarity networks in Guangzhou and Marseille but also—indirectly, in due course—to safe havens and sources of sponsorship and support elsewhere across Asia, Europe, and Africa. It was thus a combination of international opportunities and transnational revolutionary activism that ultimately enabled the making of the Vietnamese revolution as it unfolded over 1945–1954 and was belatedly extended across the full breadth of Vietnam over 1959–1975.

---

7. See, for example, Jacques Marseille, *Empire Colonial et Capitalisme Français: Histoire d'un Divorce* (Paris: Éditions Albin Michel, 1984), 124–128.

From Royal Restorationism to Reformism to Republicanism *à la Chinoise*, 1885–1925

The first waves of large-scale organized mobilization that unfolded across the territories that came to comprise Vietnam drew heavily on the discursive tradition and sociological infrastructure of Sinographic cosmopolitanism, on the one hand, and on various forms of support and solidarity from neighboring China, on the other.[8] In 1885, for example, deepening French intervention and encroachment in the Red River Delta[9] sparked a large-scale insurrection across Annam and Tonkin following the forced flight of the newly enthroned boy emperor Hàm Nghi from the court in Huế and the issuance of a royal edict in his name calling for loyalty and aid to the monarch (*cần vương*). The edict, issued in classical Chinese ideographs and invoking precedents from the Shang and Tang dynasty periods in Chinese history,[10] was disseminated in villages across Annam and Tonkin by local mandarins and networks of literati schooled in the Four Books and Five Classics of the neo-Confucian canon.[11] With an average of twelve thousand candidates for the civil service taking the provincial examinations each year,[12] these networks of local mandarins, scholars, and schoolboys provided extensive discursive and mobilizational structures for collective action across the otherwise weakly integrated rural provinces of the realms ruled by the court in Huế. Like the Catholic *cofradías* and Masonic lodges of the Philippines or the *pesantren* and Sufi *ṭuruq* of Java and Sumatra, the state-supported circuitries of Sinographic cosmopolitanism offered the foundations for translocal collective action across Annam and Tonkin in the late nineteenth century.

In addition, alongside the accumulated heritage of Sinographic cosmopolitanism, the Cần Vương insurrection also benefited from the fortuitous availability of assistance from various sources originating in southern China. French inroads along the Red River had been threatened and thwarted by the bandit-like Black Flag remnants of the Taiping Rebellion who had sought refuge in neighboring Tonkin from Qing forces, who also crossed the border in the early 1880s with the

---

8. On the more scattered resistance to French colonization in the 1860s and 1870s, see Mark W. McLeod, *The Vietnamese Response to French Intervention, 1862–1874* (Westport, CT: Praeger, 1991).

9. Kim Munholland, "Admiral Jauréguiberry and the French Scramble for Tonkin, 1879–83," *French Historical Studies* 11, no. 1 (Spring 1979): 81–107.

10. David G. Marr, *Vietnamese Anticolonialism, 1885–1925* (Berkeley: University of California Press, 1971), 49–51.

11. Marr, *Vietnamese Anticolonialism*, 52–53, 56–69. See also Charles Fourniau, *Annam-Tonkin 1885–1896: Lettrés et Paysans Vietnamiens face à la Conquête Coloniale* (Paris: Éditions L'Harmattan, 1989), 46–94.

12. Wynn Gadkar-Wilcox, "French Imperialism and the Vietnamese Civil Service Examinations, 1862–1919," *Journal of American-East Asian Relations* 21 (2014): 373–393, at 380.

encouragement of the court in Huế.[13] By 1884, the combined Chinese forces in Tonkin numbered almost fifty thousand.[14] French troops thus had to contend not only with Annamese and Tonkinese rebels but also with armed forces of southern Chinese provenance as well, and the Cần Vương insurrection drew much of its firearms from Guangxi and Yunnan provinces, with weak French (and Qing) control over the ethnically diverse upland borderlands enabling cross-border traffic to thrive throughout the late 1880s.[15]

But the underlying sources of resistance to the entrenchment and extension of French rule in the late nineteenth century ultimately proved to be very limited in their effectivity. The ideological and organizational underpinnings of the Cần Vương insurrection did not provide the bases for sustained popular mobilization or systematic command and coordination across Annam and Tonkin, enabling a French counterinsurgency campaign to achieve "pacification" within a few short years. During the early–mid 1890s, moreover, the Qing court in Beijing belatedly tightened up enforcement of the provisions of the 1885 treaty that had acknowledged French sovereign control over Tonkin, Annam, and Cochinchina, thus enabling French suppression of Black Flag and other armed formations of Chinese provenance and extinguishing residual hopes for Qing support.[16]

By the turn of the twentieth century, however, the developments and trends leading up to the Chinese Revolution of 1911 had begun to encourage new forms of political activism linking reformers and revolutionaries in Qing realms to their counterparts in neighboring Indochina. As briefly discussed above, the Qing defeat in the Sino-Japanese War of 1894–1895 had spurred a campaign for reform led by Kang Youwei and his protégé Liang Qichao, both scions of scholar-gentry families from Guangdong whose socialization and training in classical Chinese scholarship in preparation for civil service examinations was combined with immersion in the urban cosmopolitan milieu of Guangzhou, where new forms of knowledge and sources of news were circulating amidst China's ongoing revolution in modern print culture.[17] In May 1895, a month after the signing of the Treaty of Shimonoseki, Kang and Liang led a group of civil service examination candidates in petitioning the emperor to cancel the treaty; reorganize and strengthen the Qing army; and undertake sweeping administrative, educational,

---

13. Bradley Camp Davis, *Imperial Bandits: Outlaws and Rebels in the China-Vietnam Borderlands* (Seattle: University of Washington Press, 2017.

14. Lloyd E. Eastman, *Throne and Mandarins: China's Search for a Policy during the Sino-French Controversy, 1880–1885* (Cambridge, MA: Harvard University Press, 1967), 101.

15. Marr, *Vietnamese Anticolonialism*, 69–72.

16. Kim Munholland, "'Collaboration Strategy' and the French Pacification of Tonkin, 1885–1897," *Historical Journal* 24, no. 3 (September 1981): 629–650, especially 647–648; Marr, *Vietnamese Anticolonialism*, 73–76.

17. See, for example, Steven B. Miles, *The Sea of Learning: Mobility and Identity in Nineteenth-Century Guangzhou* (Cambridge, MA: Harvard University Press, 2006).

and social reforms. In the same year, Kang and Liang also founded the Self-Strengthening Society (Qiangxue Hui), which they used as a vehicle to advance New Text Confucianism and the cause of constitutional monarchy and modernization as per the model of the Meiji Reformation. In 1898, Kang and Liang won support from Emperor Guangxu and embarked on the so-called Hundred Days' Reform, only to face exile in Japan after a palace coup by the Empress Dowager Cixi and a conservative backlash later that year.[18]

By the turn of the twentieth century, Chinese reformist intellectuals such as Kang Youwei and Liang Qichao had established a base in Japan to promote the restoration of the emperor and the reform of the Qing state through New Text Confucianism and constitutional monarchy.[19] By 1905, there were more than twenty thousand Chinese students in Japan under the auspices of Kang and Liang's hosts, the Tōa Dōbunkai (East Asia Common Culture Society),[20] even as Chinese merchants in Japan helped to fund the publication of journals filled with articles promoting reforms and translations and interpretations of diverse foreign writings, which circulated widely among the growing reading public in major Chinese cities and among Chinese communities across Asia and the Americas.[21] In China, the publication of reformist journals and tracts combined with the abolition of the civil service examination system and the founding of thousands of new, self-consciously modern schools to amplify the calls and expand the audience for reform.

The circulation of New Text Confucianism and late Qing reformism began to extend into Tonkin and Annam, drawing into their orbit scions of established literati families whose immersion in the world of classical Chinese philosophy and literature and aspirations for examination-based entry, employment, and ascendancy within the imperial civil service came into question with French intervention, establishment of colonial rule, and imposition of administrative and educational reforms in the final decades of the nineteenth century. By the early 1900s, the writings of Kang Youwei and Liang Qichao were widely available across Annam and Tonkin, attracting a sizeable audience (and distribution network) of

18. Luke S. K. Kwong, "Chinese Politics at the Crossroads: Reflections on the Hundred Days Reform of 1898," *Modern Asian Studies* 34, no. 3 (July 2000): 663–695.

19. Mark Elvin, *Another History: Essays on China from a European Perspective* (Honolulu: University of Hawai'i Press, 1996), 352–389; Peter Zarrow, "The Reform Movement, the Monarchy, and Political Modernity," in *Rethinking the 1898 Reform Period: Political and Cultural Change in Late Qing China*, ed. Rebecca E. Karl and Peter Zarrow (Cambridge, MA: Harvard University Press, 2002), 17–47.

20. On the Tō-A Dōbunkai, see Douglas R. Reynolds, "Training Young China Hands: Tōa Dōbun Shoin and Its Precursors, 1886–1945," in *Japan's Informal Empire in China, 1895–1937*, ed. Peter Duus, Ramon H. Myers, and Mark R. Peattie (Princeton, NJ: Princeton University Press, 1989), 210–271; Urs Matthias Zachmann, "The Foundation Manifesto of the Tōa Dōbunkai (East Asian Common Culture Society)," in *Pan-Asianism: A Documentary History, 1850–1920*, ed. Sven Saaler and Christopher W. A. Szpilman (Lanham, MD: Rowman and Littlefield, 2011), 53–60.

21. Paula Harrell, *Sowing the Seeds of Change: Chinese Students, Japanese Teachers, 1895–1905* (Stanford, CA: Stanford University Press, 1992), 40–60.

readers of classical Chinese at a time when some thirteen thousand candidates were still taking the province-level civil service examinations each year.[22]

It was against this backdrop that the Đông-Du (Go East) movement emerged in 1905 as a new transnational network across the Sinosphere linking Annamese and Tonkinese activists to other advocates for constitutional monarchy and modernization in Japan and China. The movement's founder, Phan Bội Châu, had been swept up in the Cần Vương insurrection as an adolescent studying for the civil service examinations in his home province of Nghệ An and in 1897 moved to Huế, where he finally passed the regional exams in 1900. It was then and there that he obtained copies of Kang Youwei and Liang Qichao's reformist tracts, began to articulate his own ideas of reform in the context of the subjugation of the emperor to French rule, and started to assemble a clandestine network of supporters under the rubric of the Viêt-Nam Duy-Tân Hội (Vietnam Modernization Society), not only in Annam and Tonkin but also in Cochinchina. Over the next few years, he achieved some success in fund-raising and recruitment among the same local mandarins and extended networks of literati whose members and forebears had led the Cần Vương insurrection in the late 1880s. He also enlisted to the cause Prince Cường Để, a hitherto obscure member of the extended royal family who harbored a claim to the throne based on his direct descent from the eldest son (and one-time crown prince) of Gia Long, the progenitor of the Nguyễn dynasty.[23]

In 1904, Phan travelled to Japan, arriving in early 1905 in the bustling treaty port city of Yokohama on Tokyo Bay, the center of the textile and tea trades and "the conduit through which a massive flow of information, knowledge, and skills was brought into Japan,"[24] where Liang Qichao was based in the midst of a thriving Chinese merchant community.[25] Meetings with Liang were arranged and enabled introductions to Japanese politicians associated with the Pan-Asianist Tōa Dōbunkai, whose interest in expanding Japanese links to China and Southeast Asia was intensified by victory in the 1904–1905 Russo-Japanese War.[26] Through Liang, Phan also secured introductions to a network of sympathetic Chinese merchants

22. Emmanuel Poisson, *Mandarins et Subalternes au Nord du Viêt Nam: Une Bureaucratie à l'Épreuve* (Paris: Maisonneuve et Larose, 2004), 180. More broadly, on the sociology of the mandarinate and the classical school system in Tonkin at the turn of the twentieth century, see 61–137.

23. Trần Mỹ-Vân, *A Vietnamese Royal Exile in Japan: Prince Cường Để (1882–1951)* (London: Routledge, 2005), 9–24.

24. See Simon Partner, *A Merchant's Tale: Yokohama and the Transformation of Japan* (New York: Columbia University Press, 2018), 168, and 52–53 on the local Chinese community.

25. On Phan Bội Châu's trajectory to 1905, see Marr, *Vietnamese Anticolonialism*, 83–86, 98–119, and Vĩnh Sính and Nicholas Wickenden, eds. and trans., *Overturned Chariot: The Autobiography of Phan- Bội-Châu* (Honolulu: University of Hawai'i Press, 1999), 47–91.

26. Shiraishi Masaya, "Phan Bội Châu in Japan," in *Phan Bội Châu and the Đông-Du Movement,* ed. Vĩnh Sính (New Haven, CT: Yale University Council on Southeast Asia Studies, 1988), 2–100.

stretching from Yokohama to Hong Kong, Guangzhou, and Sài Gòn, who provided various forms of financial and logistical assistance.[27]

With Liang's encouragement, Phan adopted a two-pronged strategy. On the one hand, he began to engage in active propaganda efforts, writing tracts for dissemination in China and, in the original classical Chinese and in translation into *quốc ngữ*, in Annam, Cochinchina, and Tonkin. These tracts provided a critical analysis of French colonization and a celebration of Vietnamese resistance, while pioneering a new literary style largely borrowed from Liang Qichao and his reformist compatriots, minimizing "flowery nuance and classical allusions in favour of a direct, hard-hitting prose."[28] Thanks to the support of Liang Qichao, thousands of copies of Phan's writings were printed, reaching Huế, Sài Gòn, Hà Nội, and Hải Phòng through Chinese distributors of "new books" (*hsin-shu*), then disseminated through sympathizers among local mandarins and teachers and students in the civil service examination circuit, and subsequently translated into *quốc ngữ* for a broader Vietnamese readership.[29]

On the other hand, Phan embarked on efforts to establish a clandestine network of Vietnamese activists stretching across Annam, Cochinchina, and Tonkin, with external bases of support in Guangzhou, Hong Kong, and Siam, as well as a safe haven and educational hub in Japan. Phan established links with remnants of the Cần Vương movement and the Black Flags in Guangdong in late 1905, and by early 1906 he had facilitated the flight of Prince Cường Để into exile in Japan via Hong Kong. Over the next few years, arrangements were made for as many as two hundred Vietnamese students to be transported to Japan and installed in various schools set up for Chinese and other foreign students, including the Shimbu Military Academy. Meanwhile, a network of wealthy supporters in Sài Gòn and other cities developed a set of businesses, including a string of hotels, to help finance student travel to Japan and to facilitate further recruitment, clandestine meetings, and publishing. By 1907, the Đông Kinh Nghĩa Thục (Tonkin Free School) had been established in Hà Nội, with as many as five hundred students offered instruction in *quốc ngữ* and Chinese on the basis of the "new learning" promoted by Kang Youwei and Liang Qichao and their reformist Vietnamese fellow travellers.

---

27. Nguyễn Thế Anh, "Phan Bội Châu et les Débuts du Mouvement Đông-Du," in *Phan Bội Châu and the Đông-Du Movement*, ed. Vĩnh Sính (New Haven, CT: Yale University Council on Southeast Asia Studies, 1988), 5.

28. Marr, *Vietnamese Anticolonialism*, 115.

29. Vĩnh Sính, "Chinese Characters and the Medium for Transmitting the Vocabulary of Modernization from Japan to Vietnam in the Early 20th Century," *Asia Pacific Quarterly* 25, no. 1 (Autumn 1993): 1–16; Lorraine Marion Paterson, "Tenacious Texts: Vietnam, China, and Radical Cultural Intersections, 1890–1930" (PhD diss., Yale University, 2006), 39–54.

Through its teachings and its publishing activities, the school also served as a key hub for propaganda and recruitment across Tonkin.[30] Schools modelled on the Đông Kinh Nghĩa Thục began to spread in provinces of Tonkin and Annam. Small cells of the Việt-Nam Duy-Tân Hội remained active and retained links to residual Cần Vương strongholds in upland areas of northern Tonkin near the Chinese border and tightly clustered communities of refugees in southern China as well as northeastern Siam.

By 1908–1909, the activities of this embryonic resistance network had helped to give rise to various forms of mobilization, which in turn prompted a French crackdown and a curtailment of the network's further expansion within Cochinchina, Annam, Tonkin, and beyond. French surveillance of students travelling to Japan and intelligence gathering in Hà Nội and Sài Gòn turned up evidence of diverse conspiratorial activities, including plans for the poisoning of soldiers in the garrison in Hà Nội. These discoveries prompted a wave of arrests and the closure of the Đông Kinh Nghĩa Thục in 1908, as well as further arrests in response to demonstrations for tax reductions in areas of Annam.

Meanwhile, the signing of a treaty between France and Japan in 1907 led not only to the extension of the Anglo-Japanese Treaty of 1902 and the Entente Cordiale of 1904 into a Quadruple Entente but also the mutual recognition of spheres of influence in various regions of China, Northeast Asia (e.g., the Korean Peninsula and Manchuria), and Southeast Asia, including French Indochina.[31] Against this backdrop, Japan's provision of a safe haven and support base for Phan Bội Châu and Prince Cường Để came into question, leading to their expulsion from Japan in 1909. By 1910, Phan, Cường Để and some of the students deported from Japan had regrouped in Siam, where long-standing Vietnamese immigrant communities as well as Cần Vương refugees provided something of a base, and where King Chulalongkorn's reported resentment of the territorial borders imposed on him by France in 1907 seemingly helped to ensure a measure of official tolerance, if not protection. Having lost Japanese patronage for efforts to create a modern educated vanguard under the rubric of the Đông-Du movement, the remnants of the Việt-Nam Duy-Tân Hội began to use their safe haven in Siam to accumulate weapons and initiate plans for various forms of armed struggle in Indochina, but with little prospects for success given their small numbers and limited training and resources.[32]

---

30. Marr, *Vietnamese Anticolonialism*, 164–184; Vũ Dức Bằng, "The Đông Kinh Free School Movement, 1907–1908," in *Aspects of Vietnamese History*, ed. Walter E. Vella (Honolulu: University of Hawaii Press, 1973), 30–95.

31. For background and the text of the treaty, see John Albert White, *Transition to Global Rivalry: Alliance Diplomacy and the Quadruple Entente, 1895–1907* (Cambridge: Cambridge University Press, 1995), 254–261, 302–303.

32. Christopher E. Goscha, *Thailand and the Southeast Asian Networks of the Vietnamese Revolution, 1885–1954* (Richmond, Surrey: Curzon Press, 1999), 14–34.

In this unpromising context, the Chinese Revolution of 1911 offered new pos-sibilities for the reinvigoration of the small, struggling network established by Phan Bội Châu and for its reorientation along self-consciously republican lines. Since 1904, Phan had established contacts with his reformist patron Liang Qichao's revolutionary republican rivals affiliated with the Tongmeng Hui (Chinese Rev-olutionary Alliance), which was founded and based in Japan in 1905. This new movement drew into its ranks Chinese students who had become attracted to di-verse currents of republicanism, anarchism, and socialism during their stay in Japan,[33] as well as disparate elements in the small but growing modern educated segment of society in China and among Chinese communities across Asia and North America.

The diasporic basis of Chinese revolutionary republicanism was embodied in its president and leader, Sun Yat-Sen, who, like his reformist rivals Kang Youwei and Liang Qichao, hailed from Guangdong Province but was educated in Hawai'i and Hong Kong.[34] From the mid-1890s, Sun was engaged in revolutionary agi-tation, conspiracy, fund-raising, and intrigue among Chinese communities in Hawai'i, Hong Kong, London, Penang, San Francisco, Singapore, Tokyo, and Van-couver.[35] Expelled from Japan in early 1907 in response to Qing pressures, Sun relocated to Southeast Asia, moving between Singapore, Penang, and Hanoi, where he appears to have enjoyed a measure of sympathy and support from French officials.[36] Sun and the Tongmeng Hui used this base in Tonkin to instigate a se-ries of local insurrections across the border in Yunnan, Guangxi, and Guang-dong in 1907–1908, followed by abortive military rebellions in Guangzhou in 1910 and early 1911 organized from Hong Kong.[37] Sun's transnational peregrinations, fund-raising, propagandizing, recruitment efforts, and conspiratorial activities thus overlapped and intersected with those of Phan Bội Châu, offering him both inspiration and potential sources of assistance.

With the Wuchang Uprising of October 1911 and the onset of the Chinese Revolution, Guangzhou thus emerged as an even more promising safe haven and support base for revolutionary organizing efforts in Indochina. By Janu-ary 1912, Phan had relocated to Guangzhou, just as Sun Yat-sen was assuming

---

33. Martin Bernal, *Chinese Socialism to 1907* (Ithaca: Cornell University Press, 1976).

34. On revolutionary activism in Guangzhou, see Edward J. M. Rhoads, *China's Republican Rev-olution: The Case of Kwangtung, 1895–1913* (Cambridge, MA: Harvard University Press, 1975).

35. Harold Z. Schiffrin, *Sun Yat-sen and the Origins of the Chinese Revolution* (Berkeley: Univer-sity of California Press, 1968); Marius B. Jansen, *The Japanese and Sun Yat-sen* (Stanford, CA: Stan-ford University Press, 1970); Marie-Claire Bergère, *Sun Yat-sen* (Stanford, CA: Stanford University Press, 1998), 1–172.

36. Kim Munholland, "The French Connection That Failed: France and Sun Yat-Sen, 1900–1908," *Journal of Asian Studies* 32, no. 1 (November 1972): 77–95; Jeffrey G. Barlow, *Sun Yat-sen and the French, 1900–1908* (Berkeley: University of California Center for Chinese Studies, 1979).

37. Bergère, *Sun Yat-sen*, 173–197.

the presidency of the newly established Republic of China, with a provisional government in the central coastal city of Nanjing. Within a few months, Phan had assembled the remnants of his network, formally dissolved the Việt-Nam Duy-Tân Hội and established the Việt Nam Quang Phục Hội (Vietnam Restoration Society), now restyled along republican lines in imitation of Sun's Tungmeng Hui, with Cường Để given the honorary title of "president" to incorporate the remaining supporters of the renegade prince's claim to the Nguyễn throne.[38] From its hub in Guangzhou and bases in Siam, the Việt Nam Quang Phục Hội engaged in continuous propaganda and recruitment efforts and occasionally instigated (or inspired) violent action against the French colonial regime: assassinations and bombings in 1913, attacks on border posts in 1915, coordinated protests in 1916, and a prison revolt in 1917.[39] This *propagande par le fait* (propaganda of the deed) bore traces of the influence of Chinese anarchist groups active at the time in Guangzhou, who worked closely with Phan Bội Châu and his network in the early 1910s.[40]

But the threat and promise of Guangzhou-based revolutionary republicanism in Indochina was short lived.[41] By March 1912, military strongman Yuan Shikai had usurped the presidency of the fledgling republic, forcing Sun to flee to Japan in 1913 and leaving Yuan to reestablish the monarchy and proclaim himself emperor in late 1915, only to die of renal failure in mid-1916 amidst a series of local uprisings that initiated China's descent into provincial warlordism.[42] These developments fatally undermined Phan's hopes for a safe haven and support base in Guangzhou. By early 1914, Phan found himself arrested and imprisoned by pro-Yuan Guangdong warlord governor Long Jiguang, and upon his release in 1917 he fled the city for the comparative safety of Hangzhou (the capital of coastal Zhejiang Province, south of Shanghai), where he remained, largely inactive, until his capture by French intelligence agents in 1925 in Shanghai.[43]

38. Marr, *Vietnamese Anticolonialism*, 215–217.

39. Peter Zinoman, *The Colonial Bastille: A History of Imprisonment in Vietnam, 1862–1940* (Berkeley: University of California Press, 2001), 158–199.

40. Arif Dirlik, *Anarchism in the Chinese Revolution* (Berkeley: University of California Press, 1991), 116–147; Georges Boudarel, "L'Extrême-Gauche Asiatique et le Mouvement National Vietnamien (1905–1925)," in *Histoire de l'Asie du Sud-Est: Révolts, Réformes, Révolutions*, ed. Pierre Brocheux (Lille: Presses Universitaires de Lille, 1981), 165–192, especially 168–177.

41. Kawamoto Kuniye, "The Viet-Nam Quang Phuc Hoi and the 1911 Revolution," in *The 1911 Revolution in China: Interpretive Essays*, ed. Eto Shinkichi and Harold Z. Schiffrin (Tokyo: University of Tokyo Press, 1984), 115–127.

42. Patrick Fuliang Shan, *Yuan Shikai: A Reappraisal* (Vancouver: University of British Columbia Press, 2018).

43. Marr, *Vietnamese Anticolonialism*, 225–226, 238–239; *Overturned Chariot: The Autobiography of Phan-Bội-Châu*, translated by Vinh Sinh and Nicholas Wickenden (Honolulu: University of Hawai'i Press, 1999), 219–263.

Meanwhile, aside from the handful of violent episodes noted above, across Cochinchina, Annam, and Tonkin the 1910s and 1920s saw nothing akin to the mass mobilization pioneered by the Sarekat Islam in Java and parts of Sumatra in the same years. By this time, the phasing out of the imperial civil service examination system had begun to erode the foundations of Sinographic cosmopolitanism, thus undermining the translocal discursive and organizational infrastructure that had enabled the Cần Vương insurrection of the late 1880s. But meanwhile, other developments and trends within Indochina and across Europe and Asia during the interwar era had already begun to set the stage for a new round of revolutionary activism under new auspices, starting first in Guangzhou in the late 1920s and then belatedly bearing fruit in parts of Indochina in the late 1930s.

World War I and the Russian Revolution: L'Union Intercoloniale and the Comintern

Just as fin de siècle Great Power conquests and conflicts in Asia and the Chinese Revolution of 1911 enabled and constrained the possibilities for organizing and mobilizing within and beyond the borders of Indochina from the 1880s through the 1910s, so too did World War I in Europe and the October Revolution of 1917 in Russia extend the horizons and expand the fields and modes of operation of Vietnamese revolutionaries over the course of the 1920s and 1930s. The French war effort in 1914–1917 had involved the recruitment and deployment of hundreds of thousands of African and Asian troops and workers, including one hundred thousand from Cochinchina, Annam, and Tonkin.[44] As the revolutionary activist then known as Nguyễn Ái Quốc (later as Hồ Chí Minh) wrote in the Communist bimonthly Parisian journal La Vie Ouvrière in 1923, "Of the 159 regiments of the French army, 10 are composed of white colonials, which is to say seminatives, 30 of Africans, and 39 of natives of other colonies; half of the French army is thus recruited in the colonies."[45]

Estimates of the total number of troops and workers from French colonies in Africa and Asia by the end of the war range from nearly 475,000 to just over 660,000 to more than 750,000.[46] An additional contingent of Chinese laborers

---

44. Kimloan Vu-Hill, Coolies into Rebels: Impact of World War I on French Indochina (Paris: Les Indes Savantes, 2011).

45. "L'Armée Contre-Révolutionnaire," in Ho Chi Minh: De La Révolution 1920–1966, ed. Bernard B. Fall (Paris: Librairie Plon, 1968), 42. Translation by the author.

46. Clifford Rosenberg, Policing Paris: The Origins of Modern Immigration Control between the Wars (Ithaca, NY: Cornell University Press, 2006), 114; Richard S. Fogarty, Race and War in France: Colonial Subjects in the French Army, 1914–1918 (Baltimore, MD: Johns Hopkins University Press,

assisted the war effort in France, its numbers ranging between 140,000 to 200,000.[47] Meanwhile, the US entry into the war in 1917 brought 200,000 African American soldiers and 50,000 African American army laborers to serve in France.[48]

While the numbers of these Asian, African, and African American troops and workers in France dwindled with the end of the war and demobilization in 1918, France, and Paris in particular, retained notable traces of this cosmopolitanism for years to come. Even before the war, Paris had begun to emerge as the world capital of modernist art and literature, and by the late 1910s and early 1920s the likes of Chagall and Diaghilev, Modigliani and Picasso, and Hemingway and Joyce were installed in the cafés and salons of Montparnasse, while Josephine Baker and the other African American singers, dancers, and musicians of the Revue Nègre became the highlight of the jazz clubs of Montmartre.[49] But this much celebrated moment in the history of modernism bore testimony to a broader and longer pattern of immigration that was crucial to the making of the French working class from the final decades of the nineteenth century. With World War I, the continuing flows of Belgian, Italian, and Spanish migrant labor dating back several decades were now accompanied by a wave of new arrivals in Paris from farther afield: Bohemia, Moravia, Slovakia, Poland, and the Jewish Pale of Settlement in the former Russian Empire, the Mediterranean coasts of the former Ottoman Empire, as well as Algeria, Morocco, Tunisia, and various French colonies elsewhere in Africa.[50] By the mid-1920s, more than 10 percent of the population of Paris and an estimated 20 percent of its manual labor working class were foreign born, and by 1930, the city's immigrant population had more than doubled.[51]

It was against this backdrop that the man who became known as Nguyễn Ái Quốc and later as Hồ Chí Minh surfaced in Paris in 1919 amidst a confluence of major domestic, transnational, and international political developments. Indeed, the year 1919 witnessed an upsurge of working-class mobilization in Paris, from bloody May Day demonstrations to food riots in late July and August, tenants' protests against rising rents and evictions, and a month-long strike of over one hundred sixty thousand metalworkers across Paris and its suburban "red belt."[52]

2008), 27; Claude Liauzu, *Aux Origines des Tiers-Mondismes: Colonisés et Anticolonialistes en France (1919–1939)* (Paris: Éditions L'Harmattan, 1982), 100.

47. Nora Wang, *Émigration et Politique: Les Étudiants-Ouvriers Chinois en France (1919–1925)* (Paris: Les Indes Savantes, 2002), 20, 44.

48. Tyler Stovall, *Paris Noir: African Americans in the City of Light* (New York: Houghton Mifflin, 1996), 1–24.

49. Stovall, *Paris Noir*, 25–81.

50. See the various fine essays in André Kaspi and Antoine Marès, eds., *Le Paris des Étrangers Depuis un Siècle* (Paris: Imprimerie Nationale, 1989).

51. Rosenberg, *Policing Paris*, 29.

52. Tyler Stovall, *Paris and the Spirit of 1919: Consumer Struggles, Transnationalism, and Revolution* (Cambridge: Cambridge University Press, 2012).

Meanwhile, over the course of the same year Paris hosted the first Pan-African Congress, organized by NAACP (National Association for the Advancement of Colored People) activist and *Crisis* editor W. E. B. Dubois against the backdrop of the "red summer" of white racist violence against African Americans in cities across the United States,[53] as well as the rise of Marcus Garvey's Universal Negro Improvement Association (UNIA) and its separatist alternative to the legal activism and assimilationism of the NAACP.[54]

Finally, and perhaps most important, 1919 witnessed the unfolding of the Paris Peace Conference, in which the promise of a peace settlement based on the principle of self-determination—first and most forcefully articulated by the Russian Bolshevik leader Vladimir Ilyich Lenin—was represented by American president Woodrow Wilson. The year saw first a flurry of activist advocacy on behalf of a wide variety of nationalist causes—Chinese, Egyptian, Indian, Korean, and, as with Dubois, Pan-African—through petitioning of the conference delegates, and then, once the provisions of the Treaty of Versailles were made known, a wave of mass protests as varied as the May Fourth Movement in China, the Khilafat movement in India, and the revolution in Egypt, as part of the fabled 1919 "World on Fire" briefly described in chapter 6.[55] Nguyễn Ái Quốc's brief visits to various African ports as a *sous-chef* on a Chargeurs Réunis ocean liner in 1911–1912[56] and his reported encounter with the Harlem Renaissance and brief contacts with émigré Korean nationalists during short stays in New York and Boston in 1912–1913 thus foreshadowed the explosion of transnational political activism he found in Paris on his arrival in 1919.[57]

It was thus thanks to the convergence of diverse strands in Paris in 1919 that the field of vision and modus operandi of the Vietnamese revolution began to expand beyond the Guangzhou-based republican conspiratorial *propagande par le fait* of the 1910s. Inspired and enabled by the dramatic developments in their

53. See Barbara Foley, *Spectres of 1919: Class and Nation in the Making of the New Negro* (Chicago: University of Illinois Press, 2003), and Chad L. Williams, *Torchbearers of Democracy: African American Soldiers in the World War I Era* (Chapel Hill: University of North Carolina Press, 2010), 223–260.

54. Adam Ewing, *The Age of Garvey: How a Jamaican Activist Created a Mass Movement and Changed Global Black Politics* (Princeton, NJ: Princeton University Press, 2014).

55. Erez Manela, *The Wilsonian Moment: Self-Determination and the International Origins of Anticolonial Nationalism* (Oxford: Oxford University Press, 2007).

56. Unlike the Marseille-based Messageries Maritimes that dominated French maritime traffic in Asia, Le Havre-based Chargeurs Réunis operated routes in the Americas and Africa before extending its coverage to include the ports of Sài Gòn and Hải Phòng at the turn of the twentieth century. Employment on Chargeurs Réunis liners thus entailed far greater African and American exposure in terms of coworkers, passengers, and ports visited during the months at sea.

57. William J. Duiker, *Ho Chi Minh* (New York: Hyperion, 2000), 46–51. On the importance of his relations with Korean nationalists in the United States and Paris, see Thu Trang-Gaspard, *Hồ Chí Minh à Paris (1917–1923)* (Paris: Éditions L'Harmattan, 1992), 67–70, 106, and Sophie Quinn-Judge, *Ho Chi Minh: The Missing Years* (London: Hurst, 2003), 18. But the evidence of his stints in the United States is still questioned by some historians.

Parisian milieu detailed above, activists hailing from across the full breadth of the French colonial empire began to convene and collaborate in new forms of political activism. In 1919, the Guadaloupean Max Bloncourt and the Malagasy Jean Ralaimongo,[58] and Samuel Stéfany, all members of the Paris-based Ligue des Droits de l'Homme (League for the Rights of Man),[59] founded La Ligue Française Pour L'Accession aux Droits de Citoyens des Indigènes de Madagascar (French League for Accession to Citizens' Rights for the Natives of Madagascar), and in 1920 Louis Hunkanrin,[60] who faced arrest, imprisonment, and exile after founding a branch of La Ligue des Droits de l'Homme in Dahomey in 1910, likewise began publishing (with Bloncourt's assistance) the journal *Le Messager Dahoméen*.[61] By 1921, these African and Afro-Caribbean activists joined Nguyễn Ái Quốc in forming the Union Intercoloniale (Intercolonial Union), whose founding statutes cited aims of strengthening solidarity among colonials living in France and discussing and studying political and economic questions concerning the colonies. To this end, the Union Intercoloniale published a journal, *Le Paria*, whose circulation ran as high as three thousand by the mid-1920s, with hundreds of issues distributed in France, in the Dahomeyan cities of Porto Novo and Cotonou, in Madagascar, and across Indochina, much to the consternation and concern of the French authorities.[62]

As *Le Paria* editor and frequent contributor Nguyễn Ái Quốc distinguished himself by the transcontinental breadth of his interests,[63] which were also amply reflected in the articles, opinion pieces, and letters he submitted to other publications in Paris in the early 1920s. He even published a futuristic short story in *L'Humanité* in 1922 written from the perspective of 1998 on the fiftieth anniversary of the independence of the "African Federative Republic," a piece dedicated to an Algerian murdered by a French colonial military officer.[64] Nguyễn Ái Quốc's writings treated French (and British) colonialism holistically, rather than with sole reference to Indochina, and they extended to issues such as racism and the vio-

---

58. Jean-Pierre Domenichini, "Jean Ralaimongo (1884–1943) ou Madagascar au Seuil du Nationalisme," *Revue Française d'Histoire d'Outre-Mer* 61, no. 204 (1969): 236–287.

59. William D. Irvine, *Between Justice and Politics: La Ligue des Droits de l'Homme, 1898–1945* (Stanford, CA: Stanford University Press, 2005).

60. Guy-Landry Hazoume, Jean Suret-Canale, A. I. Asiwaju, Mathias F. Oke, and Guillaume Da Silva, *La Vie et L'Œuvre de Louis Hunkanrin* (Cotonou: Librairie Renaissance, 1977); Sylvain Coovi Anignikin, *Les Origins du Mouvement National en Afrique Noire: Le Cas du Bénin 1900–1939* (Paris: L'Harmattan, 2014), 181–201, 211–214.

61. Philippe Dewitte, *Les Mouvements Nègres en France 1919–1939* (Paris: Éditions L'Harmattan, 1985), 63–68.

62. Liauzu, *Aux Origins des Tiers-Mondismes*, 105–111; Thu Trang-Gaspard, *Hồ Chí Minh à Paris (1917–1923)* (Paris: Éditions L'Harmattan, 1992), 140–156, 202–217.

63. On this point, see Liauzu, *Aux Origins des Tiers-Mondismes*, 108–109, especially footnote 30, and for a systematic analysis of the "internationalist" coverage of *Le Paria*, 113–130.

64. Brent Hayes Edwards, "The Shadow of Shadows," *Positions: East Asia Cultures Critique* 11, no. 1 (Spring 2003): 11–49, at 36–39.

lence perpetrated against African Americans by the Ku Klux Klan.[65] As depicted in his 1923 tract *Le Procès de la Colonisation Française* (French Colonialism on Trial), slavery in Dahomey, famine in Algeria and Tunisia, and exploitation in Indochina were all of a piece.[66] The imperatives and opportunities for intercolonial resistance were also foreshadowed, as seen already in an article he wrote for *L'Humanité* in 1920 that condemned French suppression of work stoppages on the docks of Hải Phòng that were impeding the departure of a contingent of Vietnamese infantrymen for Syria.[67] By 1924, the wide-angle lens picture was clear: "Senegalese [soldiers] have the sad honor of having assisted French militarists in the massacre of their brothers in the Congo, the Sudan, Dahomey, and Madagascar. Algerians have fought in Indochina. Annamese [troops] are garrisoned in Africa."[68] Although Nguyễn Ái Quốc had begun his years in Paris boarding with the exiled reformist and republican scholar-activist Phan Châu Trinh,[69] and had joined with him in 1919 to found the Association des Patriotes Annamites and submit a petition to the Versailles Peace Conference delegates calling for autonomy, civil rights, and tax reforms in Indochina, within a few short years the ends and means, and the scale and scope of his political activism had considerably widened and become decidedly more revolutionary.

Indeed, since 1919 Nguyễn Ái Quốc and his *comrades* in the Union Intercoloniale and the editorial offices of *Le Paria* were immersed in the broader milieu of socialist internationalism in France during a period of accelerated "Bolshevization." They published opinion pieces and letters in socialist newspapers and journals, and the collaborative work that eventually bore fruit in the Union Intercoloniale and *Le Paria* enjoyed the sponsorship of the Section Française de l'Internationale Ouvrière (SFIO; (France's Socialist Party) from the outset. In 1920, moreover, the SFIO Congress in Tours saw a majority vote in support of affiliation with the Comintern, leading to the creation of the Parti Communiste Française (PCF; French Communist Party) the following year.[70] Nguyễn Ái Quốc attended the SFIO Congress in Tours in 1920 and affirmed support for affiliation with Communist International (Comintern); he likewise attended the first PCF

---

65. See Fall, *Ho Chi Minh: De La Révolution 1920–1966*, 21–170.

66. Alain Ruscio, ed., *Nguyễn Ái Quốc (Hồ Chí Minh): Le Procès de la Colonisation Française et Autres Textes de Jeunesse* (Paris: Le Temps des Cerises, 1999), 31–172.

67. Trang-Gaspard, *Hồ Chí Minh à Paris*, 129.

68. "L'Indochine et le Pacifique," *La Correspondance Internationale* 18 (1924), in Bernard B. Fall, ed., *Ho Chi Minh: De La Révolution 1920–1966* (Paris: Librairie Plon, 1968), 51–55 at 53–54. Translation by the author.

69. On Phan Châu Trinh's trajectory from schooling in the neo-Confucian canon to attraction to Chinese modernism and republicanism, his orbit in the "Sinosphere," imprisonment, and exile, and his intersections and antagonistic relations with Phan Bội Châu, see Vĩnh Sính, ed., *Phan Châu Trinh and His Political Writings* (Ithaca, NY: Cornell University Southeast Asia Program, 2009).

70. Philippe Robrieux, *Histoire Intérieure du Parti Communiste 1920–1945* (Paris: Fayard, 1980), 11–50.

Congress in Marseille in 1921, gave an address on the colonial question, and was elected to represent the district of the Seine. The newly founded and rapidly "Bolshevized" PCF subsidized and otherwise supported the Union Intercoloniale, and the affiliation with the party and the Comintern was amply clear in the Communist rhetoric and reasoning found in the pages of *Le Paria*.[71]

In mid-1923, amidst intensifying police surveillance and growing disappointment with the PCF's limited interest in colonial issues, Nguyễn Ái Quốc departed Paris for Moscow after securing an invitation to work for the Comintern, but the new transnational revolutionary linkages he had helped to establish in France endured for years to come. Over the latter half of the 1920s, a new generation of Vietnamese students began to arrive and expand in numbers, many of whom were attracted to the Communist political culture they encountered in France and exported to Indochina when they returned home after finishing their studies.[72] Even as the Union Intercoloniale and *Le Paria* faded away and were replaced by more narrowly defined activist groups such as the Ligue de Défense de la Race Nègre (League for the Defense of the Negro Race or LDRN), Messali Hadj's Étoile Nord-Africaine (ENA; North African Star), and the Parti Annamite de l'Indépendance (PAI), internationalist and "intercolonial" solidarities remained strong.[73] For example, a Vietnamese-language periodical published by the Indochinese section of the PCF-affiliated Union Fédérale des Étudiants (UFE; Federal Union of Students) featured articles in 1930 that included coverage of the US occupation of Haiti and the intricacies of Uruguayan politics.[74]

The political implications of these internationalist and intercolonial sympathies and solidarity networks inspired considerable concern among the French authorities over the course of the 1920s and 1930s.[75] For example:

---

71. On the "Bolshevization" of the PCF in the early 1920s, see Robrieux, *Histoire Intérieure*, 51–129. On PCF subsidy and support for the Union Intercolonial and *Le Paria*, and their "Bolshevization," see Michael Goebel, *Anti-Imperial Metropolis: Interwar Paris and the Seeds of Third World Nationalism* (Cambridge: Cambridge University Press, 2015), 187–199.

72. Daniel Hémery, "Du Patriotisme au Marxisme: L'Immigration Vietnamienne en France de 1926 à 1930," *Le Mouvement Social* 90 (January–March 1975): 3–54; Scott McConnell, *Leftward Journey: The Education of Vietnamese Students in France, 1919–1939* (New Brunswick, NJ: Transaction, 1989); Goebel, *Anti-Imperial Metropolis*, 137–142. But see also Erica J. Peters, "Resistance, Rivalries, and Restaurants: Vietnamese Workers in Interwar France," *Journal of Vietnamese Studies* 2, no. 1 (Winter 2007): 109–143.

73. Liauzu, *Aux Origins des Tiers-Mondismes*, 131–136; Jennifer Anne Boittin, *Colonial Metropolis: The Urban Grounds of Anti-Imperialism and Feminism in Interwar Paris* (Lincoln: University of Nebraska Press, 2010), 77–110; Benjamin Stora, *Messali Hadj, 1898–1974* (Paris: Pluriel, 2012), 46–176; Goebel, *Anti-Imperial Metropolis*, 138–139.

74. Goebel, *Anti-Imperial Metropolis*, 142.

75. See Michael B. Miller, *Shanghai on the Metro: Spies, Intrigue, and the French between the Wars* (Berkeley: University of California Press, 1995), and Kathleen Keller, *Colonial Suspects: Suspicion, Imperial Rule, and Colonial Society in Interwar French West Africa* (Lincoln: University of Nebraska Press, 2018).

In 1926, Algerian police discovered Vietnamese translations of the writings of Lenin and Marx among insubordinate Vietnamese nurses and soldiers at the Maillot military hospital in Algiers. On intercepting their letters and having them translated into French, the Sûreté traced their connections to addresses in Paris and to militants in North Vietnam. Someone in Paris had apparently told the nurses in Algiers to contact Vietnamese soldiers garrisoned in the French Concession in Shanghai, another hotspot of anticolonialism. Five years later, some of these Vietnamese troops in Shanghai were indeed arrested for distributing "seditious," "anti-French," or "communist" propaganda material. Worrying reports also came in from islands in the Indian and Pacific oceans. In 1929, the French minister of colonies reported that 129 "Creole" women from Réunion, who had married Chinese labor migrants and followed them to the Kwantung Leased Territory during the 1920s, might be exposed to "revolutionary ideas" in China and spread them back home in Réunion. A few months later, unrest among Vietnamese sailors in Papeete, Tahiti, provoked unease among colonial officials about potential repercussions in Vietnam, Shanghai, and Paris.[76]

Stretching from port to port across the oceans and continents of the globe like a "many-headed hydra,"[77] there loomed, at least in the imagination of the Sûreté, the specter of a "vagabond internationalism" comprised of the subalterns of the French Empire and the world capitalist economy—sailors and soldiers, seamen and stevedores, bartenders and bistro waiters, and panhandlers and pickpockets memorably described in the Jamaican-born Harlem Renaissance author Claude McKay's account of life in the *Port Vieux* harbor area of "motley" Marseille in his 1929 novel *Banjo*, his 1937 memoir *A Long Way From Home*, and his posthumously published novel *Romance in Marseille*.[78]

Meanwhile, by the early–mid-1920s the socialist internationalism represented in organized form by the Comintern had also begun to draw Indochinese revolutionaries-in-the-making into its orbit. Thanks to a Comintern invitation and its clandestine assistance, Nguyễn Ái Quốc surreptitiously departed Paris for Moscow in 1923, and in subsequent years other Vietnamese activists in Paris

---

76. Goebel, *Anti-Imperial Metropolis*, 34.

77. Peter Linebaugh and Marcus Rediker, *The Many-Headed Hydra: Sailors, Slaves, Commoners, and the Hidden History of the Revolutionary Atlantic* (Boston: Beacon Press, 2000).

78. Brent Hayes Edwards, *The Practice of Diaspora: Literature, Translation, and the Rise of Black Internationalism* (Cambridge, MA: Harvard University Press, 2003), 187–240; Claude McKay, *Banjo: A Story without a Plot* (New York: Harper and Brothers, 1929); Claude McKay, *A Long Way from Home* (New York: Lee Furman, 1937), 277–291; Claude McKay, *Romance in Marseille* (New York: Penguin Books, 2020).

availed of the same facilities to make similar journeys to the USSR.[79] It was through Nguyễn Ái Quốc's intermediation, moreover, that some members of the community of Chinese student-workers in France won introductions to the PCF and, in due course, invitations to Moscow as well.[80] If Paris in the late 1910s and early 1920s was truly "the capital of men without a country,"[81] then it was through Moscow, the headquarters of the Comintern and the new hub of revolutionary cosmopolitanism, that the pathways of the Vietnamese revolution began to return to Indochina, via Guangzhou, in the mid-1920s.

From the KUTV to Whampoa to *Thanh Niên*, 1924–1929

Indeed, the Moscow of the early–mid 1920s seemed to promise much in the way of solidarity and support for aspiring Asian socialist revolutionaries such as Nguyễn Ái Quốc. The Soviet leader V. I. Lenin's 1920 "Theses on the National and Colonial Questions" had encouraged Communist parties to assist revolutionary movements "among the dependent and subject nations and in the colonies," the Comintern convened the Congress of the Peoples of the East in Baku in September 1920, and successive Comintern congresses in 1920, 1921, and 1922 reiterated concern for nations oppressed under conditions of colonialism and semicolonialism, while opening the door to cooperation with movements, parties, and social classes outside the narrow parameters of proletarian internationalism.[82] As of 1921, moreover, the Comintern had established in Moscow a Communist University of the Toilers of the East (KUTV), which provided instruction in Marxism-Leninism and in revolutionary strategy and tactics to hundreds of students recruited from across Asia, Africa, and the Middle East.[83] From 1925

---

79. Goebel, *Anti-Imperial Metropolis*, 35.

80. Marilyn A. Levine, *The Found Generation: Chinese Communists in Europe during the Twenties* (Seattle: University of Washington Press, 1993), 159–160; Nora Wang, *Émigration et Politique*, 170–171, 207, 252–253; Elizabeth McGuire, *Red at Heart: How Chinese Communists Fell in Love with the Russian Revolution* (Oxford: Oxford University Press, 2018), 28. It was reportedly Nguyễn Ái Quốc's broken Cantonese and his excellent Chinese calligraphy that enabled communication, rather than shared facility in French. See Wang, *Émigration et Politique*, 170–171.

81. Michael Goebel, "'The Capital of the Men without a Country': Migrants and Anticolonialism in Interwar Paris," *American Historical Review* 121, no. 5 (December 2016): 1444–1467.

82. For background, see Charles B. McLane, *Soviet Strategies in Southeast Asia: An Exploration of Eastern Policy under Lenin and Stalin* (Princeton, NJ: Princeton University Press, 1966), and Kevin McDermott and Jeremy Agnew, *The Comintern: A History of International Communism from Lenin to Stalin* (Basingstoke: Macmillan, 1996).

83. Anatoly A. Sokolov, *Komintern i Vietnam: Podgotovka Vietnamskikh Politicheskikh Kadrov v Vuzakh SSSR 20–30 gody* (Moscow: Institut Vostokovedeniya, Rossiskaya Akademiya Nauk, 1998). See also Natalya N. Timofeeva, "Kommunistichesky Universityet Trudyashchikhsya Vostoka (KUTV) (1921–1925)," *Narody Azii i Afriki* 1 (1976): 47–57, and Natalya Timofeeva, "Kommunistichesky Universityet Trudyashchikhsya Vostoka (KUTV) (1926–1938) gg.," *Narody Azii i Afriki* 5 (1979): 30–42.

through 1938, at least sixty Vietnamese activists were enrolled, obtaining passage (under false Chinese passports) from France through the assistance of comrades in the French Communist Party or by making their way to Moscow via China.[84] Like their Chinese counterparts at the Sun Yat-sen University founded in 1925,[85] Vietnamese KUTV graduates later assumed leading positions in what became the Indochinese Communist Party (ICP) in 1930,[86] and their time in Moscow helped to school and socialize them within the institutional and intellectual discipline of the Comintern as the fractiousness of Soviet politics in the mid–late 1920s gave way to Stalinist hegemony by the end of the decade.

It was thanks to Soviet intermediation, moreover, that by the mid-1920s Vietnamese revolutionaries began to explore and experiment with new forms of activism and organization in the southern Chinese coastal city of Guangzhou. As noted above, by 1923 Sun Yat-sen had established a base in Guangzhou from which he began preparations, with Soviet assistance, to extend his republican government across China. Two earlier attempts at such a Northern Expedition had foundered in the face of military indiscipline, infighting, and intrigues among the commanding officers of the armed forces mobilized by Sun, and thus by 1923 he settled on a two-pronged new strategy to revitalize the Guangzhou-based republic and reunify China.[87]

On the one hand, Sun enlisted Soviet assistance in the form of financial support, arms shipments, and, crucially, military training, in hopes of reorganizing the Kuomintang (Nationalist Party) along Leninist democratic centralist lines and reconstituting a disciplined National Revolutionary Army much as Trotsky had achieved with the Red Army through Bolshevik-appointed people's commissars.[88] To this end, Sun accepted into his entourage a group of Soviet advisors, most notably the Comintern agent Mikhail Borodin,[89] with whom he consulted closely

84. Sokolov, *Komintern i Vietnam*, 36–39, 77–79.

85. Yueh Sheng, *Sun Yat-sen University in Moscow and the Chinese Revolution: A Personal Account* (Lawrence: University of Kansas Center for East Asian Studies, 1971); Min-ling L. Yu, "Sun Yat-sen University in Moscow, 1925–1930" (PhD diss., New York University, 1995).

86. On Trần Văn Giàu, for example, see H. N. (Julie) Pham, "Revolution, Communism, and History in the Thought of Trần Văn Giàu" (PhD diss., Pembroke College, University of Cambridge, 2008), 81–89.

87. For an excellent overview of the situation, see C. Martin Wilbur, "Problems of Starting a Revolutionary Base: Sun Yat-sen and Canton, 1923," *Bulletin of the Institute of Modern History Academia Sinica* 12, no. 1 (1974): 727.

88. Mark von Hagen, *Soldiers in the Proletarian Dictatorship: The Red Army and the Soviet Socialist State, 1917–1930* (Ithaca, NY: Cornell University Press, 1990), 13–126; Roger R. Reese, *Red Commanders: A Social History of the Soviet Army Officer Corps, 1918–1991* (Lawrence: University Press of Kansas, 2005), 12–48.

89. Borodin was born Mikhail Gruzenberg in 1884 in the Jewish Pale of Settlement in a small village outside Vitebsk, the beloved birthplace and hometown of Marc Chagall and the home of the famous "People's Art School" he founded in 1919 as commissar of arts until its closure in 1922. On Borodin né Gruzenberg, see Lydia Holubnychy, *Michael Borodin and the Chinese Revolution, 1923–1925* (New York: Columbia University East Asian Institute, 1979). On

on major policy decisions.[90] With Borodin's encouragement, Sun oversaw the establishment of a military academy on Whampoa (Huangpu), an island in the Pearl River less than 20 kilometers from the heart of Guangzhou. From its founding in 1924, the Whampoa Military Academy indoctrinated hundreds of cadets in military organization, strategy, and tactics, while inculcating them with a "Whampoa spirit,"[91] under the watchful eye of academy commander Chiang Kai-shek, a group of Soviet military advisors with recent experience in the civil war, and political instructors such as Zhou Enlai, a leading Chinese Communist Party (CCP) activist who had recently arrived back in China after several years in France, where his organizing efforts had intersected with those of Nguyễn Ái Quốc.[92]

On the other hand, Sun agreed to incorporate CCP cadres into the Kuomintang (KMT) and to endorse a formal united front between the two parties in early 1924, in hopes of absorbing and appropriating their radical energies and mass organizing techniques for purposes of strengthening his fragile republic and re-unifying China under its authority. CCP labor-organizing efforts in Guangzhou had begun with the party's founding in 1921 and started to achieve traction over the next few years. Over the course of 1925 and 1926, moreover, Guangzhou came to serve as a base for as many as two hundred thousand striking workers from Hong Kong during the sixteen-month Canton–Hong Kong general strike and boycott against British interests and as a site for a wave of local strikes involving further tens of thousands of workers and lasting into 1927.[93]

As early as 1922, moreover, a Japanese-educated[94] CCP cadre named Peng Pai had been actively engaged in organizing peasant associations and campaigning for rent reductions in his home county of Haifeng in rural Guangdong Province, with the mobilization of tens of thousands of peasants enabling the KMT-CCP united front government in Guangzhou to begin to extend its mass base into its

---

Vitebsk, see Aleksandra Shatskikh, *Vitebsk: The Life of Art* (New Haven, CT: Yale University Press, 2007).

90. C. Martin Wilbur and Julie Lien-yieng How, *Missionaries of Revolution: Soviet Advisers and Nationalist China, 1920–1927* (Cambridge, MA: Harvard University Press, 1989); Alexander Pantsov, *The Bolsheviks and the Chinese Revolution, 1919–1927* (Honolulu: University of Hawai'i Press, 2000).

91. Roderick L. MacFarquhar, "The Whampoa Military Academy," *Papers on China* 9 (1955): 146–172; Richard B. Landis, "Institutional Trends at the Whampoa Military School, 1924–1926" (PhD diss., University of Washington, 1969); Thomas M. Williamsen, "Political Training and Work at the Whampoa Military Academy Prior to the Northern Expedition" (PhD diss., Duke University, 1975). See also the account provided by the Soviet general and Kuomintang military advisor Alexander Cherepanov: Alexandr I. Cherepanov, *Zapiski Voyennovo Sovyetnika v Kitaye: Iz Istorii Pyervoi Grazhdanskoi Revolyutsionnoi Voiny (1924–1927)* (Moscow: Institut Narodov Azii, Akademiya Nauk SSSR, 1964), 83–104.

92. Chae-Jin Lee, *Zhou Enlai: The Early Years* (Stanford, CA: Stanford University Press, 1994), 151–163.

93. Jean Chesneaux, *Le Mouvement Ouvrier Chinois de 1919 à 1927* (Paris: Mouton, 1962), 409–444; Ming Kou Chan, "Labor and Empire: The Chinese Labor Movement in the Canton Delta, 1895–1927" (PhD diss., Stanford University, 1975), 200–234, 308–356.

94. On the importance and impact of his experience in Japan, see Yong-Pil Pang, "Peng Pai from Landlord to Revolutionary," *Modern China* 1, no. 3 (July 1975): 297–322.

rural hinterlands and thus undermine the authority of local warlords whose entrenchment continued to confine the republic to its urban coastal enclave.[95] By 1924, the KMT had not only established a Peasant Department headed by Peng Pai and staffed largely by CCP cadres but also, under Peng Pai's leadership, a Peasant Movement Training Institute that provided hundreds of peasant organizers over 1924–1926 with training in class analysis, organizing techniques, and military operations.[96] In 1925, as the KMT launched its Eastern Expedition from Guangzhou to wrest control over the port city of Shantou (Swatow) and other coastal areas from the local warlord Chen Jiongming, CCP-led peasant mobilization helped to swell the ranks of the recruits into the army, enabling both a successful military campaign and, with the flight of local landlords, the establishment of the Hai-Lu-feng Soviet across much of two counties in eastern Guangdong.[97]

It was thus amidst unprecedented Comintern-backed experiments in political organization and mass mobilization that Vietnamese revolutionaries such as Nguyễn Ái Quốc began to recongregate in Guangzhou in 1924–1927, and to revive the city's role as a hub for agitation and activism in nearby Indochina. After months in Moscow spent writing, participating in Comintern-sponsored and other meetings, and attending the Communist University of the Toilers of the East, Nguyễn Ái Quốc had won permission to join Borodin in late 1924 in the Comintern mission in Guangzhou, where he found signs of renewed activity among the remnants of the largely defunct network established by Phan Bội Châu in the years following his expulsion from Japan.[98] Members of a new group of young radical activists identifying themselves as the Tâm Tâm Xã (Association of Like Hearts) succeeded in enrolling in the Whampoa Military Academy, and Phan himself, perhaps through Nguyễn Ái Quốc's intervention, managed to secure the entry of more Vietnamese students upon his return to Guangzhou in 1924.[99] Over the next three years, Nguyễn Ái Quốc used his Comintern and CCP contacts to promote the entry and support the studies of as many as one hundred Vietnamese cadets at Whampoa.[100] At the same time, he also enabled Vietnamese activists to attend courses in the Peasant Movement Training Institute, whose leadership was assumed by the Hunanese CCP activist Mao Zedong in 1926.[101]

95. Robert B. Marks, *Rural Revolution in South China: Peasants and the Making of History in Haifeng County, 1570–1930* (Madison: University of Wisconsin Press, 1984), 152–229.

96. Gerald W. Berkley, "The Canton Peasant Movement Training Institute," *Modern China* 1, no. 2 (April 1975): 161–179; Roy Hofheinz Jr., *The Broken Wave: The Chinese Communist Peasant Movement, 1922–1928* (Cambridge, MA: Harvard University Press, 1977), 78–92; Fernando Galbiati, *P'eng P'ai and the Hai-Lu-Feng Soviet* (Stanford, CA: Stanford University Press, 1985), 240–254.

97. Galbiati, *P'eng P'ai and the Hai-Lu-Feng Soviet*, 203–222.

98. Duiker, *Ho Chi Minh*, 105–145; Quinn-Judge, *Ho Chi Minh: The Missing Years*, 69–115.

99. Marr, *Vietnamese Anticolonialism*, 257–258.

100. Cherepanov, *Zapiski Voyennovo Sovyetnika v Kitaye*, 92.

101. Galbiati, *P'eng P'ai and the Hai-Lu-Feng Soviet*, 243.

Thanks to these opportunities for instruction and immersion within the intellectual culture, organizational umbrella, and active political struggles of the Comintern and the CCP, the years 1924–1927 in Guangzhou saw the emergence of a new revolutionary network established by Nguyễn Ái Quốc known as the Việt Nam Thanh Niên Cách Mệnh Đồng Chí Hội (Revolutionary Youth League of Viet Nam), or Thanh Niên for short. In contrast to the *propagande par le fait* practiced by Phan Bội Châu or even the Tâm Tâm Xã (such as its failed attempt to assassinate the French governor-general of Indochine during his 1924 visit to Guangzhou), Thanh Niên was designed to be a network of disciplined cadres who would draw on the organizational and mass mobilizational techniques instilled in them by training courses in Moscow and Guangzhou and associated with the Comintern and the CCP. The lessons, legacies, and linkages of the revolutions in Russia and China were now to be applied to Vietnam. By 1927, as many as three hundred activists had been recruited from across Annam, Tonkin, and Cochinchina, and among Vietnamese émigré communities in northeastern Thailand and Laos, transported to Guangzhou, enrolled in the Whampoa Military Academy or the Peasant Movement Training Institute, or in some cases sent on to the KUTV in Moscow, and otherwise inducted and immersed within the ranks of the Thanh Niên.[102]

But by 1926–1927, this unprecedented window of opportunity to use Guangzhou as a base for Communist indoctrination and then reinfiltration back into Vietnam began to close, as the "Right" Kuomintang leader, Chiang Kai-shek, abandoned the United Front policy and initiated a violent campaign against the CCP. Assuming the leadership of the National Revolutionary Army after Sun Yat-sen's death in 1925, Chiang outmaneuvered CPP and other "Left" Kuomintang forces to seize control of the party and the city of Guangzhou in March 1926, leading to the arrest and expulsion of CCP cadres and Comintern agents from the city. Subsequent months saw efforts to reestablish a new basis for Comintern and CCP support for the Kuomintang and the New Revolutionary Army as Chiang began to undertake his long-awaited Northern Expedition to reunify China. But by 1927, the break had deepened and descended into violence, with Kuomintang forces carrying out a thoroughgoing purge of CCP cadres in their ranks, forcibly suppressing CCP organizations and activities, and executing thousands of Communists, most infamously in the Shanghai massacre in April of that year.[103]

---

102. For overviews, see William J. Duiker, "The Revolutionary Youth League: Cradle of Communism in Vietnam," *China Quarterly* 51 (July–September 1972): 475–499; Huỳnh Kim Khánh, *Vietnamese Communism, 1925–1945* (Ithaca, NY: Cornell University Press, 1982), 63–89; Goscha, *Thailand and the Southeast Asian Networks of the Vietnamese Revolution*, 64–74. For an evocative account based on the reminiscences of a Thanh Niên recruit, see Hue-Tam Ho Tai, *Passion, Betrayal, and Revolution in Colonial Saigon* (Berkeley: University of California Press, 2010), 23–52.

103. On this complex series of events, see the classic account by the American journalist Harold R. Isaacs, *The Tragedy of the Chinese Revolution* (London: Secker and Warburg, 1938).

Communist resistance—the Nanchang Uprising of August 1927, the short-lived Canton Commune in Guangzhou in December 1927, and rural soviets in Hai-feng and Lufeng counties—proved unsuccessful, and the CCP was driven under-ground and out of the cities and surrounding coastal areas, regrouping in 1928 under the Chinese Workers' and Peasants' Army as the party's conflict with the Kuomintang shifted onto new terrain in the interior of China.[104]

Against this backdrop, by the end of 1927 Nguyễn Ái Quốc and his embry-onic Thanh Niên network had essentially lost Guangzhou as a safe haven, educa-tional hub, and organizational base, and were returning to their home provinces and key urban centers in Tonkin, Annam, and Cochinchina, or dispersing to other sites of refuge and recruitment outside Indochina, most notably northeastern Siam. Some Thanh Niên activists melted into the ranks of the CCP as its cadres went underground or fled to the countryside; others remained enrolled in the Whampoa Military Academy and established new linkages with Kuomintang of-ficers. As for Nguyễn Ái Quốc, in April 1927 he left Guangzhou for Moscow via Shanghai and Vladivostok, but within a few months he had returned to Asia via Paris, Brussels, and Berlin, arriving in Siam in mid-1928. There he remained until late 1929, based in the northeast of the country near the border with Laos, where the Thanh Niên network had established training schools among the Vietnamese immigrant communities in the region.[105]

104. Bruce Elleman, *Moscow and the Emergence of Communist Power in China, 1925–30: The Nanchang Uprising and the Birth of the Red Army* (London: Routledge, 2009); Marcia R. Ristaino, *China's Art of Revolution: The Mobilization of Discontent, 1927 and 1928* (Durham, NC: Duke University Press, 1987).

105. Thanyathip Sripana, "Tracing Hồ Chí Minh's Sojourn in Siam," *Southeast Asian Studies* 2, no. 3 (December 2013): 527–558.

FROM THANH NIÊN TO THE INDOCHINESE COMMUNIST PARTY (ICP) AND THE VIỆT MINH

It was thus from beyond Indochina that a new phase of revolutionary organizing and activity began to emerge and unfold over the late 1920s and 1930s, setting the stage for the onset of the revolution in 1945 and its triumphs in subsequent decades. Thanh Niên recruits had been drawn from among the remnants of the networks established by Phan Bội Châu and expanded to incorporate a new generation of students who had participated in a wave of school strikes in cities and towns across Tonkin, Annam, and Cochinchina in 1926–1927,[1] thus providing something of an organizational infrastructure across Vietnam by the late 1920s. But by 1929, Thanh Niên had dissolved as a coherent organization, leaving in its wake a welter of new groupings: an Indochinese Communist Party (ICP), a rival Annamese Communist Party in Cochinchina, and the Annam-based Tân Việt (New Vietnam), which was renamed the League of Indochinese Communists. It was only thanks to the external intervention and insistence of the Comintern that unification was achieved in 1930, initially as the Vietnamese Communist Party and subsequently as the Indochinese Communist Party (ICP).[2] Indeed, the conference itself was initiated on the instructions of the Comintern and organized by

---

1. Micheline Lessard, "Tradition for Rebellion: Vietnamese Students and Teachers and Anticolonial Resistance, 1888–1931" (PhD diss., Cornell University, 1995), 242–268.

2. On the choice of "Indochina," see Christopher E. Goscha, *Vietnam or Indochina? Contesting Concepts of Space in Vietnamese Nationalism, 1887–1945* (Copenhagen: Nordic Institute of Asian Studies, 1995), 62–74.

Nguyễn Ái Quốc in his new capacity as the head of its Far Eastern Bureau, based in Shanghai.[3]

Throughout the 1930s, the ICP continued to rely on external safe havens, sources of support, and solidarity networks, as seen in the holding of its first National Congress in Macao in March 1935. From mid-1931, the arrests of key party activists by the French authorities had left the ICP without any real organizational leadership within Indochina, but eventually Comintern officials in Moscow created an Overseas Leadership Bureau in 1934 led by KUTV-trained ICP cadres, who were subsidized and supported by the French Communist Party (Parti Communiste Français or PCF) and corresponded with the PCF through seamen working on the ocean liners plying the routes between Asia and French ports such as Le Havre and Marseille.[4]

From its inception, the ICP's operations extended far beyond Indochina. ICP cadres maintained a safe haven and communications network among Vietnamese émigré communities in northeastern Siam and Laos, while establishing a base in the early 1930s in the town of Long Zhou in the southern Chinese province of Guangxi along the mountainous border with the provinces of Cao Bằng and Lạng Sơn, which provided a beachhead for communications, logistical support, and organizing efforts elsewhere in Tonkin.[5] At the same time, maritime connections were also crucial for the ICP:

> Nguyen Ai Quoc recruited Vietnamese and Chinese sailors working on the ships plying the South Seas to fulfil maritime duties for the Comintern. In the personal documents that the British Special Branch seized from Nguyen Ai Quoc in the wake of his arrest in June 1931 were detailed lists of Vietnamese and Chinese liaison agents—"boys," sailors, laundrymen, cooks and servants. In several of Quoc's lists, we follow sailors across the sea lanes connecting the ports of Singapore, Hong Kong, Canton and Bangkok, and on to Vladivostok and Marseilles. In a file marked "List J," we find a table of ship movements of the Compagnie des Messageries Maritimes, one of the largest shipping

---

3. Ralph B. Smith, "The Foundation of the Indochinese Communist Party, 1929–1930," *Modern Asian Studies* 32, no. 4 (October 1998): 769–805. On the Far Eastern Bureau, see Onimaru Takeshi, "Shanghai Connection: The Construction and Collapse of the Comintern Network in East and Southeast Asia," *Southeast Asian Studies* 5, no. 1 (April 2016): 115–133.

4. Young Soon Nho, "A History of the Indochinese Communist Party, 1930–1936" (PhD thesis, School of Oriental and African Studies, University of London, 2000), 186–187, 272–278. On the role of seamen in the links between the FCP and the ICP, see H. N. (Julie) Pham, "Revolution, Communism, and History in the Thought of Trần Văn Giàu (PhD diss., Pembroke College, University of Cambridge, 2008)," 99–112.

5. Pham, "Revolution, Communism, and History," 121–123.

companies in the world at that time. The dates for the Company's ships' arrivals and departures from major Asian ports are noted meticulously by Quoc for the months of February to August 1931. Accompanying them are coded lists of corresponding Vietnamese and Chinese maritime agents.[6]

Within Indochina, moreover, the ICP's activities were also informed and impelled by major shifts in Comintern policy during the late 1920s and 1930s. It was against the backdrop of the May 1928 Sixth Comintern Congress, for example, that Thanh Niên activists had begun to reconstitute themselves as Communists in line with calls for the abandonment of alliances with bourgeois nationalists, the proletarianization of revolutionary movements under Communist leadership, and the escalation of mass organizing and mobilization.[7] By 1930, the ICP had helped to promote a series of strike actions in Sài Gòn and the port city of Hải Phòng, a wave of strikes on rubber plantations in 1930,[8] and then, in 1930–1931, a large-scale peasant insurrection, culminating in the formation of local "soviets," in Nghệ An and Hà Tĩnh, the home provinces of two leading KUTV-trained ICP Overseas Leadership Bureau members in addition to Nguyễn Ái Quốc himself.[9] While this wave of mobilization subsided in the face of French repression by 1931, the hundreds of ICP cadres arrested and incarcerated over subsequent years used their time in prison for "rebuilding the organization, studying Marxist-Leninist theory, and indoctrinating new adepts," with courses taken in Moscow and Guangzhou in the 1920s informing the strengthening of the party's identity and internal discipline over 1930–1936.[10]

The Seventh Comintern Congress in 1935 likewise prompted a second phase of ICP activism in the latter half of the 1930s, in the context of the Popular Front government in France under Prime Minister Léon Blum (1936–1938) and its liberalization policies in Indochina. In line with the new Comintern policy favor-

6. Goscha, *Thailand and the Southeast Asian Networks of the Vietnamese Revolution, 1885–1954* (Richmond, Surrey: Curzon Press, 1999), 80.

7. Kevin McDermott, "Stalin and the Comintern during the 'Third Period', 1928–33," *European History Quarterly* 25, no. 3 (July 1995): 409–429.

8. Pierre Brocheux, "Le Prolétariat des Plantations d'Hévéas au Vietnam Méridional: Aspects Sociaux et Politiques (1927–1937)," *Le Mouvement Social* 90 (January–March 1975): 55–86; Tran Tu Binh, *The Red Earth: A Vietnamese Memoir of Life on a Colonial Rubber Plantation* (Athens: Ohio University Center for Southeast Asian Studies, 1985); Martin Thomas, *Violence and Colonial Order: Police, Workers and Protest in the European Colonial Empires, 1918–1940* (Cambridge: Cambridge University Press, 2015), 141–176.

9. Martin Bernal, "The Nghe-Tinh Soviet Movement, 1930–1931," *Past and Present* 92 (August 1981): 148–168. See also Sophie Quinn-Judge, "Ideological Influences on the Revolutionary High Tide: The Comintern, Class War, and Peasants," *South East Asia Research* 19, no. 4 (December 2011): 685–710.

10. Peter Zinoman, *The Colonial Bastille: A History of Imprisonment in Vietnam, 1862–1940* (Berkeley: University of California Press, 2001), 238, 221–222, and, more generally, 200–239.

ing cooperation and coalition building with other parties in antifascist popular fronts, the ICP engaged in participation alongside Trotskyists and other independents in elections to Sài Gòn's municipal council in 1935 and in the publication of the journal *La Lutte*,[11] agitation in favor of an Indochinese Congress and the formation of "action committees" across the countryside, labor organizing and strikes on the docks of Sài Gòn and along the railways, and peasant organizing to expand the party's mass base.[12] These forms of collaboration reflected the diversity of cosmopolitan left-wing currents in the political scene during this period, especially in Sài Gòn and elsewhere in Cochinchina, as seen in the strength of Trotskyist influences among activists returning from studies in France and the anarchist leanings of *La Cloche Fêlée* publisher Nguyễn An Ninh.[13]

Beyond these shifts in Comintern policies, the onset of World War II induced further changes in the ICP in the late 1930s. Nazi Germany's invasion and occupation of France in May–June 1940 brought grave economic disruption and hardship to Indochina and greatly weakened the authority of the French colonial state, prompting ICP cadres in Cochinchina to launch a poorly organized insurrection in Sài Gòn and then the surrounding countryside in November–December 1940. The ensuing French crackdown decimated the ICP's ranks, destroying its infrastructure in Cochinchina.[14]

Southern China, 1937–1945

Meanwhile, the Japanese invasion and partial occupation of China from 1937 led to the formation of a second Soviet-backed United Front between the Kuomintang and the CCP, thus enabling the reactivation of southern China as a potential safe haven and support base for Vietnamese revolutionary activities and infiltration within Indochina. By late 1938, Nguyễn Ái Quốc, after years of languishing in inactivity in Moscow (following his arrest and detention in Hong Kong in 1931, belated release in late 1932, and transit via Xiamen, Shanghai, and Vladivostok in early 1933), returned to southern China in late 1938 via the CCP's base

11. Daniel Hémery, *Révolutionnaires Vietnamiens et Pouvoir Colonial en Indochine: Communistes, Trotskystes, Nationalistes à Saigon de 1932 à 1937* (Paris: Maspero, 1975).

12. Sud Chonchirdsin, "The Indochinese Congress (May 1936–March 1937): False Hope of Vietnamese Nationalists," *Journal of Southeast Asian Studies* 30, no. 2 (September 1999): 338–346.

13. See Hue-Tam Ho Tai, *Radicalism and the Origins of the Vietnamese Revolution* (Cambridge, MA: Harvard University Press, 1992), especially 72–87, 125–131, 232–243, and the evocative account provided in Ngo Van, *Au Pays de la Cloche Fêlée: Tribulations d'un Cochinchinois à l'Époque Coloniale* (Paris: L'Insomniaque, 2013).

14. Sud Chonchirdsin, "The Indochinese Communist Party and the Nam Ky Uprising of Cochin China, November-December 1940," *South East Asia Research* 5, no. 3 (November 1997), 269–294. See also Sud Chonchirdsin, "The Indochinese Communist Party in French Cochin China (1936–1940)" (PhD thesis, School of Oriental and African Studies, University of London, 1995), 255–326.

area of Yan'an in the north-central province of Shaanxi, where he spent two weeks consulting with CCP cadres. Over the course of 1939, he circulated within the orbit of the CCP and its People's Liberation Army (PLA) bases, moving from Guangxi to Hunan and briefly visiting Zhou Enlai at the CCP's liaison office in the Kuomintang's capital, Chongqing, in the western province of Szechuan.[15]

These peregrinations helped to set the stage for efforts to revive the ICP from sites of refuge in southern China. By mid-1940, Nguyễn Ái Quốc had arrived in Kunming, the capital of Yunnan Province, where long-standing trade routes to Tonkin had been reinforced by French construction of a railroad link in the early 1900s, more than ten thousand Vietnamese railway workers and other émigrés had settled, and remnants of the Thanh Niên network and refugees from French repression after the failed Vietnamese Nationalist Party (Việt Nam Quốc Dân Đảng, or VNQDĐ) mutiny of 1930 and the abortive ICP insurrection of late 1940 had congregated.[16] In late 1940, Nguyễn Ái Quốc moved from Kunming to neighboring Guangxi Province, whose mountainous border with the Tonkinese provinces of Cao Bằng and Lạng Sơn promised access to local ICP base areas inside Indochina established in the early 1930s.

These moves coincided with the development of Japanese military strategy in China and Southeast Asia. By September 1940, Japanese pressure on the newly established French Vichy regime had enabled the movement of 6,000 Japanese troops into Tonkin, as well as the use of Tonkin for four airfields and the movement of 25,000 troops into Yunnan. By mid-1941, the Japanese military presence in Indochina had been extended to Cochinchina, a move that provoked a US freeze on Japanese assets and an extension of the 1940 embargo of scrap metal (e.g., iron ore) shipments to include a ban on the export of petroleum to Japan, helping to precipitate the Japanese attack on Pearl Harbor in December 1941 and the onset of American involvement in World War II.[17] An uneasy condominium between the Vichy French authorities and Japanese military forces persisted into early 1945. This state of affairs prefigured a strong interest among KMT forces in southern China in promoting anti-Japanese forces in neighboring Indochina, while precluding the effective empowerment of non-Communist na-

---

15. William Duiker, *Ho Chi Minh* (New York: Hyperion, 2000), 201–238; Quinn-Judge, *Ho Chi Minh: The Missing Years* (London: Hurst, 2003), 191–233.

16. On the mutiny and its aftermath, see Tobias Rettig, "French Military Policies in the aftermath of the Yên Bay Mutiny, 1930: Old Security Dilemmas Return to the Surface," *South East Asia Research* 10, no. 3 (2002): 309–331. On VNQDĐ exiles in Yunnan, see Van Dao Hoang, *Viet Nam Quoc Dan Dang: A Contemporary History of a National Struggle: 1927–1954* (Pittsburgh, PA: RoseDog Books, 2008), 169–196.

17. Jonathan Marshall, *To Have and Have Not: Southeast Asian Raw Materials and the Origins of the Pacific War* (Berkeley: University of California Press, 1995).

tionalist forces by the Japanese military administration along the lines observed in Indonesia over 1942–1945.[18]

Against this backdrop, the period from late 1940 through early 1945 saw the reemergence of Vietnamese revolutionary activity in southern China, now manifested in the form of armed guerrilla units operating along the border of Guangxi and Tonkin. By early 1941, KMT general Zhang Fakui, commander in chief of the Fourth War Area, had established a training camp for Vietnamese revolutionaries in the town of Jingxi, just sixty-five kilometers from the border with Tonkin, to assist in anticipated Chinese military operations against the Japanese forces in Indochina. Hundreds of Vietnamese trainees passed through the camp, including ICP cadres afforded a measure of protection under the rubric of the KMT-CCP United Front or otherwise able to shield their political affiliation from KMT scrutiny.[19] Meanwhile, over the course of 1941, an ICP base area was established in Pác Bó, a small village in Cao Bằng Province just three kilometers from the Chinese border, where the Party held its Eighth Plenum in May of that year. It was then and there that the Việt Nam Độc Lập Đồng Minh (Vietnam Independence League, or Việt Minh) was established, as an armed united front effectively under ICP control but aimed to encompass—or overshadow—a broader array of groups active in southern China enjoying the patronage and protection of Zhang Fakui, which he brought together under the rubric of the Việt Nam Cách Mạng Đồng Minh Hội (League for the Vietnamese Revolution, known as the Đồng Minh Hội), which excluded ICP cadres.[20]

As the war unfolded in southern China and elsewhere over 1942–1944, the Việt Minh experienced limited growth along the border of Guangxi and Tonkin. At first, the anti-Communist inclinations of the Kuomintang prevailed, as seen in the formation and promotion of the Đồng Minh Hội and the arrest of Nguyễn Ái Quốc, now carrying papers identifying him as Hồ Chí Minh, in August 1942 outside Jingxi and his imprisonment until his release in September 1943. But by late 1943, the weakness and ineffectiveness of the Đồng Minh Hội had led Zhang Fakui to draw Hồ Chí Minh and the Việt Minh into the league, a move variously explained by the influence of CCP agents and sympathizers among his advisors, deepening tensions with the KMT leadership in Chongqing, and wartime pragmatism in the forging of alliances against the Japanese.[21] Unlike the other self-styled

18. For a fine overview, see Ralph B. Smith, "The Japanese Period in Indochina and the Coup of 9 March 1945," *Journal of Southeast Asian Studies* 9, no. 2 (September 1978): 268–301.

19. King C. Chen, *Vietnam and China 1938–1954* (Princeton, NJ: Princeton University Press, 1969), 46–47, 67–71.

20. David G. Marr, *Vietnam 1945: The Quest for Power* (Berkeley: University of California Press, 1995), 167–177.

21. See Chen, *Vietnam and China*, 55–85; Hoang Van Hoan, *A Drop in the Ocean: Hoang Van Hoan's Revolutionary Reminiscences* (Beijing: Foreign Languages Press, 1988), 193–202; Peter Worthing, *Occupation and Revolution: China and the Vietnamese August Revolution of 1945* (Berkeley:

nationalist groups in the Đồng Minh Hội alliance, the ICP-led armed guerrilla units along the border with Guangxi had expanded their base of operations from the mountainous areas of Cao Bằng, Lạng Sơn, and Bắc Cạn provinces into lowland areas along the Red River Delta and elsewhere in Annam and Cochinchina, thus suggesting their greater capacity to assist in an anticipated KMT campaign against Japanese forces in Indochina.[22]

While the Việt Minh's activities and influence within Indochina itself remained rather limited through mid-1944, military developments in Europe and Asia enabled the movement's growth thereafter. By the end of 1944, Paris had been liberated, American forces were retaking the Philippines, the massive Japanese Ichi-gō campaign was underway in southern China (including Guangxi Province), and hundreds of French troops were being parachuted into Indochina, with growing anticipation of an imminent Allied invasion. By March 1945, rising Japanese concerns had spurred a coup against the increasingly unreliable Vichy French authorities and the establishment of direct Japanese military rule across Indochina under a nominally independent government headed by the Vietnamese emperor Bảo Đại and Prime Minister Trần Trọng Kim, precisely as pressures to devote troops and other resources to the last-ditch defense of the Greater East Asia Co-Prosperity Sphere were reaching breaking point.

The Japanese administrative presence—and its policing and surveillance capacities—in the countryside became increasingly attenuated, even as forced requisitioning of rice led to famine in much of Tonkin and northern Annam by mid-1945, conditions that combined to enable continuing expansion by Việt Minh units in rural areas.[23] By June 1945, a Liberated Zone had been created, covering nine provinces in Tonkin, governing an estimated one million people, and providing a base for military and political training for expansion. "In numerous rural areas throughout North and Central Vietnam local 'People's Revolutionary Committees' were created as a parallel administrative structure competing with the government authorities. Wherever possible, these committees would supplant the latter."[24]

University of California at Berkeley Institute of East Asian Studies, 2001), 41–46. On the broader military and political context of wartime Guangxi, see Graham Hutchings, "A Province at War: Guangxi During the Sino-Japanese Conflict, 1937–45," *China Quarterly* 108 (1986): 652–679.

22. Duiker, *Ho Chi Minh*, 258–282; Marr, *Vietnam 1945*, 167–194.

23. Marr, *Vietnam 1945*, 96–107; Bùi Minh Dũng, "Japan's Role in the Vietnamese Starvation of 1944–45," *Modern Asian Studies* 29, no. 3 (July 1995): 573–618; Geoffrey C. Gunn, *Rice Wars in Colonial Vietnam: The Great Famine and the Viet Minh Road to Power* (Lanham, MD: Rowman and Littlefield, 2014), 135–164; Stein Tønnesson, *The Vietnamese Revolution of 1945: Roosevelt, Ho Chi Minh, and de Gaulle in a World at War* (London: Sage, 1991), 240–249, 281–282.

24. Huỳnh Kim Khánh, "The Vietnamese August Revolution Reconsidered," *Journal of Asian Studies* 30, no. 4 (August 1971): 761–782, at 775–776. For a detailed overview, see Greg Lockhart, *Nation in Arms: The Origins of the People's Army of Vietnam* (Sydney: Allen and Unwin, 1989), 104–143.

Against this backdrop, the ICP-controlled Việt Minh was far better positioned than its counterparts in Indonesia to respond to the official Japanese surrender in August 1945. The last weeks of August 1945 saw Việt Minh–led mobilizations in Hà Nội, Huế, Sài Gòn, and other towns and cities across Tonkin, Annam, and Cochinchina in which they seized government buildings and established their provisional authority. On September 2, 1945, Hồ Chí Minh addressed a huge crowd on a main square in Hà Nội and proclaimed Vietnamese independence, a few short weeks after Indonesian revolutionaries had impelled Soekarno to issue a similar declaration in Indonesia. A revolution fully captured and commandeered by the Indochinese Communist Party was now set to unfold in Vietnam.

The Kuomintang Interregnum and Its Aftermath, 1945–1946

Indeed, compared to the abiding internal diversity and divisiveness of the Revolusi in nearby Indonesia in 1945–1949, the ICP-led Việt Minh was far better placed to establish and institutionalize monopolistic and monolithic authority over revolutionary mobilization in Vietnam during late 1945 and early 1946, especially in Tonkin and Annam. In contrast to the endurance and evolution of autonomous Islamic educational institutions and associational activities extending across the Netherlands East Indies and interlinking with the circuitries of Islamic scholarship, Sufi brotherhood, and pilgrimage across the Muslim world, the phasing out of the imperial civil service examination system by the French colonial regime in the 1910s prefigured the rapid eclipse of schooling in the Four Books and Five Classics of the Confucian canon in Vietnam, even as the scholastic circuitries of Sinographic cosmopolitanism in neighboring China had come unraveled with the collapse of Qing rule. In contrast to the enduring prominence of Javanese, Sundanese, and Madurese batik traders on Java, and the entrenched position of Acehnese, Buginese, and Minangkabau merchants in the Outer Islands of the Indonesian archipelago, the extension of French direct investment and the intensification of economic linkages between Indochina and the Pearl River Delta in southern China during the late nineteenth and early twentieth centuries left the emerging Vietnamese entrepreneurial class sidelined and subordinated to French and Chinese capital. Thus, the intellectual, institutional, and economic bases for a sociological and political counterweight to the ICP—such as Islam had provided vis-à-vis the PKI and the Sayap Kiri in the Indonesian Revolusi—were notably underdeveloped in Vietnam, as seen in the weakness of republican groups such as the Constitutionalist Party in Cochinchina during the interwar period.[25] The only partial exceptions to this pattern were the Cao Đài and Hòa Hảo religious sects that emerged and expanded in and around the Mekong Delta before World War II and established autonomous organizations, including armed militias, which were primed for mobilization at the end of World War II.[26]

Beyond Indochina itself, moreover, the tumultuous political developments in southern China in the decades following the 1911 overthrow of the Qing dynasty presented opportunities for diverse new Vietnamese experiments with Sino-graphic cosmopolitanism, but republican successors to Phan Bội Châu's Việt Nam Quang Phục Hội did not fare as well as the ICP. A Vietnamese Nationalist Party (Việt Nam Quốc Dân Đảng, or VNQDĐ) modelled after the Chinese Kuomintang was founded in 1927, but French repression following a VNQDĐ-orchestrated mutiny in the Tonkinese garrison town of Yên Bái in 1930 led to the party's implosion, with many remaining VNQDĐ members regrouping and taking refuge in Yunnan Province over subsequent years.[27] Meanwhile, other remnants of the VNQDĐ in Vietnam reconstituted themselves in the liberalized environment of the Popular Front era of the mid-late 1930s in new parties such as the Đại Việt Quốc Dân Đảng (ĐVQDĐ; Greater Vietnamese Nationalist Party, or Đại Việt), which were then driven underground with renewed repression under the Vichy regime from 1940, only to resurface in early 1945 with some hopes of support and sponsorship by the Japanese military, especially after the coup in March of that year. Thus, while VNQDĐ activists in Yunnan and Guangxi had provided the initial recruits to Kuomintang general Zhang Fakui's Đồng Minh Hội, they could not lay claim to a cohesive party network of their own within Indochina and their tentative efforts to cooperate and coalesce with Đại Việt activists deepened Kuomintang doubts as to their reliability, especially compared with the Việt Minh. In this context, it was, ironically enough, with effective Kuomintang encouragement and assistance that tightly organized, ICP-led Việt Minh forces had begun to establish an expanding base area in northern Vietnam over the summer of 1945 in anticipation of an Allied invasion of Indochina, even as the welter of nationalist "parties" remained divided, disorganized, and thus fatally

25. Ralph B. Smith, "Bui Quang Chiêu and the Constitutionalist Party in French Cochinchina, 1917–1930," *Modern Asian Studies* 3, no. 2 (March 1969): 131–150; Hue-Tam Ho Tai, "The Politics of Compromise: The Constitutionalist Party and the Electoral Reforms of 1922 in French Cochinchina," *Modern Asian Studies* 18, no. 3 (June 1984): 371–391; Megan Cook, *The Constitutionalist Party in Cochinchina: The Years of Decline, 1930–1942* (Clayton, Victoria: Monash University Centre of Southeast Asian Studies, 1977).

26. Jayne Susan Werner, *Peasant Politics and Religious Sectarianism: Peasant and Priest in the Cao Dai in Vietnam* (New Haven, CT: Yale University Southeast Asia Studies Monograph Series, 1981); Jérémy Jammes, *Les Oracles du Cao Đài: Étude d'un Mouvement Religieux Vietnamien et de ses Réseaux* (Paris: Les Indes Savantes, 2014); Hue-Tam Ho Tai, *Millenarianism and Peasant Politics in Vietnam* (Cambridge, MA: Harvard University Press, 1983); and Tran My-Van, "Beneath the Japanese Umbrella: Vietnam's Hoa Hao during and after the Pacific War," *Crossroads* 17, no. 1 (2003): 60–107.

27. Ho Tai, *Radicalism and the Origins of the Vietnamese Revolution*, 184–185, 217–223.

diminished as a republican counterweight to Communist control over the Vietnamese Revolution.[28]

These accumulated advantages of the ICP vis-à-vis potential republican rivals were augmented by international and regional circumstances that further intertwined the fortunes of the revolution in Vietnam with those of the revolution in neighboring China. At the Potsdam Conference in late July 1945, at US president Franklin Delano Roosevelt's insistence, responsibility for the liberation of Indochina north of the 16th Parallel had been awarded to the Nationalist Chinese government of Kuomintang generalissimo Chiang Kai-shek, in avowed recognition of the putative status of China among the Allied victors of World War II. Yunnanese troops from the Chinese 1st Army Group under General Lu Han were dispatched to Indochina to accept the surrender of the Japanese 38th Army, to oversee the disarming, demobilization, and repatriation of Japanese troops, and to establish law and order in northern Vietnam. By late August, tens of thousands of Chinese troops were crossing over the border from Yunnan and Guangxi into Tonkin, and by early September General Lu Han had established his headquarters in Hà Nội, even as British and Indian forces of the Southeast Asia Command (SEAC) responsible for the liberation of Indochina south of the 16h Parallel, accompanied by a company of French troops, were establishing control in Sài Gòn.[29]

From early September 1945 through March 1946, the occupation of northern Vietnam by more than one hundred thousand Kuomintang troops provided an unparalleled opportunity for the ICP-led Việt Minh and the embryonic Democratic Republic of Vietnam (DRV) to consolidate power. Kuomintang general Lu Han was reportedly very unsympathetic to French aims of restoring colonial rule in Indochina and relatively indifferent to the complexion of the Việt Minh, or at least willing to allow its forces to retain administrative control over Hà Nội. In October 1945, moreover, Chiang Kai-shek's maneuvers to remove Lu Han's cousin and mentor, 1st Army Group commander in chief General Long Yun, from his longtime position as governor of Yunnan Province, led to the enlistment of Lu Han as his replacement, distracting him from his duties in Hà Nội and leading to his departure for Kunming before the end of the year. Lu Han's preoccupation with political developments in Yunnan, moreover, left considerable operational latitude in the hands of one of his key aides, General Xiao Wen, whose previous service under General Zhang Fakui in Guangxi in 1942–1945 had involved

28. On the complex history of these nationalist parties from 1927 through 1945, see François Guillemot, *Dai Việt, Indépendance et Révolution au Việt-Nam: L'Échec de la Troisième Voie (1938–1955)* (Paris: Les Indes Savantes, 2012), 46–219.

29. Worthing, *Occupation and Revolution*, 54–68; Lin Hua, *Chiang Kai-Shek, De Gaulle Contre Hô Chi Minh: Việt-Nam 1945–1946* (Paris: Éditions L'Harmattan, 1994), 109–137.

intimate working relations, and close personal and perhaps political sympathies, with Hồ Chí Minh.[30]

Overall, the six-month occupation of northern Vietnam by Kuomintang Chinese troops had three critical consequences. First, the nature of the occupation encouraged the ICP-led Việt Minh to engage in nominal coalition building with various nationalist parties while simultaneously enabling the ICP to outmaneuver and eliminate them over the first six months following the proclamation of Vietnamese independence. On the one hand, to avoid antagonizing the Kuomintang authorities (whether in Hà Nội or in Chongqing), Hồ Chí Minh invited figures associated with the VNQDĐ and the Đồng Minh Hội to join the provisional government in positions of public prominence if not actual power. In November 1945, moreover, the Indochinese Communist Party announced its formal dissolution, even as the Việt Minh remained firmly under its effective control. After elections were held in January 1946, a Việt Minh victory was proclaimed (on the basis of an estimated 97 percent of the popular vote), and a veneer of democratic pluralism was preserved, with the VNQDĐ and the Đồng Minh Hội accorded fifty and twenty seats, respectively, alongside the three hundred occupied by the avowedly non-Communist Việt Minh.

On the other hand, the concentration of coercive and regulatory powers in the hands of the ICP-controlled Việt Minh enabled restriction and repression of the non-Communist nationalist parties, as seen in DRV minister of the interior (and leading ICP cadre) Võ Nguyên Giáp's outlawing of two of the Đại Việt parties in early September 1945, followed by his interdiction of several youth groups and a vaguely worded decree enabling the arrest of "those who threaten the DRV." Subsequent months saw the formation of military tribunals, restrictions on the possession of firearms, arrests of non-Communist nationalist party activists, a steady stream of attacks in the Việt Minh-controlled press against nationalist parties for their "unpardonable" pro-Japanese sympathies during World War II, and a campaign of abductions and assassinations escalating over the final months of 1945. The Việt Minh's claim of a 90 percent victory in the elections held in early January 1946 excluded localities where various nationalist parties enjoyed something of a presence, reflecting and reinforcing their effective marginalization under the nominally non-Communist coalitional government in Hà Nội.[31]

---

30. For various accounts, see Chen, *Vietnam and China*, 65–68, 73–77, 82–85, 94–97, 115–127; Worthing, *Occupation and Revolution*, 84–88, 104–106; Lin Hua, "The Chinese Occupation of Northern Vietnam, 1945–1946: A Reappraisal," in *Imperial Policy and Southeast Asian Nationalism, 1930–1957*, ed. Hans Antlöv and Stein Tønnesson (Richmond: Curzon Press, 1995), 144–169; and Guillemot, *Dai Viêt*, 315–321.

31. See Guillemot, *Dai Viêt*, 276–315, and François Guillemot, "Au Cœur de la Fracture Vietnamienne: L'Élimination de l'Opposition Nationaliste et Anticolonialiste dans le Nord du Vietnam (1945–1946)," in *Naissance d'un État-Parti: Le Viêt Nam depuis 1945*, ed. Christopher E. Goscha and Benoît De Tréglodé (Paris: Les Indes Savantes, 2004), 175–216.

Second, the Chinese occupation delayed the return of French forces to Tonkin and northern Annam even as they were reestablishing control over Cochinchina and southern Annam over late 1945 and early 1946. In contrast to the early and unconditional transfer of authority from the British to the French authorities south of the 16th Parallel, the Kuomintang government in Chongqing and the Kuomintang authorities in Hà Nội dragged out negotiations with the French government for the return of French forces north of the 16th Parallel until the end of February 1946, insisting, inter alia, on a separate French–Vietnamese agreement prior to the landing of French forces at Hải Phòng in early March 1946. It was in the context of escalating tensions and brief armed hostilities between French and Chinese forces in Hải Phòng harbor that a preliminary accord was signed between France and the DRV, with the Chinese presence and pressure effectively sealing the deal.

On the one hand, the agreement provided for French recognition of the DRV as a "free state" within the Indochinese Federation and the "French Union," as the French Empire was restyled in early 1945 in line with the reforms and new modes of representation promised at the January 1944 conference of Free French and colonial offices in Brazzaville, the Congolese capital of Afrique Equatoriale Française (AEF; French Equatorial Africa). The agreement meshed well with the new *politique de Brazzaville*, under which Indochina and other Associated States would enjoy a measure of autonomy even as the grandeur and Great Power status of France was restored in the aftermath of its humiliating defeat and occupation during World War II.[32] But the anxieties inspiring the *politique de Brazzaville* increased with the abortive Sétif uprising and ensuing massacres in Algeria in May and June 1945,[33] the railway strike and riots in the key Cameroonian port city of Douala in September 1945,[34] and the vitriol and violence with which insurrectionary mobilization, unilateral proclamations of independence, and the withdrawal of French forces unfolded in Lebanon and Syria over 1945 and early 1946.[35] Thus, the Chinese occupation combined with developments and trends across the French Empire to prefigure a deferred and delimited return of French forces to northern Vietnam, even as French authority was restored to the cities, major towns, and key transportation routes south of the 16th Parallel by early 1946.

---

32. See Martin Shipway, "Creating an Emergency: Metropolitan Constraints on French Colonial Policy and Its Breakdown in Indo-China, 1945–47," in *Emergencies and Disorder in the European Empires after 1945*, ed. Robert Holland (Abingdon: Frank Cass, 1994), 1–14.

33. Jean-Louis Planche, *Sétif 1945: Chronique d'un Massacre Annoncé* (Paris: Perrin, 2006); Martin Thomas, "Colonial Violence and the Distorted Logic of State Retribution: The Sétif Uprising of 1945," *Journal of Military History* 75, no. 1 (January 2011): 125–157.

34. Richard A. Joseph, "Strikers, Settlers, and *Sans-Travail*: The Douala Riots of September 1945," *Journal of African History* 15, no. 4 (October 1974): 669–687.

35. See Martin Thomas, "Divisive Decolonization: The Anglo-French Withdrawal from Syria and Lebanon, 1944–46," *Journal of Imperial and Commonwealth History* 28, no. 3 (2000): 71–93.

On the other hand, the agreement entailed DRV acceptance of 15,000 French troops alongside 10,000 DRV troops to "relieve" Chinese forces, with the French contingent to be fully phased out by 1951 and the French government committed to respect the results of a referendum on the possible unification of Tonkin, Annam, and Cochinchina. These terms provided the basis for the continued entrenchment of the DRV in northern Vietnam over nine more months, even as tensions between DRV and French forces continued to escalate during the year, leading to the outbreak of open hostilities in mid-December 1946. Thus, thanks to the Chinese occupation of northern Vietnam, an ICP-controlled, Việt Minh-led government was able to establish itself and extend its authority north of the 16th parallel over the fifteen months from early September 1945 through mid-December 1946.[36]

Third and finally, the Chinese occupation of northern Vietnam and the subsequent nine-month interlude of uneasy coexistence between French and Vietnamese forces enabled the ICP-controlled, Việt Minh-led Democratic Republic of Vietnam to engage in accelerated forms of state formation and mass mobilization during late 1945 and 1946. As of September 1945, the ICP counted no more than 5,000 members out of a total Vietnamese population of 23 million, with party membership growing to 20,000 by the end of 1946, 50,000 by the end of 1947, 180,000 by the end of 1948, and half a million by 1950.[37] But already by August 1945, armed brigades of the ICP-led Việt Minh had established a local infrastructure of government in villages and towns, first in upland areas along the border with Guangxi, then extending across six provinces north of Hà Nội and expanding across the Red River Delta. These Việt Minh units "approached a few individuals in each locality to form a Việt Minh group.

> Members then began to learn how to read and write, to memorize the basic political platform, undertake military drills, and solicit donations. It was hoped that as the number of participants increased, separate hamlet associations for farmers, youth, women, and elders would be created, with each association electing its own representative to the local *Việt Minh* committee. ICP cadres would then select the most promising activists to make up the hamlet's first party cell.[38]

As this infrastructure was established and entrenched across much of Tonkin and northern Annam in 1946, the ICP-led DRV maintained its command, control,

36. Worthing, *Occupation and Revolution*, 113–169; Stein Tønnesson, *Vietnam 1946: How the War Began* (Berkeley: University of California Press, 2010), 39–64.

37. Christopher Goscha, *Vietnam: Un État Né de la Guerre 1945–1954* (Paris: Armand Collin, 2011), 67–76.

38. David G. Marr, *Vietnam: State, War, and Revolution (1945–1946)* (Berkeley: University of California Press, 2013), 443.

and communications structures thanks to early infiltration and appropriation of the central offices of the Service des Postes, Télégraphes et Téléphones offices in Hà Nội, even as the early British-assisted restoration of French authority in Sài Gòn and conditions on the ground in southern Annam and Cochinchina impeded the extension of Việt Minh (and ICP) rule below the 16th Parallel. "Thanks to colonial post office and the wireless radio station at Bach Mai, south of Hanoi, the Viet Minh telephoned, cabled, and radioed instructions to civil servants in most of Vietnam's provincial and district towns."[39] From early September 1945 through mid-December 1946, the DRV's Voice of Vietnam aired its broadcasts across the country, transmitting information and instructions to millions of listeners.

The DRV's centralized command, control, and communications infrastructure was extended into rural Vietnamese society. A mass mobilizational campaign to promote literacy among the population at large unfolded in late 1945 and 1946 in line with a September 1945 decree mandating compulsory literacy for all Vietnamese over the age of eight years old within a year. As of July 1946, some 37,000 instructors dispatched by the Mass Education Bureau were said to be teaching some 600,000 Vietnamese men, women, and children how to read, with more than 100,000 reaching proficiency. By September 1946, official figures claimed that 2.5 million Vietnamese had been taught to read by nearly 100,000 instructors.[40] However exaggerated these figures might have been, the overall impact of the campaign was to extend the penetration of the ideological (party-)state apparatuses of the DRV deep into Vietnamese society, drawing hundreds of thousands of ordinary Vietnamese men and women into the orbit of the ICP's lexicon, much as "speaking Bolshevik" became established across the early postrevolutionary Soviet Union:[41]

> From late 1945, ordinary Vietnamese learned how to use positive revolutionary terms like liberation, struggle, progress, sacrifice, comrade, unity, and national front, as well as negative terms such as traitor, counterrevolutionary, reactionary, and exploiter. They had to denounce publicly all aspects of French rule and hide or destroy evidence of prior participation in the colonial system. Literate individuals sought clues to proper revolutionary behavior in newspapers and leaflets, while illiterates relied on word-of-mouth, activist speech-making, and observing the conduct of visiting cadres.[42]

---

39. Christopher Goscha, "Wiring Decolonization: Turning Technology against the Colonizer during the Indochina War, 1945–1954," *Comparative Studies in Society and History* 54, no. 4 (October 2012): 803.

40. Marr, *Vietnam*, 530–536.

41. On "speaking Bolshevik" in early postrevolutionary Soviet society, see Stephen Kotkin, *Magnetic Mountain: Stalinism as a Civilization* (Berkeley: University of California Press, 1997), 198–237.

42. Marr, *Vietnam*, 565–566.

This process of DRV (party-)state formation, mass mobilization, and institutional-cum-ideological penetration of Vietnamese society went hand in hand with the construction of a modern army under centralized party-state control. As of September 1945, thousands of local militias emerged in villages, towns, and cities across the full breadth of Vietnam, and over the remaining months of 1945 and over 1946 most of those above the 16th Parallel were systematically incorporated into the DRV's National Armed Forces, forming a regular army consisting of some seventeen province-based infantry regiments and nine centrally commanded infantry battalions by September 1946, with political officers down to the battalion and company levels predominantly drawn from the growing ranks of ICP members. Organizational discipline and ideological indoctrination were enhanced by the establishment of military schools supervised and staffed by Chinese-trained officers, who instructed military officers and cadres in combat skills and military tactics and strategy.

Meanwhile, efforts to extend the embryonic DRV's military mobilization south of the 16th Parallel were undermined by the British-backed landings of French Expeditionary Corps troops and the restoration of French control over Sài Gòn and other major towns of the Mekong Delta in September 1945. Against this backdrop, so-called Nam Tiến (Southern Advance) groups mobilized and headed down along the coast in a poorly organized and ill-fated effort to counter the restoration of French rule in major towns and roadways over the remaining months of 1945. But as of late 1946, "no reliable chain of command extended yet to the majority of armed independence groups operating in the southern countryside."[43]

In Annam, however, a major reorganization effort was initiated in March 1946 under the leadership of Nguyễn Sơn, a leading ICP cadre, longtime exile in China, and veteran of the CCP's Long March and its subsequent establishment of a base area in Yan'an in the central Chinese province of Shaanxi. Nguyễn Sơn established three brigades, each consisting of three or four regiments, as well as a special military academy in the central Annam coastal province of Quảng Ngãi where some four hundred students were trained to command companies, serve on battalion and regimental staffs, and form specialized units (e.g., engineering, counterintelligence, logistics) in the DRV's National Armed Forces. Through his teachings, his translations of Mao's works, and his own military treatises, Nguyễn Sơn helped to inform and enhance Vietnamese revolutionary warfare with extensive experience and expertise drawn from China.[44]

---

43. Marr, *Vietnam*, 171.

44. Marr, *Vietnam*, 161–166; Christopher E. Goscha, "Building Force: Asian Origins of Twentieth-Century Military Science in Vietnam (1905–54)," *Journal of Southeast Asian Studies* 34, no. 3 (October 2003): 535–560, at 545–546.

Alongside this reliance on organizational models for party/state building and military mobilization drawn from experiences and indoctrination in China, the ICP-led DRV worked to develop close linkages to concrete sources of logistical support beyond the borders of Vietnam as it struggled to establish its authority over the course of 1946. Drawing on the well-established solidarity networks among Vietnamese communities, by late 1945 the Việt Minh had established armed guerrilla units in Laos and assisted in the founding of the Lao Issara (Free Laos) movement led by Lao princes opposed to the restoration of French colonial rule. Military operations leading to French reoccupation of the major towns of Laos in the weeks following the March 1946 accords spurred tens of thousands of Vietnamese refugees to flee into neighboring Thailand, where they were incorporated into established Vietnamese émigré communities and enjoyed safe haven and quiet support from the sympathetic civilian government of Pridi Phanomyong in Bangkok.[45]

Thanks to this protected base in Thailand, the DRV gained access to a thriving arms market. "The disarming of more than 100,000 Japanese troops, the demobilization of much of the Royal Thai Army . . . and the arrival of almost 27,000 Allied troops" in late 1945 had left Thailand "awash with arms," and Bangkok emerged as "the major Southeast Asian crossroads for arms shipments coming from abroad—from the Philippines, Singapore, Indonesia, Hong Kong, Macao and China on the one hand; and from Italy, Sweden and Czechoslovakia on the other."[46] While Vietnamese émigré networks provided an overland pipeline for weapons, equipment, explosives, and medicines to be smuggled from Thailand via Laos and Cambodia, maritime trade links enabled the DRV to source war matériel both from Thailand and elsewhere. DRV agents dispatched agents to Manila and Rangoon to source weapons from among the vast surplus of arms left from the bloody battles that had devastated the Philippines and Burma over the course of late 1944 and early–mid 1945. CCP and other networks among the Chinese émigré communities across Southeast Asia and in Hainan, Hong Kong, and Macao helped to facilitate maritime smuggling via the small-scale junk trade along the long, snakelike coastline of Vietnam.[47]

Survival, 1947–1949

With the forced displacement of the DRV from its seat of government in Hà Nội by French military operations at the end of 1946 and the onset of armed

45. Goscha, *Thailand and the Southeast Asian Networks of the Vietnamese Revolution*, 145–157.
46. Goscha, 185 and 189. See 181–235 for a comprehensive overview.
47. See Christopher E. Goscha, "The Maritime Nature of the Wars for Vietnam (1945–1975): A Geo-Historical Reflection," *War and Society* 24, no. 2 (November 2005), 53–92, especially 55–66.

conflict between French troops and Việt Minh forces, the organizational models borrowed from China and the war matériel sourced from Thailand, elsewhere in Southeast Asia, and the port cities of southern China provided crucial survival tools as the revolution faced the threat of extinction. By early 1947, DRV forces had been forced to evacuate Hà Nội and other major towns and cities, relocating its government headquarters, military command center, supply base, and training ground northward to the hilly areas along the Chinese border. Over the course of the year, the French Far East Expeditionary Corps (Corps Expéditionnaire Français en Extrême-Orient, or CEFEO) undertook a large-scale military offensive against Việt Minh forces, especially in Cochinchina, where the Việt Minh also became embroiled in a civil war with religious groups such as the Cao Đài and the Hòa Hảo (and, by 1948, with the gangster-style Bình Xuyên organization), which enjoyed considerable strength in the Mekong Delta.[48] Meanwhile, Cao Đài and Hòa Hảo leaders joined figures affiliated with the VNQDĐ and Đại Việt parties in a broad-based non-Communist coalition to support the return of Emperor Bảo Đại to Vietnam to lead a national government within the French Union, a plan that soon won strong French support.[49]

But thanks to the internal organizational strengths and cross-border logistical support networks established by the DRV over late 1945 and 1946 as noted above, revolutionary forces survived the French onslaught, especially in Tonkin and Annam.[50]

> Throughout 1947 most DRV local committees continued to function despite erratic or non-existent contact with central authorities. They collected taxes and donations, stockpiled food, billeted soldiers, tightened security, and tried to prepare inhabitants against arrival of French troops. Roads were dug up, culverts destroyed, underground caches and hiding places constructed, and scenarios for defense rehearsed. For months the majority of villages north of the sixteenth parallel saw enemy soldiers only at a distance, as [CEFEO] focused on control of urban centers, main roads, and river ways.[51]

---

48. Jessica M. Chapman, *Cauldron of Resistance: Ngho Dinh Diem, the United States, and 1950s Southern Vietnam* (Ithaca, NY: Cornell University Press, 2013), 30–39.

49. Mark Atwood Lawrence, "Recasting Vietnam: The Bao Dai Solution and the Outbreak of the Cold War in Southeast Asia," in *Connecting Histories: Decolonization and the Cold War in Southeast Asia, 1945–1962*, ed. Christopher E. Goscha and Christian F. Ostermann (Washington, DC: Woodrow Wilson Center Press, 2009), 15–38.

50. For a concise overview of the French campaign and its consequences, see Bernard B. Fall, *Street without Joy: The French Debacle in Indochina* (Harrisburg, PA: Stackpole Books, 1961), 27–31.

51. Marr, *Vietnam*, 571.

By the end of 1947, "recruitment in villages under Viet Minh control had begun to rebound after losses from the French offensive, and the size of revolutionary armed forces was steadily on the rise."[52] In Tonkin, the Việt Minh

> controlled the whole area northeast and east of the Red River and Ha-noi as well as the fertile provinces south of the Red River Delta down to northern Annam, including the towns of Thanh Hoa and Vinh. In north-ern and central Annam, between the towns of Vinh and Qui Nhon, the French held only a narrow coastal strip beginning just north of Quang Tri and ending slightly south of Tourane (Da Nang), in addition to part of the thinly populated highland; the rest of the territory, perhaps 80 percent of the total, was from the start of the conflict in Viet Minh hands. In southern Annam and in Cochin China, French control was more extensive. They held all the cities . . . and they had at least nomi-nal control (though not at night) of the major roads. Even here, though, guerrilla action was frequent, and a few areas were under Viet Minh con-trol. . . . Saigon, meanwhile, featured regular grenade attacks on cafés and bars frequented by *colons*, and French authorities felt compelled to maintain a strict curfew of eleven P.M.[53]

By the end of 1948, the number of armed guerrillas mobilized by the DRV was estimated to have expanded to 250,000, with Việt Minh forces enjoying control over more than half of all the villages across Vietnam and a population of as many as twelve million people.[54] While focused on the countryside, the "People's War" was also extended to the cities, with an extensive network of underground cells established in Hà Nội and a campaign of urban guerrilla warfare waged in Sài Gòn, including a grenade attack on the famous Chinese-run casino Le Grande Monde in 1947 and the bombing of the Majestic cinema in 1948.[55]

Meanwhile, developments across the vast expanse of the French Empire com-bined to constrain French efforts to obliterate the Việt Minh, the DRV, and other obstacles to the reestablishment of colonial authority across the full breadth of

52. William J. Duiker, "Ho Chi Minh and the Strategy of People's War," in *The First Vietnam War: Colonial Conflict and Cold War Crisis*, ed. Mark Atwood Lawrence and Fredrik Logevall (Cambridge, MA: Harvard University Press, 2007), 152–174, at 164.

53. Fredrik Logevall, *Embers of War: The Fall of an Empire and the Making of America's Vietnam* (New York: Random House, 2012), 175.

54. Logevall, *Embers of War*, 165.

55. See Christopher E. Goscha, "Colonial Hanoi and Saigon at War: Social Dynamics of the Viet Minh's 'Underground City', 1945–1954," *War in History* 20, no. 2 (April 2013): 222–250, especially 245–249. For further contextualization and detail, see Christopher E. Goscha, "'La Guerre Par D'Autre Moyens': Réflexions sur la Guerre du Việt Minh dans le Sud-Vietnam de 1945 à 1951," *Guerres Mondiales et Conflits Contemporains* 206 (2002): 29–57.

Indochina over 1947. A string of incidents—the massacre of repatriated *tirailleurs sénégalais* in a camp outside Dakar in late 1944, indiscipline in the ranks of troops in Syria in 1944–1945, and the violent suppression of an insurrection in the Algerian town of Sétif in May 1945—had raised concerns about the reliability of African troops, thus leading to their official exclusion from service in Indochina in October 1945 and leaving the overstretched CEFEO constrained in recruitment and reinforcements.[56] Indeed, a general strike in Senegal in 1946 set the stage for a railway strike across French West Africa in October 1947, involving 17,000 railwaymen and 2,000 port workers, enduring into early 1948, and exacerbating French anxieties about the African bases of the empire.[57]

In March 1947, moreover, just as the dwindling of CEFEO troops from 67,000 to 62,000 had forced a reversal of this ban on African troops, an insurrection erupted in Madagascar that led to the diversion of 12,000 troops originally bound for Indochina. The insurrection broke out in response to intensifying French repression of the Mouvement Démocratique pour la Rénovation Malgache (MDRM), whose two *députés* to the Constituent Assembly—former members of the short-lived Parti Communiste de la Région de Madagascar during the Popular Front period—had drafted a law declaring Malagasy independence within the French Union, a move reportedly inspired by the Vietnamese example and also enthusiastically endorsed by Hồ Chí Minh in a private meeting with the two men in Paris amidst his negotiations with the French government in the summer of 1946.[58] From its outbreak in late March 1947, the insurrection spread from the eastern garrison town of Moramanga across much of Madagascar, surviving violent French suppression over subsequent months and not fully dying out until the end of 1948, at the cost of tens of thousands of Malagasy lives. By diverting much needed French and African troops away from the conflict in Indochina, the insurrection deprived the CEFEO of much needed reinforcements at the peak of its aggressive campaign against the Việt Minh in 1947.[59]

By mid-1947, moreover, this deepening crisis across the breadth of the French Empire began to intensify and expand with the pressures of the Cold War in Europe. In May 1947, the Parti Communiste Français (PCF; French Communist Party) withdrew from the coalition government in Paris and shifted into outright opposition to the war in Indochina. With the PCF's departure, the French gov-

56. Julien Fargettas, *La Fin de la "Force Noire": Les Soldats Africains et la Décolonisation Française* (Paris: Les Indes Savantes, 2018), 19–43.

57. Frederick Cooper, "'Our Strike': Equality, Anticolonial Politics, and the 1947–48 Railway Strike in French West Africa," *Journal of African History* 37, no. 1 (March 1996): 81–118.

58. For an account of the meeting with Hồ Chí Minh, see Jacques Tronchon, *L'Insurrection Malgache de 1947: Essai d'Interprétation* (Paris: Karthala, 1986), especially 335–337. For background, see also Martin Shipway, "Madagascar on the Eve of Insurrection, 1944–47: The Impasse of a Liberal Colonial Policy," *Journal of Imperial and Commonwealth History* 24, no. 1 (January 1996): 72–100.

59. Michel Bodin, *La France et Ses Soldats: Indochine, 1945–1954* (Paris: L'Harmattan, 1996), 29.

ernment, already increasingly suspicious of the Communist affiliations and inclinations of the MDRM in Madagascar and the Rassemblement Démocratique Africain (RDA) in Afrique Occidentale Française (AOF; French West Africa) and Afrique Équatoriale Française (AEF), shifted from condominium and cooptation vis-à-vis African nationalists into a much more conservative and confrontational policy.

Much as French (and American) suspicions of Communist influence and orientation in the MDRM informed and enabled violent repression before and after the insurrection in Madagascar,[60] so too did similar fears about PCF linkages impel a crackdown on the RDA in West Africa in 1948 and efforts to contain the growth of the militant Union des Populations du Cameroun (UPC), which was founded by left-wing union activists in the port city of Douala in the same year.[61] With the costs of the war in Indochina reaching 60 billion francs and 5,000 casualties by the end of 1947,[62] the realities of imperial overstretch were increasingly evident, foreshadowing the adoption of a *eurafricain* policy by the likes of the Socialist *ministre de France d'outre-mer* (minister of overseas France) François Mitterand of "abandonner l'Indochine pour mieux conserver l'Afrique."[63]

Indeed, with every passing year, the war in Indochina became more difficult and dangerous to sustain for France and its empire. From nearly 60,000 in early 1946, the numbers of French troops in Indochina fell to 43,000 by 1949, climbing no higher than 53,000 by 1954, requiring increasing reliance on Africans, North Africans, and Foreign Légionnaires, whose numbers rose to nearly 20,000, almost 37,000, and more than 18,000 respectively by 1954, totalling nearly 60 percent of all armed personnel other than those locally recruited.[64] CEFEO reliance on such troops prefigured abiding fears and persistent problems with military effectiveness, discipline, and morale: more than 80 percent of the African troops were inexperienced fresh recruits, as were a similar percentage of the Légionnaires.[65]

Meanwhile, even with increasing reliance on more poorly paid non-French troops, the costs of the war in Indochina continued to grow, rising threefold

---

60. Douglas Little, "Cold War and Colonialism in Africa: The United States, France, and the Madagascar Revolt of 1947," *Pacific Historical Review* 59, no. 4 (November 1990): 527–552.

61. Alexander Keese, "A Culture of Panic: 'Communist' Scapegoats and Decolonization in French West Africa and French Polynesia (1945–1957)," *French Colonial History* 9, no. 1 (2008): 131–146; Thomas Deltombe, Manuel Domergue, and Jacob Tatsitsa, *Kamerun! Une Guerre Cachée aux Origines de la Françafrique (1948–1971)* (Paris: La Découverte, 2011), 74–95.

62. Mark Atwood Lawrence, *Assuming the Burden: Europe and the American Commitment to War in Vietnam* (Berkeley: University of California Press, 2005), 180.

63. François Mitterand, *Aux Frontières de l'Union Française: Indochine-Tunisie* (Paris: René Julliard, 1953), 25.

64. Sarah Jean Zimmerman, "Living beyond Boundaries: West African Servicemen in French Colonial Conflicts, 1908–1962" (PhD diss., University of California at Berkeley, 2011), 101.

65. Michel Bodin, *Soldats d'Indochine 1945–1954* (Paris: L'Harmattan, 1997), 13.

between 1947 and 1952.[66] Although French public opinion remained largely indifferent to the ongoing war in Indochina,[67] the rising costs—40 percent of the defense budget by 1947[68] and more than 10 percent of the national budget by 1949—increasingly vexed policymakers attentive to the competing imperatives of early postwar reconstruction and, from 1949, contributions to the newly established North Atlantic Treaty Organization (NATO).[69] Tightening budget constraints meant worsening pay and conditions for soldiers, rendering recruitment of French soldiers ever more difficult.[70]

From mid-1947, moreover, PCF opposition to the war in Indochina enabled various forms of resistance in avowed solidarity with the embryonic and embattled DRV. From December 1949 through March 1950, the PCF-affiliated Confédération Générale du Travail (CGT) sustained a stevedores' strike in the crucial southern port city of Marseille,[71] elsewhere in southern France, and in the Algerian ports of Oran and Algiers, vowing that "not a single firearm for the dirty war in Indochina will depart from the ports of the Mediterranean."[72] Such solidarity with the DRV in famously multicultural Marseille arguably reflected the pronounced strength of the PCF in the city and the signature prominence of African (and North African) stevedores, such as the Senegalese activist, writer, and film director-to-be Ousmane Sembène,[73] on the docks of its bustling La Jolliette harbor.[74]

But the threat of left-wing disruption of the French war effort in Indochina extended far beyond Marseille, as seen in the Dreyfus-like Henri Martin Affair in Toulon, home to France's premier naval base. Martin, a French sailor sent to Indochina in 1945, deserted the navy in late 1946 and returned to Toulon,

66. Hugues Tertrais, *La Piastre et le Fusil: Le Coût de la Guerre d'Indochine 1945–1954* (Paris: Comité pour l'Histoire Économique et Financière de la France, 2002), 119.

67. See Alain Ruscio, "L'Opinion Française et la Guerre d'Indochine (1945–1954): Sondages et Témoignages," *Vingtième Siècle: Revue d'Histoire* 29 (January–March): 35–46.

68. Elizabeth Buettner, *Europe after Empire: Decolonization, Society, and Culture* (Cambridge: Cambridge University Press, 2016), 133.

69. Tertrais, *La Piastre et le Fusil*, 225.

70. Michel Bodin, *La France et Ses Soldats: Indochine, 1945–1954* (Paris: L'Harmattan, 1996), 31–32; Tetrais, *La Piastre et Le Fusil*, 180–181.

71. On the importance of Marseille for the transport of CEFEO troops bound for Indochina, see Michel Bodin, "Le *Pasteur*: Un Rouage Essentiel du Transport des Troupes dans la Guerre d'Indochine, 1945–1956," *Guerres Mondiales et Conflits Contemporains* 216 (2004): 59–69.

72. Alfred Pacini and Dominique Pons, *Docker à Marseille* (Paris: Éditions Payot et Rivages, 1996), 73–96, at 73.

73. On Sembène's experiences as a stevedore and activist in Marseille, see his novel *Docker Noir* (Paris: Debresse, 1956) and Samba Gadjigo, *Ousmane Sembène: The Making of a Militant Artist* (Bloomington: Indiana University Press, 2010), 89–129.

74. Minayo Nasiali, "Trouble on the Docks: Strikes, Scabs, and the Colonial Question in Marseille's Port Neighborhoods," *Journal of Urban History*, 42:5 (2016), 900–918. For background, see also: Jacques Loew, *Les Dockers de Marseille: Analyse Type d'Un Complexe* (L'Arbresle: Documents Économie et Humanisme, 1945), 40.

where he engaged in leafleteering and agitating against the war at the naval base.[75] Arrested in 1950, he stood trial and was convicted and sentenced to five years of imprisonment, with the PCF publicly defending him and no less than Jean-Paul Sartre, whose journal *Les Temps Modernes* had opposed the war in Indochina since December 1946,[76] founding a committee to lead a campaign for his release.[77] Overall, L'Affaire Henri Martin served as a cause célèbre rallying opposition to the war in Indochina during 1950–1953, nearly two decades before protests against the Vietnam War that swept the United States in the late 1960s and early–mid 1970s.[78] Thus, as the Việt Minh and the DRV struggled to withstand the onslaught of French military operations beginning in 1947, their survival was enabled if not by steady sources of sustenance, support, and solidarity from beyond Indochina, then by increasingly tight constraints on the exercise of French imperial power.

1949–1954: From Cao Bằng to Điện Biên Phủ

While conditions across the breadth of the French Empire thus helped to limit the effectiveness of French military operations in Vietnam from 1947 to 1949, other circumstances beyond Indochina combined to isolate the Việt Minh and the DRV during these same years. The formal dissolution of the ICP in late 1945 left the party without recognition or reward from Moscow, even as the Chinese civil war focused CCP and PLA energies on the conquest of Manchuria and northern China, leaving the southern provinces of Yunnan and Guangxi largely in KMT hands and thus Vietnamese comrades without a safe haven across the border.[79] In 1947, solidarity with the DRV across Asia led dockworkers in Burma, Ceylon, India, Malaya, and Singapore to refuse "to service French ships carrying war matériel or troops to Indochina," and "new nationalist administrations in India and Burma, in the process of attaining sovereignty from Britain, limited the

---

75. Alain Ruscio, ed., *L'Affaire Henri Martin et la Lutte contre la Guerre d'Indochine* (Pantin: Temps des Cerises, 2005).

76. David Drake, "*Les Temps Modernes* and the French War in Indochina," *Journal of European Studies* 28, no. 1 (March 1998): 25–41; Paige Arthur, *Unfinished Projects: Decolonization and the Philosophy of Jean-Paul Sartre* (London: Verso, 2010), 43–54.

77. Jean-Paul Sartre, *L'Affaire Henri Martin* (Paris: Gallimard, 1953).

78. Alain Ruscio, *Les Communistes Français et la Guerre d'Indochine 1944–1954* (Paris: Éditions L'Harmattan, 1985), 266–287.

79. On the international circumstances of the ICP's estrangement from Moscow during this period, see Christopher E. Goscha, "Courting Diplomatic Disaster? The Difficult Integration of Vietnam into the International Communist Movement (1945–1950)," *Journal of Vietnamese Studies* 1–2 (2006): 59–103.

number of French aircraft that could refuel at their airfields or pass through their skies."[80] But the military coup in Bangkok in November of the same year left the Việt Minh's crucial supply route through northeastern Thailand and Laos without the tacit protection enjoyed under the civilian-led government of Pridi Phanomyong. Overall, throughout 1947–1949, the Việt Minh and the DRV survived with minimal external support.

But with the victory of the CCP in October 1949, external conditions shifted dramatically and decisively for the Việt Minh and the DRV, much as Hồ Chí Minh and his comrades had already begun to anticipate as CCP victory approached during 1948 and 1949. Small-scale arms sales to the Việt Minh and coordination and communication between the CCP and ICP had intensified from 1947 to 1949, with occasional cross-border forays by both pro-CCP guerrilla groups and, notably, Việt Minh troops as well.[81] In 1948, moreover, following the Maoist mass mobilizational techniques developed in Yan'an in the early–mid 1940s, the party-state moved to consolidate its hold over the countryside through "emulation campaigns." Cadres "fanned out across the countryside," gathering villagers together through farmers, women, and youth associations and encouraged them to

> eradicate illiteracy, produce more rice, step up their local weapons production, and support the resistance financially. . . . . Emulation campaigns served as the main mechanism through which the state recruited for the local militia and requisitioned labor to clear new land to increase agricultural production . . . [and] to help the party politicize peasants and bring them into its mass associations.[82]

Such Maoist-style "emulation campaigns" also helped to set the stage for the next stage of revolutionary mass mobilization in line with the strategy for protracted people's war developed by Mao in the mid-1930s. Indeed, in his mid-1947 tract "The Resistance Will Win," ICP general secretary Trường Chinh ("Long March") had elaborated a three-stage plan along lines familiar from Mao's 1937 pamphlet *Yu Chi Chan* (Guerrilla Warfare), moving from a strategic defensive posture to an equilibrium in which experiments with mobile warfare allowed for larger concentrations of troops and, in due course, a general counteroffensive.[83] Thus, beyond survival and overcoming "weariness, discouragement, and tendencies to compromise and defeatism" from 1947 to 1949, Chinh suggested, the

---

80. Mark Atwood Lawrence, "Transnational Coalition-Building and the Making of the Cold War in Indochina, 1947–1949," *Diplomatic History* 26, no. 3 (July 2002): 453–480, at 463.

81. Chen, *Vietnam and China, 1938–1954*, 187–201.

82. Christopher Goscha, "A 'Total War' of Decolonization? Social Mobilization and State-Building in Communist Vietnam (1949–54)," *War and Society* 31, no. 2 (August 2012): 136–162, at 147–148.

83. Mao Tse-Tung, *On Guerrilla Warfare* (New York: Frederick A. Praeger, 1961).

ICP's aim should be "to strengthen our forces, training more cadres, producing more weapons, establishing more regular and guerrilla forces, developing and consolidating revolutionary organizations preparing conditions for the switch-over to the stage of general counter-offensive."[84]

Thus, just as Mao's general counteroffensive was drawing to a close in China, Chinh's movement into strategic equilibrium and escalation into mobile warfare shifted into higher gear in Vietnam and elsewhere in Indochina. On November 4, 1949, little more than a month after the CCP's proclamation of victory and the establishment of the People's Republic of China (PRC), the DRV announced the imposition of mandatory military service on all Vietnamese men between the ages of eighteen and forty-five, thus enabling the creation of a regular army, the People's Army of Vietnam (PAVN).[85] With the CCP's victory and the founding of the PRC, the ICP had high hopes that once again it could use southern China as a base for waging revolution, even beyond what it had undertaken in the mid-1920s.

Indeed, the newly founded PRC offered the DRV what the French war correspondent and scholar Bernard Fall termed an "active sanctuary," providing "shelter, training facilities, equipment, and—if it can get away with it—troops."[86] By early 1950, the DRV had won formal recognition by the PRC and, thanks to Chinese intercession, the USSR (and then its satellite states in Eastern Europe), with Hồ Chí Minh quickly travelling to Beijing and Moscow for meetings with Mao and Stalin. By 1950, Chinese military assistance began flowing to the DRV, with delivery of 14,000 guns, 1,700 machine guns, cannons, and significant supplies of ammunition, grain, medicine, and communications equipment between April and September of that year, and no less than 21,500 tons of aid over the course of 1950–1954.[87] Alongside such material assistance, the Chinese also provided military training to as many as 30,000 Vietnamese troops comprising thirty infantry battalions and six artillery battalions over the same years in special schools established in Yunnan and Guangxi.[88]

Strengthened and sustained by Chinese military assistance and steered by dozens of Chinese military advisors under the Chinese Military Advisory Group (CMAG), the newly formed People's Army of Vietnam (PAVN) moved promptly into a new phase of mobile warfare. September–October 1950 saw a swift and

---

84. Truong Chinh, *The Resistance Will Win* (Hanoi: Foreign Languages, 1960), 75.
85. Greg Lockhart, *A Nation in Arms: The Origins of the People's Army of Vietnam* (Sydney: Allen and Unwin, 1989), 183–221.
86. Bernard B. Fall, *Street without Joy: The French Debacle in Indochina* (Harrisburg, PA: Stackpole Books, 1961), 375.
87. Goscha, "Building Force," 550.
88. Goscha, "Building Force," 551; Charles Kraus, "A Border Region 'Exuded with Militant Friendship': Provincial Narratives of China's Participation in the First Indochina War, 1949–1954," *Cold War History* 12, no. 3 (August 2012): 494–514, at 502–505; Laura M. Calkins, *China and the First Vietnam War, 1947–54* (London: Routledge, 2013), 51.

successful border campaign force thousands of French troops to evacuate Cao Bằng and the other garrison towns along the Tonkin–Guangxi border, "leaving behind 11,000 tons of ammunition and abandoning virtually all of Vietnam north of the Red River delta," thus ensuring unimpeded transfers of war maté-riel and military personnel from China. With the extension of this campaign into the western Tonkinese province of Hòa Bình, moreover, the DRV's effec-tive control extended not only from the Chinese border down to the Red River Delta but on its western flank down into northern Annam. Emboldened by these victories, PAVN commander in chief and DRV minister of Defense Võ Nguyên Giáp, with grudging CMAG support, launched a second military cam-paign across the Red River Delta in early 1951, but this general counteroffensive proved to be premature, forcing a retreat into the DRV's base area and a CMAG-led reorganization of the PAVN and restructuring of the DRV's governing structures.[89]

Against this backdrop, 1952–1953 saw the extension of the DRV's area of con-trol through a CMAG-coordinated campaign in the northwesternmost reaches of upland Tonkin, stretching into neighboring Laos. Since 1948, the ICP had adopted an explicitly Indochina-wide strategy of intensified cooperation and co-ordination with the Lao Issara (and the Khmer Issarak in Cambodia), with Giáp in 1950 treating Indochina as "one strategic unit and one battlefield."[90] With France's formation of the Associated States of Laos, Cambodia, and Vietnam (each ruled by a French-sponsored monarch) in 1949[91] came the dissolution of the In-dochinese Communist Party in early 1951 and its transformation into the Viet-namese Workers' Party (VWP), but the newly constituted VWP soon embarked on the task of creating a Khmer People's Revolutionary Party in Cambodia and its counterpart in Laos as junior partners for an envisaged Vietnamese-led Indochina-wide federation of socialist republics.[92] With this long-term objective and the short-term imperative of protecting supply routes from Thailand in mind, the Vietnamese Communists dispatched thousands of "cadres, soldiers, secretar-ies, doctors, nurses, radio operators, navigators and teachers" to Laos and Cam-bodia to set up and sustain an "inter-connected Indochinese politico-military administration," complete with a clandestine postal and transport network across DRV-controlled areas of Indochina.[93]

89. Qiang Zhai, *China and the Vietnam Wars, 1950–1975* (Chapel Hill: University of North Car-olina Press, 2000), 31, 34–36.

90. Goscha, *Vietnam or Indochina?*, 111.

91. Christopher Goscha, *The Penguin History of Modern Vietnam* (London: Allen Lane, 2016), 256–268.

92. Christopher E. Goscha, "Une Guerre Pour L'Indochine? Le Laos et le Cambodge dans le Con-flit Franco-Vietnamien (1948–1954)," *Guerres Mondiales et Conflits Contemporains* 211 (2003): 29–58.

93. Goscha, *Vietnam or Indochina?*, 124–125.

By 1953, this Indochina-wide extension of Vietnamese party-state power was combined with its intensification within the boundaries of Vietnam through new forms of Chinese-inspired and Chinese-assisted mass mobilization. The year 1953 witnessed the onset of a large-scale land reform campaign across DRV-controlled areas of Tonkin and northern Annam in line with Chinese experience and advice, further consolidating the party-state's penetration of Vietnamese society and thus its disciplinary, extractive, and mobilizational capacities.[94] By late 1952, moreover, the PAVN had launched a CMAG-coordinated Northwest Campaign to extend the DRV's state-making efforts into the furthermost reaches of northwestern Tonkin, the upland Black River region largely governed by the French-backed local leaders of the Tai Federation.[95] From October to December 1952, the PAVN secured control over most of Sơn La, Lai Châu, and Lào Cai Provinces, moving into eastern Laos by early 1953. This campaign not only incorporated the ethnic Thái and Hmong upland areas of the Black River region into the authority structures of the DRV but also enabled the party-state to assume effective control over the lucrative opium trade, thus considerably enhancing the fiscal base for its war effort.[96]

It was thus in the context of expanding DRV (party-)state and PAVN military capacities—and diminishing French mobilizational strength and morale—that the long siege of Điện Biên Phủ unfolded over late 1953 and early–mid 1954. By 1953, faith in the prospects of French victory in Indochina had precipitously declined in the ranks of the French civilian and military leadership and also among US policymakers, who had been subsidizing and directly supporting the French war effort since 1950, thus leading newly appointed CEFEO commander Henri Navarre to launch a new campaign to seize the initiative against the PAVN and the DRV.[97] But his plan to reestablish a French beachhead in northwestern Tonkin by airlifting thousands of CEFEO troops to the garrison town and transport hub of Điện Biên Phủ in a remote valley in the mountains along the border with Laos ran aground in the face of the mobilizational capacities of the DRV and the PAVN enhanced and expanded by the Chinese-inspired and Chinese-assisted (party-)state- and war-making developments of the preceding years. Already in 1950, the DRV had reportedly mobilized 121,700 "people's laborers" (*dân công*) over

---

94. See Alex-Thai D. Vo, "Nguyễn Thị Năm and the Land Reform in North Vietnam, 1953," *Journal of Vietnamese Studies* 10, no. 1 (2015): 1–62, and Alec Holcombe, *Mass Mobilization in the Democratic Republic of Vietnam, 1945–1960* (Honolulu: University of Hawai'i Press, 2020), 119–178.

95. Philippe Le Failler, *La Rivière Noire: L'Intégration d'une Marche Frontière au Vietnam* (Paris: CNRS Éditions, 2014), 415–467.

96. See John T. McCalister Jr., "Mountain Minorities and the Viet Minh: A Key to the Indochina War," in *Southeast Asian Tribes, Minorities, and Nations*, ed. Peter Kunstadter (Princeton, NJ: Princeton University Press, 1967), 2:771–844, 821–822, and Christian C. Lentz, "Cultivating Subjects: Opium and Rule in Post-Colonial Vietnam," *Modern Asian Studies* 51, no. 4 (2017): 879–918, especially 894–903.

97. On this context, see Logevall, *Embers of War*, 334–378.

1.7 million working days for its border campaign, 300,000 *dân công* over 2.8 million working days in the failed campaign to take Red River Delta in early 1951, and 333,000 "fighter laborers" over 11.9 million work days in the battle for control over Hòa Bình in late 1951–early 1952, and overall, according to official DRV figures, "between 1950 and 1954, the DRV mobilized 1,741.381 people as civilian porters, almost all of them peasants. Together, these men and women clocked up a mind-boggling 53,787,470 working days."[98]

Such mobilizational capacities proved crucial for PAVN success at Điện Biên Phủ. The autumn 1952 PAVN Northwest Campaign had involved 36,000 soldiers and an estimated 70,000 *dân công*, including 9,000 locally conscripted laborers, setting the stage for the eight-month Điện Biên Phủ campaign involving 70,000 soldiers and more than 260,000 *dân công*, including 30,000 locals. Preparations for the campaign required the improvement and extension of roads and riverways to transport troops, war matériel, rice and other foodstuffs, and medicine over distances of hundreds of kilometers from China and DRV-controlled areas of Tonkin and Laos. Just one ninety-two-kilometer road segment, for example, "ran up, over, and around mountain ranges," with more than fourteen thousand *dân công* "felling trees, hauling dirt, and enduring bouts of illness" under the supervision of Chinese advisors and Vietnamese cadres.[99] Drawing on this elaborately secured, sustained, and staffed logistical infrastructure as well as extensive Chinese military advice, intelligence, and material assistance—including, crucially, 37-mm Soviet-made anti-aircraft artillery weapons—the PAVN began to encircle Điện Biên Phủ in late 1953, initiated the first of a series of major assaults in March 1954, and entirely overran the embattled garrison by May of that year. On the eve of the final attack, China supplied two battalions with 75-mm recoilless cannons and Katyusha multiple rocket launchers to enable a "total victory."[100]

With the CEFEO's humiliating defeat at Điện Biên Phủ came France's forced withdrawal of its forces from Indochina but less than "total victory" for the Vietnamese Revolution. With the USSR and the PRC mediating for (and "moderating" the demands of) the DRV and the United States and the United Kingdom assuming a similar broker role for France, an agreement was forged in July 1954 in Geneva, Switzerland, with compromise and concessions forced on the DRV and the French.[101] Under the Geneva Accords, French and Vietnamese troops with-

98. Goscha, "A Total War for Decolonization?", 156.
99. Christian C. Lentz, *Contested Territory: Điện Biên Phủ and the Making of Northwest Vietnam* (New Haven, CT: Yale University Press, 2019), 134, 111, and, more generally, 133–203.
100. For an overview of the Chinese role at Điện Biên Phủ, see Zhai, *China and the Vietnam Wars*, 46, and 46–49.
101. See, for example, Chen Jian, "China and the Indochina Settlement at the Geneva Conference of 1954," in *The First Vietnam War*, 240–262; Ilya V. Gaiduk, *Confronting Vietnam: Soviet Policy toward the Indochina Conflict, 1954–1963* (Stanford, CA: Stanford University Press, 2003), 28–53; and James Waite, *The End of the First Indochina War* (London: Routledge, 2012).

drew from Cambodia and Laos, and a demarcation line (and surrounding demili-
tarized zone) was established in Vietnam along the 17th Parallel, with DRV
forces regrouping to the north and French forces to the south, where the French
Union's State of Vietnam nominally headed by Emperor Bảo Đại remained in
place, with US economic and military assistance, and in due course American
troops, quickly supplanted the French, whose withdrawal was completed by 1956.
Thus, as of 1954, the hopes and dreams for revolutionary socialist transformation of the full extent of Vietnam—and Indochina—had yet to be realized. If the
resumption of armed revolutionary struggle south of the 17th Parallel in Vietnam was already in evidence by 1959, it was not until 1975, after much violence
and suffering, that Communist Party–led regimes established themselves across
the full breadth of Indochina.

But arguably much the same conditions that had enabled the establishment of
the DRV in 1945, its endurance in the face of French military campaigns, and its
entrenchment from 1954 helped to set the stage for these subsequent Communist victories across Indochina. From 1959 if not earlier, the DRV served the National Liberation Front (NLF) and its forces in South Vietnam, as well as its allies
in Laos and Cambodia, as an active sanctuary, much as it had been served by the
PRC since late 1949. From the mid–late 1950s onward, moreover, the DRV pursued this Indochina-wide strategy in the face of successive American efforts to
establish and entrench credible alternatives to DRV-backed Communist Party–
led forces in South Vietnam, Laos, and Cambodia, efforts no more successful than
those undertaken by their French predecessors in 1946–1954. Finally, from the
mid-1960s onward, these American efforts, like those of the French before them,
ran aground in the face of their own internal limitations and contradictions,
American imperial overstretch, the DRV's enduring patronage of armed revolutionary movements across Indochina, and continuing sympathy, solidarity, and
support for the Vietnamese Revolution, not only from the PRC and the USSR,
but from many other fellow travellers across the world. As in the period leading
up to the early establishment of the DRV in 1945–1954, the Vietnamese Revolution up to 1975 and beyond remained profoundly shaped by complex international circumstances and transnational connections.

Conclusions

As detailed and demonstrated in the previous pages, the Vietnamese Revolution
was, like the revolutions in the Philippines and Indonesia, a struggle that exceeds
the limitations of a narrowly national(ist) framework of analysis. As with the Philippine and Indonesian revolutions, the onset, unfolding, and ultimate outcomes

of the Vietnamese Revolution were profoundly shaped by developments and trends in the international realm, in this case most obviously World War II, but also successive seismic shifts in neighboring China, from the overthrow of the Qing and the warlord era to the rise and fall of the KMT-CCP United Front in the 1920s, the Japanese invasion and occupation of 1937–1945, the civil war of 1945–1949, and the establishment of the People's Republic of China in October 1949. Meanwhile, in sharp contrast to Indonesia, the condominium between the Vichy French regime and Japanese military authorities between 1940 and March 1945 precluded the entrenchment and empowerment of non-Communist forces under conditions of Japanese occupation and preparation for Allied invasion through mass mobilization of local paramilitary forces, thus leaving the Việt Minh to champion the cause of independence without the kind of competition and countervailing power that both Soekarno and Masyumi represented in Indonesia. In further contrast to the British and Australian roles in restoring Dutch rule across the full breadth of the Indonesian archipelago in late 1945 and early 1946, moreover, the allocation of responsibility for the liberation of Indochina north of the 16th Parallel to the Chinese nationalist government left Tonkin and northern Annam in the hands of Kuomintang forces inclined toward condominium with the Việt Minh, thus providing the fledgling Democratic Republic of Vietnam an opportunity for early (party-)state-building efforts.

Finally, this brief Kuomintang interlude exemplified the broader importance of China's role in enabling Vietnamese revolutionary mobilization, from the heyday of Phan Bội Châu in the 1900s and early–mid 1910s through Thanh Niên in the 1920s, and the ICP and the Việt Minh during the early–mid 1940s. Indeed, the diplomatic, logistical, and, crucially, military support provided by the PRC from early 1950 was absolutely essential for the formation of the PAVN and the fortunes of its successive campaigns up to and including the long siege of Điện Biên Phủ over late 1953 and early–mid 1954. In all of these ways, international circumstances favored revolutionary mobilization—and a Communist-led revolution in particular—far more than in Indonesia or other countries in Southeast Asia.

As with the Philippine and Indonesian revolutions, moreover, the underlying discursive and mobilizational infrastructure of the Vietnamese Revolution was profoundly shaped by the enduring legacies of Vietnam's idiosyncratic experience of deepening immersion within transcontinental and transoceanic currents of global commerce and cosmopolitan culture over the *longue durée*. On the one hand, in contrast to Catholicism and Islam, the Sinographic cosmopolitanism adopted by Vietnamese literati was, from its crystallization under the late Song dynasty and its consolidation and canonization as the Four Books and Five Classics under the Ming, integrated into successive dynastic states through civil service examinations and thus a state orthodoxy ultimately dependent on state employment for its sustenance and sustainability, whether in the Middle Kingdom, in Đại Việt in the Early Modern Era, or under the Nguyễn in the nineteenth century.[102] In contrast to Catholicism in the Philippines and Islam in Indonesia, moreover, the infrastructure of Sinographic cosmopolitanism remained essentially confined to the literati over the centuries even as the diverse religious and spiritual beliefs and practices prevailing in Vietnamese society at large never cohered in any translocal ecclesiastical or institutional form.[103] It was against this backdrop that the exclusively male literati networks that provided the discursive and mobilizational infrastructure for the Cần Vương insurrection of the mid–late 1880s disintegrated with the termination of the civil service examination system in the 1910s (much as they had under the Qing in the preceding decade), leaving the field of revolution making without a conservative cosmopolitan counterweight to communism such as Islam provided in Indonesia.

On the other hand, from the mid-nineteenth century, the tightening integration of Cochinchina, Annam, and Tonkin into the world economy unfolded under French imperial auspices and arrangements that strengthened Vietnamese connections with southern China and with the rest of Indochina, across the full breadth of the French Empire, and beyond. With the transformation of the Mekong Delta and its hinterlands into a vast rice bowl for the provisioning of Guangzhou and Hong Kong and the conversion of Tonkin into a staging post for riverine and rail links to Yunnan came expanding flows of commodities, capital, and labor connecting the circuitries of Vietnam's emerging market society with those of southern China. This tight symbiosis between the Indochinese and southern Chinese economies combined with colonial segregation of Cantonese, Teochiu, Hakka, and other Chinese immigrants into separate *congrégations* to preclude the emergence of a class of indigenous Vietnamese or assimilated Sino-Vietnamese— landowners, moneylenders, and merchants—sufficiently strong to steer the Vietnamese Revolution toward a liberal republican rather than a socialist outcome as observed in the Philippine Revolution, or even to sustain other counterweights to communism as Muslim merchant support for Islamic educational and associational

---

102. See Thomas A. Wilson, *Genealogy of the Way: The Construction and Uses of the Confucian Tradition in Late Imperial China* (Stanford, CA: Stanford University Press, 1995), especially 23–71. For further, deeper historical contextualization of the "Confucian" tradition dating back to the Han period, see Michael Nylan, *The Five "Confucian" Classics* (New Haven, CT: Yale University Press, 2001).

103. For mid-eighteenth and mid-twentieth century accounts, see Father Adriano di St Thecla, (*Opusculum de Sectis apud Sinenses et Tunkinenses: A Small Treatise on the Sects among the Chinese and Tonkinese*, trans. Olgar Dror (Ithaca, NY: Cornell University Southeast Asia Program 2016), and Léopold Cadière, *Croyances et Pratiques Religieuses des Viêtnamiens* (Paris: École Française d'Extrême-Orient, 1957). Many thanks to Peter Zinoman for his astute articulation of this argument and for his suggestion of Cadière's book as a key source.

networks ensured vis-à-vis the PKI and the Sayap Kiri during the Indonesian Revolusi.

With the establishment of French protectorates in Cambodia and Laos and the incorporation of Khmer and, to a lesser extent, Lao, peasants into the burgeoning rice trade centered in Sài Gòn (and to a far lesser extent, Hải Phòng), moreover, came Vietnamese market linkages and migrant communities extending and expanding across Indochina and into neighboring Siam. From the 1920s onward, these networks across Indochina and beyond provided crucial logistical support for the revolutionary struggle within Vietnam itself. Furthermore, with the inclusion of Indochina within the broader ambit of the French Empire, with the recycling of Banque de l'Indochine profits into new investments in Africa, and with the recruitment of Vietnamese coolies and soldiers alongside *les tirailleurs sénégalais* and other colonial laborers and troops came the kinds of political possibilities embodied and advanced by the short-lived Union Intercoloniale in the early 1920s. Indeed, even without much active "intercolonial" cooperation with African sympathizers in the late 1940s and early–mid 1950s, increasing French anxieties about imperial overstretch constrained the CEFEO's efforts to annihilate the DRV during its period of essential isolation from 1947 through much of 1949. As Nguyễn Ái Quốc had foreseen and foreshadowed in the early 1920s, the interconnected nature of French imperialism across Africa and Asia proved crucial for the Vietnamese Revolution in the end.

Finally, as with the Freemasons and religious confraternities in the making of the Philippine Revolution and the variously Islamic and socialist networks, *lasykar*, and political parties associated with Masyumi and the Sayap Kiri during the Indonesian Revolusi, the very institutional bases and egalitarian promises of revolutionary brotherhood and, far more than in the Philippines or Indonesia, sisterhood, undergirding the Vietnamese Revolution were profoundly cosmopolitan rather than national or nationalist in their origins and orientations. In the case of the Vietnamese Revolution, it was an unalloyed Communist cosmopolitanism that provided the discursive and mobilizational tools, the institutional mechanisms of socialization, the organizational blueprints, and the concrete resources for the establishment of a party-state and the waging of guerrilla and conventional revolutionary warfare. From the Comintern and the KUTV in Moscow to the Whampoa Military Academy and the Peasant Movement Training Institute in Guangzhou, from Yan'an to the military training camps established in Guangxi and Yunnan in 1950, Vietnamese revolutionaries were introduced to the writings of Marx, Lenin, and Mao, instructed in mobilizational and military techniques, and imbued with a Communist ethos and esprit de corps. They learned to "speak Bolshevik,", a language whose grammar determined the internal structures of the DRV party-state and the PAVN and the ultimate aims and objectives of the Vietnamese revolution beyond the securing of independence to the transformation of Vietnamese—and Indochinese—society. In all of these ways, the Vietnamese Revolution was the product of Communist internationalism.[104]

Overall, as with the Philippine and Indonesian Revolutions, the international conjuncture in Indochina in the early aftermath of World War II combined with the idiosyncratic constellation of cosmopolitan legacies and linkages enabling revolutionary mobilization in Vietnam to determine the specific trajectory and outcome of the Vietnamese Revolution. On the one hand, the peculiarities of the Vichy French–Japanese condominium from 1940 into early 1945, the Kuomintang interlude north of the 16th Parallel in late 1945 and 1946, the anxieties and exigencies of the overstretched French Empire across Africa, and the inauguration of the People's Republic of China in 1949 combined with the earlier establishment of linkages to southern China and across Indochina into Siam to present Vietnamese revolutionaries with unique advantages unparalleled in either the Philippine Revolution at the turn of the twentieth century or the Indonesian Revolusi of 1945–1949. On the other hand, the contraction of the scholastic networks of Sinographic cosmopolitanism with the abolition of the civil service examinations in the 1910s and the constraints on the growth of a properly Vietnamese landowning and mercantile class imposed by French and Chinese capital combined to diminish the prospects for royalist, reformist, or republican mobilization, even as the accessibility of Communist cosmopolitanism through Paris, Moscow, Guangzhou, and elsewhere in southern China enabled far more effective party- and (party-)state building, at least in northern Vietnam, than anywhere else in Southeast Asia, including Indonesia. In all of these ways, international circumstances and cosmopolitan connections proved decisive for the forcefulness, the forms, and the fortunes of the Vietnamese Revolution.

---

104. For a forceful articulation of this argument, see Tuong Vu, *Vietnam's Communist Revolution: The Power and Limits of Ideology* (Cambridge: Cambridge University Press, 2017). For a picture of the emergence of Communist internationalism, see Brigitte Studer, *The Transnational World of the Cominternians* (New York: Palgrave Macmillan, 2015). For a very illuminating treatment of Vietnam's immersion in a broader "socialist ecumene," see Susan Bayly, *Asian Voices in a Postcolonial Age: Vietnam, India and Beyond* (Cambridge: Cambridge University Press, 2007).

COMMONALITIES, COMPARISONS, CONCLUSIONS

In the preceding chapters, this book has suggested a set of commonalities in its contextualization of the Philippine, Indonesian, and Vietnamese Revolutions over the proverbial *longue durée*, commonalities that might serve as the basis for an alternative or complementary template for modern Southeast Asian history alongside that provided by the state-centered telos of the rise of national consciousness, nationalist mobilization, and new nation-states. Here the common drivers and dynamics emphasized in the emergence and evolution of Philippine, Indonesian, and Vietnamese societies were commercial and cosmopolitan, rather than primarily rooted in state institutions, practices, and boundaries that were both so colonizing and so nationalizing in their impact. Thus, the historical contextualization of the Philippine, Indonesian, and Vietnamese revolutions in this book has synthesized the works of successive generations of historians to suggest a potentially unifying and illuminating template for the framing of the modern history of Southeast Asia as a whole.

Viewed from this perspective, the making and remaking of modern Southeast Asian societies can be traced back to the Early Modern Era (c. 1350–850 CE), the period depicted by Victor Lieberman as one of mutually reinforcing war making and state making,[1] and described by Anthony Reid both as an Age of Commerce and an era of large-scale religious proselytization and conver-

---

1. Victor Lieberman, *Strange Parallels: Southeast Asia in Global Context, c. 800–1300*, vol., 1, *Integration on the Mainland* (Cambridge: Cambridge University Press, 2003); Victor Lieberman, *Strange Parallels, Southeast Asia in Global Context, c. 1300–1830*, vol. 2, *Mainland Mirrors: Europe, Japan, China, South Asia, and the Islands* (Cambridge: Cambridge University Press, 2010).

sion.[2] Long-distance trade enabled and impelled state formation, marketization, monetization, land settlement and reclamation, as well as the increasing homogenization of language, culture, and religion in expanding zones of central state power (especially across mainland Southeast Asia). With transcontinental and transoceanic commerce, moreover, came cosmopolitan connections, communications, and conceptions, whether Indic, Islamic, Buddhist, Catholic, or Sinographic, which linked various parts of Southeast Asia to other regions of the world. These diverse cosmopolitan currents not only informed kingship, court culture, and statecraft; they also imparted enduring legacies in local languages, literatures, and institutions of learning, as seen in the establishment of forms of schooling that linked Southeast Asians—in particular, Southeast Asian boys and men—to sites of knowledge production and sources of intellectual authority outside the region, whether in China, the Middle East, or Europe. Thus, the emerging societies of Southeast Asia were profoundly transformed by the incorporation of the region into transcontinental and transoceanic commercial and cosmopolitan circulation, of commodities, discourses, and practices in the Early Modern Era.

Following the Early Modern Era came what Eric Hobsbawm termed the Age of Empire,[3] which saw the deepening incorporation of Southeast Asia into the world economy over the latter half of the nineteenth century and the early twentieth century, under the auspices of colonial rule, Pax Britannica, and the transportation revolution of accelerated railroad construction and steamboat traffic across the region and beyond. The expanding and intensifying commercialization of agriculture and commodification of land produced market societies across Southeast Asia, societies in which increasing flows of commodities, capital, and labor linked cities ever more tightly to their hinterlands through the local circuitries of the world economy. Throughout the region, these processes overlaid the webbed fabric of cosmopolitan legacies and linkages of the Early Modern Era with a dense latticework of new transcontinental and transoceanic connections between Southeast Asia and other parts of the world. Immigrants from the southern provinces of China, the Hadhramaut region of the Arabian Peninsula, and the Indian subcontinent played crucial roles as commercial and financial intermediaries in the expanding market economies of Southeast Asia, as merchants, moneylenders, revenue farmers, rice millers, and shippers, pioneering new forms

---

2. Anthony Reid, *Southeast Asia in the Age of Commerce, 1450–1680*, vol. 1, *The Lands Below the Winds* (New Haven, CT: Yale University Press, 1988); Anthony Reid, *Southeast Asia in the Age of Commerce, 1450–1680*, vol. 2, *Expansion and Crisis* (New Haven, CT: Yale University Press, 1993); Anthony Reid, "Islamization and Christianization in Southeast Asia: The Critical Phase, 1550–1650," in *Southeast Asia in the Early Modern Era: Trade, Power, and Belief*, ed. Anthony Reid (Ithaca, NY: Cornell University Press, 1993), 151–179.

3. Eric Hobsbawm, *The Age of Empire, 1875–1914* (London: Weidenfeld and Nicolson, 1987).

of capital accumulation and new kinds of associational activism, in sprawling business empires and school networks across the region.

With the rise of market societies across Southeast Asia came the hallmarks of modernity: new forms of status, wealth, and power challenging established "traditional" hierarchies, new forms of consciousness, expression, authorship, and audience among the emerging and expanding reading publics in the port cities and market towns of the region, with new social imaginaries coming into view. This modernity was profoundly cosmopolitan rather than protonational in its shape and substance, not only within the rarified world of elite educated dandies and *flâneurs* but also in the expanding realm of urban popular culture, as seen in the diversely foreign inflections and hybrid forms of street opera and theater found in Southeast Asian cities by the turn of the twentieth century (e.g., *komedya*, *Komedie Stamboel*, *cải lương*). With market societies and modernity (or modernities) came modern modalities of organizing and mobilizing, presenting more egalitarian challenges to existing hierarchies of wealth, status, and power, church and crown, aristocratic lineage, and traditional religious and social authority, as seen in Masonic lodges, labor unions, political parties, and other vehicles for associational activity and activism in the public sphere. These translocal organizational and mobilizational structures not only brought together Filipinos, Indonesians, and Vietnamese in new ways and in protonational forms but also linked them to transnational sources of solidarity and support across the region and beyond, whether in Bohemia, Berlin, or Baku, Cairo, Mecca, Paris, Moscow, or Guangzhou. In the Philippines, the Netherlands East Indies, and the territories of Cochinchina, Annam, and Tonkin today known as Vietnam, these common developments and trends unfolded over the late nineteenth century and the first four decades of the twentieth century, as they did elsewhere across Southeast Asia.

But if in retrospect these common transformations can be seen to have portended and prefigured the Philippine, Indonesian, and Vietnamese revolutions, they did not suffice to precipitate revolutionary mobilization in and of themselves. Nor did the uneven and incomplete unfolding of these developments and trends across Southeast Asia over the late nineteenth and early–mid twentieth centuries suffice for purposes of predetermining variance in the timing, forms, and trajectories of these three revolutions, or for that matter the contrast between these three revolutions and the nonrevolutionary outcomes observed elsewhere across the region. Beyond the commonalities, some kind of comparative analysis is also in order.

As signalled in the title and sketched out in the chapters above, this book has suggested that the origins of the Philippine, Indonesian, and Vietnamese Revolutions were profoundly, but also diversely, cosmopolitan in nature. In this vein, the book has suggested that the explanation for the differences observed between these revolutions lies not in innate, intrinsic, internal features of the three societies in which they unfolded, but rather in the varying ways they were integrated into the broader circuitries and currents of transcontinental and transoceanic commerce, into the world capitalist economy, and into diverse forms of cosmopolitan connectedness across the region and beyond. In terms of the varying timing of the three revolutions, for example, the book has followed scholars of Southeast Asian history as well as specialists on revolutions beyond the region in emphasizing the varying conjunctural impact of interimperial competition and international conflicts in undermining established state institutions and in enabling revolutionary mobilization across the region. For example, the Spanish-American War both uniquely enabled and ultimately constrained the Philippine Revolution, while having little in the way of consequences elsewhere in Southeast Asia. The Sino-Japanese War of 1894–1895, the Russo-Japanese War of 1894–1905, and World War I likewise helped to stimulate new forms of association and mobilization in both the Netherlands East Indies and French colonial Indochina, as seen in the rise of the Sarekat Islam in the former and the various initiatives spearheaded by Phan Bội Châu in (and beyond) the latter context over the 1910s and early–mid 1920s. As for the diverse disruptions and dislocations of World War II, they proved decisive in very different ways for both the Indonesian Revolusi and the Vietnamese Revolution, with the varying forms of Japanese occupation and Allied liberation favoring republican and Islamic forces in the former and Communist forces in the latter. Meanwhile, revolutionary struggles in other parts of the world also contributed in different ways and to varying extents to revolutions in Southeast Asia, as seen most clearly in the crucial timeliness of the Cuban Revolution for the Philippine Revolution and the centrality of the Chinese Revolution of 1911 and the Chinese Communist Party's revolutionary struggle from the 1920s and its victory in 1949 for the trajectory and triumph of the revolution in neighboring Vietnam. Southeast Asians made revolutions—with ample courage and creativity, resilience, resourcefulness, and ruthlessness—but in international circumstances not of their own making.

In suggesting explanations for the variegated forms and diverging trajectories of the Philippine, Indonesian, and Vietnamese Revolutions, moreover, this book has also stressed the importance of both the distinctive legacies of cosmopolitan connections dating back to the Early Modern Era and the different constellations of social forces that crystallized during the Age of Empire with the deepening integration of the region into the world economy over the late nineteenth and early twentieth centuries. The absorption of the Philippines into the global circuitries of the Catholic Church, for example, drew the inhabitants of the archipelago not only into the transoceanic Jesuit republic of letters but also into the transcontinental culture wars between Ultramontanist Catholicism and the anticlerical forces of science, Freemasonry, liberalism, and republicanism of late nineteenth-century Europe, thus prefiguring both the Masonic origins and organizational form of the Katipunan and the local mobilizational infrastructures of the *cofradías* in the Philippine Revolution. The assimilation of Chinese immigrants and their offspring into Philippine society, moreover, enabled an emerging class of mestizo rural landowners, local worthies, provincial merchants, and urbane *ilustrados* to assume leadership of a Filipino revolution (uninhibited by their *chino* paternal origins) and to assert a narrowly liberal rather than more radically egalitarian vision of a Philippine Republic broadly compatible with the colonial democracy imposed by the United States in the wake of its "pacification" of the archipelago in the early 1900s.

In contrast, the incorporation of the Indonesian archipelago within the transoceanic circuitries of the Muslim world and the intensifying traffic of Islamic pilgrims and scholars across the Indian Ocean in the era of the steamboat Hajj enabled and impelled the establishment and expansion of institutions of Islamic learning across the Netherlands East Indies and the emergence of forms of authority and associational activity that enjoyed considerable autonomy from both the colonial state and local aristocracies, thus prefiguring the prominence of Islamic forms of revolutionary discourse, leadership, and organization during the Revolusi. At the same time, even as the segregation and stigmatization of Chinese immigrants as "foreign" inhibited the rise of an Indonesian counterpart to the *ilustrado* leadership of the Philippine Revolution and the hegemony of a liberal vision of a Republik Indonesia, the early establishment and expansion of an agroindustrial complex of large-scale plantations linked by railroads to the port harbors of Java and Sumatra entailed the emergence of a sizeable class of wage laborers available for unionization and revolutionary socialist mobilization, under the leadership of the PKI and other left-wing parties, thus ensuring the prominence of Communism alongside—and against—Islam in the Indonesian Revolusi, albeit without a solid organizational base among the peasantry in rural areas outside the plantation belts.

Finally, the incorporation of Vietnamese literati within a broader Sinosphere of classical Chinese scholarship—the Confucian canon of the Four Books and the Five Classics—during the Early Modern Era diverged from the patterns of Catholic and Islamic scholasticism observed in the Philippine and Indonesian archipelagos in crucial and consequential ways. Unlike their Filipino and Indonesian counterparts, these Vietnamese literati were integrated into successive dynastic states through the examination system, thus enabling the early demise and effective disappearance of this conservative, patriarchal form of cosmopolitanism in Cochinchina by the 1860s and in Annam and Tonkin over the 1910s in the face of the expansion of the modern bureaucratic state under French colonial auspices. Consequently, the radical egalitarianism of the Indochinese Communist Party was not countered or constrained by the more conservative and patriarchal forms of all-male socialization found in the schoolboy networks of the Philippine Revolution or the Islamic schools of the Indonesian Revolusi, allowing Communist forms of revolutionary brotherhood—and, notably, sisterhood—embodied by the ICP-led Việt Minh to assume a hegemonic and essentially monopolistic position within the Vietnamese revolution. At the same time, the relegation of Indochina to the roles of rice bowl for Guangzhou and Hong Kong and platform for French agribusiness, mining, and investment in southern China ensured the emergence of a Vietnamese commercial and landowning elite squeezed by, and subordinated to, Chinese and European capital and thus ill equipped to champion a republican form of revolution. Thus, even before the CCP's victory in China in late 1949, it was, ironically enough, the ICP rather than the weak welter of Vietnamese nationalist parties that benefited most from the Kuomintang's interest and interventions in Indochina. In all of these ways, the variously republican, Islamic, and Communist complexions and conclusions of the Philippine, Indonesian, and Vietnamese Revolutions were profoundly determined by both the diverse cosmopolitan connections of the Early Modern Era and the differing modalities of integration into the world economy in the Age of Empire.

Beyond the Philippine, Indonesian, and Vietnamese Revolutions, moreover, the analytical framework and arguments of this book can also be further extended across Southeast Asia through a set of paired comparisons with other absent or unconsummated, revolutionary struggles elsewhere in the region. In the case of Siam (later Thailand), for example, the emergence of a class of assimilated Sino-Thai merchants, moneylenders, rice millers, and revenue farmers by the turn of the twentieth century suggests obvious parallels with the Philippines, as does the development of diverse commercial linkages and cosmopolitan connections between Bangkok—contemporaneous with Manila, Cebu, and Iloilo—and various parts of Europe during the same period.[4] But in contrast with the deepening conflict between Chinese mestizo elites and the conservative Catholic Church during the late nineteenth century that gave rise to the Philippine Revolution, the twentieth century in Thailand saw the gradual accommodation, absorption, and ascendancy of similarly new (Sino-Thai) social forces alongside and within a centralizing, modernizing state (with control over the Theravada Buddhist *sangha*), first under absolutist monarchical auspices and then under military, if not fully

---

4. G. William Skinner, *Chinese Society in Thailand: An Analytical History* (Ithaca, NY: Cornell University Press, 1957); Akira Suehiro, *Capital Accumulation in Thailand, 1855–1985* (Bangkok: Silkworm Books, 1989).

republican, rule that only grudgingly, haltingly, and provisionally gave way to parliamentary democracy.[5]

In the case of Malaya, moreover, the bifurcation between immigrant Chinese capital accumulation and aristocratic Malay rule likewise suggests obvious parallels with the Netherlands East Indies, as does the scale and significance of plantation agriculture and tin mining in terms of early proletarianization and opportunities for revolutionary socialist forms of unionization and mass mobilization. But distinctive features of the "plural society" in Malaya inhibited the patterns of revolutionary mobilization observed in the Indies. The Malay sultans, in sharp contrast with the Javanese *priyayi*, enjoyed custodial control over the institutions of Islamic worship, education, and publishing, thus precluding the emergence of autonomous Islamic associations, movements, or political parties such as Muhammadiyah, Nahdlatul Ulama, Sarekat Islam, and Masyumi in Indonesia.[6] Workers for the tin mines and rubber plantations of Malaya were recruited from southern China and the Indian subcontinent, even as the Malay peasantry was preserved and protected from the agricultural involution and immiseration that produced a steady flow of Javanese coolie laborers onto the plantations of Java and Sumatra over the late nineteenth and early twentieth centuries.[7] Thus, even with the disruptions and dislocations of World War II, Malaya saw little in the way of Islamic or other challenges to aristocratic hegemony among the Malays, and the armed guerrilla struggle mounted by the Malayan Communist Party (MCP) in the late 1940s and early 1950s remained largely confined in its appeal to the ethnic-Chinese working class, thus foreclosing the possibility of an Islamic and/or Communist revolution on the Malay Peninsula.[8]

Finally, in the case of Burma, the emergence of the Irrawaddy River Delta as a zone of accelerated population growth and commercialized rice production for export—and an ethnically segmented "plural society"—in the late nineteenth and early twentieth centuries suggests obvious parallels with Cochinchina, Vietnam, and, more broadly, Indochina during the same period.[9] Just as the form and tra-

---

5. Maurizio Peleggi, *Lords of Things: The Fashioning of the Siamese Monarchy's Modern Image* (Honolulu: University of Hawai'i Press, 2002); Matthew Phillip Copeland, "Contested Nationalism and the 1932 Overthrow of the Absolute Monarchy in Siam" (PhD thesis, Australian National University, 1993).

6. William R. Roff, *The Origins of Malay Nationalism* (New Haven, CT: Yale University Press, 1967).

7. Lynn Hollen Lees, *Planting Empire, Cultivating Subjects: British Malaya, 1786–1941* (Cambridge: Cambridge University Press, 2017).

8. Cheah Boon Kheng, *Red Star over Malaya: Resistance and Social Conflict during and after the Japanese Occupation of Malaya, 1941–1946* (Singapore Singapore University Press, 1983); Nina Belogurova, *The Nanyang Revolution: The Comintern and Chinese Networks in Southeast Asia, 1890–1957* (Cambridge: Cambridge University Press, 2019).

9. Michael Adas, *The Burma Delta: Economic Development and Social Change on an Asian Rice Frontier, 1852–1941* (Madison: University of Wisconsin Press, 1974).

jectory of the Vietnamese revolutionary struggle was profoundly shaped by Indochina's deepening integration into a regional economy centered on Guangzhou and Hong Kong and by developments and trends in southern China, so too were the nature, extent, and prospects of revolutionary mobilization definitively determined by the tight linkages between Burma and neighboring India, within whose colonial administrative circuitries Burma remained enfolded as late as 1937.[10] Thus, much as the first decades of the twentieth century saw successive mobilizational efforts championed by members of the last generations of Vietnamese literati schooled and socialized within the orbit of Sinographic cosmopolitanism, so too did the interwar era in Burma see a series of social movements led by *pongyi* (monks) from within the Theravada Buddhist *sangha*, whose autonomy from state control and patronage (in sharp contrast with neighboring Siam) enabled their continued immersion within the broader circuitries of Buddhist cosmopolitanism stretching across the Indian subcontinent, Ceylon (Sri Lanka), and beyond.[11] Just as Phan Bội Châu's reformism and republicanism was giving way to Hồ Chí Minh's Communism in the mid-late 1920s, a simultaneous shift unfolded in Burma, where, as in Indochina, the predominance of foreign (i.e., British and Indian) control over the rice trade and the commanding heights of the economy suggested the potential appeal of revolutionary socialism as a critique and alternative vis-à-vis free market liberalism.[12]

But in contrast with its French, Soviet, and Chinese circuits and sponsors in Indochina, Marxism arrived in Burma via Britain, India, and Indian immigrant workers in Rangoon and remained overshadowed by the Fabian, Gandhian, and Nehruvian variants of socialism that prevailed among Anglophone critiques of the Raj and British imperialism.[13] These weaker prospects for Communist revolutionary struggle in Burma combined with the specific local circumstances of World War II—Japanese occupation and installation of a nominally independent but essentially puppet Burmese government—to favor the postwar and postindependence triumph of (anti-Indian) economic nationalism and avowedly Buddhist socialism, while the armed guerrilla struggle of the Communist Party of Burma (CPB) failed to achieve the organizational solidity, military strength, or

10. Swapna Bhattacharya (Chakraborti), *India-Myanmar Relations, 1886–1948* (Kolkata: K P Bagchi, 2007).

11. Erik Braun, *The Birth of Insight: Meditation, Modern Buddhism, and the Burmese Monk Ledi Sayadaw* (Chicago: University of Chicago Press, 2013); Alicia Turner, *Saving Buddhism: The Impermanence of Religion in Colonial Burma* (Honolulu: University of Hawai'i Press, 2014).

12. Khin Yi, *The Dobama Movement in Burma (1930–1938)* (Ithaca, NY: Cornell University Southeast Asia Program, 1988).

13. Robert H. Taylor, "The Burmese Communist Party and Its Indian Connection: Formation and Factionalism," *Journal of Southeast Asian Studies* 14, no. 1 (March 1983): 95–108; Robert H. Taylor, *Marxism and Resistance in Burma, 1942–1945: Thein Pe Myint's Wartime Traveler* (Athens: Ohio University Press, 1984).

political success of the ICP-led Việt Minh in nearby Vietnam. Overall, viewed within this comparative perspective, the parameters of possibility for revolution making in Southeast Asia were determined by a mixture of the varying opportunities created by international conjunctures and the varying availability and appeal of cosmopolitan discursive and organizational infrastructures—such as those associated with republicanism, communism, and Islam—within the diverse societies of the region.

In conclusion, *Republicanism, Communism, Islam: Cosmopolitan Origins of Revolution in Southeast Asia* has, in descriptive terms, provided a denationalized, internationalized, and transnationalized account of the Philippine, Indonesian, and Vietnamese Revolutions, an account contextualized within the history of Southeast Asia and the broader global backdrop of the making of the modern world. In historiographical terms, the composite account and comparative analysis in the pages above has presented a synthesis of, and an admiring tribute to, the rich body of scholarship produced by historians of Southeast Asia and of other regions of the world, rather than an individual work of original empirical research. In analytical terms, moreover, the book has offered a set of answers to questions that have remained essentially unanswered—and are arguably unanswerable—within a narrowly national(ist) framework for understanding the Philippine, Indonesian, and Vietnamese revolutions, and perhaps for understanding other instances of mass mobilization usually interpreted simply as struggles for national independence elsewhere across the world.

Finally, in political terms, the book has advocated both a more critical interpretation and a more generous—that is, capacious and magnanimous—appreciation of the diversity of actors and aspirations contributing to the making of Southeast Asia than that provided by narrowly nationalist narratives. For example, the book's emphasis on the anticlerical and elitist colorations of the Philippine Revolution, the centrality of Islam and Communism to the Indonesian Revolusi, and the crucial contributions of both the Kuomintang and the CCP to the Vietnamese Revolution—and of China to the making of Vietnam as a whole—challenges official and otherwise established allocations of credit and blame for the tribulations and triumphs of these three revolutionary struggles. In addition, the book has suggested a nonnationalist basis for sympathy and support for the egalitarian aspirations and emancipatory energies animating Southeast Asians' revolutionary struggles during the late nineteenth and early–mid twentieth centuries. After all, these variously republican, Communist, and Islamic struggles contained within them the potential to upend and transcend the inequalities and injustices of the established colonial order through the revolutionary transformations envisaged as accompanying transitions to national independence.

At the same time, however, these variously republican, Communist, and Islamic struggles also contained within them organizational practices and authority structures that portended new forms of hierarchy and domination once colonial states were replaced by independent nation-states. Thus, today as Filipino, Indonesian, Vietnamese, and other Southeast Asian citizens of the region continue to struggle for political freedom and social justice they might find inspiration not only from established "national heroes" and the nationalist elites who came to assume state power after independence but also among those whose contributions to the making of history have been downplayed, disavowed, and debarred from official nationalist pantheons and panegyrics. To acknowledge and understand the cosmopolitan origins of revolutions in Southeast Asia is thus to appreciate the diversity and complexity of the forces that helped to fuel revolutionary mobilization in different parts of the region, forces variously absorbed, appropriated, and eviscerated by new nation-states in the aftermath of independence, but forces that may be revived and redirected into new struggles for *100 Percent Merdeka* today and in years to come.

Index